MEDITERRANEAN MOSAIC

PERSPECTIVES ON GLOBAL POP

GENERAL EDITOR, GAGE AVERILL, NEW YORK UNIVERSITY

Perspectives on Global Pop explores the global traffic in musical sounds that is reconfiguring the world's sonic map. Popular musics of the "west," from jazz to techno, have long sought new audiences and meanings in their global march; and subaltern popular musics—such as soukous, soca, rai, or bhangra—have also garnered international markets and influence. *Perspectives on Global Pop* showcases a cross-disciplinary dialogue on issues, theories, and regional studies in global popular musics and seeks to evaluate the repercussions of accelerated globalization and cultural hybridity.

PUBLISHED TITLES IN THE SERIES

MEDITERRANEAN MOSAIC

POPULAR MUSIC AND GLOBAL SOUNDS

EDITED BY GOFFREDO PLASTINO

Perspectives on Global Pop

Routledge
Taylor & Francis Group
NEW YORK AND LONDON

Published in 2003 by
Routledge
29 West 35th Street
New York, NY 10001
www.routledge-ny.com

Published in Great Britain by
Routledge
11 New Fetter Lane
London EC4P 4EE
www.routledge.co.uk

Printed in the United States of America on acid-free paper.

10 9 8 7 6 5 4 3 2 1

Cataloging-in-Publication Data is available from the Library of Congress.

ISBN 0-415-93655-1 (hbk.)
ISBN 0-415-93656-X (pbk.)

CONTENTS

ACKNOWLEDGMENTS

Like many of the musical forms with which it deals, this book is the result of many and varied connections, both local and global, which I am happy to record here. In addition, like a sailor who has finally reached port, I wish to remember here my companions on the voyage. Above all, then, I wish to thank Gage Averill, who wanted to include this book in the series edited by him and has always been generous with his advice and his encouragement. I thank Richard Carlin (and, through him, the whole staff at Routledge). I have often sorely tried his patience, but he knew how to hold on and wait. I thank all those who accepted my invitation to collaborate and who subsequently have had to put up with my (often persistent) requests.

Then I should like to thank Roberto Catalano, Joško Ćaleta, Naila Ceribašić, Franco Fabbri, Antonello Fazio, Mario Gros, Ellen Harold, Christine Head, Anna Lomax Chairetakis, Josep Martí y Perez, Svanibor Pettan, Antonio Samà, Annamaria Sanzi, Joe Sciorra, and Benedetto Sestito, to whom I have turned many times to seek information, suggestions, documents, help: their responses to me were always prompt and friendly. I have made frequent use of the works of Predrag Matvejević as a compass in this sea of paper; I wish to take this opportunity to acknowledge my debt to him.

This book has kept me company for several months in the course of my travels, and has been written and revised in various cities: begun on the Mediterranean, it was completed in England. I thank all my colleagues at the Department of Music of the University of Newcastle (in particular Richard Middleton, Ian Biddle, Bennet Hogg, and Karen Tweed with whom I have spoken at greatest length on various aspects of this publication) for the calm seas they have created round about me and for their friendship: all this has helped me bring to fruition a long labor of love.

INTRODUCTION

SAILING THE MEDITERRANEAN MUSICS

GOFFREDO PLASTINO

Arriving at the Mediterranean, let us first select a point of departure (Matvejević 1991: 17).

Zaragoza, April 2001. Before going to Bajo Aragón, to hear once again the drum rhythms performed there during Holy Week, I stop for some days in this beautiful and hospitable city. During my explorations, as usual, I visit some record stores. One of them offers free copies of the magazine *Batonga! La Revista de las músicas del mundo,* with a cover featuring the Spanish musician David Cervera and his *nuevo sonido mediterráneo.* In the cover story, Cervera tells a journalist about his latest record, *Talaüd,* and explains his "new Mediterranean sound":

> I think there are some very clear characteristics at the level of the sound spectrum, types of instruments and intonation: there is also something very significant and highly essential in the melismas and chord patterns. In any case, I have a very necessary explanation. Nations which are accustomed to a very hot climate, like us [Spaniards], have a type of cadence very different from people who endure the cold. To counter this you need to drink and, clearly, this makes people happier. Here people suffer and celebrate their suffering in song. This is another characteristic of the Mediterranean sound. (Amorós 2001)

I buy the record. *Talaüd* is a work of synthesis, an example of "Mediterranean crossover": different styles and musical instruments are superimposed on every track. The CD allows you to hear a symphony orchestra, a boys' choir, *dolçaines* (shawms), a hurdy-gurdy, a *clarinet de pastor* (a generic name for a traditional wind instrument), an ocarina, bagpipes such as Catalan *sac de gemes*, Bulgarian *gaida*, Irish *uillean pipes*—and also *saz*, *'ud*, bouzouki, *lauto*, *nay*, *txalapartas* (Basque wooden percussions). The compositions portray soundscapes shifting through constant sudden changes of perspective, in the attempt to depict a musical Mediterranean that is heterogeneous but, as visualized by Cervera, self-contained.[1]

Newcastle-upon-Tyne, April 2001. In the HMV music store in Northumberland Street, in the world music department, I find another interesting disc: *Mediterranean Café Sound*. Hamid Zagzoule, in the introductory CD booklet, considers musical influences between diverse countries and cultures, cuisine, landscapes, and climate as elements of a unitary representation of the Mediterranean:

> The music of Algeria, France, Greece, Italy, Morocco, Spain and Tunisia shares more than the common denominator of history and geography; the Arab, Gypsy, Latin and Maghreb traditions co-exist within each and every genre of the music. This collection of songs attempts to illustrate the links and connections inherent in the music. For instance, the Arab influence is to be found in *Flamenco*, Andalusian and *Fado* music. Similarly, you will be surprised not to detect the Latin, Gypsy traditions in *Raï* and *Shaabi*, the music of the Maghreb—Algeria, Morocco and Tunisia.
>
> The Mediterranean has been an attractive and popular destination for visitors in search of *joie de vivre*. Beautiful landscapes, hot climates, exotic cuisine and a vibrant musical culture, all combine to make the region an ideal place to retreat to. Here then, is a hand-picked collection of songs capturing the essence of the *Mediterranean sound*.

Mediterranean Café Song is a compilation, and includes tracks by musicians and bands varying widely from one another. For instance, Italy is represented by the world-music band Agricantus, which "creates a hybrid sound rooted in tradition with a contemporary feel"; Spain, by

Radio Tarifa, authors of an "intoxicating blend of Arabic and medieval singing, with a beady eye on the contemporary flamenco scene"; and Tunisia by the singer Amina Annabi, who has "experimented with Arab rap" and released an album, *Zahra*, "where oriental melodic singing reverberated against cool programmed backing." The CD, Hamid Zagzoule assures me, documents "the *real* sound of the Mediterranean."

New York, August 2001. In the big, new department devoted to world music at the Tower Records music store on Broadway, my attention is attracted by the cover of a record at a listening post. It is not a recent disc, but the store managers have decided to promote it alongside new releases. It is *Mediterranea: Songs of the Mediterranean*, by Greek singer Savina Yannatou. On the back of the cover, the contents of the CD are described:

> From the fertile landscape of the Mediterranean rim comes this evocative offering of songs: a shimmering mosaic of spellbinding voice and sultry rhythms reflecting the nearly lost traditions of Greece, Tunisia, Sicily, the Holy Land, and more.

In the booklet, Sophia Yannatou—quoting Braudel's book on the Mediterranean (1987), Italo Calvino's novel *Le città invisibili* (*Invisible Cities*), and an unpublished text by Thanos Manousopoulos (*The Music of the Mediterranean*)—explains her idea of the Mediterranean and its musics

> The successive migrations and the crossbreeding among peoples that for centuries traced their history across the Mediterranean, carrying with them in their language their native land as they journeyed by frigate or by camel train, tilting with the banners of their religions, and exchanging legends, names, traditions, songs in peaceful existence, have recorded their distinctive presences in the colored tesserae of this mosaic map.

Savina Yannatou performs songs from Greece, Albania, Italy (Apulia, Sardinia), Israel, Lebanon, Turkey, Spain, France, Corsica, and Tunisia. She is accompanied by the Primavera en Salonico Ensemble, a group of six musicians playing exclusively acoustic instruments such as

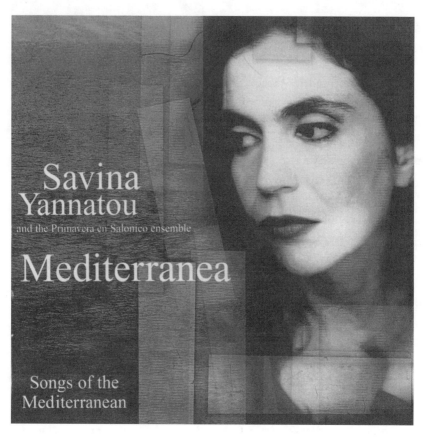

Mediterranea: Songs of the Mediterranean

the *toumbeleki* (goblet-shaped drum), *bendir* (frame drum), *daouli* (double-headed drum), guitar, 'ud, *kanonaki* (plucked zither), nay, violin, and double bass. Many songs come from the oral tradition; all have been arranged by the group, which uses the melodies as points of departure for the singer's vocal improvisations and for the musicians' solos. Elements common to all the performances are the vocal contributions of Yannatou and the idea that the musical traditions of the Mediterranean can be revived and reasserted through the subjective feelings of an artist (in this case, Yannatou herself).

Some days afterwards, I ask the head of the world music department in the Tower Records music store near Lincoln Center if he can suggest a recent "Mediterranean" record to me. "Yes," he replies at once, "there's

GOFFREDO PLASTINO

this one by the group Esta, they're really good, they're Israeli and quite well known here in New York. They play well, they're excellent musicians." Unfortunately the CD, *Mediterranean Crossroads*, is temporarily out of stock and nobody can say when the store will have it available again. I find it in another Tower Records store, having in the meanwhile visited the Esta web site, intrigued by the impassioned description of the group's music I heard. Esta describes themselves in this way:

> Proclaimed by music critics as Israel's most original instrumental band, Esta has created a unique, innovative and energetic sound that is part of a new era of music. Esta combines the aromas of World Music, the power of Rock, and the spirit of Jazz into a powerful, energetic sound that crosses genres, styles and borders. Coming from Israel, a crossroads of many different cultures, it is only natural that Esta has based their music on the various musical influences of the ethnic traditions of their parents' generations. With this background, Esta has created a rich, hot musical stew simmering with Mediterranean, Balkan, African, Asian, Celtic and Western flavours.[2]

Mediterranean Crossroads opens with an arrangement of a traditional Yemenite tune, "Deror Yikra," introduced by the sound of the *zourna*; the next track, "Go-Go," is introduced by a march played on the Highland bagpipes and repeated more than once. On the CD, a solid jazz-rock groove underpins the Mediterranean (or rather Middle Eastern) melodies and solos played on electric guitar and saxophones. On another page of the website, Shlomo Deshet, Esta's drummer and percussion player, explains the music of the band: "People like to categorize music. This is Irish music, that is Middle Eastern music. But we don't want to be obligated to any forms or any traditions. . . . What we play is accessible, it always has elements of Western music, but it is also a window to understand what goes on in other cultures."[3] The cover of the CD, a fourteenth-century map, visually reinforces the cultural and musical links between the various countries of the Mediterranean.

There is such a thing as "Mediterranean music"; it is currently known and appreciated even outside of and far from the Mediterranean, as I believe this more or less chance sampling has shown. As Predrag Matvejević has written, the Mediterranean is "more

Mediterranean Crossroads

than a matter of geography" (Matvejević 1991: 17), and attempting to understand it solely as a "lake" could be misguided: "Its boundaries are not defined by space or time. We do not know how or as what to define them: they cannot be reduced to sovereignty or history, they are not those of states or nations: they are like the chalk circle which keeps being drawn and rubbed out" (ibid.: 18). Images and sounds of the Mediterranean and its music can be found almost everywhere, as ultimate confirmation of the fact that the Mediterranean extends (in part thanks to its representations) beyond what we perceive as its geographical limits. It is thus possible to commence different Mediterranean voyages leaving from New York, England, or central Spain—in the aim of drawing a new circle.

The Mediterranean and discourses on the Mediterranean are
inseparable from one another (Matvejević 1991: 20).

The Mediterranean has at many times and in many ways been the center of attention for historians, politicians, economists, anthropologists,
sociologists, musicologists, and ethnomusicologists—and of many spe-
cialists in other disciplines. Many of them have proposed (or referred
to) a definition of the Mediterranean. An exhaustive study of concepts
of the Mediterranean cannot be attempted here (it would provide material for at least another book, probably several), but it is possible to
describe briefly some of the most important theoretical positions, lim-
iting our inquiry to the field of history and anthropology. The best-
known account is undoubtedly that of Fernand Braudel (1949), whose
seminal work on the Mediterranean at the time of Philip II of Spain has
had a profound resonance and importance far beyond the field of historical studies. Greatly oversimplifying, and also employing arguments
advanced in another work by the French historian, we may say that
Braudel believes the distinguishing trait of the Mediterranean to be its
status as "an ancient crossroads," a place in which "for millennia all has
. . . coalesced, complicating and enriching its history" (Braudel 1987: 8).
By this definition, the Mediterranean is an area of overlapping civilizations, of cultures that each speak with their own voice, and which taken
as a whole, while maintaining their own peculiarities, constitute a sub-
stantially unitary Mediterranean (see Driessen 1999: 56).

The text that may be of greatest significance for the history of
Mediterranean studies from an anthropological point of view, following the publication of Braudel's work, is that of John Davis (1977).
Davis turned his attention (and continued to do so subsequently) to
the anthropological studies on the Mediterranean, shedding light on
their contradictions and findings, focusing on different but recurring
models of analysis of the Mediterranean as a cultural region. We can
accordingly adopt his writings to illustrate the most important theoretical positions. First, Davis reminds us that the Mediterranean has
been seen as the region that produced an autonomous culture, now
extinct but for a few traces. Then again, from a different anthropological perspective, it is only during the past millennium that an "aboriginal" culture has grown up in the Mediterranean. Finally, the

Mediterranean has been perceived as nothing but a product that is (also) cultural, "an instrument of imperialist domination" (Davis 1993: 91). The model most widely accepted describes the Mediterranean as a well defined entity determinable from the inclusion of countries bordering it and by the exclusion of all others. Davis has offered criticism of this concept (Davis 1977: 11), emphasizing that is cannot be correct to exclude, say, Stuttgart from the "Mediterranean" on account of the large number of Mediterranean workers settled there, and on account of the complex relationships between this city and countries such as Italy and Turkey.

Even if Davis does not see the Mediterranean as a culturally and geographically separate entity, it is still possible to look upon it from a precise anthropological perspective. The Mediterranean has nurtured cultural, social, and economic contacts over a period of six or seven thousand years. It is not a single society, from the point in time at which it grows impossible to specify a Mediterranean economy, system of government, religion, or family organization, but it has been and remains a "melting pot" (Davis 1993: 105), and this renders it anthropologically relevant: "Mediterranean social facts are the product of the interaction of people of diverse kinds from time to time in a period to be counted in thousands of years, and they are to be investigated historically and comparatively" (Davis 1977: 14–15).

Davis's work has been seen as a milestone in the anthropological debate on the Mediterranean, arousing numerous discussions (see Boissevain 1979). Subsequently, in the attempt to define the category "Mediterranean" in a way satisfactory for all, anthropologists have at one time or another highlighted as characteristics essential to the Mediterranean area: cultural unity transcending differences; social and cultural forms of communication; tendencies to change; but also, contrary to this, the existence of sometimes insurmountable limits and oppositions, barriers, and enmities, and a certain degree of fragmentation (Pina-Cabral 1989: 404).

It is probably more useful, these days, to consider the Mediterranean as "a cultural construct that has been fostered by intellectuals for centuries and in that regard pretty close to the image of the nation, while it has nowadays developed into more of a folk-concept founded upon tourism and a general interest in roots and traditions"

(Frykman 1999: 283). For a better analysis of the cultural characteristics of the present-day Mediterranean, we may therefore accept the fact that this area has undergone and is still undergoing constant internal and external modification, and that it is necessary to reflect on the Mediterranean forms of cultural identification (Driessen 1999: 59, 61): "The category 'Mediterranean' is not solidly uniform. On the other hand it would be presumptuous or arrogant to deny matters Mediterranean. The anthropologist who claims that the Mediterranean culture does not exist, neglects that for many different actors 'Mediterranean' *is* a cultural reality" (ibid.: 61). Not one Mediterranean, then, but a variety of "Mediterraneans" propose themselves and are proposed, and demand to be included.

In the field of ethnomusicological studies, there has been constant attention to the musical cultures of the Mediterranean, and it has produced a number of basic texts (among many others: De Martino 1961; Weis Bentzon 1969; Picken 1975; Lortat-Jacob 1996; Sugarman 1997). The Mediterranean has been adopted also as an area of study. Tullia Magrini on many occasions has initiated theoretical reflections on the Mediterranean area, at first taking up (critically) Davis's concept of the Mediterranean as a melting pot, but also emphasizing the presence of musical cultures that are "non-communicating" or at least have a strong identity and only offer weak evidence of intercultural communication (Magrini 1993: 20–23). Magrini stipulates that, from the ethnomusicological point of view, the Mediterranean "is fascinating because it represents better than others a place in which one encounters countless diversities, and because it enables us to observe the ways in which these diversities manage to coexist, ignore each other, know each other, come into conflict, or blend" (Magrini 1999: 174–75). Magrini has also suggested adopting the definition of "Mediterranean music", "for those musical phenomena which cross the sea, which have in their DNA a genetic patrimony that unites elements of different cultures, and which carry the historical memory of contacts within the Mediterranean," extending it further to the new repertoires resulting from the "postmodern tendency to contamination" (ibid.: 175–76).

The approach adopted in this volume is somewhat different. I consider that it is necessary to take account of the fact that the present-day Mediterranean is a space (not purely geographic) in which various models (internal and external) and various musical experiences coexist and continually interact, sometimes integrating with one another, sometimes opposing one another, sometimes ignoring each other. Braudel's "heteroclite" Mediterranean (1987: 9) deserves the attention of ethnomusicologists, because it is through its music that the Mediterranean is continually and variously defined, and defines itself. In the Mediterranean (and, as we have seen, elsewhere) there are many "Mediterranean musics" to be heard, each of them an expression of identity, of economic, social, and musical relationships, each of them a result of local, regional, national, and global circumstances. These forms of music must not be redefined or reduced to a model (of whatever sort): they already exist, they are performed, they can be heard, they are disseminated by the media. The task of ethnomusicology, as I see it, is to understand their history and their characteristics, to verify and analyze the ways in which they acquire and give meaning to communities of musicians and listeners, to explain how and in what direction they change, to see how they are labeled and diffused around and outside the *Middle Sea*.

The Mediterranean is accordingly *also* the sum total of discourse on the Mediterranean, including those very arguments that define, analyze, and propose the idea of a "Mediterranean music" or of a complex of musics having clear and recognizable Mediterranean characteristics: discursive practices that precede or follow the musical experience. These musical discourses spread rapidly within and beyond the present-day Mediterranean; they are resumed, deepened, reworked, and eventually recast, forming the basis for other discourses and other performances. In particular, after the proclamation of "world music" as a musical genre (Taylor 1997: 1–4), those "circular" discourses in which the accent is currently placed on "tradition," "roots," and "authenticity" (Feld 1994: 265; Plastino 1996: 25–29) in the Mediterranean have acquired a particular modality of expression. Within "Mediterranean music," "authenticity" is highlighted as resulting from musical practices such as "contamination," "fusion," and "hybridization." These lines of discourse often relate to the model of the Mediterranean as the area within which the relationships were and are principally musical and are drawn out over a long (and often indefinable) period of time. Once again, then, the Mediterranean is perceived as a hub of communications, exchanges, and cultural influences. From any point in the Mediterranean, it is often claimed in these new avenues of discourse, music can be used as the channel to any other point (as the cover of the Esta CD suggests). Any musical superimposition or borrowing is possible, from the moment that it represents a new chapter in the long history of the complex relationships between the peoples of the Mediterranean and their forms of music.

Before and beyond musical performances, this model of "Mediterranean music" is repeated incessantly, and so it is relatively easy to find a clear explanation of it in musicians' own words, or in the texts that accompany their compositions. Each specifies the links regarded as most significant. For Esta, Israel being "a crossroads of many different cultures," it is "natural" that their music should mix genres and styles. Savina Yannatou's work is based on the idea of "migrations and . . . crossbreeding among peoples" of the Mediterranean. In the booklet accompanying her CD, Kostas Vomvolos goes into greater detail on these musical migrations:

> In any endeavor to identify the elements common to all these [Mediterranean] traditions, a good place to start is with the instruments they use. Here indeed, there are striking similarities in sonority and philosophy of construction, regardless of the variations in the way they are played and in their role in local tradition. Membranophones like the tambourine, the *darabuka* and the *daouli*, stringed instruments, bowed like the lyre and the violin and plucked like the lute, the *oud*, the tamboura and the guitar, wind instruments like the reed pipes, the *zournas* and the bagpipe, are found in a variety of sizes and types with similar or differing names in most places around the Mediterranean basin.
>
> Another feature is the overwhelming importance of the human voice. Song, as an infrangible composite of word, music, and dance, is probably the nearest thing there is to a Mediterranean tradition. Indeed, despite individual differences, the placing of the voice and the vocalization are remarkably comparable.

Many of the preceding observations regarding musical instruments might well be shared by the ethnomusicologists whose field is the Mediterranean.[4] However, while some believe the similarities between the musical instruments and their timbres is what associates the various musical cultures with one another in this region, others suggest that it is the lyrics of the songs that provide the features essential for a comparison. In the booklet introducing the compilation *Mediterranée: Les Musiques du Sud* (three CDs devoted to women's voices, accomplished performers, and "new creators"), Taoufik Bestandji (within a reasoned discussion that takes account of the geographical, cultural, and musical aspects of the Mediterranean) asks:

> Which are the common elements which have provided and continue to provide the musical wealth of the Mediterranean basin? Its riches are at one and the same time concrete and abstract, and rest in the musical language and the ideas conveyed by its melodies and its rhythms. Even if the Mediterranean languages (essentially Latin and Semitic) appear distant from one another, their poetic themes reveal a common source. This is the very essence of the oral music tradition.

Considerations that (while simplifying it) partially reproduce the anthropological model of the Mediterranean as a privileged environment and a cultural hub can be observed in recent "world music" oriented releases. The compilation *A Mediterranean Odyssey: Athens to Andalucia*, for example, places the accent on common musical features overriding cultural differences:

> The Mediterranean is one of the most culturally diverse regions of the planet. Each of the four countries featured on this collection [Spain, France, Italy, and Greece] have unique histories, distinct cultures and languages, individual styles of art, food, literature, and, of course, music. Yet, for all the differences, there are many common threads that link the music of the northern Mediterranean. Influences from the Arab world, both historical and contemporary, can be felt in every corner of the region. The echoes of Jewish culture have left their mark, from the Sephardic melodies of Spain to the Eastern European clarinet riffs that resonate in Greek traditions. Tinges of the ancient Celtic world can be heard in the music of nearly every country. And the wandering Gypsy minstrels passed through all corners of the Mediterranean, leaving an indelible mark on the style, instrumentation and attitude of music from *Athens to Andalucia*.

A Mediterranean Odyssey: Athens to Andalucia

The CD brings together tracks by musicians and bands from the folk music revival and world music who all come from Mediterranean-basin countries and, more important, have a shared perspective on music. In the music of the Italian band Novalia, "world, ambient and folk join to create an accessible and exciting new blend." The music of Greek duo Anemos "blends flavors as varied as Western classical music, renaissance themes, ancient Mediterranean music and the traditional music of Greece." This is a musical debate centering on the "Mediterraneanness" resulting from the expression in music of "fusion" between genres and styles almost all drawn from Mediterranean "roots."

The model of the Mediterranean as a defined cultural entity emerges in other discographical works, in which at times the unifying element is identified with the "influence" of one (musical) culture on the others. For instance, the first issue of the encyclopedic Italian part-work *Musiche dal Mondo: Atlante sonoro della World Music*, devoted to the Mediterranean and the Middle East, tells us that "[t]he calm, clear waters of the Mediterranean are bordered by countries with millennia of tradition, guardians of customs and histories that are diverse yet draw on common sociocultural roots that emerge intact and vital in their music" (Guaitamacchi 2000: 2); in the booklet accompanying the enclosed CD, the assertion is made that "[d]espite experiencing realities of cultural history that are profoundly different from one another, the countries washed by the warm waters of the Mediterranean have in common thousands of years of history, a Gypsy attitude and shared Arab influences." If it is "music" in general that is first invoked to express the unity of the Mediterranean, the subsequent approach is to state that within music, other (unspecified) aspects are "Mediterranean."

It would be mistaken to discount these discursive practices as irrelevant, at best nothing more than comments on a new type of world beat. They form the conduit for a conception of music in the Mediterranean, or a "Mediterranean music" right and proper. They often contain clear reference to (or the echo of) historic, anthropological, or ethnomusicological analyses. One could easily regard these discourses as nothing more than the outcome of somewhat confused attempts to create a unitary standard of valuation within the multifarious musical expressions of the contemporary Mediterranean. In reality they are a new expression of that many-sided Mediterranean familiar to historians and anthropologists. These descriptions serve to elaborate and postulate a Mediterranean both real and imaginary.

Not all the discourses on the Mediterranean are, however, based on a clear musical concept. At times, "Mediterraneanness" appears difficult or impossible to define:

> A certain way of life developed around the Mediterranean Sea, but this Mediterranean "style" is in fact a complex ensemble, altogether one and many. Full of contradictions and tensions, it is held together nevertheless by a strong bond, a spirit of "Mediterranean-ness" so to speak, a feeling of belonging to that Mediterranean world, which animates all its inhabitants. . . . The Mediterranean world of olive-trees and cheese is also a world of subtle variety: a blend of sugar and salt, a taste of sweet pepper.[5]

The model of the Mediterranean as a "lake" is again found in record releases that offer, for example, a "heartfelt collection of lullabies gathered along the sun-warmed shores of the Mediterranean sea."[6] *Parfums de Méditerranée* represents a collection of old and new recordings of music described as *Judèo-Arabe*, while Italian compilations like *Anime Mediterranee, Mare Nostrum, An Xplosion of World Music from the Mediterranean Area*, and *Mediterraneo* include some field recordings and compositions by world music, world beat, and folk music revival musicians and bands, from several Mediterranean countries. The Mediterranean thus becomes "the great sea of music" (Assante and Castaldo 1995).[7] Even more generally, the Mediterranean may be considered solely as a geographical setting or else as a source of inspiration. Following this path, it is of interest to note in particular that various contemporary guitarists have dedicated compositions of theirs to the Mediterranean. Again without claiming to offer an exhaustive survey, it is possible to illustrate this latter tendency through various works released on disc. In 1990, John McLaughlin composed and performed a concerto for guitar and orchestra in a Spanish style entitled *The Mediterranean*, declaring that "The title is firstly one of inspiration: since my home overlooks that splendid sea, it was instrumental in helping me."[8]

A few years later, another jazz guitarist, Chuck Loeb, released an album with the same title—but it is hard to detect clear "Mediterranean" influences on his disc. In 2001, the "gypsy jazz" Robin Nolan Trio released a CD entitled *Mediterranean Blues;* on the title track, an instrumental number in an orthodox Django Reinhardt style, the sole "Mediterranean" element seems to be the flamenco-style *palmas* accompaniment. The Sardinian guitarist Marino de Rosas similarly inserted among the numbers on his album *Meridies* (2001) a track called "Mediterraneo" that seems little different from his other personal reinterpretations of traditional Sardinian music, except for the fact that (again) it features a *palmas* accompaniment. *Mediterraneo* is also the title of a CD published by the Andalusian guitarist (born in Tangiers) Eduardo Niebla and Palestinian 'ud player Adel Salameh (born in Nablus): a "crossover" collaboration, that has been considered "rather an exploration of territory, looking not only towards Spain and Palestine for its roots, but also to a place where their music, in all its modern aspects, can sit" (El-Ghadban 2001).

The reference to the Mediterranean as a backdrop, as a sea that metaphorically and physically unites the countries abutting on its coastline, has not only been expressed by Western world, popular, or jazz music performers. Simon Shaheen, an 'ud and violin player born in Tarshiha (Northern Galilee) and educated at the Jerusalem Music Academy and in the United States from 1980 (where he formed the Near Eastern Music Ensemble), released a CD in 2001, *Blue Flame*, with his ensemble Qantara. *Blue Flame*, says Shaheen, "explores the possibilities of music rooted in Arabic traditional sound that crosses cultures and styles"—of the Middle East, North Africa, India, and Western classical and jazz. One track of the CD is called "Dance Mediterranea": it is an example of "crossover" between Western classical (notably Shaheen's own violin playing) and Arabic musical traditions, and "evokes the sunny countries surrounding the Mediterranean and the glinting waters that connect them."[9]

The Mediterranean can ultimately be used as an expedient, to give an arbitrary title to a collection of tracks. This tendency is particularly evident in new-age music releases, a good example being the *Mediterranea* sampler, none of whose numbers (with the possible exception of a "rhumbasalsa" by the guitarist Ottmar Liebert) can be related to the musical cultures of the Mediterranean.

The paths followed here are simply a few lanes through the sea of so-called "Mediterranean music," and many others could be added. It is not always easy, in fact, to recognize them all, because this totality of musical trends is in a constant process of change: it is like a single landscape changing with the seasons and the years, like the sea itself. All the same, if only provisionally (and in the awareness that any generalization may be modified or challenged by subsequent acquisitions and by new analyses of new musical phenomena dubbed "Mediterranean"), it is possible to draw a new map and plot other routes across the sea that are inevitably bound up with the stories (the discourses) told about them (Matvejević 1991: 116).

To summarize the various interpretations currently in circulation of "Mediterranean music" or "musical Mediterraneanness," the Mediterranean has been regarded and put forward as:

· an area of intense contacts and exchanges: meaning that every expression of Mediterranean music has, may have, or has previously had an evident or concealed relationship with another expressive form or musical culture, and that this history may be revealed, reiterated, or for that matter invented, as of the present day, by means of collaboration, contamination, fusion, hybridization between various styles, and by the simultaneous use of musical instruments employed in different Mediterranean countries.

· an area in which a culture (that may be musical) is notable for having left its traces everywhere: meaning that every local expression of music may be reformulated utilizing or inventing the formal style and structures of a different [musical] culture declared predominant, as in the case of "Arab world music" in Italy.[10]

· an area which unites the countries bordering upon it: meaning that, tautologically, the term "Mediterranean" applies to every form, performance, and musical instrument of the Mediterranean countries, even in the absence of relationships or exchanges between them, whether evident, claimed, or invented.

· a source of inspiration for musicians, Mediterranean or otherwise: meaning that some musical forms, real or "invented," and musical instruments belonging to traditions and cultures of the Mediterranean, or even at times the very name "Mediterranean," may be used in various compositions belonging to genres or styles such as popular music, folk music, world beat, jazz, hip-hop, early, and contemporary art music.[11]

· a simple arbitrary label: meaning that a collection of musical items may be brought together as "Mediterranean" although any other title would have done just as well.

Even if we seek to pursue these lines of inquiry alone, the task just outlined remains complex. Each discourse, performance, or product that we may be offered or may consider as belonging to "Mediterranean music" is located at one point or another on our map. Indeed, a single musical project may change direction from one track or composition to the next. At times there are clear points of departure (jazz, or popular music, or a traditional tune) and arrival (the "Mediterranean"), but the route followed, or to be followed, may not be so clear, or at all direct.

It is difficult to see what makes us keep trying to rearrange the Mediterranean mosaic, to keep compiling the catalogue of its components (Matvejević 1991: 18).

This book accordingly arises from a discovery and a desire: from the discovery that a multiform, contemporary "Mediterranean music" exists and is listened to and appreciated not only in the countries bordering on the Mediterranean; and from the desire to verify and analyze each of the questions connected to the reception and the diffusion of "Mediterranean music" by carrying out a properly systematic survey in various places and in different musical cultures, including:

· the use of musical forms, songs, musical instruments of the Mediterranean in popular musics (Mediterranean and otherwise);

· the use of popular music instruments and languages in the different musical cultures of the Mediterranean;

· the grouping of the popular musics of the Mediterranean under the title of "world music," and the characteristics of what has sometimes been defined and is sometimes recognized as "Mediterranean world music";

· the generation of discourses on "Mediterranean music," including those resulting from a globalization of musical languages;

· "Mediterranean music" as an element of the musical identity of young Mediterranean people;

· and some of the concepts and questions relating to musical globalization in a complex area such as the Mediterranean.

There are many questions to be answered: and the essays collected in this volume set out to answer them, each reviewing one or more aspects and together offering a broad and reasoned view of the phenomenon.

Franco Fabbri's essay is devoted to "Mediterranean" influences in rock and popular music. Fabbri begins by analyzing the definition of "Mediterranean music," observing how vague it is, and how it is often impossible to relate this label to precisely identifiable content. According to Fabbri, it is more productive to consider the concept of "Mediterranean music" "as just an 'other' that was created (by Mediterraneans and non-Mediterraneans alike) as a mythical counterpart to the popular music mainstream," and, adopting a literary comparison, he relates this concept to the nonexistent knight who is the hero of the famous novel by Italo Calvino: Agilulfo, an empty suit of armor, existing as a knight because of a will to do so and because this knight is perceived as one by those looking at him. Fabbri—who on more than one occasion has analyzed recent changes in the music of the Mediterranean derived from oral tradition (Fabbri 1998, 2001)—correctly observes that almost any knight could wear the armor, just as the umbrella of "Mediterranean music" may shelter practically any form of musical expression. By analyzing popular music, mainly in the Anglo-American tradition, from the mid-1960s up to the establishment of world music, Fabbri demonstrates how the creation of this new musical stream within popular music has often had recourse to the Mediterranean—whether real or invented. Fabbri makes an important contribution to an understanding of the knights who have inhabited this armor (to continue along the lines of his useful metaphor), and introduces us to the territories of popular music in which this nonexistent knight has been seen. (Many other essays in this volume go on to look at who has constructed or modified the armor and for what purposes.)

Sílvia Martínez analyzes the Mediterranean characteristics in Spanish folk, popular, and world musics, from the 1950s to the present day. Over the years, the Mediterranean has been taken in Spain as a constant point of reference for a variety of musical practices of varying significance. In the '50s, it represented an area from which to draw influences to elaborate a "solar" popular music (also of use as an element in the promotion of tourism). In the '60s and '70s, the folk revival and the "Nova Cançó" movement in Catalonia regarded the musics of the Mediterranean as a source of inspiration from which to draw elements of a new musical identity. It was during this period that ways were found and developed to rework musical forms coming from various Mediterranean musical cultures. Martínez also analyzes the contemporary phenomenon of "Mediterranean" popular music, reviewing the frequent alliances between Spanish musicians and musicians and bands from countries such as Algeria or Morocco. According to Martínez, the genre of *nuevo flamenco* can be partly incorporated within the "Mediterranean" musical scene: it does in fact accommodate quite a number of hybrid productions featuring non-Andalusian musicians. Martínez's essay shows that "Mediterranean music" in Spain has a long history of contacts and exchanges between different musical environments, many and varying meanings, and a wide distribution both within the country and outside it. Spain figures in the fullest sense as a "laboratory" that has been used over the years to experiment with various "Mediterranean" modalities of music making.

Antonio Baldassarre considers the relationships between music and the establishment of channels of mass communication in twentieth-century Morocco, showing how these relations represent an important aspect of the country's social and political development. Morocco has a long history of contacts between local styles of music and forms introduced from abroad, beginning in the 1950s with the introduction of genres of music characteristic of the Near East, particularly those from Egypt. These musical links continued with increasing intensity in the '60s with the arrival in Morocco of musicians from the so-called "Alternative Culture" and the emergence of local bands, were consolidated in the '70s and '80s, and constituted a solid reality in the '90s, a decade during which collaboration between Moroccan and foreign musicians was intensified, various musical genres from Morocco acquired a value on the international market, and intercultural bands appeared in which the Moroccan musical element remained prevalent. Baldassarre illustrates how this long history of musical contacts, influences, and exchanges has always been accompanied, and at times encouraged, by the media, whose role has been critical both in the introduction of new genres and sonorities in Morocco and in the promotion within the country of the new musical experiences.

Gabriele Marranci analyzes the recent establishment of *pop-raï*, showing how, in this latest phase of the genre, the musical characteristics of local and global origin are often interwoven, and jointly serve to give fresh expression to the identities of the musicians and their audience. Marranci offers a detailed analysis of record releases and the activity of the best-known singers and producers, to illustrate how the raï genre has from the start been a local music based on cultural transplantation; in pop-raï, the mediation is through the Algerian cultural tradition, the specific constituent elements of the raï, and the multicultural aspects of France, together with the expectations regarding music and sonority of Western audiences and of the market in world music. It is possible within pop-raï to distinguish among different senses of musical authenticity: the transformations to which raï has been subjected in its transition from a "local" to a global reality take account of different factors, such as "artistic collaboration, disjunctive places, identity complexity, as well as market strategy. In other words," asserts Marranci, "'French Raï' or 'international Raï' has its own 'authenticity' that is not the 'authenticity' of the Algerian Raï." Accordingly, pop-raï may be assessed as a significant example of *glocalization* (that is to say, of relationships and interactions between the local environment and diffusion and reception on a global level), which is one of the principal musical processes in the contemporary Mediterranean.

Ruth Davis analyzes the reinterpretations of the *ma'luf* by Tunisian media stars, at the same time telling the story of the diffusion of ma'luf via the media, illustrating the role played by the media in determining its success. A musical genre seen as standing within a long tradition (going back to the Tunisian communities' antecedents in medieval Spain), ma'luf includes numerous musical influences emanating from the Middle East. Widely disseminated and appreciated, and thus "popular" (in the sense of belonging to the Tunisian population as a whole), ma'luf currently enjoys widespread popularity, particularly thanks to the singing of media stars like Lotfi Boushnak and Sonia M'Barek. The latter, however, do not see themselves as mere executants of an ancient musical tradition but are more interested in "molding" the ma'luf to their personal expressive requirements. These media stars, Davis explains, consider themselves innovative, and "claim to sing the ma'luf in their own way." Their innovations consist of adopting Western musical instruments, writing new lyrics, and shaping and modifying the ensemble accompanying the song. In addition, their activity is not limited to the execution of the ma'luf, but extends to other Middle Eastern and Mediterranean musical styles. Through describing the transformations in ma'luf performances, Davis ably demonstrates the manner in which it is possible in a "popular" music genre to ascertain the relationships between local and global aspects, the links with the past, and the attention of the contemporary world. In the case of these performers, it is more than local attention, when they are at one and the same time within a musical tradition and innovators, as is demonstrated by recent intercultural alliances. For example, Lotfi Boushnak is featured on the latest CD of the Italian popular singer Pino Daniele (*Medina*, 2002), a musician noted already for having developed a new form of *canzone napoletana* (Neapolitan song) and an "Arab rock" (De Simone 1994: 83).

Michael Frishkopf analyzes the part played by Spanish and Latin musical styles in Egyptian popular music. Frishkopf presents a detailed survey of this "Spanish Tinge," based on the activity of the most important Egyptian performers and their records released to date, establishing in what manner these two new styles have been integrated into the language of Egyptian popular music. Frishkopf gives significant attention, in the course of an ethnohistorical investigation, to the effect that such influences have had and currently have on the Egyptians. After having retraced the threads of Egyptian popular music (which experienced an "explosion" during the 1970s and 1980s, in part through the fusion of Eastern and Arab elements), Frishkopf dwells on the growth and the definitive establishment of Latin and Spanish styles within the past 10 years, and on the readings that Egyptians have assigned to them. Frishkopf's essay is notable for its systematic recognition of discourses on the "Spanish tinge," explained as arising from associations of a historico-cultural and musical nature (with Andalusia, the Western world, modern Latin America, the Mediterranean), and as reflecting associations of a politico-economic nature (Westernization, globalization, marketing, technological change). In particular, the "Mediterranean" reading, asserting that "the presence of Spanish (and by extension Latin) music reflects more general cultural mixing and borrowing around the Mediterranean, including also North African, French, Greek, Italian, Turkish," and that "[t]hroughout history, Mediterranean peoples mixed and shared, due to proximity, and similar environments," clearly favors the model of the Mediterranean as a privileged area for musical exchanges.

Edwin Seroussi explores the various meanings assigned to "Mediterraneism" in the cultural history of Israel, a concept also found in Judaic studies around the end of the nineteenth century, and its bearing upon music. Seroussi distinguishes three models of Mediterraneism: a "synthesis model," pursued in search of a synthesis between the Jewish cultures of East and West and the civil societies of the Middle East; an "orientalist model," with its principal accent on the music-making of the "other" (Sephardic and Oriental) Jews; and a "subversion model," a defined form of Arabness, Turkishness, or Greekness in music, in opposition to the Western orientation of official culture in Israel. From time to time he relates Mediterraneism, in various ways, to a complex of musical facts (scales, modes, rhythms, instruments), and sees the Mediterranean as a context in which Mediterranean musics are played and heard. Seroussi looks at *musiqa mizrahit* (Oriental music), an alternative term for a genre of popular music established in Israel in the 1980s as *musiqa yam tikhonit* (Mediterranean music). As he sees it, the musiqa mizrahit genre is not specifically Israeli but imported from Greece, Turkey, and the Arab world and set to new lyrics. In the '80s it turned into popular music, and some characteristics were emphasized or added (the vocal treatment, the use of instruments such as the bouzouki, an accentuated use of the Phrygian mode). In the '90s it became *the* popular music of Israel, because it reflected the wish for a synthesis between East and West, and seemed to constitute the best way to, in a sense, evade direct confrontation with the Arab world, at the same time developing a sense of belonging to the culture of the Middle East. Seroussi also speaks of the discrimination experienced by musiqa mizrahit musicians in Israel, reconstructing the stages of a difficult and sometimes paradoxical establishment of the genre, which resulted, among other things, in the Mediterraneanization of Israeli popular music. Seroussi's article ties in with the other analyses in this book through its discussion of the diverse musical influences and the constant appeal to the Mediterranean (visualized and invoked in many ways) in the development of different musical identities in Israel.

Yektin Özer reviews the characteristics of the *Akdeniz* (Mediterranean) music scene in Turkey, locating it within the context of its medium-term cultural history. Özer tells the story of rock music and its diffusion in Turkey in the 1950s, and of the assessment of non-

Turkish popular musics in the '60s. In the course of this narrative, Özer sheds light on some relationships between Turkey and the musical cultures of the Mediterranean, illustrating how non-Turkish popular musics have been understood: in general, through the channel of the *aranjman* (arrangement), based on famous Italian, French, and Greek songs whose lyrics have been translated into Turkish and performed by aranjman singers. Özer accordingly analyzes Akdeniz music, established in Turkey at the start of the 1980s, as an "alternative" musical form, a reaction to entertainment music, or to commercial music. The cultivation of akdeniz music (that includes Greek elements and makes use of the bouzouki, but generates a sound that is neither Greek nor Turkish, despite the evidence of a Greek musical influence) expresses the wish to enter into musical relations with the Eastern and European Mediterranean. The estimation of Mediterranness has various meanings on the Akdeniz music scene. In the first place it possesses "a connotation of 'extrovertness' as opposed to 'introvertness,'" while also referring to the use of Greek, Italian, and Spanish (Andalusian) elements, which get extensive radio airplay in Turkey. Özer opportunely underlines the fact that the Akdeniz music scene does not seem to evince direct links with the global music market, rather constituting a further example within the Mediterranean of processes and relations between local musics and global contexts: definitions of what is actually "Akdeniz" may vary from one musician or one band to the next, and this flexibility is perceived as advantageous for the emergence of different identities and musical discourses with Mediterraneanness as a common point of reference.

Kevin Dawe discusses the peculiarities of popular music in Greece over the course of a decade (1990–2000), setting it in a broad sweep of cultural history extending from the 1960s to the present day. Dawe identifies a recurring model, developed to make sense of contemporary Greek music-making: that of Greece as a country of borders and contacts with a diversity of cultural worlds. Proceeding from this positive perception of Greece as a frontier, "musical orientation and indeed consciousness is explored, negotiated, contested, worked out, developed, defined, expressed." Greek musicians, explains Dawe, are aware of the dynamics of globalization, which they use to define their product and to define themselves; they take full account, moreover, of Greek musi-

cal traditions and of the sounds and musical instruments of their locality, considering them essential elements of inspiration and identity.
The musical mix that reproduces in sounds the model of the cultural
frontier includes among other things the melodies, rhythms, and
instruments of Arab, Turkish, and Middle Eastern cultures. In a close
reading of different compositions by musicians who are Greek by birth
or by choice, and by evaluating various musical genres, Dawe reveals
that within Greek popular music, identity is perceived as a mix,
achieved by the superimposition of different musical styles (many of
which come from Mediterranean countries), and is the result of various
attempts to find and establish a "right mix" in the sounds and in the
music. Here, then, we encounter a "between world" musical aesthetics,
based on the concept that intercultural collaboration, hybridization,
and crossover are not negative experiences if directed "from within."[12]

Joško Ćaleta embarks on a detailed analysis of the characteristics of
traditional music in Mediterranean Croatia, the regions of Dalmatia,
Istria, and Kvarner. Ćaleta outlines the establishment of local forms of
popular music, presenting combinations of local musical elements with
global styles and demonstrating that traditional musics and popular
local musics share the same place of origin and are performed within the
same cultural environment. This common localization gives these
musics a Mediterranean connotation, even if the links with the
Mediterranean remain undeclared (although it may be possible to identify influences and borrowings from other musical cultures). Ćaleta first
considers the phenomenon of *klapa* singing in Dalmatia, illustrating the
differences between the various forms of klapa: the traditional form; the
"festival klapa," which arose out of festival appearances by klapa singers;
and the "modern klapa," which sees the area of use expand from
Dalmatia to take in areas such as Zagreb and Rijeka as well as remote
locations like Australia, New Zealand, Canada, Germany, and Sweden,
where groups of klapa singers are active. The "modern klapa" performances include non-local musical elements such as rock, rap, blues, funk,
and "alternative" music. According to Ćaleta, the new style developed in
the '90s constitutes an element of the popular music scene in Croatia,
reflecting and enhancing a positive idea of Mediterraneanness. Ćaleta
also reviews the music scene in Istria, illustrating the activity of musicians and bands playing a mix of music forms from oral and global tra-

ditions (pop, rock, jazz, and electronic music). This is a music open to a greater diversity of influences, where the choice of a single expressive style seems impossible. The musicians active in Istria often affirm their distance from the world of traditional music, Ćaleta tells us, but they do not depart from it, using traditional forms as an element of local connotation, and understanding that, in fact, this use represents an essential element of their success outside Istria.

Goffredo Plastino highlights a disc that has left its mark on the history of popular music in Italy: *Creuza de mä* by Fabrizio De André (with Mauro Pagani). It is a work that introduced a model of "Mediterranean music" still appreciated and imitated today by numerous Italian performers. Plastino reconstructs the context of Italian popular music and in particular that of the progressive rock scene in the 1970s, a period in which there was already a marked interest in the traditional musics of the Mediterranean. It was this context that gave birth to the idea of *Creuza de mä*, which, however, distances itself from the musical experiences that preceded it. The record is in fact based on the idea that Mediterranean music can be the result of cultural mediation, expounded by performers who have no direct link with the musical traditions adopted in the elaboration of their style. *Creuza de mä* is put together in such a way that the musical elements "borrowed" from various musical cultures of the Mediterranean are not immediately identifiable and consequently represent, in the view of its creators, a "no man's land": an "invention" combining certain formal structures of popular music with a non-localizable "Mediterranean" sound. Released before the assertion of "world music" as a musical genre, this recording by De André and Pagani anticipates a number of its characteristics, such as the exploitation of traditional musical instruments and melodies and the use of sounds outside their cultural context. *Creuza de mä* thus proves important not only for its role in pioneering certain musical tendencies that emerged in the years that followed, but because it depicts a Mediterranean identity within Italian popular music, one reaffirmed in subsequent years by many performers, notably within the ambit of the folk music revival. This record upholds the idea of Italy as a place of passage and of synthesis of various Mediterranean musical cultures, which may therefore be liberally reinterpreted and re-enacted—an idea still strongly held today by many Italian musicians.

Philip Bohlman examines the repertories in which it is possible to identify a rapport between the sacred and popular musics of the Mediterranean. Rather than thinking of the two camps as separate and reciprocally in opposition, Bohlman studies the extent to which they have interacted, in particular in a period of history marked by the globalization of modes of religious expression and by the "explosion" of forms of popular devotion. Proceeding from the analysis of music product issued for the Christian Millennium Jubilee, Bohlman studies "the ways in which sacred musical practices become popular through the creative use of music by worshipers moving along personal and collective sacred journeys," and identifies in the topics of the journey toward and the passage through the holy places that renders possible the expression of the sacred in performances of popular music. Bohlman's reading of this situation presents us with a Mediterranean in which sacred popular musics are shaped by the superimposition of different musical features, clearly audible in realities that are diverse and distant from one another, and jointly constitute a diagram of points through which a constant flow of musical information passes. Bohlman's text closes the circle, in a sense, and adds essential information that—along with that contained in the articles of the other contributors—tells us of the Mediterranean as a place of new and intense musical communications.

The more we are able to know of this sea, the less we look at it on our own: the Mediterranean is not a sea of solitude (Matvejević 1991: 151).

Many connections are clearly identifiable in the essays presented in this volume, many can be discovered. I will confine myself to a few suggestions. It is important to note the use that has been made of certain musical instruments in different real-life cultural and musical situations: the bouzouki, for instance, is often found outside Greece—in rock music, in Italy, in Turkey, and often employing techniques that are incorrect but do not affect its role as one of the symbolic timbres of the Mediterranean. Then again, relations with Spain and some musical cultures of Spain may be encountered elsewhere (Morocco, Tunisia, Egypt, Turkey). There is then clear evidence of the influence on different local forms of music exerted by the diffusion and hearing (from Spain to

Turkey) of a model of song such as the Italian, from the Sanremo festival (Borgna 1986). More generally, there clearly emerges a broad spectrum of intercultural collaborations, based on attentive listening to and sometimes participation in recordings of music differing from those made locally.[13] One of the merits of the essays in this volume is undoubtedly that of having shed light on many "relevant connections . . . across the Mediterranean" (Stokes and Davis 1996: 256).

The relationship between musical expression and identity is present in all the articles, and it is possible to see how much these identities are shaped and established through music. The claim of "Mediterraneanness" often represents the element fundamental to the development of a local musical identity, *glocal* and sometimes global. But the "Mediterranean" is not always the same for all: we see the differences in the conception of "Mediterranean music" in Spain, Israel, Turkey, or Italy. We also see how in Egypt the Mediterranean reading of popular music has been advanced alongside many others, sometimes overlapping, sometimes remote.

One constant element appears to be a recourse to local realities in all musical experiences. Local musical cultures are revisited, redeveloped, relaunched via the acquisition of other repertories, whether global, Mediterranean, or local. The dialogue is between that which is at hand and familiar and that which is perceived as distant (though sometimes not that far off) but similar, or in some way assimilable. The process of change never appears sudden or inevitable, but always as the result of reflection on various possibilities of change: instrumentation, style, expression. The relationship with global musical reality has always been closely assessed and carried to its conclusion without ever losing sight of local links (included here, adopted in many different ways). It may therefore be emphasized once more that these musicians of the Mediterranean "have . . . established connections with other musical cultures and music markets, in this instance by emphasizing some of the distinct musical characteristics akin to their own or else by forming new alliances through whom they are represented" (Guilbault 1993: 39).

Many of the musical repertories considered here are currently disseminated through the market for world music, even if they have sometimes been created or elaborated without direct reference to this new "hyper-genre." At the same time, it is correct to state that they have come together (and will probably continue to come together) within world music, because the model of the Mediterranean as an area of musical communications and exchanges in all directions (on which many musical experiences in the contemporary Mediterranean are based, or to which they are related) represents on a reduced scale and for a precise geographico-cultural reality that which world music seeks to achieve for the whole world. The welcoming of many Mediterranean musical realities beneath the umbrella of world music then appears both "natural" and inevitable: in great part, as we have had opportunity to observe, it has already taken place. In seeking to read and interpret the musical facts documented in this volume through the discourses of and about world music (Frith 2000), it is possible to offer in evidence many aspects such as (among others): the postmodern condition of some traditional musical cultures; the disappearance or attenuation of boundaries; musical creativity and cultural borrowing; changes in musical traditions; and hybridity and (as) authenticity. Many hybrid musical forms and productions analyzed in this book are "situated in the intestices of numerous cultural borders" (Joseph 1999: 2); are the result of processes of exchanges not only between a center and a periphery but also between different peripheries, and work as the metaphors "for the form of identity that is being produced from these conjunctions" (Papastergiadis 1997: 274); develop new senses of self, not through the marginalization but through the awareness (Klopper 2000: 229). But we must not overlook that many of these elements appeared in various musical traditions of the Mediterranean before the establishment of world music. In a sense, the Mediterranean has been a privileged environment in which the musical dynamics successively lifted by world music have been repeatedly tried out; for this reason, world-music-oriented recordings look attentively at, and seek to "cover" completely, the contemporary Mediterranean—which nevertheless seems unable to mesh completely with this musical dimension.

The pieces of this mosaic could have been joined by many more, and many more will be added.[14] Every presentation of the evidence restores to us an aspect, necessarily and fortunately partial, of this complex, multifaceted reality—as usual, one feels like saying. The Mediterranean, then, is always taking on new form: this explains the fascination that it exerts.

More than once, finishing my work on this book, I have thought of a song which I heard and recorded ten years ago, during a religious festival in a little village in Calabria (Southern Italy). At the end of September 1992, I was in Riace for the feast of Saints Cosmas and Damian, the patron saints and protectors of the village, who gather to their sanctuary, year after year, a vast crowd of devotees, including throngs of Gypsies. I spent one afternoon in the church listening to the singing of one man: Giovanni Schipilliti. I had encountered him at other festivals that year; he was known, heard, and appreciated by all as an accomplished and tireless singer. In church, Giovanni Schipilliti sang religious songs, in which the congregation sometimes joined. Outside of the church, he sang love songs, receiving invitations to the houses of friends and acquaintances for this purpose. On this particular afternoon, I joined him as he entered a house so that I could hear him sing some more and make some recordings. Before he started, Giovanni Schipilliti explained that to reach Riace from his village he had traveled for about seven hours (including station stops along his train journey), covering the whole coast of central-southern Calabria from the Tyrrhenian to the Ionian Sea, well aware that the same journey could be made by car in less than two hours. However, he did not own a car, and in any case, he *had* to be present at the festival. Then he began singing: some *muttette* for solo voice (a style of song commonly found in Southern Calabria, usually with guitar accompaniment), among them one with these lyrics:

Volia iettari nu lignu nta mari
mi navigu e mi vaiu a n'Arbania
mi vidu la me bella se o viva o morta
si o viva o morta mi la portu cu' mia

Vaiu e l'arrivu comu gigliu all'ortu
cu nu libbru a manu chi leggia
vaiu e l'arrivu comu gigliu all'ortu
cu nu libbru a manu chi dormia

Marinareddhu chi veni di Londra
dimmi l'amuri comu s'accomencia

e s'accomencia cu soni e cu balli
o puramenti cu chianti e lamenti

I wanted to launch a boat on the sea
to sail and go as far as Albania
to discover whether my beloved is alive or dead
alive or dead, I will bring her back with me

I am going to join her, she is as a lily in a garden
with a book in her hand, may she be reading
I am going to join her, she is as a lily in a garden
a book in her hand even as she sleeps

Sailor who comes from London
tell me how love begins
it begins with music and dancing
or else in weeping and wailing

For me, this song represents many of the questions that will be
explored in this book. It reminds me of a man who, to sing again, went
from sea to sea by the longest route he could, always feeling himself to
be at home. Most important of all, perhaps, it speaks of voyages on and
to the Mediterranean: this song is a vivid reminder to me that that sea
has also been a place of contacts, of requests, of exchanges.

Notes

1. For more information, see http://www.davidcervera.com, http://www.talaud.com.
2. See http://teev.com/esta/index.htm.
3. See http://teev.com/esta/press.htm.
4. See Magrini 1993: 22, which quotes the case of the Cretan *lyra* and instruments similar to it as an example for the Mediterranean of "exchanges that are more complex and more difficult to locate in time."
5. Notes from the compilation *Empreintes méditerranéennes*, 1998.
6. Notes from the compilation *Mediterranean Lullaby*, 2000.
7. In other CDs, the musical performances have no clear element in common: "In this compilation we unite Mediterranean music;" notes from *The Mediterranean. Traditional and Ethnic Music*, 2001.
8. John McLaughlin, notes in *The Mediterranean*, 1990.

9. Simon Shaheen, notes in *Blue Flame*, 2001. See also Bessman 2001: 84. Shaheen's CD has been viewed as one of the most relevant examples of a "new" musical phenomenon, which could be defined as "Arabic world beat." The interest in such forms of crossover in Arabo-Mediterranean countries has among other things produced compilations such as *Arabic Groove* (2001), which states: "Modern Arab artists are taking traditional melodies, rhythms, instrumentation and singing styles and superimposing them over Western pop styles. The results are irresistible blends that do not require the listener to understand the lyrics or comprehend the subtleties of the singing." *Arabic Groove* includes performances of musicians from Algeria, Morocco, Lebanon, Egypt, Libya. Other recordings of the same type are *Desert Roses and Arabian Rhythms* (2001), *Arabica* (2002), and *Arabica II* (2002).

10. In this connection, the work done by Roberto Catalano (1999) is of great importance.

11. See, for example, these words by the composer Eleni Karaindrou, written as introduction to her last published *corpus* of compositions, *Trojan Women* (2002): "Costantinople lyra, kanonaki, nay, santouri, outi, laouto, harp, daires, daouli, sounds which comes from the depth of time. Sound which caress the shores of Asia Minor, travel to the Black Sea, nest in the domes of Costantinople and bind with the wail of Smyrna burning. Sounds recognisable not only in Greece but also in the Balkans and in all the countries wetted by the Mediterranean." In Italy, many rappers and raggamuffin bands have been associated with has been referred to as "Mediterranean reggae" (Mitchell 2001: 198, 208), because of the use of regionals dialects, samples of Italian traditional musical instruments, and influences of Middle Eastern musics (see Plastino 1996).

Furthermore, numerous jazz musicians have associated themselves with Mediterranean musical cultures or musical elements, and recently there have been many Mediterranean musicians who have released works making ample use of the language of jazz (such as Kudsi Erguner in *Islam Blues*, 2001, which includes a track entitled "Mediterranien"; or the French Orchestre National de Jazz, that released in 2002 a CD entitled *Charmediterranéan*, with Tunisian 'ud player Anouar Brahem). It is not possible to attempt an analysis of this complex musical phenomenon here: for a brief introduction, see Chambet-Werner 2000: 95–97; on Italy, see Plastino 1990, Piras 1985.

12. See, as a final example, the description of *Bahar*, the latest work by Makis Ablianitis, released by Libra Records (2000): "*Bahar* is the ultimate musical expression of contemporary multicultural identity. It is a musical journey that begins from the soil of the Balkans, opens up into the big blue of the Mediterranean, to end in the trails of the East. The inspired compositions are by Makis Ablianitis. It is music shed by the sun of the Mediterranean. The deep melodic voice of Manolis Lidakis, graces the two songs of the album. Poetic lyrics performed by, perhaps, the best Greek male vocalist. The album also features four very prominent artists: Hariprasad Chaurasia, the greatest Indian flutist, internationally acclaimed, known for his collaborations with Ravi Shankar, John McLaughlin and Jan Garbarek, among others; Dragan Dautovski, the kaval and gaida virtuoso from FYROM; Haig Yazdjian, the great Armenian 'ud player; Petros Tabouris, the Greek canun virtuoso.

In times when the borders of nations are falling and a new cultural identity is emerging, *Bahar* takes on the role of the sound sample of this new culture. A sound that respects the diversities and individualities of the cultures that comprise this album, but at the same time is the media that presents us with a contemporary musical direction" (http://www.libramusic.gr/new.html).

13. This may cause us to regard as definitively superseded the viewpoint of Sorce Keller (1993), which, on the basis of radio listening, postulated that the Mediterranean had not experienced a circulation of popular musics outside their countries of origin—a hypothesis which seems unsustainable for the past and even less plausible for the present if one considers the level of musical communication in the contemporary Mediterranean.

14. While this book was in preparation, there was held at Venice (June 2001) the 5th Meeting of the ICTM Study Group on the "Anthropology of Music in Mediterranean Cultures", on the subject *Trends and Processes in Today's Mediterranean Music*. In the account of the meeting, the accent falls in part on those musical repertoires "discovered by a wider audience and marketed thanks to the new fad for the so-called "world music"" (see: http://www.provincia.venezia.it/levi/eventi/musica_ contemporanea_medioevo/musica_contemporanea_medioevo.html).

Bibliography

Amorós, Miguel. 2001. "David Cervera. La música mediterránea como forma de expresión," *Batonga! La revista de las músicas del mundo* 16: 4.

Assante, Ernesto and Gino Castaldo. 1995. "Il grande mare della musica," in *Mediterraneo / Il disco del mese*. Roma: Edizioni La Repubblica. 4–11.

Bessman, Jim. 2001. "Arabic Music moves West. Cheb Mami, Simon Shaheen, Others Spread the World," *Billboard* August 11: 1 and 84.

Boissevain, Jeremy. 1979. "Towards a Social Anthropology of the Mediterranean," *Current Anthropology* 20/1: 81–93.

Borgna, Gianni. 1986. *La Canzone di Sanremo*. Roma-Bari: Laterza.

Braudel, Fernand. 1949. *La Méditerranée et le Monde méditerranéen à l'époque de Philippe II*. Paris: Librairie Armand Colin.

———. 1987. *Il Mediterraneo. Lo spazio e la storia—gli uomini e la tradizione*. Milano: Bompiani.

Catalano, Roberto. 1999. *Mediterranean World-Music: Experiencing Sicilian-Arab Sounds*. Ph.D. Dissertation in Ethnomusicology. Los Angeles: University of California.

Chambet-Werner, Oriane. 2000. "Entre jazz et 'musiques du monde.' Regards croisés sur la rencontre de l'autre," *Cahiers de musiques traditionnelles* 13: 91–102.

Davis, John. 1977. *People of the Mediterranean. An essay in comparative social anthropology*. London, Henley and Boston: Routledge and Kegan Paul.

———. 1993. "Modelli del Mediterraneo," in *Antropologia della musica e culture mediterranee*, edited by Tullia Magrini. Venezia: Fondazione Ugo e Olga Levi / Società Editrice il Mulino. 89–105.

De Martino, Ernesto. 1961. *La terra del rimorso. Contributo a una storia religiosa del Sud*. Milano: Il Saggiatore.

De Simone, Roberto. 1994. *Disordinata storia della canzone napoletana*. Ischia: Valentino Editore.

Driessen, Henk. 1999. "Pre- and Post-Braudelian Conceptions of the Mediterranean Area. The Puzzle of Boundaries," *Narodna umjetnost*, 36/1: 53–63.

El-Ghadban, Yara. 2001. "Shedding Some Lights on Contemporary Musicians in Palestine," *Middle East Studies Association Bulletin* (http://w3fp.arizona.edu/mesas-soc/Bulletin/35-1/35-1Al-Ghadban.htm)

Fabbri, Franco. 1998. "Generi in trasformazione: l'elettrificazione di alcune musiche nel Mediterraneo," in *Norme con ironie. Scritti per i settant'anni di Ennio Morricone*, edited by Sergio Miceli. Milano: Suvini Zerboni. 81–102.

——. 2001. "Alcune musiche popolari del Mediterraneo e la loro ricezione come World Music," in *Musica come ponte tra i popoli*, edited by Giuliano Tonini. Lucca: LIM. 121–126.

Feld, Steven. 1994. "From Schizophonia to Schismogenesis: On the Discourses and Commodification Practices of 'World Music' and 'World Beat'," in Charles Keil and Steven Feld, *Music Grooves. Essays and Dialogues*. Chicago and London: University of Chicago Press. 257–289.

Frith, Simon. 2000. "The Discourse of World Music," in *Western Music and Its Others. Difference, Representation, and Appropriation in Music*, edited by Georgina Born and David Hesmondhalgh. Berkley, Los Angeles, and London: University of California Press. 305–322.

Frykman, Jonas. 1999. "Culturalization of the Mediterranean Space," *Narodna umjetnost*, 36/1: 283–287.

Guaitamacchi, Ezio. 2000. "Mediterraneo e Medio Oriente," in *Musiche dal Mondo. Atlante sonoro della World Music—6*, edited by Ivo Franchi, Enzo Gentile and Ezio Guaitamacchi. Milano: Fabbri Editori. 2–3.

Guilbault, Jocelyne. 1993. "On Redefining the 'Local' Through World Music," *The World of Music* 35/2: 33–47.

Joseph, May. 1999. "Introduction: New Hybrid Identities and Performance," in *Performing Hybridity*, edited by May Joseph and Jennifer Natalya Fink. Minneapolis and London: University of Minnesota Press. 1–24.

Klopper, Sandra. 2000. "Re-dressing the Past: the Africanisation of Sartorial Style in Contemporary South Africa," in *Hybridity and its Discontents. Politics, Science, Culture*, edited by Avtar Brah and Annie E. Coombes. London and New York: Routledge. 216–231.

Lortat-Jacob, Bernard. 1996. *Canti di passione. Castelsardo, Sardegna*. Lucca: Libreria Musicale Italiana.

Magrini, Tullia. 1993. "Introduzione," in *Antropologia della musica e culture mediterranee*, edited by Tullia Magrini. Venezia: Fondazione Ugo e Olga Levi / Società Editrice il Mulino. 7–33.

——. 1999. "Where Does Mediterranean Music Begin?," *Narodna umjetnost*, 36/1: 173–182.

Matvejević, Predrag. 1991. *Mediterraneo. Un nuovo breviario*. Milano: Garzanti. [Original edition: *Mediteranski brevijar*. Zagreb: SN Liber, 1987.]

Mitchell, Tony. 2001. "Fightin' da Faida. The Italian Posses and Hip-Hop in Italy," in *Global Noise. Rap and Hip-Hop outside the USA*, edited by Tony Mitchell. Middletown: Wesleyan University Press. 194–221.

Papastergiadis, Nikos. 1997. "Tracing Hybridity in Theory," in *Debating Cultural Hybridity. Mutli-Cultural Identities and the Politics of Anti-Racism*, edited by Pnina Werbner and Traq Modood. London and New Jersey: Zed Books. 257-281.

Picken, Lawrence. 1975. *Folk Musical Instruments of Turkey*. London: Oxford University Press.

Pina-Cabral, João de. 1989. "The Mediterranean as a Category of regional Comparison: a Critical View," *Current Anthropology* 30/3: 399–406.

Piras, Marcello, ed. 1985. *Jazz e cultura mediterranea*. Roma and Reggio Calabria: Ismez / Gangemi Editore.

Plastino, Goffredo. 1990. "L'invenzione del Mediterraneo," *Viceversa* 28: 30–33.

——. 1996. *Mappa delle voci. Rap, raggamuffin e tradizione in Italia*. Roma: Meltemi.

Sorce Keller, Marcello. 1993. "La 'popular music' come riflesso dei contatti culturali nell'area mediterranea. Un'occasione per riconsiderare la definizione corrente di cultura," in *Antropologia della musica e culture mediterranee*, edited by Tullia Magrini. Venezia: Fondazione Ugo e Olga Levi / Società Editrice il Mulino. 133-145.

Stokes, Martin and Davis, Ruth. 1996. "Introduction," *Popular Music* 15/3 (Middle East Issue): 255–257.

Sugarman, Jane. 1997. *Engendering Song. Singing and Subjectivity at Prespa Albanian Weddings*. Chicago: University of Chicago Press.

Taylor, Timothy D. 1997. *Global Pop. World Music, World Markets*. New York and London: Routledge.

Weis Bentzon, Andrea Fridolin. 1969. *The Launeddas. A Sardinian Folk Music Instrument*. Copenhagen. Akademisk Forlag.

Discography

A Mediterranean Odyssey. Athens to Andalucia. Putumayo World Music PUTU 148–2. 1999.

Ablianitis, Makis. *Bahar*. Libra Music LM 020–2. 2000.

An Xplosion of World Music from the Mediterranean Area. Edizioni Musicali Il Pontesonoro PVD 965.18. No date.

Anime mediterranee. Pontesonoro OM0013. 1997.

Arabic Groove. Putumayo World Music PUT 189–2. 2001.

Arabica. A North African Voyage into Sound. Bar de Lune LUNECD07. 2002.

Arabica II. Bar de Lune LUNED10. 2002.

Cervera, David. *Talaüd*. Chrysalis 7243 5 27672 2 9. 2000.

Daniele, Pino. *Medina*. BMG Ricordi 74321835222. 2001. (Includes "Via Medina," with Lotfi Boushnak.)

De Rosas, Marino. *Meridies*. Amiata Records ARNR 199. 2001. (Includes "Mediterraneo.")

Desert Roses & Arabian Rhythms. Mondo Melodia 186 850 018 2. 2001.

Empreintes méditerranéennes. L'empreinte digitale ED 13069. 1998.

Erguner, Kudsi. *Islam Blues*. ACT 9287–2. 2001. (Includes "Mediterranien.")

Esta. *Mediterranean Crossroads*. Newance E1002. 1996.

Jefira. *Rencontres. Musique d'Une Méditerranée Inventée*. Buda Musique 82971–2. 1999.

Karaindrou, Eleni. *Trojan Women*. ECM 1810. 2002.

Kithara. *Musica Mediterranea*. Chandos CHAN 0562. 1994.

Loeb, Chuck. *Mediterranean*. DMP CD-494. 1993.

Mare Nostrum. Antologia di musica mediterranea. Libera Informazione Editrice A 483797. No date.

McLaughlin, John. *The Mediterranean*. CBS MK 45578. 1990.

"Mediterranea" sampler. New Age Music & New Sounds NANS 033. 1994.

Mediterranea—Voices of the Sun. Audibis Tempo A6206. 1999.

Mediterranean Café Songs. Nascente NSCD 061. 2000.

Mediterranean Lullaby. Ellipsis Art . . . CD 4290. 2000.

Méditerranée. Les musiques du Sud. Al Sur ALCD 1002. 1998. 3 CDs.

Mediterraneo. Edizioni La Repubblica DdM-38. 1995.

Mediterraneo. Hellenic Music for Classical Guitar. Pearl SHECD 9634. 1999.

Musiche dal mondo: Mediterraneo. Fabbri Editori. 2000.

Musiques de fêtes en Calabre. Maison des Cultures du Monde / Audivis W 260051. 1993. (Includes Muttetta.)

Niebla, Eduardo and Adel Salameh. *Mediterraneo*. Riverboat TUGCD1012. 1996.

Orchestre National de Jazz. *Charmediterránéan*. ECM 1828.

Parfums de Méditerranée. EMI Music France / Atoll Music 4 98228 2. 1998.

Robin Nolan Trio. *Mediterranean Blues*. Refined Records RR 1003. 2001.

Shaheen, Simon (& Qantara). *Blue Flame*. ARK 21 Records 186 850 022 2. 2001. (Includes "Dance Mediterranea.")

The Mediterranean. Traditional & Ethnic music. Adama music ad-20506. 2001.

Yannatou, Savina. *Mediterranea. Songs of the Mediterranean*. Sounds True STA MM 00118D. 1998.

PAINT IT BLACK, CAT:
ROCK, POP, AND THE MEDITERRANEAN

FRANCO FABBRI

Garlic Bread, Olives, and Lobster:
"Mediterranean Food"

"Garlic bread: as an Italian you must be fond of it," says my Canadian friend.

"Well, I am, but the only place where I usually eat it is England."

"Are you kidding?"

We are sitting at a table in a small restaurant, on a Greek island. We are talking about "Mediterranean food." Italians are supposed to be eating garlic bread at any time of the day. "I'm sorry, but you won't find anything like garlic bread in a bakery in Italy. We have *bruschetta* which is served in restaurants (rather unlikely if you go north of Florence, anyway): it consists of a slice of bread, grilled, brushed with raw garlic, served with salt and olive oil. It can be served also with fresh tomato and basil. In the past, if you ordered *bruschetta* you would get the garlic and oil version; now the default is with tomato, and if you want it just with garlic you have to ask—at least in Rome—for a *bruschetta bianca* (white). You will not have to ask for basil with tomato, it will come anyway."

"Ah, basil" says our friend Dimos, who at last is bringing the fish we ordered some time ago (almost an hour, actually). "We don't eat it."

"I understand. It's a kind of ornamental plant here, also with some religious significance."

"Of course. Its name means 'royal,' 'of the Lord.'"

"In Italy we can't imagine tomato salad or pizza without basil. By the way, why don't you ever cook fish in the oven? It would be ready in twenty minutes! With potatoes and olives, it's great!"

"Olives? In the oven? How can you put olives into the oven?" The conversation could continue for a long time. It is interrupted by the sound of a mobile phone. Another Italian sitting at the next table is almost shouting: "*Sì mamma, stiamo benissimo, mangiamo pesce tutti i giorni!*" ("Yes, mom, we are fine, eating fish every day!"). So I spare my British, Canadian, and Greek friends the old story of Greek fishermen throwing lobsters back into the sea, because nobody would want them (this was during World War II, and everyone was starving, then). We join multicultural forces, and firmly ask the fish-eating Italian to go elsewhere for his very important phone calls.[1]

"Mediterranean food": everyone knows about it. Italian pasta or Greek *moussaka*? Oily Spanish vegetables, or grilled meat with raw onions in Croatia? *Soupe du pêcheur à la Provençale*, or Sardinian roasted pig? *Couscous*, or lentil soup? And, to finish, what about a cup of coffee? Café crème? Espresso? Turkish?

Prototypes, Best Examples, and Empty Armors

Few concepts have vaguer contours (do concepts have contours?) than "Mediterranean food."[2] One that comes to mind immediately is "Mediterranean music." It could be used as a probe to test current theories about categories (see Lakoff 1987 and Fabbri 1999; or, also as an homage to the "Mediterranean food" discussants, see Tagg 1982). Many people talk about it, many people seem to believe that some category, class, concept, or cultural unit like "Mediterranean music" does exist. For an entity like this, it is more than enough (according to Stefani 1978, music is just any activity around sounds). But then, what is it? Apparently there is no clear definition to help us distinguish between music items or events that should be in or out, represented or not represented by the label. So it is not a class like the ones created within scientific taxonomies (for example: insects and arachnids; see Lakoff 1987 and Eco 1997). It doesn't seem to be a genre, either: when a genre is accepted by a community, there is an agreement about features of the musical events that are allowed in the context (Fabbri 1981, 1982a, 1982b, 1996, 1999, 2001). Some of these norms are quite precise, sharp, defined by significant oppositions; nothing like this seems at work in the "Mediterranean music" concept. If it is a very broad, fuzzy category, then it doesn't seem to be defined by prototypes or best examples (Lakoff 1987). Yes, of course there are music items that will be immediately recognized as "Mediterranean music," but they are very different from one another, so the category would admit many prototypes, each one possibly in conflict with the others. And even family resemblances do not seem to help: Plucked sounds? Reeds? Modality? Is it true, then, that some people would accept music from Pakistan or Turkmenistan as "Mediterranean"?

Of course there is another, practical solution to the problem. One can first define the concept geographically, including music events originated in Mediterranean countries and excluding those which do not belong to countries that share the Mediterranean coastline. Then one will have to consider to which degree musics belonging (*belonging?*) to Mediterranean countries but based in regions far from that coastline (say, Brittany, Galicia) can be included. Then one will have to discuss genres, and wonder if compositions by Luigi Nono, born in Venice and—according to his own declarations—influenced by the music culture and soundscapes of one of the most important cities in the Mediterranean and its history, should be treated as "Mediterranean music." Or (to remain in Italy), one will have to ask if music like the collection of songs included in Fabrizio De André's album *Creuza de mä* (that many commentators would consider the epitome of Italian "Mediterranean music," although it was constructed by a singer-songwriter and a former progressive-rock musician using Turkish, Greek, and Middle Eastern models, with lyrics in a "fake" Genoese dialect) must be included in the category.[3] In the end, we would probably come to a definition of "Mediterranean music" based on a collection of musics geographically based around the sea, acceptable by a community (ethnomusicologists, World Beat fans, jazz composers, or anything else).

Honestly, although I understand that this is the only possible framework for our discussion, I prefer the vaguer fuzzy category that resembles "Mediterranean food." That is, I find it more productive to consider "Mediterranean music" as just an "other" that was created (by Mediterraneans and non-Mediterraneans alike) as a mythical counterpart to the popular music mainstream. As such, it has the same consistency of Italo Calvino's *The Nonexistent Knight*, an empty suit of armor fighting against injustice, kept together and made alive by the poor people's wishes. The knight's squire, Gurdulù, likes to take the character and shape of anything he sees—another useful literary metaphor, as we shall see.

The Construction of "Mediterranean"

Usually it takes time for a genre to be named. Genre names are often retroactive; decades after the naming process took place, people use the genre name to indicate musics that existed before the name was agreed on (see Blesh and Janis 1950 about the birth of the term "ragtime" in 1897, quite some time after the music to which the label referred had been in existence; the same happened for the blues, *rembetika*, and so forth). A similar process seems to be at work with "Mediterranean music." But we still know very little about the process. Certainly the term is used, and in some countries institutions were established that refer to the concept: there is a Mediterranean Music Centre in Lamia, Greece, an Arab and Mediterranean Music Centre in Tunisia. Would it be a useful international research project, to trace the origins of this cultural unit in all countries (even non-Mediterranean ones), and to compare processes that led to its construction? Some suggestions that the empty armor image might apply on a larger scale than just my own heuristic usage came from informal talks with colleagues from other countries, and of course this book spontaneously provides much relevant information on the ideology of "Mediterranean." However, even answering collectively very simple questions like, "When was 'Mediterranean music' first named like this in this country?" or "Which genres in this country are thought to belong to 'Mediterranean music' and which are not?" would form the basis for more solid theoretical ground.

But there are various levels and communities for which such questions might make (common) sense, not just national ones. I suspect the idea of "Mediterranean" has common traits across different communities within the Islamic, Orthodox, Catholic, or Hebrew worlds. May I also wonder, then, if the idea of "Mediterranean" has the same form among Sephardim compared to Ashkenazim? Is "Mediterranean" the same for Northern and for Southern Italians? And what about other communities, like the transnational community of popular music? Is there a pop musician's common sense about "Mediterranean"?

Pop and the Mediterranean

If there is one, a crucial period in time for the construction of a meaning for "Mediterranean music" may be centered in the mid-'60s. Before that, pieces of "Mediterranean" exoticism (in a broad sense) abound in the history of popular music and jazz, including: jazz classics like "Caravan" and "Night in Tunisia"; comedy songs like "Istanbul (Not Constantinople)"; and quite a number of Roman or Neapolitan souvenirs like "Mandolins in the Moonlight" or "The Man Who Plays the Mandolin"—it may be useful to know that the Italian original text for "The Man Who Plays the Mandolin (Guaglione)" never mentions that musical instrument–sung by American singers of Italian origin like Perry Como or Dean Martin in the late '50s. In the early '60s, while Elvis Presley was singing *O sole mio* ("It's Now or Never," top selling hit in the United Kingdom in November 1960) and "Torna a Surriento (Surrender)," Greek music enjoyed a sudden popularity: in 1960 "Never on Sunday" (music by Manos Hadjidakis, sung by Melina Mercouri) won an Academy Award for best song, and in 1964 bouzoukis triumphed again with Theodorakis's "Zorba's Dance." It is of little or no importance, then (and it is still so today), that there be no such folk dance in Greece as *sirtaki*, as the "small" *sirtòs* invented by Theodorakis worked very well, as an exemplary kind of "internal" exoticism.[4]

All these pieces contributed with their success—probably then also functioning as "best examples" although contradictory ones, as in cognitivists' theories (Lakoff 1987)—to the construction of a "Mediterranean music" category accepted by North American and European audiences, including musicians. However, in the mid-'60s, a different approach to the exotic becomes apparent. One of its earliest traces is the sitar, first played by George Harrison, on "Norwegian Wood (This Bird Has Flown)," released on The Beatles' album *Rubber Soul* in late 1965. That sitar doesn't sound more exotic than fuzz bass in "Think for Yourself," on the same album; it's just strange, different, a new sound. The original sleeve notes point out instruments and sounds uncommon for the group: "Paul on piano," "Mal 'organ' Evans on

Hammond," "George Martin on harmonium," and so on. The sitar (unlike in later Harrison songs) doesn't mean "India"; it means that pop is ready to incorporate any sound.

Within a dozen of months, every sound source—from spliced or reversed tape to tablas, from early electronic instruments to steam organs, from dulcimers to manually braked tape flanges—will become part of the mix. The mixer has been the real medium of pop, since then, and is probably a large part of the message. And there is an ideological counterpart for this technological appropriation: an attitude to consider other musics (from Stockhausen to raga), other cultures, as something that can easily become part of "our" culture, if approached and experienced with an open mind, with Schillerian naïveté (see the cover of *Sgt. Pepper's Lonely Hearts Club Band*, 1967) or with an attitude similar to that Italo Calvino character, Gurdulù, who—seeing a goose—starts to swim in a pond and quack. Superficial as it can be, this attitude toward the musical exotic is anyway different from the previous (and following: think of songs like "Fernando," by ABBA) postcard-like treatment of "the other."[5] Technical means have changed—in over 35 years—from rudimentary multitrack to samplers and computers, but still relations between the multinational "mainstream" and "local" music cultures can be viewed under the old dichotomic perspectives of appropriation and representation that could be used for late nineteenth and early twentieth century classical music (national schools and various exotic portraits of faraway countries). It may be added that in popular music this dichotomy overlaps others, like "rock" versus "pop," "authentic" versus "commercial," "progressive" versus "standardized." And the polarities (the different vectors' directions) do not neccesarily always remain the same. In the mid-'60s, musicians willing to appropriate other musics used to name themselves "pop," but under that different (compared with today's) naming convention, the game to play was: "Make it your own." And this was good.

But would all sounds be really good? Not exactly so. Everything with a "mainstream" color or smell could be suspect, and should be treated carefully or avoided. Even the strings in "Yesterday" sounded dubious: is that a Beatles record or is it Sinatra? So we shouldn't be surprised if, given the mainstream success of Italian and Greek songs in the late '50s and early '60s, that part (not a small one) of the

"Mediterranean music" concept didn't have immediate appeal for non-Mediterranean (mostly English) pop musicians. While the "Mediterranean music" concept was created as an "other" with respect to the mainstream, one shouldn't forget that at various times during the twentieth century some musics from the Mediterranean (especially Neapolitan songs) were indeed *the* pop mainstream. "Mediterranean music" isn't all the same.

So, when in the mid-'60s the quest for new sounds begins, there is another dichotomy to be accounted for: "uncontaminated exotic" and "mainstream exotic." What belonged to Perry Como and Dean Martin couldn't be easily appropriated by John Lennon or Mick Jagger.

"Paint It Black"

Listening to "Paint It Black" (Rolling Stones, 1966, released as a single and included in the American edition of *Aftermath*), after talking about new sounds and exoticism, is a strange learning experience. Where are the new sounds? Do we mean the sitar played by Brian Jones? What is exotic? Do we mean the heterophony performed by Mick Jagger's voice and Jones's sitar? Or toms accompanying the chorus, with weak hints of *darbukkas*? Or the chorus itself, when it is sung in unison *a bocca chiusa*? In the age of samplers and World Music, or just after Jimmy Page's and Robert Plant's re-issue of "Kashmir" performed with Moroccan musicians, "Paint It Black" sounds like any other Rolling Stones hit of that same period. But everyone who listened to it when it was released most probably remembers "Paint It Black" as a very strange, characteristic piece, definitely Arabic (with a sitar? Yes, with a sitar!). It was part of the myth that the single climbed Moroccan charts (were there charts in Morocco in 1966? There is no reason to doubt it).[6] After the sitar's debut in "Norwegian Wood," and in the same year of "Love You To" (on the Beatles' *Revolver*, 1966), "Paint It Black" helped set the standard of at least one exotic piece per album/concert. It was one of the opening songs during the Stones' European tour in spring 1967, just while the Beatles were recording *Sgt. Pepper*, that would include George Harrison's *Within You Without You*—which climbed Indian charts, of course.

"Paint It Black" is Brian Jones's nonexistent knight. Jones actually went to Morocco two years after the release of the single, in 1968, visited the village of Jajouka, and made recordings with the local Berber musicians (The Master Musicians of Jajouka). An album including these recordings was released in 1971, two years after Brian Jones's death, and has been known since then as one of the earliest representatives and building blocks of the "World Music" concept, contributing (even with its evident technical tricks and/or flaws) to the definition of the genre's sound. *Brian Jones Presents: The Pipes of Pan at Jajouka* isn't "Mediterranean," for obvious reasons: there are no traces of the Arab-Andalusian tradition, and Berber musical traits can be (at least superficially) understood as pointing to "Africa," "desert," or "mountain." It is a real music from Morocco that can be interestingly compared to the music Brian Jones and the other Rolling Stones (and their fans) thought could be understood as Moroccan.[7]

"Matilda Mother"

"Matilda Mother" is another precursor, not of "World Music," but of fairy tale suggestions in many progressive rock lyrics. Written by Syd Barrett, it is one of the songs released on *The Piper at the Gates of Dawn* (1967), the first of Pink Floyd's albums. There's an instrumental interlude, a kind of comment to the lyrics, that sounds deliberately "Arabic," especially in the rhythm and in the *maqam*-like melody, if not in the sound of the distorted electric organ—although that sound would be at home in today's Arabic pop. What makes this short interlude interesting is that, contrary to many of the examples given above, there appears to be at least an ambiguous behavior toward the exotic material, a kind of ironic postcard from a psychedelic Scheherazade. Pink Floyd's visual attitude seems to be confirmed even by this small piece of music: it isn't a matter of mastering other musics and capturing them in one's own language, but of being able to portray also exotic images, using appropriate(d) music structures. The augmented fourth in the scale, resulting from an augmented second over the (minor) third step, probably appears here in rock for the first time. It will become one of the recurring features in Bartók-influenced progressive rock, at the beginning of the next decade.

"Ruby Love" and "O Caritas"

When the first non-Arabic hint at the Mediterranean appeared in English popular music, in 1971, progressive rock was already flourishing. "Ruby Love," by Cat Stevens (included in the album *Teaser & the Firecat*), isn't progressive at all, although its 7/8 meter suggests a relation (and probably Cat Stevens is the most "prog" of all singer-songwriters). Before then, one should at least notice another postcard, the macaronic "Sun King," in the Beatles' *Abbey Road* (1969), marked by its mixture of fake Spanish and Italian (*paparazzi*), and mariachi-style vocals. A *divertissement*, and also a suggestion that the semantic space[8] for "Latin" in English covers a very wide geographic space, from Italy to Spain to Mexico and beyond, pointing at another "other," a non-postcolonial one. In fact, if we make an exception for "Sun King," "Ruby Love" is not only the first notable English pop song with "Mediterranean" flavor that doesn't sound Arabic, it's the first "exotic" song related to a nation, a culture, that wasn't part of the British Empire. It isn't a surprise, then, that the real name of its author is Stephen Dimitri Georgiou, son of a Greek father and a Swedish mother.[9]

"Ruby Love" is actually partly sung in Greek, and the most distinguishable sound is that of bouzoukis playing in parallel thirds. More than an English pop song influenced by Greek moods, it sounds like an ever-repeated fragment of a Vassilis Tsitsanis song recorded in a London studio, arranged without clarinet and with more guitar. If a musical recipe for "Mediterranean" is plucked strings in thirds and (not obligatory, but well received) compound meter, then "Ruby Love" is at least as Mediterranean as Yorgos Dalaras or Fabrizio De André.

The bouzouki appears again in Stevens' "O Caritas," a song included in *Catch Bull at Four* (1972), the album that followed *Teaser & the Firecat*. It is played by Andreas Toumazis, who is also coauthor of the song. "O Caritas" is indeed a peculiar song. Lyrics are in Latin (Latin proper, the language of ancient Rome and of the Catholic Church until few decades ago) in the first part, then in English. We are informed by a vertical writing on the inside of the album cover, where all the lyrics are printed, that the English part is a translation of the Latin part (which includes lines like "nos perituri mortem salutamus"). The bouzouki plays some very idiomatic (Greek) fills at the end of some lines, but in general, it sounds more like a guitar or mandolin, played in a Spanish style. Chord sequences and hand claps are much closer to flamenco than to *rembetika*. Although the vocal line has a definite

Spanish flavor, the sound of the Latin language immediately evokes Gregorian chant. Such daring mixes of sounds and moods from all three main Mediterranean peninsular countries (Greece, Italy, and Spain) and from different times are emerging now, three decades after "O Caritas." It isn't most likely the best of Cat Stevens' songs, but probably a symptom of his growing discomfort about mainstream pop culture, and a step toward his shift to more spiritual interests and his eventual conversion to Islam.

Progressive Rock and the Balkanic "East"

Compound meter and modality become, in the early '70s, part of the technical norms of the progressive rock genre.[10] The ideological hierarchy of the genre, in the musicians' as well as in the audience's community, confirms and supports the importance of these musical features. This is unlike the following constitution[11] of punk rock (as an "anti-progressive" genre), when an ideological norm will establish that playing skills are not necessary, while in fact most punk musicians are skilled (although maybe not virtuosi): in progressive rock compound meter and modality (and virtuosity) are both ideologically and factually important.[12] They are a real part of the game. Musicians practice uncommon rhythms, look for them in other musics, and members of the audience (many of them musicians, or would-be musicians) try to recognize them, and are pleased if they do. As mentioned many years later in Tony Levin's *King Crimson Barber Shop*, "If you really want some fun, and tap your foot in twenty-one," the "King Crimson band" is all you need.

In our search for "Mediterranean" influences, it is of no little importance that one of the main sources for compound meter in early progressive rock was Dave Brubeck's *Time Out*. This 1959 jazz album became a must among English (and generally European) virtuoso keyboardists and drummers around '67–'68. Its 9/8 opening piece (divided as 2+2+2+3), "Blue Rondo à la Turk," was especially admired; it became just "Rondo" for Keith Emerson's The Nice (although Emerson, in that first recording, squared the 9/8 meter into 4/4!) Ottoman rhythms, not just strictly Turkish, but also from other areas in the Balkans, often mediated by Bartók (the "Bulgarian rhythm"), were soon sought out by a new generation of rock musicians who can actually read music as well as buy folk recordings.[13] Modality is also part of the advanced training of musicians aware of jazz techniques, and becomes a tool not only for improvisation, but also for composing. Whole-tone, "Bartók," and other scales or modes can be found in the music of King Crimson, Gentle Giant, Henry Cow, and other groups in the early '70s. However, an unsuspected connection between "art rock" and the Mediterranean anticipated most of British groups, and came from the United States. In 1970 the New York Rock & Roll Ensemble, established by some Juilliard students including Michael Kamen (of later film-music fame, from *Brazil* to *Die Hard* and *Lethal Weapon*), collaborated with Manos Hadjidakis, the well-known Greek composer we encountered as the author of "Never on Sunday." The third album by the group, *Reflections*, includes nine songs and one instrumental piece; all music composed by Hadjidakis. The main character of the work is "classical" (mostly in the instrumentation, where harpsichord and oboe share the foreground), not unlike the almost contemporary *Concerto grosso n. 1* (1971), by New Trolls (an Italian group) with orchestral arrangements by another (future) Academy Award winner, Luis Bacalov. But in some pieces Hadjidakis's Greek vein emerges. Once again, we hear plucked strings in parallel thirds, and modal melodies.

Modalism has been a resource for popular musicians since the early '60s, to avoid and counteract tonic-dominant-tonic and sensible-tonic clichés in "light music." Many known examples of modal behavior can be found in Lennon-McCartney's songs. When pop and rock musicians start looking at "serious music" as a source or a model, it isn't surprising that they look at composers that completely fulfill and give sense to traditional tonal relations, like Bach, or avoid or question them, for historical or national reasons: from Mussorgsky to Prokofiev, from Bartók to Messiaen. In an interview in 1992,[14] Robert Fripp (King Crimson's leader, guitarist, and composer) told me that much of his work at that time was with the "symmetric scale" (alternated tones and semitones), one of the modes Messiaen described as "limited transposition modes." Such scales can be found in King Crimson pieces before the mid-'70s. Fred Frith (guitarist and founder of Henry Cow and Art Bears), when asked why some of his pieces had a distinctly Balkanic sound (like Art Bears' "Moeris, Dancing"), answered that he started in Cambridge as a folk guitarist, and his teacher was a Yugoslav friend. Like many other jazz and rock musicians from his generation, Frith read Ernö Lendvai's *Béla Bartók: An Analysis of His Music* when it was first translated into English in 1971, and began composing using the Golden Section. Another reader of this book—according to his own declarations—was Keith Jarrett.[15] Temporelli discovered detailed and almost incredible Golden Section coincidences in the structure of the piano introduction and synth solo (by Tony Banks) of Genesis' "Firth of Fifth," in *Selling England by the Pound*.[16]

Speechless after Punk

So Bartók and folk musics from the Balkans, compound meter, and modality definitely have a role in the development not just of progressive rock, but of other more or less related genres. After the punk revolution ended in the mid-'70s, some progressive rock musicians—as Fred Frith put it—"recycle[d] themselves into the new wave."[17] Many of progressive rock norms were done away with,[18] like long compositions, exaggerated showmanship, virtuosity, and heavy equipment, while some musicians were able to continue their activity in smaller contexts, with shorter forms, still working with the same stylistic elements. Frith's solo albums include material from Greek dances (*Gravity*) or sound Balkanic even if recorded in Switzerland with the French group Etron Fou Leloublan (*Speechless*, side one); modality is still at the base of Fripp's compositions (like "Breathless," from *Exposure*); and Peter Gabriel experiments with compound meter ("Solsbury Hill") and starts exploring a huge collection of cassettes from all over the world to "steal" new rhythms.[19] Home multitrack and cheap studios (punk's main resources against gigantic progressive productions) became tools for experimental musicians. Even before the first samplers become available, Fripp theorized the usage of urban noises as components of a rhythm track (for a *Discotronic* project, never implemented).[20] At about the same time (1979-80), his colleague in a couple of earlier tape-music projects, Brian Eno, and David Byrne collected live and radio recordings and folk records (Lebanese, Egyptian, and Algerian voices, as well as an American choir) and synchronized them on multitrack tape with a rock rhythm section. With their *My Life in the Bush of Ghosts*, the sound of "World Music" (as a genre) is born, long before the label is formulated.[21] Though the recording equipment is still analog, "exotic" voices are put

The cover for Brian Eno's and David Byrne's *My Life in the Bush of Ghosts*; the image is from a video by Brian Eno.

into perspective in a frame of riffs, ostinato figures, and electronic sequences, with great clarity and neat contours. A relation is established between different foregrounds (there is no background, no accompaniment, actually), which recalls the relation between figures and geometric ornaments in ancient Greek pottery, or between right and left hand in some piano pieces by Bartók.

When digital recording and post-production become available later on, this new aesthetics of sound recording will prove to be more suitable to the balance of until then "non-phonogenic" acoustic instruments of world musics, than to the magmatic "wall of sound" of rock. Musicians and producers who, since 1980–81 have kept as their sound reference Peter Gabriel's third album (including pre-Real World "Biko") and Eno-Byrne's *My Life in the Bush of Ghosts*, will eventually discover that for the first time, after almost three decades, rock isn't the genre that benefits most from technological innovation.

Sahara Elektrik

In 1980, members of the German band Embryo (a '70s experimental group that didn't survive the end of the decade in its original collective form, becoming a trademark for the leader's production) formed Dissidenten. Oriental suggestions could be found already in Embryo's and in other German groups' music: Holger Czukay (member of Can, film composer) included a radio recording of an unknown Iranian singer in "Persian Love Song," for his album *Movies* (1980), when Eno and Byrne were still in the studio, their project unknown. But Dissidenten pushed the concept further, and their first record, *Germanistan* (1982), was recorded in India, with local musicians (the Karnataka College of Percussion). Possibly under the influence of *My Life in the Bush of Ghosts*, the period 1982–83 was a busy one for rock musicians traveling and/or recording with musicians from "Third World" (as it was called at that time) countries, including Peter Gabriel's work on his fourth solo album, presented at the first WOMAD Festival. It was a crucial time for the definition of what will be later named "World Music." Dissidenten played an important role, here. In 1983 they moved to Tangiers, placing their recording equipment at the Sultan's Palace. Paul Bowles and Abdessalam Akaboune helped them contact Moroccan musicians. Their album *Sahara Elektrik*, featuring Cherif Lamrani (mandoloncello, vocals), Lbark Chadili (vocals), and Mohammed Ayoubi (vocals, percussion), was released in Germany in 1984. By 1985 one of the songs, "Fata Morgana," had become a huge success all over Europe (especially in Spain) as a single and as a disco "floor filler."

The overall sound wasn't as fashionable as in Eno-Byrne's record, and the rhythm section is just basic. But the live unison singing (remember "Paint It Black"?) of the Arab voices and the repeating notes from the mandoloncello's plucked strings had a "local" appeal that made this deliberately fake "Arabic/Mediterranean" thing somehow "authentic." After nearly twenty years, "Fata Morgana" still sounds new: it is, in fact, the sound one expects to find today anywhere in Arab countries whenever young musicians perform with electric instruments and a drum kit. Today's standards (genre rules) are probably more sophisticated in terms of rhythmic and instrumental variety, but the mid-'80s records by Dissidenten—including *Life at the Pyramids* (1985)—are still close to the common sense of "Mediterranean music" in the pop-rock community. Differences among genres and individuals must be accounted for: while for some musicians performing with colleagues from Mediterranean countries is now an established practice (Sting with Cheb Mami or George Dalaras; Robert Fripp with Cheikha Rimitti; and of course many Real World productions), for others the Mediterranean is above all an abstraction, that can even be evoked by practices like placing the word "Aman" haphazardly in the lyrics, or playing a *darbukka* with a conga technique (to name just a couple of examples from recent Italian recordings).

Back to the Foods

After the constitution of the World Music genre, and with the introduction of affordable sampling equipment, *nonexistent knights* like "Mediterranean music" found better conceptual and technical tools to stay alive. So our historical overview of "Mediterranean" influences in multinational mainstream pop and rock can stop here. Information about this music is not more available now, but individual elements of the musics—sounds, instruments, techniques—are readily available. To return to the "Mediterranean food" discussion, you will rarely encounter the real cuisine of any chosen Mediterranean country elsewhere (even within the Mediterranean, but certainly if you go north), but on the other hand you can buy *feta* cheese in Germany (it is also made there) or *harissa* hot sauce in Milan, and think what you are preparing is a real peasant salad or *couscous*. Or you can believe that your own recipe has a Mediterranean taste because you put garlic or basil or fresh coriander in it. And if someone disagrees, you could go on talking about it forever.

Notes

1. This is a combination of a few real conversations, with some literary reworking. All details are true, however, including the mobile phone call. Thanks to Karen Collins, Philip Tagg, Dimos Koukakis, Alessandra Gallone, and the unidentified Italian tourist.

2. About the kind of space where concepts or genres can be "placed," and the multidimensional "borders" that separate them, see Eco 1975 (the "Q Model"); Fauconnier 1997; Fabbri 2000.

3. About Fabrizio De André's *Creuza de mä* and the idea of a Mediterranean music in Italy, see Chapter 11.

4. For a comment about Theodorakis' invention of sirtaki, see Fabbri 1998.

5. For an ideological critique based on exemplary analysis, see Tagg 1981.

6. It is true, anyway, that "Paint It Black" was number one in the U.K. charts in the last week of May 1966. See Jasper 1984.

7. Or generically Arabic. I remember hearing one song where drumming and unison singing sounded very much like "Paint It Black," though in the major mode: it was the hymn of Al Fatah.

8. For "semantic space" see Ullmann 1962; for mapping processes see Fauconnier 1997 and Fabbri 1999.

9. In fact, Cat Stevens' father originates from Cyprus; I'd suggest that historic relations between United Kingdom and Greece or Cyprus do not make these countries and cultures as familiar to the British as India or the Arab world.

10. About technical and formal rules, see Fabbri 1982b. For a discussion of "genre" and "style" see Moore 1993; Moore 1998; Fabbri 1999.

11. See Fabbri 1999 for "constitution" as the process of putting together genre rules.

12. For ideology in genre rules, see Fabbri 1982b. For a definition of ideology as a hierarchy of codes, see Eco 1975.

13. One of the most amazing examples of almost straight transcription from ethnic recordings to progressive rock is Italian popular group Area's "Cometa rossa" (from *Caution Radiation Area,* 1974), taken from "Krivo Horo," included in a collection of village music of Bulgaria first released in 1970. See Chapter 11, pp. 271–272.

14. Unpublished.

15. See Yamashita and Hill 1990.

16. Unpublished paper.

17. Personal communication.

18. For those unfamiliar with my writings about genres, I'd like to point out that generic norms need not to be outspoken. They are quite often conventional, without any convention being explicitly stipulated. See Lewis 1969.

19. This is nicely documented in an ITV documentary about Peter Gabriel's fourth album, filmed in 1982–83. Gabriel actually uses the term "stealing."

20. See sleeve notes for *God Save the Queen/Under Heavy Manners,* 1980: "Discotronic is defined as that musical experience resulting at the interstice of Frippertronics and disco." The statement is ironic; however, the *musique concrète* version of Discotronics was commented on in the press.

21. It is of course true that ethnomusicologists were using the term "world music" decades before its adoption as a genre label. For a discussion of the birth of the term World Music, see Fabbri 2001; Frith 2000.

Bibliography

Blesh, Rudi, and Harriet Janis. 1950. *They All Played Ragtime: The True Story of an American Music*. New York: Knopf.

Calvino, Italo. 1977. *The Nonexistent Knight and the Cloven Viscount*. San Diego: Harcourt Brace & Co. Harvest Books.

Eco, Umberto. 1975. *Trattato di semiotica generale*. Milano: Bompiani.

——. 1997. *Kant e l'ornitorinco*. Milano: Bompiani.

Fabbri, Franco. 1981. "I generi musicali: una questione da riaprire," *Musica/Realtà* 4: 43–65.

——. 1982a. "What kind of music?" *Popular Music* 2: 131–143.

——. 1982b. "A Theory of Musical Genres: Two Applications", *Popular Music Perspectives*, edited by David Horn and Philip Tagg, Göteborg & Exeter: IASPM. 52–81.

——. 1996. *Il suono in cui viviamo*. Milano: Feltrinelli.

——. 1998. "Generi in trasformazione: l'elettrificazione di alcune musiche nel Mediterraneo," in *Norme con ironie. Scritti per i settant'anni di Ennio Morricone*, edited by Sergio Miceli. Milano: Suvini Zerboni. 81–102.

——. 1999. *Browsing Music Spaces. Categories And The Musical Mind*, paper presented at the 3rd Triennial British Musicological Societies' Conference, Guildford, U.K.: <http://www.theblackbook.net/acad/tagg/xtrnltxts.html>

——. 2000. "Musiche, categorie, e cose pericolose," *Annex 3*, edited by Egidio Pozzi. Venezia: La Biennale di Venezia. 87–93

——. 2001. "Alcune musiche popolari del Mediterraneo e la loro ricezione come World Music," in *Musica come ponte tra i popoli*, edited by Giuliano Tonini. Bolzano: Istituto Musicale Vivaldi. 121–127.

Fauconnier, Gilles. 1997. *Mappings in Thought and Language*. Cambridge, U.K.: Cambridge University Press.

Frith, Fred. 2000. "The Discourse of World Music," in *Western Music and Its Others*, edited by Georgina Born and David Hesmondalgh. Los Angeles: University of California Press. 305–322.

Jasper, Tony. 1984. *The Top Twenty Book. The Official British Record Charts 1955–1983*. Poole, U.K.: Blandford Press.

Lakoff, George. 1987. *Women, Fire and Dangerous Things. What Categories Reveal about the Mind*. Chicago: The University of Chicago Press.

Lendvai, Ernö. 1971. *Béla Bartók. An Analysis of His Music*. London: Kahn & Averill.

Lewis, David K. 1969. *Convention. A Philosophical Study*. Cambridge, MA: Harvard University Press.

Moore, Allan. 1993. *Rock: The Primary Text. Developing a Musicology of Rock*. Milton Keynes, U.K.: Open University Press.

——. 1998. *Issues of Style, Genre, and Idiolect in Rock*. Unpublished paper. Lecture at Bologna University.

Stefani, Gino. 1978. *Capire la musica*. Milano: Espresso Strumenti.

Tagg, Philip. 1981. *Fernando the Flute*. Stencilled Papers from the Gothenburg University Musicology Department no. 8106, Göteborg, Sweden: Gothenburg University.

——. 1982. "Analysing popular music: theory, method and practice," *Popular Music* 2: 37–67.

Ullmann, Stephen. 1962. *Semantics: An Introduction to the Science of Meaning.* Oxford: Basil Blackwell & Mott.

Yamashita, Kunihiko and Timothy Hill. 1990. *Inner Views. Conversations with Kunihiko Yamashita.* Tokyo: Masamichi Asaishi/Rising Inc.

Discography

(Note: for CDs, years before 1982 are release years of original LP.)

ABBA. *Fernando.* Epic EPC 4036. 1976.

Area. *Caution Radiation Area.* Cramps CRS LP 5102. 1974. (Includes "Cometa rossa.")

Art Bears. *Hopes and Fears.* RéR abCD2. 1978. (Includes "Moeris, Dancing.")

Beatles, The. *Help!* Parlophone CDP 7 46439 2. 1965. (Includes "Yesterday.")

——. *Rubber Soul.* Parlophone CDP 7 46440 2. 1965. (Includes "Norwegian Wood" and "Think For Yourself.")

——. *Revolver.* Parlophone CDP 7 46441 2. 1966. (Includes "Love You To.")

——. *Sgt. Pepper's Lonely Hearts Club Band.* Parlophone CDP 7 46442 2. 1967. (Includes "Within You without You.")

——. *Abbey Road.* Parlophone CDP 7 46446 2. 1969. (Includes *Sun King.*)

Dave Brubeck Quartet, The. *Time Out.* Columbia CK 65122. 1959. (Includes "Blue Rondo à la Turk.")

Como, Perry. *Mandolins in the Moonlight.* RCA Italiana 45N 0725 JKAW 4724. 1958.

Czukay, Holger. *Movies.* 1980. (Includes "Persian Love Song.")

De André, Fabrizio. *Creuza de mä.* Ricordi SMRL 6308. 1984.

Dissidenten. *Germanistan.* EXIL. 1982.

——. *Sahara Elektrik/Life at the Pyramids.* EXIL 05508. 1984–85.

Eno, Brian and David Byrne. *My Life in the Bush of Ghosts.* EG EGCD 48. 1981.

Ellington, Duke. *The Great Chicago Concerts.* Limelight 844 401 2 2. 1994 (Includes a 1946 recording of "Caravan.")

Fripp, Robert. *Exposure.* EGCD 41. 1979. (Includes "Breathless.")

——. *God Save the Queen/Under Heavy Manners.* Polydor 2311005. 1980.

Frith, Fred. *Gravity.* Ralph Records FF-8057. 1980.

——. *Speechless.* Ralph Records FF-8106. 1981.

Gabriel, Peter. *Peter Gabriel.* ATCO 36-147-2. 1977. (Includes "Solsbury Hill." This is Peter Gabriel's first solo album.)

——. *Peter Gabriel.* Charisma PGCD3. 1980. (Includes "Biko." This is Peter Gabriel's third solo album.)

——. *Security.* Geffen 2011-2. 1982. (This is Peter Gabriel's fourth solo album. *Security* is the title of the American release; the original U.K. release, like all preceding albums, has no title.)

Genesis. *Selling England by the Pound.* Atlantic SD 19277-2. 1973. (Includes "Firth of Fifth.")

King Crimson. *Frame by Frame—1981–4.* Virgin KC BOX 1 C. 1991. (Includes "The King Crimson Barber Shop.")

Martin, Dean. *The Man Who Plays the Mandolin* (*Guaglione*). Capitol CL 14690. 1956.

Master Musicians of Jajouka. *Brian Jones Presents The Pipes of Pan at Jajouka.* Point Music 446 487-2. 1971.

Mercouri, Marina. *Never on Sunday.* HMV 7EG 8701. 1960.

New Trolls. *Concerto grosso n. 1.* Cetra LPX 8. 1971.

New York Rock & Roll Ensemble. *Reflections.* Atlantic 7567 80635 2. 1970.

Nice, The. *The Thoughts of Emerlist Davjack.* Immediate 3 C062-90785. 1967. (Includes "Rondo.")

Page, Jimmy and Plant, Robert. *No Quarter.* Fontana 526 362 2. 1994. (Includes "Kashmir.")

Parker, Charlie and the All-Stars. *Summit Meeting at Birdland.* CBS 466550 2. 1977. (Includes a 1951 recording of "Night in Tunisia," with author Dizzie Gillespie.)

Pink Floyd. *The Piper at the Gates of Dawn.* EMI 7243 8 31261 2 5. 1967. (Includes *Matilda Mother.*)

Presley, Elvis. *The Collection Volume 2.* RCA 74321 33071 2.1984. (Includes "It's Now Or Never.")

———. *The Collection Volume 3.* RCA 74321 40053 2.1984. (Includes "Surrender.")

Rolling Stones. The. *Paint It Black.* Decca F-12395. 1966.

———. *Aftermath.* Abkco 74762. 1966.

Stevens, Cat. *Teaser & the Firecat.* Island 842 350-2 IMCD 104. 1971. (Includes "Ruby Love.")

———. Catch Bull at Four. Island ILPS 19206. 1972. (Includes, "O Caritas.")

They Might Be Giants. *Flood.* Elektra 9 60907-2. 1990. (Includes a recent version of *Istanbul [Not Constantinople].*)

Various Artists. *A Harvest, A Shepherd, A Bride: Village Music Of Bulgaria.* H-72034. 1970. Produced by Ethel Raim and Martin Koenig. (Includes "Gankino Krivo Horo," by Bitov Orchestra.)

Various Artists. *A Story of Popular Music—20 original Recordings—Glamour and Glitter Love 9199 994.* No date. (Includes original soundtrack version of "Zorba's Dance.")

Various Artists. *Dances of the World.* Elektra/Nonesuch 979 167-2. 1987. (Includes above mentioned recording of "Gankino Krivo Horo.")

CHAPTER TWO

SEEKING CONNECTIONS THROUGH A SEA: MEDITERRANEAN SOUNDS IN SPANISH FOLK AND POPULAR MUSIC

SÍLVIA MARTÍNEZ

Concerning the formulation of a concept, politicians ask whether the Mediterranean is a bridge or a wall, a border or a passage, a line of contact or a zone of friction. Anthropologists raise the debate about the existence of a possible cultural area or an imperialist construct. In answer to these questions, some respond that the Mediterranean is surely all this and much more. Ethnomusicologists would assert that this affirmation does not explain much when confronting the existence of a supposed "Mediterranean Music."

As John Davis (1993: 89–106) synthesizes, Mediterranean has successively been considered: (1) a presupposed and non-conflictive category which joins geographical territory and culture; (2) a unit that existed centuries ago, of which traces remain; (3) an identity construct which has gradually been consolidating in the last few centuries; and (4) an imaginary product posited by Northern Europe.

Actually, the countries on this sea, from the Mashreq to the southern coast of Western Europe, including the Balkans and the Maghreb, encompass a variety of languages, forms of social organization, and cultural traditions.[1] In addition, there is no tendency toward economic and social uniformity. On the contrary, according to Bichara Khader, the last few decades have seen an "increasing economic imbalance between the two coasts: in the early '90s, the four major Euro-Mediterranean countries, (France, Italy, Spain and Greece), generated 88 percent of the GNP of the region . . . such that a Spaniard is today statistically 10 times richer than Moroccan, and a French citizen 13 times richer than an Egyptian" (quoted in Míguez 1995, 14).

In this context, Spain has gone, in a short time, from being a country of exiting emigrants to a country of incoming immigrants. Due to increasingly more restrictive immigration policies, people immigrating from other countries either arrive or die, in many instances, in small boats crossing the perilous Strait of Gibraltar. Although the presence of Maghrebi and Latin American students in Spanish universities is significant and growing, as is the number of foreign workers integrated into the productive and social structures of the country, the living conditions for poor immigrants in Spain are generally very difficult and often inhuman. With respect to the peoples of the Mediterranean, this reality is especially true for Moroccans, given that they constitute the most numerous group of immigrants (aside from those who are citizens of the European Union [EU]). Despite many centuries of common history with Berbers and Arabs, Moroccans are viewed negatively by many Spaniards, who recall recent episodes such as the participation of Moroccan troops on the Peninsula to repress the miners' revolt in Asturias (1934), or the collaboration of many Moroccans—voluntary or forced—with Franco's troops in the coup d'état of 1936. All of this contributes toward configuring a social landscape in which expressions of xenophobic rejection—including those of persons in power—increasingly appear, as well as sporadic demonstrations in which some celebrate multicultural presence, which is already a reality around Spain.

In order to understand the initiatives struggling to recreate a Mediterranean identity in the Spanish musical scene through the selective appropriation of specific cultural traditions of the area, another social-political element should be considered. In barely thirty years, Spain has gone from being an autarchic country that repressed its internal cultural diversity to having a political and territorial organization structured in autonomous communities that have, in some cases, co-official language and identity discourses that differentiate them from the whole of Spain. Among the political and cultural claims advanced during the last years of the dictatorship, for example, was that of distinguishing Catalan-speaking areas ("Catalan Countries"). This was often interwoven with an idea of Mediterraneanness encompassing, among other territories, the Balearic Islands, Valencia, and Catalonia.[2]

In one way or another, all these elements will appear in the creations of the musicians and bands that have qualified their musical style with adjectives related to the Mediterranean. However, the first question to formulate in approaching this issue would seem to be, Is there a distinctive music of the Mediterranean area that can be understood as self-contained or as having some common trait or collective identity? Davis states that there are peoples living along the Mediterranean who are distinct in terms of language, religion, politics, economics, kinship, literature, and music; and who, in most cases, share these characteristics with various non-Mediterranean neighbors (Davis 1993: 105). Following from this idea, he concludes that there exists neither a distinctive nor a homogeneous cultural area.[3]

Scarnecchia (1998: 11–12), in turn, speaks of the existence in the Mediterranean of great traditions ("musical cultures that have diffused, impregnating and unifying diverse and extensive geo-political territories, such as the Arab-Moslem civilization"), which appear together with smaller traditions ("middle- and large-sized islands of local musical cultures which have maintained their own characteristics"). The point of view put forth in the present chapter is that although the Mediterranean does not constitute a homogeneous cultural area, it does currently function as a point of reference in terms of a particular identity for some performers and publics of the Spanish musical scene. The references to the "Mediterranean culture" can be seen as an expression of the will toward a distinct way of being. This discourse coexists with other parallels: one expressing the will to exist as European without ceasing to exist as Mediterranean (with the differences in the scale of values and customs designated as distinct from Central European or Nordic); and the other using the Mediterranean in attempting to keep the barriers between the North and the South (with these regions being conceived as much more than geographical points of reference). In this way, the northern part of the Mediterranean of Europe is unified with the southern, Maghrebi, and oriental part. It ought not be forgotten that on occasion this same idea of Mediterraneanness includes an aspect of "Latinness," which allows the willing linkage of the musical traditions of Iberia with those of the countries of Latin America, principally of the Caribbean area.

To sum up, there seems to be a potpourri of proposals, in whose expression and advancement music may be seen to play an important role. Thus, there is not one sole Mediterranean music in recent Spanish musical production. Instead, there are distinct connotations, uses and "othernesses" at constant variance with the label "Mediterranean." The translation of the Mediterranean onto the current traditional music scene, for example, invokes a concept of a pan-Mediterranean culture and ideal sonority—necessarily simplified and immediately recognizable through the use of specific rhythms, melodic designs, or instrumental timbre. Still, this construct may deliberately intend to seek a Mediterranean sonority necessarily anterior to and often the fruit of personal initiatives.

In order to lay claim to a common past beyond armed conflict, some historians state their intention of exhuming little-known passages from the history of both the Christian countries of the Mediterranean as well as the Ottoman Empire. They do so on the basis of working "for a more beneficial exchange between peoples and their cultures in an important process of cultural intermingling which makes a Mediterranean identity increasingly more evident."[4] Likewise some musicians lament that Mediterranean music has not yet acquired the naturalization papers that other musics already enjoy, such as "Latin music" or "Celtic music."

As Scarnecchia (1998: 14) affirms, "There do not exist direct and egalitarian exchanges between different places in the Mediterranean, but bilateral channels between the centre and the outskirts. These channels occasionally include or exclude, arbitrarily, those whom the market for music in the world elects as representatives of different genres and countries; thereby offering distorted perceptions of the musical realities of concrete places." Hence, it is probable that if the project of joint construction within the European Union takes increasing account of the region's economic, political, cultural, security, and other interests, and "rediscovers" the European Mediterranean space as a strategic point for its interests (Míguez 1995), then there will be no delay in seeing this South—mythical and Mediterranean—empowered as a representation of another whole drawn with a profile all its own in the global musical market.

Mediterranean Song in the '50s: Sun, Beach, and Tourism

One of the most important reference points of the Mediterranean, insofar as concerns Spanish music, is found at the end of the '50s. At this time, the hardest years of postwar misery were being slowly overcome and the development of the tourist industry was beginning. Tourism seemed to offer not only a way to crack the lethargy brought by the autarchy but also an important source of foreign currency. The Spain sold was a land of sun and beaches. Such a concept was also used by song festivals in order to promote the tourist image.

Following the model of the Italian Festival of Sanremo (which enjoyed great popularity in Spain from its inauguration in 1951 and throughout the decade), the city council of Benidorm, a small town on the "Costa Blanca" (White Coast) of Valencia, convoked the first "Festival Español de la Canción de Benidorm" (Spanish Song Festival of Benidorm). From the outset, the festival had the support of the Ministry of Information and Tourism and the Broadcasting "Emisoras del Movimiento" (Network of the Government). This festival has been habitually described as an excellent marketing operation in which the Franco regime succeeded in presenting Benidorm as a perfect summer city, also effecting that a good portion of the pop production of that period would adhere to that venue (Fabuel 1998: 27). Songs had "catchy" melodies, "sugary" arrangements, and maximum simplicity, and the lyrics portrayed love and life without complications. To gain an idea of the repertoire and personalities promoted, it is not necessary to look any further than the winners at the Festival, who are today still celebrated singers on the national panorama: Raphael (first prize, 1962) and Julio Iglesias, singing, symptomatically, "La vida sigue igual" (Life Goes On the Same) in 1968.

Within a few months after the first Festival of Benidorm, the Festival of Mediterranean Song was undertaken. Created in Barcelona, the project was explicitly to be comprised of "international performers from Mediterranean countries." Yet obviously, this Mediterranean did not include the national Catholicism of the regime, or oriental or North African Mediterraneanness. Thus, the roll of melodic singers was limited to Italian, Greek, and French performers, in addition to those from Spain. A Mediterranean restricted to its coast along the northeast, unproblematic and happy, was the image drawn in the first years of the festival. The festival's soundtrack included songs of trivial subject matter and the same attractive pop that could be found in the rest of the festivals.

Conflict arrived with the fifth festival in 1963, when the winner was a song sung by Salomé and Raimon in Catalan, "Se'n va anar" (Going Away). A great controversy was unleashed and the authorities prohibited singing in this language for four years. The Franco regime had done what it could for decades to nullify the linguistic and cultural variety of Spain, to the point of prohibiting the use of any language other than Spanish. Thus, allowing into the festival a song that was sung in Catalan constituted a provocation. It is clear that the distance had been continuing to widen between the image that was officially sought and what festivals actually succeeded in organizing: advancing rock groups, innovative for the time, as well as singer-songwriters with important, albeit camouflaged, messages of protest in their lyrics, and so on. The festivals had become a means of earning a living for a large number of musicians and were a priority for the recording industry (Ordovás 1987: 131–136). It is not surprising that participants ranged from the Duo Dinámico, the first Spanish pop group associated with the phenomenon of fans, which won first prize at the Festival of Mediterranean Song in 1966, to Lluís Llach, a singer emblematic of the Catalan movement, who won the festival's second prize in 1968.

The career of singer-songwriters such as Raimon, Llach, and some others developed along paths distinct from the song-festival circuit. Although their beginnings in the festivals are no more than anecdotal, their trajectories as musicians related to a movement for change with Catalan nationalist aims—in Valencia and Catalonia—reflect another musical image of the Mediterranean, radically opposed to that popularized by the song festivals.

The Mediterranean Sound in the Claim on Behalf of the "Països Catalans"

Between the late '60s and the early '70s, the "Nova Cançó" (New Song)[5] movement, to which Raimon and Llach were closely bound, was forged. Following the steps of the French *chanson* and taking as models such musical artists as Jacques Brel, Léo Ferré, and Georges Brassens, the

Catalan group Setze Jutges (Sixteen Judges) was formed. This development propelled the writing of lyrics in Catalan and stimulated the promotion of young singer-songwriters deliberately seeking to move away from the unconcerned pop song. The Nova Cançó, Joan Fuster (1987: 13) explains, "Already from the beginning centered on a concisely culturalist proposition" which "was markedly distanced from the blah-blah-blah and the *chim-chim-chim* of the little songs in fashion."

The close connection between the movement of singer-songwriters, the claim and defence on behalf of Catalan linguistic rights, and the political idea of the "Països Catalans" lead toward another Mediterranean image present on the current musical scene. While at first the politicization overshadowed any aesthetic position of the movement of the Nova Cançó, when democracy was more or less normalized in Spain, the tie between language and the song became closer and closer. Already in the '80s, the struggle was not so much to demand social rights as to defend language: facing the hegemony of Spanish and English, to continue to sing in Catalan—despite its wretched situation in the market in most cases—remained an option in terms of identity for all the territory comprising the Països Catalans. This territory is often framed as a sound and geographical ideal of pan-Mediterraneanness: "As the ambit of our language is that of the Països Catalans, so is the ambit of our musical idiom the breadth of the Mediterranean," commented the group Al Tall with reference to their collaboration on the record *Cançons de la nostra Mediterrània* (Songs of Our Mediterranean).

Lluís Llach is one of the most important members of this movement, which has experimented with sonorities from various places in the Mediterranean. His principal claim has always been the defense of the Catalan language, but this commitment has brought him to take on what Fuster (1987: 15) calls "all that has been marginalized." The sea and the cultures along its shores are specific constants in Llach's work. One of the first works in which Lluís Llach shows a sensibility for other Mediterranean cultures is *Viatge a Itaca* (*Voyage to Ithaca*), published in 1975. With this CD, Llach followed his previous habit of translating poems by other authors. However, instead of using lyrics poems written by Catalan poets (Màrius Torres, Joan Salvat-Papasseit, and others), he chose the poem *Itaca* by the Greek poet Kavafis. With a Catalan version by Carles Riba and Llach himself, he created one of the most beautiful and representative songs in his repertoire.

Llach has also occasionally made use of Greek-inspired melodic-rhythmic designs and timbres for songs (including "Vaixell de Grècia" [Vessel from Greece], "A la taverna del mar" [At the Tavern of the Sea]). He has also invoked texts that exalt the fellowship of the peoples of the Mediterranean. His 1993 work, *Un pont de mar blava* (A Bridge of Blue Sea), contains a suite of pieces with an Arabian theme sung by Amina Alaoui, a Greek theme sung by Nena Venetsanou, and other verses that conclude: "A bridge of blue sea so that we feel one together with another/a bridge that unites different skins and lives."[6] The critics hailed the recording as "a stirring cantata claiming the Mediterranean as a cradle of cultures and intermingling."

Llach's commitment to sharing the stage with singers from the Maghreb or any other place "of the South" also supports his claim of Mediterranean fellowship. At a time when Spain is beginning to recognize its status as a recipient of immigration and where the presence of a foreigner—especially a Maghrebi—arouses frequent demonstrations of xenophobic rejection, public attitudes claiming common traits across cultures or the mere artistic interchange with musics stemming from Africa or Latin America imply a clear social and political commitment. Certainly, such attitudes are specific in celebration of intermingling; they have a permanent venue in events for solidarity or multicultural festivals, where it is possible to hear raï, *chaab*, salsa, reggae. At times, these attitudes also entail access to the list of hits, as in the case of the band Mano Negra. The value of these initiatives is undeniable at the moment of advancing a proposal of coexistence and cultural interchange, provided that the risk of encapsulating the "exotic" image that these musics might represent has been taken into account, so as not to impede these musics from negotiating their rightful place as whole, full-fledged, local identities.

Just as Llach has made musical traditions of Greece or the Maghreb his own, he has likewise experimented with another of the Mediterranean musics par excellence, flamenco, playing the piano and sharing the stage with the dancer Cristina Hoyos, who choreographed various dances to his music (Festival del Milenio, December 2000, Barcelona). Not all followers of the singer-songwriter, however, are capable of assimilating this design in Llach's aesthetic. In a press conference before to the concert with Hoyos, Llach declared: "If a follower accuses me of being unfaithful, this means s/he has not followed me well. I am nationalistic, stemming from respect and openness toward all that comes from elsewhere. We are speaking of two cultures [Catalan and Andalusian] which have been mingling for centuries, and which in this last century have done so in an impressive way." The reference to the two cultures leads to the juxtaposition often underlying the evocation of the Mediterranean: the musical cultures of different areas along the coast are taken as distinct wholes that, nevertheless, have a willingness to collaborate in marking out a common present or future. In order to understand Llach's "defense" before part of his public, it should not be forgotten that, to a large extent, Catalan nationalism has been con-structed an opposition to "Spanish" ("Castilian," "Andalusian," etc.) identity. This has resulted in a contradiction that is difficult to recon-cile: on one hand, there is the use of the Catalan musical tradition within the framework of a nationalist claim of the Països Catalans; on the other hand, there is the pan-Mediterranean discourse that also includes flamenco as an aesthetic point of reference. Today, while the most exclusivist positions of Catalan nationalism have become dated, flamenco has been regaining the position it formerly had in Catalonia. The foremost singers and dancers of flamenco from Catalonia have shared the stage with other musicians (Toti Soler, Marina Rossell, Juan Manuel Serrat, and Maria del Mar Bonet, among others).

Pan-Mediterranean Folk

If Llach has sporadically made use of the Mediterranean as a referent in his work, the progression toward a pan-Mediterranean musical pro-posal has been followed with much greater ease by the fans of Maria del Mar Bonet. This results from her convoking, in her early work, the song of the singer-songwriter and the revival of the musical heritage of the Balearic Islands. The evolution, in Bonet's own words referring to the album El·las with adaptations from songs of Theodorakis, stems from

> following this journey that I began with singing songs of Tunisia with Fethi Zghonda and the members of the Ensemble de Musique Traditionelle de Tunez, and also performing songs of Sardinia, etc. . . . I

know that this is only to begin to know and discover this very wide world of old and modern songs and their authors; so fantastic is it to discover likewise that we have so many things in common and so many that are in our culture, traditions. . . . That is to say, many more that do unite us than do not; and any effort is valid; which in my case, within the music and my space in which I like to live, the Mediterranean, occupies first place.[7]

In Llach's case, the Mediterranean sound is based on an idea of juxtaposition of neighboring cultures, from which he borrows determined characteristics (ornamental, timbral, melodic) for his creations. However, Bonet's work is founded on the revival of Mediterranean folklore that she considers as a whole, with a Majorca "which has never stopped being Moorish" as a meeting point. Her objective is "to learn what I can with music from all the Mediterranean: Greeks, Italians, Turks, Tunisians, Moroccans. . . . Because it is the way to love your culture, which interests me profoundly. To learn its songs and respect them, and to show that here too the songs form part of this cultural Mediterranean, so fine and with so much intermingling as there has been in Majorca. I consider the Mediterranean musical culture to be part Greek, Italian, North African" (Manresa 1994: 112).

Bonet's musical proposal offers a stylized vision of popular song from distinct points of Mediterranean geography. The revival of forms, texts, and traditional instruments is accompanied by a sophisticated artistic proposal, from which perhaps comes the trait most characteristic of Bonet: a timbre and very fine treatment of voice, far from the version of the same traditional song offered away from the stage. This characteristic, along with another constant of her work, the translation and adaptation into Catalan of everything she performs—whether traditional Israeli songs or original Greek or Turkish themes by Theodorakis or Livaneli, respectively—differentiate Bonet's proposal from similar ones in the ambit of Mediterranean folklore. Along her musical trajectory, Bonet has coincided with other musicians representative of the recuperation of Mediterranean music. There have been collaborations in concerts as well as joint recording projects such as *Cançons de la nostra Mediterrània* (1982), a beautiful collection of popular ballads and songs of the Catalan countries performed by Bonet and the group Al Tall.

Front cover of Maria del Mar Bonet's and Al Tall's *Cançons de la nostra Mediterrània*

A third tendency is that represented by the Valencian group Al Tall. Along with Bonet, this group understands Mediterranean music as a common whole of a shared substratum; however in their case, the proposal is based fundamentally on the creation of new compositions departing from the traditional canon (following what in Italy is called *riproposta*).[8]

In considering the artistic trajectory of Al Tall on their last anniversary, a journalist pointed out the fact of "having revived with their songs an identity that was vanishing at vertigo velocity," defining "a new vernacular sound later fitting into the Mediterranean referential ambit which they themselves had contributed toward inventing"

(Frechina 2000: 30–31). In the case of Al Tall, the contradiction of joining a nationalist discourse while coming nearer to other cultures of the Mediterranean has also caused clashes with their followers: "If [we suffered pressures in order to avoid deviations in the artistic line of the group], especially at a moment when we were carrying out the collaboration with the Muluk el Hwa for the album *Xarq Al-Andalus*, there were people who reproached us directly, in a frank manner" (ibid.: 33).

The active promotion by Al Tall of the establishment of a musical idiom to revive a "Mediterranean standard," as opposed to others more favored by the industry, such as "Celtic music," is fruit of the necessity to impel this repertoire to territories where the musical tradition has a rather scarce social incidence, which, in this case, refers to Valencia. Al Tall proposes "a process of de-regionalization and de-folklorization of the musical tradition" allowing it to take on "greater dimensions, more open, more elastic, more international," although the group is conscious of the difficulties of the proposal. Al Tall sees as a significant barrier the fact that some Mediterranean musics already possess "a very strong mark and great social implantation in their territory: flamenco, Greek rembetika, the music of the south of Italy, Turkish music, etc. are traditions with deep roots and great personality, and perhaps it will be difficult to find a recognizable standard" (ibid.: 36).

The proposals of Llach, Bonet, and Al Tall synthesized here represent three significant cases into which the majority of the musical proposals of current Mediterranean music of the traditional scene may fit: (1) the song of the singer-songwriter that incorporates distinctive musical elements from other parts of the Mediterranean; (2) the revival of the folklore of the countries along the Mediterranean Coast; and (3) the folklorist recreation of new compositions following the traditional model. The most numerically representative case is perhaps the second of these possibilities, if the most historicist angle is included, represented by initiatives to revive ballads, such as with Rosa Zaragoza, author of *Nanas del Mediterráneo* (1992) and *Cançons de jueus, cristians i musulmans* (1995); or that of musicians who orient their efforts to the revival of the multicultural roots of Iberia, recording medieval, Andalusian, or Sephardic music (Adolfo Aosta, Toni Xuclà, María Valverde). All of these musics have managed to establish a minimum infrastructure of record companies and festivals that both allow promotion and also give an idea of the vitality of the different "Mediterranean connections" offered by the folk and traditional scene.

Before concluding the analysis of this scene, it seems useful to briefly contrast the creators' point of view with the public's drawing nearer to the scene, as well as the public's use of the scene. Here, it becomes pertinent to question whether the concert-going public, which nourishes the singer-songwriter and folk circuit, fully adopts the musicians' proposals. A revealing example may be found in the follower identified with the most nationalist facet of the repertoires, who responds with suspicion and disapproval to musics considered "not indigenous," especially when these musics are identified with some Spanish territory. However, in the case of folk, the nationalist reading is blurred, so the integration of elements from "other's" musics appears to be more for amusement.

In the case of the Catalan scene, more specifically Barcelona, circuits are available to folk groups that can be considered already consolidated (with monographic programs on cable television and various radio channels, specialized publications, cycles and festivals throughout the year). These circuits glue together the offerings of dozens of groups under the label of "traditional music" or the denomination most recently used of "music with roots." Here, Jaume Aiats' analysis of these circuits seems highly relevant. Aiats observes that the discourse that accompanies the adaptation from this music suggests the existence of "a supposed musical tradition, distinctly characteristic and genuine." It also repeatedly evokes "purity," "authenticity," "naturalness," which does not imply the actual acceptance of the tradition, with such acceptance concurring with reasonably structured arguments. This discourse does, however, limit itself to serving as a support to a set of attitudes and social models (Aiats 1999: 2–3). On one hand, according to Aiats, the musical product is advanced as stemming from a genuine and distinct particular past; on the other hand, the observation of the musical product totally contradicts the basis of the argument.

In regarding the highly recreational use of the music made in these circuits, it can be understood that, despite the prevailing discourses in defense of Catalanness and pan-Mediterraneanness, the coherence of this distinct sound universe is not broken before the presence of elements that have nothing to do with the construct of "autochthonous music." The bands that have gone through the twelve meetings of the Cycle of Traditional and Popular Music (Tradicionàrius), principal promoter of the scene, provide an example. These bands supposedly recreate the traditional music of the Països Catalans; however, an examination of the musical instruments reveals that, along with those typical of the area, such as the *gralla*, *tarota*, *flabiol*,[9] others, not at all inheritors of the local tradition, such as the ocarina, didgeridoo, whistle, or *cajon* (Figueras 2000: 96–98), are also integrated without problems. Jordi Fàbregas, coordinator of the activities of C.A.T.,[10] confirms the prevalence of the recreational factor and the festive meeting at the margin of the "commitment to tradition" when he observes that those in attendance do not participate with the same enthusiasm in concert proposals as in other events in which free rein may be given to social relations:

> The way I see it, I wish that when people were listening to a concert, they would put in the same passion that they feel when dancing, but I don't see it. And I would like it to be there. Anyway, the fact is that there are people interested in traditional music because they have a good time and learn to dance to different musics, and I believe that this is what someone will take who is interested and wishes to get more involved . . . dance can be the doorway. (Orriols 1999)

Aiats affirms that the references to a past tradition are perceived "as a pretext or setting where personal relationships are activated" and that these references ought to be read not so much as a "solid base of conceptions but as a convenient stage design" given that "the appeal and references to the past are more rhetorical than effective" (Aiats 1999: 4, 10).

Thus, on one hand, there are the transcendental, purist attitudes of some musical groups that even propose to scientifically demonstrate the origin of Mediterranean music: "If a cultural or anthropological study about our traditions is done, we will understand the existence of a great variety of nexus between peoples of the Mediterranean coast." They would also eliminate the not strictly traditional elements: "It is necessary to know what Majorcan music is, because within a few years songs made in the '70s that are pseudo-popular and that people have accepted as popular music despite that they are not strictly so, have been consolidating on our island" (Delgado 2000). On the other hand, there is a much more relaxed idea that exploits a model of sociability: "healthy," "natural." Above all, this idea is opposed to the model of diversion represented by milieus such as discotheques as well as forms of entertainment that center around "mainstream" music—which is considered to be "empty," "without roots," "from outside."

What about popular music?

While the traditional music scene continues to conserve purist attitudes toward Mediterranean musics, the discourses on the popular music scene have always been much more relaxed. However, the dividing line between the musical camps is not so clear: many groups straddle the middle. Yet there are a series of traits that allow the discussion of a specific treatment in the ambit of popular music: the prevalence of classic rock instruments, complemented by such instruments as the *gralla, tenora,* and Maghrebi drums; a greater flexibility in fusions with jazz, reggae, and musics of Anglo-Saxon origin; and some specific communications media.

Having emerged from the same context as folk groups or the Nova Cançó, what in the '70s was denominated "Mediterranean rock" designated a series of groups who were seeking to connect the background of some performers of blues, jazz, and rock with the local musical tradition. This tradition was understood on two levels: one strictly local, of the Catalan ambit; and another more general, that would encompass the "Mediterranean musical tradition." Bands shared billing with salsa orchestras or performers of the Nova Cançó in concerts and festivals that joined a vocation of modernity with the spirit of social engagement, on behalf of the restoration of the public space in the first years of democracy. As opposed to the hieratic proposal of the singer-songwriters, the proposal of Mediterranean rock produced a highly festive and danceable music that would accompany, along with folk groups, many of the first popular celebrations of the time.

The most emblematic of the Mediterranean rock groups is undoubtedly the Companyia Elèctrica Dharma. Currently named Elèctrica Dharma, the group has pioneered the fusion of local sounds with rock and jazz; that is, "jazzy" arrangements of traditional melodies, with a lead role for the *tenora* in the melodic section. The band has been defined as author of "an unmistakable sound world which contributes to the autochthonous musical tradition and is, at the same time, one of the most modern and exportable musical proposals." In addition, their music gives "a personal and current sound, always with a strictly instrumental rendering of traditional Catalan pieces."[11]

Collaborations with flamenco singer-songwriter Mayte Martín, arrangements with Maghrebi reminiscences, or versions of pieces of Eric Satie are also found in the work of Elèctrica Dharma. At the moment, Elèctrica Dharma is one of the groups that has best known how to fit their proposal into the wave of World Music. They have gone from recording with small local producers to recording with Mondicor, participated in the 2001 Rock in Rio festival, and are preparing anthologies of their songs to be presented in various countries of Latin America. (They anticipate the release of two volumes entitled *The New Music of the Mediterranean* in Brazil.)

In a manner parallel to the lasting capacity of the pioneer bands, in recent years there have emerged a series of groups that bear witness to this spirit of fusion, such as El Diablo Mariachi, Mano Negra, and Dusminguet. Although these groups do not constitute examples of strictly Mediterranean music, given that the fusion they propose encompasses many other points of reference, there are some aspects that connect them to this sound universe. Dusminguet, for instance, records and releases with Chewaka (an offshoot in Madrid of Virgin that also contains important figures, such as Enrique Morente, emblematic in the renewal of flamenco). In addition, they made a long visit to Morocco in order to prepare their last album. Yet, however much Maghrebi references appear in their two records that have been released (instruments such as the darbukka, melodic designs, outlines of raï, songs with texts in Arabic), the members of Dusminguet themselves point out that they did not go to Morocco to be inspired by the sound of that land. Still, even though the group advances an especially festive and light spirit, they also assert a clear message of commitment to anti-racism and the claim for North-South solidarity. Their compositions reveal rhythms of cumbia, merengue, rumba, and reggae, among others, in a mix that defies the "essential." As Dusminguet themselves affirm, "What music is not the fruit of diverse cultures, in other words, a mixture? Purity in a living expression and [one] in constant movement such as music is a fallacy" (Pons 2000: 24). With proposals such as this one, the Mediterranean sounds on the popular music scene are becoming detached from their political origins in order to explore the "music with roots" in a manner much more free of nationalist slogans, without limitations in the use of other languages, and championing the intermingling that is characteristic of the new century.

Naturally, the use of the adjective "Mediterranean" or "Oriental" sounds on the Spanish scene encompasses many other tendencies. The particular reference is found in proposals of experimental electronic music, such as that of the Orquesta del Caos. They present their music as "a style that is found between jazz, contemporary music, Mediterranean music and techno." The project of Soul Mondo, an electronic group, states its intention of "endowing dance music with a Mediterranean and Latin identity," creating an "advanced" music based on the use of cybernetics and rhythms "belonging to us or close to our culture."[12] These include Afro-Cuban folklore and Andalusian or Maghrebi music. (One of this group's CDs is dedicated to the memory of the Algerian musicians Cheb Hasni and Rachid Baba.)

Moreover, Scarnecchia's interpretation of the Mediterranean sound today as "an oriental tendency that is generically expressed through the *arabesque* and *local colour* of oriental flavor" (1998: 15), brings to mind El Último de la Fila. Until their dissolution in 1998, this band, formed by Quimi Portet and Manolo García,[13] had a regular presence on the Spanish list of top hits at the end of the '80s and the beginning of the '90s. Their sound was characterized by a melismatic vocal expression with a clear oriental echo.

Before ending this review of the Mediterranean sounds in Spain, mention of flamenco ought to be made, especially considering its use as a specific point of reference. Even in its most traditional form, flamenco constitutes one of the most emblematic musics of the northern coast of the Mediterranean; indeed, a specialized and highly complex field of study, "flamencology," has developed. For lack of space and knowledge, it is not possible to go into the arduous polemics about the degree of Arab influence in flamenco, whether traces of Andalusian music appear, or the many more questions on the table in the discussions of flamencologists today.[14] Moreover, recent proposals of the fusion of flamenco and Andalusian music, such as the collaborations between Enrique Morente and the Orquesta Andalusí de Tetuán, however criticized by the purists of the genre, constitute yet one more point in the image of a common Mediterranean: a point that has a vocation on the Spanish popular music scene.

Coda

By way of synthesis, it may be concluded that the discourse about Mediterraneanness in the Spanish musical scene has evolved from a lure for tourism to a claim to the intermingling that is characteristic of the musical production of recent years. In the '50s, the Mediterranean identified little more than the gathering of musics stemming from the countries along the northeastern shore in order to promote tourism. With the last years of the dictatorship, a pan-Mediterranean set of ideas concerning music began to take shape. This was seen in the Nova Cançó, the folk groups, and some rock groups, which would support the claim in defense of the country's cultural diversity and the political program that would accompany such claims. With the nationalist charge deactivated, groups began to emerge that would exploit elements identified with the "Mediterranean sound." Some have appeared in a pop version of a melodic-oriental style (El Último de la Fila); others have taken the form of diversion in the kind of intermingling exportable under the broad umbrella of World Music (Elèctrica Dharma, Dusminguet); and others seek a language of their own in the latest electronic tendencies through the incorporation of rhythms with "local color" (Soul Mondo).

In any case, the expression of a supposed Mediterraneanness in these proposals seems to respond to the necessity to find a distinct creative alternative to the pressure that the globalized and Anglo-centric market exerts on the musical scene situated on the periphery. Thus, the conception of what is distinctive in terms of "one's own" may be invoked. This idea is quite versatile regarding musical tradition, which currently permits bands and the public to identify with the "Mediterranean sound" with the same facility they do with some musics from Latin America. All are gathered to defend a sportive claim on behalf of the "multi-culti," which does not necessarily reflect a harmonious coexistence and may, in fact, contradict the way the multicultural reality is lived day to day.

Notes

1. Braudel affirms that the Mediterranean is "a thousand things at once: a crossroad and a boiler of economic, political and cultural systems with four religious cosmo-visions, about 22 languages, around 17 specific forms of social organization, a geo-political space with north-south and east-west axes going through, and a complex interlaced with forces and tendencies grappling between tradition and modernity" (quoted in Pérez-Plaza 1989: 492).

2. The claim for the recognition of Països Catalans (Catalan Countries)—i.e., territory where Catalan is spoken, including various regions in both Spain and southern France—still forms part of the agenda of some political parties and the Catalan nationalist movement.

3. This is not to say, evidently, that there exists no trait in common. There are traits in common, as Peter Manuel argues (1989). However, it ought also be pointed out that many of these traits are not exclusive to the Mediterranean area and, above all, that neither are they the base of a common music.

4. For example, Giovanna Motta's intention is to "bring to light lesser known episodes in order to point out the presence of early embryonic forms of cultural integration—in work, family, nutrition, music" (Motta 2000).

5. Obviously, the proliferation of singer-songwriters in this period was not limited to Catalan-speaking territory. The discussion is focused on this area because of its relationship to Mediterranean musics. Concerning the large number of singer-songwriters from the whole of Spain, see Turtós and Bonet 1998.

6. "Un pont de mar blava per sentir-nos frec a frec/un pont que agermani pells i vides diferents."

7. Note of the artist on the album cover.

8. Here, the group Al Tall is proposed as a model for the doyen, but many other groups can be mentioned that bear witness with similar proposals: Uc, Música Nostra, Siurell Elèctric, Sis Som, Trajinada.

9. The *gralla* and *tarota* are like popular oboes; the *flabiol* is a small flute which is generally played with just one hand. All of these are traditional instruments of the area of the Països Catalans, although their names are distinct in each region.

10. C.A.T. stands for "Centre Artesà Tradicionàrius," a space where most of the activities throughout the year are held, and which serves as organizational headquarters.

11. Comments of Xevi Planas on the album cover of *Catalluna* (Planas 1994).

12. All these quotations are from press dossiers and from comments on web pages.

13. This is the same Manolo García who collaborates with María del Mar Bonet on the song "Noies Voramar—Ligna Koritsia" from the album *El·las*.

14. In order to get inside the world of flamencology with a reading critical of many of its presupposed traditions, the work of Gerhard Steingress (1998) is recommended.

Bibliography

Aiats, Jaume. 1999. "Los grupos de *Música Tradicional* en Catalunya o la construcción de una identidad alternativa," paper presented at ICTM Colloquium *Musics in and from Spain: Identities and Transcultural Processes*, Oviedo, Spain, December 16–19 (forthcoming).

Davis, John. 1993. "Modelli del Mediterraneo," in *Antropologia della Musica e Culture Mediterranee*, edited by Tullia Magrini. Bologna: Il Mulino. 89–106.

Delgado, Lau. 2000. "S'Albaida. Sons de la Mediterrània," *FOLC* 1: 7.

Fabuel, Vicente. 1998. *Las chicas son guerreras. Antología de la canción popular femenina en España*. Lleida, Spain: Milenio.

Figueras, Joan. 2000. "Música tradicional i identitat. Preguntes sense resposta?" *Caramella* 3: 96–98.

Frechina, Josep Vicent. 2000. "Al Tall. Vint-i-cinc anys de tossudesa," *Caramella. Revista de música i cultura popular* 2: 30–42.

Fuster, Joan. 1987. "Introduction," in: Lluís Llach, *Poemes i cançons*. València: Eliseu Climent Ed. 9–19.

Manresa, Joan. 1994. *Maria del Mar Bonet*. Barcelona: La Magrana.

Manuel, Peter. 1989. "Modal Harmony in Andalusian, Eastern European, and Turkish syncretic Musics," *Yearbook for Traditional Music* XXI: 70–93.

Míguez, Alberto. 1995. *Europa y el Mediterráneo. Perspectivas de la Conferencia de Barcelona*. Madrid: Fund. para el Análisis y los Estudios Sociales.

Motta, Giovanna. 1998. *I turchi, il Mediterráneo e l'Europa*. Milano: Franco Angeli.

——. 2000. "La identidad mediterránea y sus vínculos con Europa," in *Seminario "La identidad mediterránea en el seno de la UE,"* Tarragona (Spain), 8–9 June <http://www.urv.es/noticies/sem-cursos/mediterranea/ponencia4.htm>

Ordovás, Jesús. 1987. *Historia de la música pop española*. Madrid: Alianza Editorial.

Orriols, Xavier. 1999. "L'entrevista: Jordi Fàbregas, músic i director del Centre Artesà Tradicionàrius," *Caramella. Revista de música i cultura popular* 1: 6–10.

Planas, Xevi. 1994. *El toc llunàtic*. Barcelona: La Magrana.

Pérez-Plaza, Vicente. 1989. "Comentarios sobre intercambios y sinergias Norte-Sur en el Mediterráneo," in *Movimientos Humanos en el Mediterráneo Occidental*, edited by Maria Àngels Roque. Barcelona: Insitut Cátala d'Estudis Mediterranis. 491–495.

Pons, Pere. 2000. "Dusminguet. Música d'esperit nómada," *Enderrock* 60: 22–27.

Scarnecchia, Paolo. 1998. *Música popular y música culta*. Barcelona: Icaria.

Steingress, Gerhard. 1998. *Sobre flamenco y flamencología*. Sevilla: Signatura Ed.

Turtós, Jordi and Magda Bonet. 1998. *Cantautores en España*. Madrid: Celeste.

Discography

Al Tall. *Xarq Al-Andalus*. RNE N3-20003C. 1985.

——. *Xavier el coixo*. Iberfon 5854. 1988.

——. *Europe-eu!* PDI 803523. 1994.

——. *Deixeu que rode la roda*. PDI 804508. 1998.

Al Tall / Maria del Mar Bonet. *Cançons de la nostra Mediterrània*. Ariola 12044678. 1982.

Cheb Samir. *Cheb Samir.* K-Industria AFBSA01. 1999.

Companyia Elèctrica Dharma. *L'Oucomballa*. PDI 43729. 1976.

——. *Catalluna*. PICAP 11411. 1994 [1983].

——. *Sonada*. Mondicor 20152. 2000.

del Mar Bonet, Maria. *El·las. Maria del Mar Bonet canta Theodorakis*. Ariola 74321 14668 2. 1993.

——. *Primeres cançons*. Blau CDM 124. 1997.

——. *El cor del temps 1967–1997*. Picap 92 0010 04. 1997.

Duo Dinámico. *20 Éxitos de Oro*. EMI-Odeón 1217111. 1980.

Dusminguet. *Vafalungo*. Chewaka-Virgin 846940-2. 1998.

El Último de la Fila. *Como la cabeza al sombrero*. EMI 7981592. 1991.

——. *Astronomía razonable*. EMI 7890292. 1993.

Iglesias, Julio. *Yo canto*. Columbia 716189J. 1969.

Llach, Lluís. *Viatge a Itaca*. Fonomusic M-29455. 1987 [1975].

——. *Campanades a morts*. Fonomusic 1022. 1987 [1977].

——. *I si canto trist*. Fonomusic 1087. 1991 [1974].

——. *Un pont de mar blava*. Picap 900051 1993.

Osta, Adolfo. *Lonja Paraula d'Amar*. Tecnosaga KPD 10894. 1992.

Rasha. *Let Me Be*. Nubenegra INN 1103-2. 2000.

Soul Mondo. *Nada malo en la casa*. Fonomusic 8080. 1997.

Toni Xuclà. *Conte del mediterrani*. Edigsa. 1978.

Toti Soler. *Epigrama*. PDI 80.3398. 1994 [1985].

Toti Soler / Ester Formosa. *M'aclame a tu*. Pequeñas Cosas PCCD 0002. 1997.

Urbàlia Rurana. *Sarau Mediterrani*. Tram TRM 0113. 1999.

VVAA. *Dies i hores de la Nova Cançó*. Edigsa CM 440/1. 1976.

VVAA. *Tradicionàrius. 7è Cicle de Música Tradicional i Popular*. TRAM 0036. 1994.

VVAA. *Cançons de la Mediterrània*. RNE N3–20014–1. 1987.

Zaragoza, Rosa. *Nanas del Mediterráneo*. Tecnosaga KPD 10938. 1987.

——. *Cançons de jueus, cristians i musulmans*. Tecnosaga KPD 10969. 1995.

C H A P T E R   T H R E E

MOROCCAN WORLD BEAT THROUGH THE MEDIA

ANTONIO BALDASSARRE

The relation between Moroccan music culture, mass communication, and information technology is tightly connected to the broader context of the historical and political events of twentieth-century Morocco. In particular, it should be referred to as the encounter, and clash, between the native traditional culture, largely Arab-Islamic in its roots, and modern Western culture. Mass communication media—like newspapers, radio, television, sound and video recorders (first analog, then digital), and more recent technologies—have now become, or are quickly becoming, familiar among Morocco's population, both in towns and the rural countryside. This is having a strong impact on their way of playing music and listening to it, as well as affecting the process of publishing and distributing music. In this chapter, I focus on the complex relationship between Moroccan music and mass-communication media, and on what seem to be the main cues of a global process of transformation, today extending to all local traditions of popular culture.

The Mass Media at the Time of the Protectorate

The Algeçiras Conference (1906) and the Treaty of Fez (1912) marked the beginning of Moroccan colonization: Spain occupied the territories of northern Morocco, France ruled over all remaining areas of the country. During the 44 years of the Protectorate, French colonial policy was mainly concerned with a process of social acculturation, especially aiming to create a local cultural elite that could profitably side with the colonial officers in their attempts to modernize and restructure the entire country. The native people who were to become Morocco's ruling class were taught Western customs and standards. As students, they frequently moved to the "metropolis," Paris and other large French towns, to pursue further studies and educational programs. These scholarship programs became an important credential in order for them to secure a career in state administration or trade. Based on their previous successful experience with the colonization of Algeria, the French government's goal was the *équipement du pays,* the creation of all public infrastructures and industrial production plants, as required, in order to develop a modern economy. To this end, they sent a number of "cultural officers" to Morocco. These were appointed to supervise local usages and customs, and to find a way of functionally converting these practices to meet French standards and interests.[1]

The planning of urban spaces and transportation systems during the Protectorate offers a tangible example of the centralizing interests that animated the French colonization process. Roadways were planned to fit the demands of a large transportation system all across the country; the necessity of feasible access to the Atlantic Ocean led to the building of new large seaport settlements (a case in point is Casablanca); the need for central political and administrative control caused the sites of state power to move from Fez and Marrakech to Rabat, a city completely reshaped by the architect Henri Prost with the aim of centralizing the administration offices of the colonial power; in the main Moroccan towns, the hygienic and healthcare norms of the French *résidents* caused the appearance of a *ville nouvelle* separated from the traditional *medina.* Theaters, concert halls, and libraries (as well as *boulevards* and *café-terrasses*) were the actual public sites where the Protectorate cultural policy was pursued.[2]

As far as music is concerned, pioneering work was pursued by the officers of the *Service des Arts Indigènes*, who started what we today would call ethnomusicological investigations in the field. They created the *Laboratoire de Musique Marocaine*, a group of music scholars including Alexis Chottin, whose musicological research work was the most rele-

ANTONIO BALDASSARRE

vant in the group.[3] Matching the political interests of the colonization process, these scholars focused primarily on the "ethnic differences" of Moroccan music culture, putting special emphasis on Berber music and largely disregarding the Arab musical tradition, which was more popular among the Moroccan ruling class.[4]

The mass media were instruments of cultural colonization (clearly, here I refer to the "cold" media available at the beginning of the twentieth century). Newspapers and magazines offered room for cultural debates, thus supporting the education and rise of local intellectual elites. Regular concerts of Moroccan folk music and dance were organized, for the first time, both in Morocco and abroad.[5] The gramophone and the radio entered the country; the music of the natives became the object of 78 rpm record production (labels and producers included Odéon, Columbia, and Pathé). These recordings today represent an archive of the utmost relevance in the study of folk music repertoires and playing styles.

Radio broadcasting, first introduced for colonial propaganda, often included performances of Moroccan music. These events, however, were not intended to foster a large diffusion of local music culture, as live music concerts were attended by larger audiences than radio programs and the use of gramophones was not yet popular. Rather, they made possible the coalescence of a local intelligentsia: once simple lovers of music and naïve listeners, the young elites now became interested in the revitalization of the musicological literature of Arab tradition, and in a comparison between such tradition and the various styles of Western music.[6]

The defeat of the overall French Protectorate policy was initially caused by a "cultural accident," the so-called *Dahir Berbère*, a law established in 1930 (yet never accepted by the Sultan Mohammed ben Youssef). It affirmed that a difference existed between the legal treatment of Moroccan people of Berber roots and mother tongue on the one hand, and the Moroccan people of Arab culture on the other. This was a typical "divide and conquer" approach, but it was soon emphasized by both the elites and the masses, giving birth to modern Moroccan nationalism. Popular protests and other events led to the Moroccan resistance (passive, "blank" resistance in the first place; active, armed, and guerrilla resistance later). These events also led to the fall and exile of the Sultan, and to the bloody insurrection that finally caused the French to retreat. Eventually, the French authorities had to accept the return of Sultan Mohammed ben Youssef from exile in Madagascar, as required by the activitsts and the *Istiqlal* independentists (Independence Party).

In the years between the stipulation of the *Dahìr Berbère* and the Sultan's exile, and even in the bloody period that followed (1953–56), radio music broadcasts were sharply divided: some followed the dictates of the colonizers (their music included European classics and some local folk music that could provide an example of "ethnic difference"); others were influenced by the Moroccan nationalists, with their hope for political independence. The latter, clearly, welcomed all musical genres of Moroccan origin, and particularly the *nuba*, the Arab-Andalusian music, that they described as "Andalusian-Maghrebin," to emphasize its specifically local nature, as opposed to foreign influences.[7] For both the elites and the lay population, the *Nuba Istihlal* expressed the feelings of Moroccan independence, in much the same way Giuseppe Verdi's *Nabucco* was perceived by Italians as the popular expression of Italy's national independence.

The Mass Media and the Establishment of Moroccan National Identity

After the independence declaration (1956), Morocco went through a time of dense and lively cultural activity. Music personalities such as Bouchaib El Bidaoui and Houcine Slaoui set the basis for Moroccan modern popular song, developing from traditional musical forms like *'aità* and *melhun*.

The radio supported this renaissance, as it brought modern song to all areas of the country, also contributing to the creation of new "musical stars." Particular attention was paid to the traditional "high music" repertoire (the Arab-Andalusian *nuba* and the melhun), which became a symbol for regained national unity. By the end of the 1950s, the Radio Nationale Marocaine recorded and circulated the complete melhun repertoire, and played an influential role in the popular success of musical masters such as Houcine Toulali. At that time, the Orchestre Nationale was also created, with the task of taking up and disseminating Morocco's "classic" music, consisting of 11 different forms of nuba.

However, the radio (and to some extent the gramophone record) supported not only the local music but also that of foreign cultures, especially those coming from the Near East. The 'aṣrī (modern) song, especially of Egyptian origins, greatly influenced the musical taste of the Moroccan audience, and ended up influencing many musicians as well. The modern song imported from the Near East was also the object of cultural debates bearing on issues of modernization and cultural authenticity (issues already discussed as early as the 1932 Cairo Congress). The music recording industry and the radio broadcast program were subject to the significant influence of musical products created by the cultural industry of Egypt and the Near East, which was already consolidated and capable of meeting the demands of mass production. This situation was experienced as a symptom of a presumed inferiority of the Moroccan music culture compared to that of the Near East. By the 1960s, the music of the Near East had become the predominant reference model for the majority of Moroccan musicians and producers.[8]

Among the plethora of musicians passively adopting the Egyptian and Near East 'aṣrī song model (often with poor results, except in the case of artists such as Mohammed Fouitah and Ahmed El Bidaoui), two artists stood on their own: Brahim El 'Alami and Hamid Zahir. The former followed a very personal and original path to urban popular (cha'abi) song; the latter merged the different rhythms, timbres, and sarcastic lyrics peculiar to the music of the Marrakech area, thus shaping a kind of vaudeville that expressed very precisely and even with a humorous vein the desires, frustrations, and hopes of the lay population.

The lively musical scene set up by Bouchaib El Bidaoui, Houcine Slaoui, Brahim El 'Alami, and Hamid Zahir contrasted with the cultural policy pursued by the political power. The goal, for the latter, was the consolidation of a national cultural identity, whose musical manifestation was represented by the Moroccan classical music tradition preserved in the National Music Conservatory. However, national identity was even more heavily stressed, in spite of foreign influences, in the oughnya al wataniya, the "patriotic song" that was brought out at every possible official ceremony. This was a national folkloric type of song, created for the purpose of channeling the imagination and creativity of the masses toward expressive forms strictly useful to the lines of political power. This kind of song often used lyrics that served as mere rhetorical devices void of artistic content. In short, it represented a degenerate outcome derived from the centuries-old tradition of panegyrical chant in tribal Morocco.

During the 1960s, the Radio Nationale Marocaine musical program was divided into two main branches: entertainment music (Near Eastern in either its origins or stylistic influence), and "high music" Moroccan tradition (nuba and melhun, emblems of reborn national identity). The latter was in the air at all times on the occasion of civil or religious celebrations, only to be interwoven with political speeches and, of course, the ubiquitous patriotic songs. The rich and varied local traditions of popular music, rarely included in radio programs, were occasionally revisited only to give a sense of genuine Moroccan national heritage.

This emphasis on national identity met political demands to establish a rather monolithic, clear-cut, and reassuring image of the newly born State of Morocco, contrasting with the emphasis put forward by the former French governors on minorities and ethnic differences. Like other Arab countries regaining political independence from their colonizers, Morocco underwent a massive and pervasive process of reappropriation of its Arab roots. In the 1960s, the Arab cultural element was privileged in all aspects of cultural activity, to the detriment of other specific local traditions and to the detriment of the Western (primarily French) influence, of course.[9] The will to leave behind all Western cultural tutoring was mirrored by the main issues raised at the Arab Music Conferences held in Iraq (1964), Morocco (1966), and Egypt (1969). There the growing influence of Western musical constructs was analyzed (scales, tonality, harmony, instruments) and compared with the evident effects of linguistic diglottism all over the Arab world.

The Media and the "Alternative Culture" in the 1960s

The advent of television brought about little change in the agenda of Moroccan cultural politics. On the one hand, musical programs remained largely a matter of the entertainment industry (especially the

Near East *'asrì* song style), while on the other they continued to foster some kind of national musical identity (nuba, melhun, and "patriotic song"). However, some room was left for the interesting musical proposals of artists such as Brahim El 'Alami and Hamid Zahir. The music of more ethnically connotated styles was rarely featured, and when it was, it went under the umbrella definition of "national folklore music," with a strongly decontextualizing and impoverishing effect. This is somewhat paradoxical, as in fact this kind of music was the one closest to the musical taste of the majority and the one most deeply rooted in the customs and imagery of the people. It was frequently played at family gatherings and celebrations, as well as at large scale meetings organized by and for the urban and rural masses.

This scenario, seemingly very stagnant, suddenly and radically changed by the end of the 1960s, when a number of events led to the emergence of the new Moroccan "pop music" scene, including bands such as Les Frères Megri, Jil Jilala, and Nass El Ghiwane. This last band quickly rose to popularity especially among the young (and, indeed, the absolute majority of the total population was young).[10] There are several reasons behind this huge success: most people, and especially the intellectuals, loved the music played by Nass El Ghiwane because it represented an effective reaction against the stereotyped *'asrì* song, while at the same time it also revitalized stylistic traits of the music typical to peasant communities and Sufi brotherhoods. Young Moroccans preferred the music and lyrics of artists their own age, who became spokesmen of an entire generation with its frustrations and its ambitions for social change.

The protest against the hegemonic political system, and the repressive, stereotypical lifestyle, was clearly a characteristic issue of the then growing "counterculture" that was being disseminated by the new musical style itself. As is well known, it was a worldwide phenomenon that, starting from within the United States and French universities, in only a few years extended to the young people of many countries. The earlier manifestations of this international, or better transnational phenomenon, are found in the work of avant-garde artists and intellectuals searching for new cultural and expressive identities. It is not by chance that several such artists and intellectuals, American and European protagonists of this "alternative culture," used to spend a lot of time in Morocco in close contact with local artists, thus absorbing new concepts and new lines of research in their work.

The forerunners of this movement were proponents of new cultural trends eager to experience a leave, or escape, from their own native culture, to face exotic civilizations. Among them was the musician and writer Paul Bowles, a principal figure of the generation of so-called "new immigrants," somewhere between the lost generation and the beat generation. After World War II, Bowles traveled all around Morocco, then moved to India and Ceylon, finally settling down back in Tangiers, in 1959, where, in the same year, William Burroughs completed his novel, *The Naked Lunch*. In July 1961, Timothy Leary, Allen Ginsberg, and Gregory Corso were in Tangiers. Their work opened the way for the flower power movement and alternative life styles, for the followers of which Morocco became one of the most important destinations.[11]

A crucial year for this "new culture" was 1969, when the Rolling Stones guitarist Brian Jones settled in the area of the Rif, fascinated by the flavor of the *kif* and the Jajouka traveling musicians. The latter participated in his historic album *Brian Jones Presents The Pipes of Pan at Jajouka* (1971).[12] The jazz pianist Randy Weston, searching for the cultural roots of Afro-American music, moved to Tangiers where he started the African Rhythms Club, there developing a fertile artistic partnership with Gnawa musicians. In the summer of 1969, Jimi Hendrix and the members of the Living Theatre visited the *Djabat* village, near the Atlantic coast and the town of Essaouira. In Essaouira, the Living Theatre first performed their *Paradise Now*. Julian Beck and Judith Malina met with Tayeb Saddiqi, an actor, director, and playwright born in Essaouira, and following his suggestion the Living Theatre produced their new piece with the soundtrack provided by a young Gnawa master, Paqa (alias 'Abderrahman Kirouch). In exchange, as a gift for their Western friends, the Gnawa performed a complete *lila*, the night long ritual of the Morocco Gnawa.[13]

The Essaouira artistic events in the summer of 1969 provided the context to the birth of Nass El Ghiwane. This band was created when four young men from the popular quarters of Casablanca (Boujmah Hgour, Omar Sayed, Larbi Batma, and Allal Ya'ala), all actors and musicians, met Tayeb Saddiqi, who became their adviser. Saddiqi introduced

'Abderrahman Paqa to them, and the latter eventually joined the band, as vocalist and *ganbrì* player.[14]

Following the wave of enthusiasm that arose in the summer of 1969, thousands of "beautiful people" from North America and Europe, visited Morocco's Atlantic coast. They were attracted by the chance for cheap exotic vacations, immersed in the fascinating colors and scents of what appeared to be the "nearest of the farthest countries." Notwithstanding the peaceful coexistence of native people and these *hippyà* (the local nickname for the many-colored sons and daughters of the West), the Moroccan political authorities looked at them with a skeptical eye, worried about this new Western "invasion." The local mass media soon raised their voice against the bad habits and corrupted costumes presumably encouraged by these "degenerate and idle children of an exceedingly tolerant, immoral society." They also accused the hippies of causing an increase in the circulation and abuse of illegal drugs, thereby exerting an overall negative influence on Moroccan young people.[15]

With the flower power movement, a new mass media entered Morocco: the audio cassette tape (often written K7 in Francophone areas). Launched by the Philips corporation, the cassette tape began a true revolution in the recording market and significantly changed the way people listened to music. In Morocco, between the two world wars, the gramophone and the 78 rpm vinyl record had remained elitist goods, and even the 33 rpm record and the more popular 45 (the "single" record) never really became mass products. The K7, by contrast, soon became popular among different social classes. It was cheap and easy to use, and it allowed one to tape favorite songs and form any preferred collection of music.

The K7 diffusion also brought rock music to Morocco. This music, however, never had a strong impact on the young people of Morocco. It became merely an easy token for communicating with Western people of the same age. The composition and the instrumentation typical of rock music never really affected the taste of Moroccan listeners and hence did not influence the music produced by local musicians. That was also the case with the *chanson française* always featured on radio and television programs more as a tribute to Morocco's liaison with French culture than to match the taste of the audience. Also, there was little room for the commercial exploitation of this music, because the wild dubbing of K7s all over the country and the *trabando* (black market smuggling) impeded the music industry authorities from any practical chance to protect copyright income, thereby also impeding the development of any legal market for K7 music products.

Regarding composition, the greatest influence determined by technological innovations on Moroccan music was one of volume and timbre. This was mainly due to the possibilities offered by sound amplification and reinforcement systems, as well as by cheap sound-effects units (such as reverberation). Indeed, modern sound technologies were first and foremost utilized by bands like Nass El Ghiwane just to amplify the voices (the melodies remaining in essence the same as those of the local music tradition) as well as the traditional acoustic instruments, all as in the local traditions, with the exception of the banjo, preferred over local plucked strings (such as the *suissàn* and the *lotàr*) because it offers a more stable and precise tuning, yet its timbre is similar to those of traditional instruments.

The Mass Media in the 1970s and 1980s

The 1970s represent the years of the color TV set and a huge K7 diffusion (legal and illegal) of several musical genres, either originating from within or outside Morocco. However, it was a difficult time for the political integrity of the country, with two coups d'état attempted at the beginning of the decade. The overthrow of the status quo was pursued by a number of different groups animated by different motives, including some heads of the army as well as groups of students, intellectuals, and religious integralists. The need to smooth out this political turbulence forced the government to introduce censorship, which in turn caused dozens of artists and politicians to leave the country as more innovative efforts were banned.[16] However, when Spain renounced its Sahara colony, Rio de Oro (1975), Morocco took the opportunity to occupy this area, an effort that in the end allowed a re-aggregation of the national media in what was described as a dutiful reappropriation of territories as integral to the country as all other areas.

For many international diplomatic departments, the "Sahara question" remains an unresolved political problem to this day. What is relevant to our discussion, however, is that at the time of the so-called Green March (the peaceful "invasion" of the former Spanish Saharan area by 350,000 unarmed Moroccans), all local mass media were supportive of the government action, and helped create a large popular consent. Slowly, a sense of national identity was restored, and the strong, explicit censorship exerted over artists and politicians in the early 1970s gave way to a milder policy ("dissuasive censorship"). Yet, the music of Nass El Ghiwane was still suspected to be a vehicle of ideologies potentially dangerous for the general political situation. The band was forced to change their inspiration, leaving aside any issue of social injustice or the impoverishment of the potential of human existence. This caused an inevitable decline. 'Abderrahman Paqa left the band, Larbi Batma passed away, and the band finally broke down.

In the late 1970s and at the beginning of the 1980s, two new large radio broadcasting stations were started: Radio Méditerranée Internationale (often called Médi 1) and FM Chaîne Internationale. Both devoted more room to "new music" than the Radio Nationale did. The new program supported also as national music the 'asri song of Moroccan musicians, making them known to the audience of other Arab countries, and promoting those musicians who frequently worked with Egyptian and Near Eastern composers, directors, and orchestras, such as 'Abdelhoueb Doukkali, Samira ben Said, Rhaja ben Melieh, and Ghita Bent 'Abdessalam. A place was also given to the oughniya Maghrebiya (Moroccan song) of Naima Samih and 'Abdelhadi Belkhayat, and a folk repertoire was featured as well, including Berber musicians such as Najat Attabou, Hada Ouaki, and Mohamed Rouicha. International pop music genres were represented mainly by Jamaican reggae musicians whose work stressed the African roots of their music, and whose lyrics focused on libertarian and Third World issues.

Toward the end of the 1970s, a significant promotional activity began for the traditional music culture of Morocco, especially through numerous festivals (beginning with the Festival des Arts Populaires in Marrakech). This activity usually offered the image of a reconciled community, one which in the end might favor the enormous economic potential of Moroccan tourism in the international context.

The rise of a movement for civil rights and social emancipation, though firmly hindered by the censorship and repressive attitude of civil and religious authorities, continued during the 1980s. In the summer of 1981, a crowd demonstrating in the streets of Casablanca, consisting of thousands of students, workers, and unemployed, was attacked by the Army. In the terrible fight that arose, many of the demonstrators were killed (300, according to government spokesmen; 3,000 according to local independent observers). The actions and communications of the women's rights movement have been censored many times: the magazine *Kalima* was forced to discontinue publication in April 1989, and the essay *Le harem politique* by Fatima Mernissi (1987) was published in France but never found an editor in Morocco.

Music and Media in the Global Village

After the fall of the Berlin Wall, the political scenario based on the opposition between the Atlantic and Soviet blocs came to an end, and a worldwide process of "globalization" ensued, involving all aspects of politics as well as the media. In the Islamic countries, the Gulf War caused an acceleration of this process, especially in that it marked a clear-cut separation between those countries that supported the Western forces and those that retained a more "integralist" position. Largely due to its peculiar geographic location, between the Atlantic and the Mediterranean European countries, Morocco opted for the Western forces.[17] As a corollary to these events, another product of Western thinking broke in, accompanied by the technologies and economic models of the West: democracy. Political and economic partners demanded reliable warranties as a basis for considering Morocco a part of the community of democratic countries. Indeed, a revision of the internal political models finally led to the present situation, with two large political coalitions leading the country in turn.

With regard to media and technologies, Morocco is not a foreigner to the extraordinary developments of recent years. A new TV network was created, called 2M. Satellite parabolic aerials became widespread and today appear as an integral element in the urban Moroccan environment.[18] Digital technology came in with the new media, first sound media technologies (the compact disc) then multimedia supports, like the CD-ROM. The world of Maghreb music started using digital instruments, such as synthesizers and rhythm machines, to rearrange the rhythms and tunes of traditional local repertoires.[19] A new North

African "sound" emerged, which spread all over the worldwide music market, especially represented by people like Cheb Khaled and Cheb Mami, the *Cheb* (youth) of *raï* Algerian music.

Raï music was the first music product of the "globalized'" Maghreb to become internationally renowned. It consists of various traditional styles (either "cultivated" styles like melhun, or more folkloric ones, like 'aità and cha'abi) mixed with digital sounds. It is largely based on a particular *beat* created with either electronic drum-pads and rhythm machines, or with local drums whose sound is then digitally processed. The vocal lines are mainly focused on well-tempered tuning pitch scales, so that the overall harmony is compatible with Western music, while at the same time featuring microtonal variations that follow Arab scales.

The roots of raï are to be found in the typical music of *cheikhat,* the "free women" who used to sing at marriage feasts and parties, as well as in bistros and coffee-bars reserved for "men only."[20] Raï should also be considered as a music of strong social impact (the word means opinion, free choice), often mocking the political powers and contradicting religious fanaticism. It gives place to values perceived as "hedonistic" (pleasure, eroticism, sexuality), as opposed to the puritanism proper to traditional Islamic communities. People dance to raï in discos, where the eroticism of young North African women emerges from the shadows of the harem, as the male body dances close to the female body. It marks a departure from traditional customs that demanded that a distance between men and women be maintained.

It happened that, in a very few years, this music—first coming from West Algeria and very soon appreciated in the Paris *soq* of Barbès (where it was circulated on K7 and VHS tapes, often far from any copyright protection)—was featured in most Western mass media and eventually reached the top positions of international music charts. Beside the hedonistic and libertarian element, the popularity of raï was also due to the technological sophistication of the recording process and to Western-like marketing strategies (digital instrumentation, sound engineering, massive distribution). From Oujda (a town both geographically and culturally close to Oran, the birthplace of this music), raï gradually moved to the discos of the main urban areas of Morocco. Hence it reached the local radio and television stations and, as a result, became a pale imitation of the original Algerian raï. As something made to fit the demands of the media, it was essentially impoverished of the potential of Algerian raï music, born in a different social context based on traditional values of the patriarchal family.

A quite different situation is found overseas, on the French Mediterranean coast, where the second generation of Maghreb immigrants created bands like Orchestre Nationale de Barbès and Gnawa Diffusion, opening a territory for the encounter of musicians from Algeria, Morocco, Tunisia, and France. These musicians mixed the drive of Afro-Arab-Berber rhythms with elements of funk and rock music. The subjects of their lyrics are predominantly social and political, addressing issues of sociocultural exclusion and marginalization, cultural *métissage* (perceived as vital to cultural diversity), and people's rights to self-determination and the freedom to seek a satisfying and happy life.

It is at this time that discourses and protagonists of the 1960s "alternative culture" reappeared, signaled by internationally acclaimed pictures filmed in Morocco, like Bernardo Bertolucci's *The Sheltering Sky*, from the Paul Bowles's novel, and Martin Scorsese's *The Last Temptation of Christ*.[21] The soundtrack to the former was composed by Ryuichi Sakamoto and that of the latter by Peter Gabriel; both included samples of Moroccan folk music, especially the music of popular Sufi brotherhoods like Deqqa Marrakechiya, Aissawa, and Gnawa. Suddenly, this music came to be known by a much larger international audience.

In 1992 and 1993, three compact discs of Gnawa music were launched internationally, titled *Gnawa Night Spirit Masters*, *The Splendid Gnawa Masters*, and *Gnawa Lila*. The Gnawa are descendants of black African peoples who had moved to Morocco in earlier times. They are inhabitants of a peculiar "Third World" situation, living in the poorest and most marginalized Moroccan ghettos. Nonetheless, these musicians today easily obtain visas and move abroad whenever they need to, which is a rare privilege in a world where the barriers between North and South are increasingly difficult to cross and have become insurmountable to many.[22] These possibilities are due to the rising popularity of ethnic music repertoires and the World Music circuit.

After releasing *Gnawa Night Spirit Masters*, the musician and pro-

Front cover of Orchestre Nationale de Barbès's *En Concert*

ducer Bill Laswell continued searching for new Mediterranean and African sounds. This brought him to *The Trance of Seven Colours*, an album testifying to the artistic encounter between jazz saxophonist Pharoah Sanders and the Essaouira Gnawa master Mahmoud Ghanya. Then Laswell produced the album *Digital Sheika*, by the Moroccan singer (of Jewish origins) Sapho, creating a mixture of funk and North Africa sounds. Maybe the ultimate impact of Gnawa music on Western media came when rock stars Robert Plant and Jimmy Page (former members of Led Zeppelin) worked with Gnawa musicians for the recording of *No Quarter*. Also, Peter Gabriel's recording label, Real World, produced the compact disc *Trance* by Hassan Hakmoun, a young Gnawi whose fusion of Gnawa, reggae, and rap music follows in the line of global pop, and who also played with the Kronos Quartet on their album *Pieces of Africa*.

The widespread interest in the music of the Gnawa is mainly due to its capacity to provoke trance in a ritual context. Western scholars and musicians who have developed our knowledge of the ritual practices of popular Sufi brotherhoods find themselves confronted with a way of living Islam quite different from the official scriptural orthodoxy, a way of living and interpreting this tradition that also offers women the opportunity to be actively involved.[23]

In 1998, following the interest in the musical tradition of Moroccan women, Peter Gabriel invited the group B'net Houariyat to the WOMAD festival in Reading, England. B'net Houariyat is an ensemble of five women from Marrakech who had come out internationally just a few years earlier with their first compact disc, *Poèmes d'Amour des Femmes du Sud Marocain*. In Reading, B'net Houariyat had an extraordinary success, and was welcomed by the British press as the true revelation of the festival.[24] Later, they participated in the Real World Recording Week in Bath, working out some tracks for their new compact disc and playing with Gabriel himself for a track on his album, *Up*. More recently, B'net Houariyat committed to projects of new global music. In the album *Maghreb & Friends* they joined a transnational band consisting of pop-jazz musicians from several countries, under the guidance of Vietnamese guitar player Nguyên Lê and Algerian drum player Karim Zyad. B'net Houariyat also set up a live show entitled *Marrakech Connection*, playing with the Italian band Mau Mau and the Gnawa Sidi Mimoun of Casablanca.

The musical globalization that has made raï a big international success has increased also the cooperation among Western and North African musicians. Some Moroccan musicians have participated in "high music" projects of European composers too. Michael Nyman, for example, was the proponent of an interesting borderline musical experiment involving masters of Arab-Andalusian nuba, like 'Absadeq Cheqara. Simon Elbaz, an actor and musician of Jewish origin, following the ancient traditions of Moroccan Jewish music, renovated the repertory of *matrùz* music, that consists of a mixture of Arab and Jewish styles. Vocalists Amina 'Alaoui and Touria Hadraoui (who is very committed to the social and cultural battle for women's rights), turned to

"classic" musical repertoires like *gharnati* and melhun, which historically had always been exclusively played by male singers. Women's gradual entry into the political scene solicited the local media to focus their
attention on a new "family rights act," first proposed by Moroccan
womens' organizations spontaneously established around the country.
This process arose without doubt from the gradual wave of democrati-
zation currently taking place in Moroccan society. However, it is heavily contrasted with the conservative Islamic ideology, which has
millions of proselytes among the more humble lay population.[25]

In the age of the personal computer, the Internet, and the mass diffusion of gadgets such as GSM phones, videogames, and DVD players,
at the very dawn of a new millennium, the politics of culture driven by
the media in Morocco generally lag behind the phenomena that are
characteristic of the growing global culture.[26] The reactions of the
media to these stimuli resemble mere "conditioned reflexes." The re-
evaluation of "national patrimony" (a stereotyped formula commonly
used in Morocco to refer to the richness and variety of popular culture)
is pursued primarily by following, and blatantly imitating, choices and
directions that "foreign" artists and cultural producers make. No serious efforts are concretely devoted to a deeper understanding of the
phenomena. So it happens, for example, that musicians like Gnawa and
B'net Houariyat, once snobbishly disregarded by the local intelligentsia, and then suddenly brought to the attention and appreciation
of an international audience, have now become fashionable in
Morocco's mass media too. At the same time, their perfomances remain
largely misunderstood with regard to the cultural values they express.
Experiments in crossing cultural boundaries, like those pursued by
Michael Nyman, are locally replicated without much thinking, simply
exchanging traditional Moroccan instruments, like the *qanun* (table-
zither) and 'ud (Arab lute), for synthesizers and electric guitars.
Research, such as Simon Elbaz's on the *matrùz* tradition, witnessing
the centuries-old exchanges between Arab and Jewish cultures, are
turned into a melting pot on TV night shows, with opera singers, sometimes talented international stars of *bel canto,* singing along with Arab
vocalists in a meaningless soup presumed to represent the feasible coexistence of diverse religions.

This is enough evidence, in my view, to indicate important gaps in the cultural politics pursued by the Moroccan media. The media do not sufficiently recognize the complex transformations to which the socio-cultural environment of Morocco, rooted in centuries-old traditions, is subjected, and fails, moreover, to successfully work toward integrating these traditions into the larger processes of globalization characterizing the recent years. The contrast between the spontaneous collaboration of artists and cultural producers (on a transnational level) and the attempt of the media to impose a cultural policy (on a national level) mirrors on a global scale the contrast between *gemeinschaft* and *gesellschaft* (community and society) as stipulated by Ernest Gellner (1995). New communication technologies, if used within a truly democratic context, could allow for the overcoming of this traditional impasse, favoring the transition toward a globalized but open society made up of self-governed communities.

Notes

1. As an example of how far the French policy went with this "cultural mystification," consider the history textbooks written for North African children in primary school, usually bearing titles such as *Our Ancestors the Gauls*. However, there were exceptions to this trend. The culturally more respectful position held by Hubert Lyautey, first Résident Général, was one such exception. Other examples, testifying to a more humane exchange between French colonizers and the Moroccan population, are discussed in Knibiehler, Emmery and Leguay 1992.

2. For an anthropological view of the territory colonization, see Rabinow 1989: 277–319, and Berque 1958. For a general approach to the geography of Morocco, see Beguin 1973.

3. Chottin 1924, 1933, 1938.

4. The French managed the alliance with the Marrakech *pacha* Thami El Glaoui (governing the Berber populations in South Morocco) to counterbalance the power of Arab aristocrats, represented by the Sultan Mohammed ben Youssef (later crowned King Mohammed V).

5. The *Trois journées de musique marocaine*, that took place at the Oudaia Gardens in Rabat, in 1928, were probably the first "festival" of Moroccan music.

6. A first-rate intellectual, Mohammed El Fassi (at some point Minister and then also President of the UNESCO operative committee), ackowledged his debt to the French-based education programs he had pursued as a young Moroccan. He admitted that his love and understanding of music were first stimulated by Emile Dermenghem—author of an important study on Moroccan popular Islam (Dermenghem 1954)—during his university years in Paris (El Fassi 1962).

7. The *nuba* (turn, tour) is a kind of traditional music, somewhat in the form of a *suite*, with strict rhythmical and melodic rules. The nuba repertoire first developed in Muslim Andalusia between the ninth and thirteenth centuries. After the

Catholic *Reconquista*, it slowly migrated toward North Africa (see Guettat 1980). The definintion "Arab-Andalusian music" was put forth by European musicologists Jules Rouanet and Rodolphe d'Erlanger (see d'Erlanger 1930/1949), while Moroccan tradition refers to *al 'ala* (profane repertoire) and *al sam'a* (sacred song).

8. During the 1960s, the movies having the largest circulation in Morocco were "music movies" produced in Egypt, much in the vein of light comedies and "operetta."

9. In the 1970s, this general cultural policy eventually failed, only to give way, in the 1980s, to a reverse orientation aimed at both the reappropriation of local languages and customs (themselves described as "national heritage") and the opening up of the country to the Western economy.

10. In the late 1960s, 70 percent of the Moroccan population was less than 21 years of age.

11. A description of the Tangier encounter between Timothy Leary, Allen Ginsberg, Allen Ansen, Gregory Corso, Bill Burroughs, Brion Gysin, and Paul Bowles is in Leary 1968 (Journey 11).

12. The *Jajouka* musicians came from the Tatoufèt villages around the town of Ksar El Kebir, nearby the Rif (an area inhabited by the Jebala tribe). Their ritual practices had already been described at the beginning of the twentieth century (Westermark 1926). According to a native legend, the shepherds of the area were taught the art of playing the *ghaita* (double reed instrument played by circular breathing) by the mythical *Bou Jelloud*, a faun living in caves, brushes and underwoods, partner of the nymph of the waters and the mountains, *'Aicha Qandicha*. On the Morocco *kif* culture, see Bowles 1961.

13. This event is described in Beck 1972.

14. The *ganbrì* is the drum-lute of the Gnawa. About musical instruments, structures and the context of the Gnawa music, see Baldassarre 1999a.

15. The voice raised by the newspapers, the radio and the television, was supported by the political Mighty Hand. Hundreds of *hippyà* were arrested and expelled from the country. The *kif* business was forcefully taken up by "professional organizations."

16. Among the best known exiled opinion leaders were 'Abderrahman Youssoufi (currently Prime Minister of Morocco), Abraham Serfaty, and 'Abdellatif La'abi. Censored novelists included Mohammed Choukri (*Le pain nu*) and many others. About the 1970s crisis, initially begun with the problem of the Liberation Army, the revolt of Casablanca in 1965, and the Ben Barka affair, see Hassan II 1976 and 1993; Perrault, 1990.

17. The Arab name of Morocco, *Maghreb al Aqsa,* means "Country of the Far West." In the 1990s, King Hassan II engaged himself with much commitment to opening Moroccan politics to European countries: "Il faut absolument montrer que la Méditerranée peut devenir une zone de solidarité et d'équilibre. Un véritable lac de Tibériade, autour duquel les trois religions et les fils d'Abraham, unis par des liens historiques, pourraient bâtir un merveilleux tremplin pour le siècle à venir" ["It is absolutely necessary to show that the Mediterranean can become a zone of solidarity and equilibrium; a veritable Lake of Tiberias, around which the three religions and the sons of Abraham, united by historic links, can build a marvelous spring-board for the centuries to come"] (Hassan II 1993: 297).

18. Set up by a group of entrepreneurs close to the government, 2M TV did not receive the same popularity that paid TV received in Europe and the U.S. After an apparently successful launch, most people declared themselves completely dissatisfied, refused to pay the monthly fee, and sent the signal decoders back to the corporation. A complete crisis was only prevented by the government, which moved the network under the wing of the State, making of it a national TV network, with costs covered by the usual tax income. The utilization of satellite parabolic aerials was an alternative to the insufficient quality of local TV stations. In the beginning, satellite broadcasting was simply tolerated by the authorities, but later it was officially accepted as a due homage to the "freedom of information." On socio-cultural transformations that the satellite TV broadcast phenomenon introduced into the geopolitics of Morocco, see Cattedra 1996.

19. In the early 1980s, some electronic music corporations designed keyboards capable of alternative tunings, allowing the musician to stretch the pitch intervals to quarters and eighths of the whole tone, and even to a single cent (hundredths of a tone). This made it possible to enlarge the marketplace of such keyboards to Arab countries.

20. Khaled and Mami have often acknowledged their debt to folksingers such as Cheikha Remitti and Chaba Zaouania. In Morocco, the best known *cheikhat* included Hajja Hamdaouiya and Fatna Bent Houcine. On raï and its socio-cultural aspects, see Virolle 1995.

21. Martin Scorsese, *The Last Temptation of Christ*, U.S.A., 1988; Bernardo Bertolucci, *The Sheltering Sky*, U.K.–Italy, 1990. "Exotic" Morocco had already been featured in several pictures like Orson Welles' *Othello* (U.S.A.–Morocco–France–Italy, 1949/1952) and David Lean's *Lawrence of Arabia* (U.K., 1962).

22. "For four centuries we Gnawa have not traveled, and the last time we traveled we were hiding in camel knapsacks or crammed in small shipholds by the dozens. Our journeys have never been as comfortable as they are today" ('Abdallah El Gourd, Gnawa master based in Tangier, personal communication).

23. About the ritual context of the Gnawa of Morocco, see Pâques 1991. About the contrast between scripturalism and living religious practices in the traditional Moroccan culture, see Geertz 1968. About female ecstatic rituals, see Baldassarre 2000.

24. This event was completely overlooked, or hushed up, by the Moroccan media. This was probably because the Moroccan music "professionals" felt the unforeseen exploitation of B'net Houariyat was not an effect of their own efforts. Just a few days before the Womad festival, the French newspaper *Liberation* published an article by a Maghreb journalist, "Les pseudo-révélations du Womad," depicting the B'net Houariyat as one of the several dozen semi-professional bands playing at popular feasts and meetings in Morocco, a phenomenon void of any artistic or cultural significance. With a stark polemic tone, the article explained that, in such an internationally renowned World Music festival as Womad, Morocco should be represented by great interpreters of Arab song, rather than five women coming from the poorest quarters of the Marrakech *medina*.

25. A peaceful demonstration was to take place, in support of women's civil

rights, on March 12, 2000; this was opposed by no less than three million people (half themselves women) who filled the streets and squares of Casablanca, easily preventing the demonstration.

26. The diffusion of the Internet in Morocco has led to the construction of websites dedicated to the music of the Gnawa, such as www.gnawa.net and www.dargnawa.nl. For multimedia articles about Gnawa and B'net Houariyat, see Schuyler 1997 and Baldassarre 1999b. For an interactive work on the musical culture of Morocco, see Baldassarre 1998.

Bibliography

Baldassarre, Antonio. 1998. *Morocco. Sound from an Ancient Land*. Firenze, Italy, and Casablanca: Si.Lab./Planète Intéractive.

——. 1999a. "Musique et danse Gnawa. La *lila/derdeba* comme hypertexte," in *L'Univers des Gnawa*, edited by 'Abdelhafid Chlyeh. Grénoble, France, and Casablanca: La Pensée Sauvage/Le Fennech. 87-103.

——. 1999b. "With the Daughters of Houara: from Fieldwork to World Music," *Music & Anthropology* 4 <http://research.umbc.edu/eol/MA/index/number4/baldassarre/baldae0.htm>

—— 2000. "La Hadra des Femmes au Maroc," in *La Transe*, edited by 'Abdelhafid Chlyeh. Rabat, Morocco: Marsam. 149-156.

Beck, Julian. 1972. *The Life of the Theatre*. San Francisco: City Lights.

Beguin, Hubert. 1973. *L'organisation de l'espace au Maroc*. Brussels: Académie Royale des Sciences d'Outre-mer.

Berque, Jacques. 1958. "Medinas, villes neuves, et bidonvilles," *Cahiers de Tunisie* 21-22.

Bowles, Paul. 1961. "The Kif in North-African Civilization," *Kulchur* 3: 68-72.

Cattedra Raffaele. 1996. "Marocco: frammenti urbani fra parabole e minareti," *Terra d'Africa* 5: 185-219.

Chottin, Alexis. 1924. "Airs Populaires recueillis à Fès," *Hespéris* 1: 275-285.

——. 1933. *Corpus de Musique Marocaine*. Paris: Heguel. 2 vols.

——. 1938. *Tableau de la Musique Marocaine*. Paris: Paul Geuthner.

d'Erlanger, Rodolphe. 1930/1949. *La musique arabe*. Paris: Paul Geuthner. 5 vols.

Dermenghem, Emile. 1954. *Le culte des Saints dans l'Islam maghrébin*. Paris: Gallimard.

El Fassi, Mohammed. 1962. "La musique marocaine dite musique andalouse," *Hespéris/Tamouda* III/1: 79-106.

Geertz, Clifford. 1968. *Islam observed. Religious development in Morocco and Indonesia*. New Haven and London: Yale University Press.

Gellner, Ernest. 1995. *Anthropology and Politics. Revolution in the Sacred Grove*. Oxford: Blackwell Publishers.

Guettat, Mahmoud. 1980. *La musique classique du Maghreb*. Paris: Sindibad.

Hassan II. 1976. *Le défi*. Paris: Albin Michel.

——. 1993. *La Mémoire d'un Roi*. Paris: Plon.

Knibiehler, Yvonne, Geneviève Emmery, and François Leguay. 1992. *Des Français au Maroc—La présence et la mémoire (1912–1956)*. Paris: Denoël.

Leary, Timothy. 1968. *High Priest*. New York: The World Publishing Company.

Mernissi, Fatima. 1987. *Le harem politique*. Paris: Albin Michel.

Pâques, Viviana. 1991. *La religion des esclaves*. Bergamo, Italy: Moretti & Vitali.

Perrault, Gilles. 1990. *Notre Ami le Roi*. Paris: Gallimard.

Rabinow, Paul. 1989. *French Modern. Norms and Forms of the Social Environment*. Cambridge: Massachusetts Institute of Technology Press.

Schuyler. Philip. 1997. "Rewiew of Gnawa Lila," *Music & Anthropology* 2 <http://research.umbc.edu/eol/MA/index/number2/gnawa/gnawa.htm>

Virolle, Marie. 1995. *La chanson raï*. Paris: Khartala.

Westermark, Edward. [1926] 1968. *Ritual and Belief in Morocco*. New York: University Books.

Discography

Anthologie "Al "Ala"—Musique Andaluci-Marocaine. Maison des Cultures du Monde/INEDIT. 1992/97. 72 CDs.

Anthologie d'al-Melhûn. Maison des Cultures du Monde/INEDIT W 260016. 1990. 3 CDs.

B'net Houariyat. *Poèmes d'amour des femmes du sud marocain*. Al Sur/Musisoft, ALCD 126. 1994.

——. *Voices of Marrakech*. Harmony MRF 005/2. 2001.

Brian Jones Presents The Pipes of Pan at Jajouka. Point Music B0040. [1971] 1995.

Elbaz, Simon. *Matrouz*. Al Sur/Musisoft ALCD 245. 1999.

Gabriel, Peter. *Passion. Music for The Last Temptation of Christ*. Real World RWCD1. 1989.

——. *Passion—Sources*. Real World RWCD2. 1989.

Gnawa Lila. *Les Maîtres du Ganbri*. Al Sur/Musisoft ALCD 101/145/146/147/148. 1992/95. 5 CDs

Gnawa Night Spirit Master. Axiom/Island 314-510-147. 1992.

Haddarat—Chants sacrés des Femmes de Fès. Al Sur/Musisoft ALCD 243. 1998.

Hakmoun, Hadraoui and Zahar. *Trance*. Real World CDRW 38. 1995.

Hakmoun, Hassan and Don Cherry. *Gift of the Gnawa*. Flying Fish MSI FF70571. 1995.

Kronos Quartet. *Pieces of Africa*. Nonesuch 79275. 1996.

Mahmoud Ghanya with Pharoah Sanders. *The Trance of Seven Colors*. Axiom/Island 314-524-047-2. 1994.

Nass El Ghiwane. *Essiniya*. Edition Cléopatre/Ouhmane OCD 1013. 1973.

Lê, Nguyên. *Maghreb & Friends*. ACT 9261-2. 1998.

Orchestre Nationale de Barbès. *En Concert*. Tajma'at/Virgin LC 3098. 1997.

Page, Jimmy and Robert Plant. *No Quarter*. Atlantic 7567 82706 2. 1994.

Sapho. *Digital Cheikha*. Barbarity, CFA 263 QS, 1997.

The Splendid Gnawa Masters Featuring Randy Weston. Verve/Polygram 521-587-2, 1993.

Touria, Hadraoui. *Extraits de chants soufis marocains*. Ouhmane TH 001. 1999.

——. *Malhoun*. BMDA JAM 311261. 2000.

CHAPTER FOUR

POP-*RAÏ*:

FROM A "LOCAL" TRADITION TO GLOBALIZATION

GABRIELE MARRANCI

Nowadays, it may happen that while we are surfing the Internet, visiting music stores, listening to radio stations, watching MTV, or shopping in supermarkets, we might come across Sting's "Desert Rose." Because of its virtuosic melismas, this music has an exotic and oriental, suggestive atmosphere, hypnotizing listeners. That is the result of the *raï* singer Cheb Mami's clear and limpid voice.

Writing in the early 1990s, Sorce Keller (1992: 136) defined pop-*raï* as an Algerian hybrid repertoire with a limited diffusion and an extremely localized audience. Although raï music was principally a local repertoire, it has always been a musical genre in which *transculturation* (Marranci 2000a) and musical exchanges have played a fundamental role. Consequently, as the quotation marks in the title underline, the concept of "local" is to be interpreted in relation with its opposite, the "global." Indeed, seven years later, the international pop star Sting decided to select the Algerian raï singer Cheb Mami for the "Desert Rose" duet on his new album *Brand New Day*. What brought about this radical transformation and international diffusion of the former local Algerian pop-raï?

In this chapter, I observe the different phases that allowed pop-raï to move from a local musical tradition to a global music reality and market. Indeed, while there are some works about Algerian pop-raï history and its role in Algerian society (Shade-Poulsen 1999; Daoudi and Miliani 1995; Virolle 1995) and even fewer about raï in France (e.g. Marranci 2000a and 2000b; Derderian 1996; Miliani 1995; Gross et al. 1992), there do not appear to be any studies about the different phases of pop-raï's globalization.

The term "globalization" "may be understood as referring to the process, procedures and technologies—economic, cultural, and political—underpinning the current 'time space' compression which *produce a sense of immediacy and simultaneity* about the world" (Brah, Hickman, Mairtin 1999). Moreover, through globalization, people may cross boundaries to imagine new time-space (or space-time) dimensions and power relations. The recent globalization of raï is very different from its earlier diffusions through the Mediterranean area because of the Algerian immigrant network. Although raï music has always been a multicultural genre, and music styles such as reggae, *chanson françaies*, and fox trot have played an important role in its development, nowadays three principal factors are central to its globalization: new types of commodification, new forms of musical identity, and new representations of raï's meaning.

Pop-raï, however, has suffered from misleading representations and descriptions both of its cultural meaning and its song texts because of political exploitation and market strategies. First of all, during the process of raï's Western commodification, major record companies have overemphasized those aspects of raï music that protested against restrictive Algerian customs, in order to develop a Western audience. At the same time, raï was represented as a repertoire against Islamic extremists, referred to as "the rebellious music of Oran" or "the battle of raï." Additionally, pop-raï's singers have been portrayed as the new martyrs of the Islamic *jihad* against Algerian society and music. On the contrary, pop-raï singers have always rejected these stereotyped representations and have stressed that their music has no political connotations or anti-Islamic intentions. The mass media, in particular in France, have been promoting this "caricature" of pop-raï to reinforce, as we shall see, the Western political distinction between acceptable, positive Arabic traditions, such as raï music, and dangerous, disruptive, Islamic customs.

Some recent articles and books, even within academia (e.g., Mitchell 1996), have accepted and reproduced this questionable representation of pop-raï. This may create unclear delimitation between the study of pop-raï and its commercial and political promotion (e.g., Lorai and Chawky 1999). For instance, Tony Mitchell, stressing the hostility that raï suffered in Algeria because of Islamic antagonism, reports that, "These culminated in the death of raï singer Cheb Hasni at the hands of an angry crowd in Oran in September 1994" (Mitchell 1996: 71). The official police report did declare that an Islamic commando was responsible for the murder of Hasni, yet the reason for his murder was more likely associated with the payment of an old debt rather than Islamic terrorism.[1]

In 1985, however, not many French people were interested either in Hasni's murdered or in raï music itself. In fact, in France, raï singers and musicians principally played in Oriental cabarets and weddings parties. Khaled, for instance, was only really known by people living in the Maghrebi quarters of French cities. Some French newspapers and magazines, in contrast, had published articles on raï, describing the incredible effects on Algerian youth of this revolutionary repertoire. On the one hand, the Algerian press was stressing the disruptive consequences that raï had on young people. On the other hand, the French press (e.g., *Actuel* and *Libération*) was underlining the contested vulgarity discussed in Algeria as positive rebellious and westernized aspects of raï (Shade-Poulsen 1997: 76). That was the consequence of the fact that raï music was becoming a positive aspect within the difficult relations existing between French society and the Magrhebian community in France.

Indeed, during the early 1980s, most young people coming from the second generation of French Algerians expressed their difficult position within French society through rap music. Yet French society, and in particular French politicians, associated this musical culture with the United States' ghetto's lifestyle, violence, and drug selling. The Maghrebians' preference for rap was interpreted as a possible escalation of the violence in the French suburbs (Boucher 1998). The narrative of raï music, on the contrary, was, and is, completely acceptable from a Western point of view, because the texts address love, sex, and alcohol, categories that are not "scandalous" in our societies.

As a result, during 1986 some immigrant associations of Paris and the Parisian municipality decided to organize a four-day concert of raï at Bobigny, a Parisian suburban quarter. This event represents an important milestone in the internationalization of pop-raï. Not only was it the first concert of raï to be held in France, it was also the first concert of raï to be held outside the Maghreb. It allowed the singers to achieve contracts with major international record companies and, consequently, to settle in France.

To survey the developments about pop-raï after the Bobigny concert in a relatively short space is a daunting task. I think that to look at the personal artistic pathways of raï singers may allow for a more focused and comprehensive exploration of its globalization process. Yet ethnomusicologists have been reluctant to study the work of single artists, particularly those who are famous. However, Danielson argues that, "To say that talented performers working in commercial domains are simply marketing to the unsuspecting public seems naïve" (1997: 15). Therefore, the following pages will take reader into the recent history and musical production of pop-raï (in France) through its principal artists in order to understand the new developments of this repertoire.

Khaled and the Internationalization of Raï Music

One of the most famous singers performing at Bobigny was Cheb Khaled.[2] Known as the "King of Raï" in Algeria, during the concert he showed that his success had crossed the Mediterranean because of the "music cassette immigrant's network." His great success in Algeria had been the result of his incredible voice, his simple texts, his vernacular language, and his danceable music. Indeed, in Algeria, raï singers and their listeners set up networks of emotive relationship through the songs that mirror the listeners' daily life experience. Listeners can reinterpret Khaled texts and music by creating personal metaphors of their own lives (see Shade-Poulsen 1999: 97–132). In other words, in the first part of Khaled's career, his success came from the capacity to represent Algerian youth and their quest for fewer societal restrictions and more freedom of inter-gender relations.

Certainly, Martin Meissonier, one of the promoters of the Bobigny concert, had other reasons for his interest in Khaled's music. At that time, Algerian music was absent from the landscape of World Music; yet the successes of Peter Gabriel's WOMAD[3] was showing the potential of this new product. Hence, the album *Kutché* was the result of Meissonier's efforts to bring pop-raï within the increasingly successful label of World Music. *Kutché* can be seen as the first international album of pop-raï. Recorded in London, Paris, and Algiers, with high-digital technology, *Kutche*, for the first time, mixes traditional raï with reggae and jazz, thanks to the ability of Algerian jazzman Safy Boutella. Moreover, Khaled considered this album his "revenge against the producers of pirate cassettes and the fraudulent music editors of Oran" (Khaled 1998:130). His revenge took the form of "remaking" some of his most popular songs at the time, such as "Baroud," "El-Léla," "Minuit," "Cheba," or "La Camel," which may be the best example of Martin Meissonier's and Safy Boutella's modifications of Khaled's original style.

"La Camel" is a famous Cheikha Rimitti hit that Khaled had arranged with new music. In the first version, it is possible recognize the typical recording procedure that the Oran publishers adopted. In fact, "the most important thing was that the rhythmic cycle not die. As soon as the singer had done his job, he hurried out of the studio, leaving behind the studio musicians" who arranged music (Shade-Poulsen 1999:67) sometimes with electronic keyboard and synthesized sounds, as in the case of "La Camel." The Algerian version is characterized by the synthesized sound of a trumpet, which is constantly present, to recall the typical instrumentation of the football supporters' music bands in Oran.[4] This greatly influenced raï music through the famous musicians Bellemou (Daoudi and Miliani 1996). However, it is the voice of Khaled that catches the ears of listeners as much as the text of the song. The hypnotic rhythm cycle, stressed by the darbukka, complements the expressiveness and meaningfulness of Khaled's voice.

If in the first version of "La Camel" the music emphasizes Khaled's voice, in the remade *Kutche* version, music, with its complex structure and texture, distracts the listeners from both Khaled's voice and the text. In fact, in the *Kutche* version, Khaled remade "La Camel" in 4/4 funky style, with electric guitars and sophisticated musical effects. Additionally, a choir intones the refrain, breaking the rhythm cycle with syncopated parterres in alternation with Khaled's voice, which seems to lose its traditional centrality. In other words, the most important and salient modifications took place in the domain of the sound, rhythm, and music textures, producing a result very different from traditional raï. The quality of the sound and the instrumentation are very important aspects in Western pop music today; on the other hand, Algerian listeners focus, in particular, on the song texts and rhythm structure. Many Algerians told me that one could listen to raï in two different ways: first, with your mind and your heart, second, with your body and your feet. In the case of the funky version of "La Camel," the focus was on dancing, and because of the 4/4 rhythm, on Western dancing style.

"Didi," the "third[5] winning ticket" (Khaled 1998:143) of Khaled, and hitherto his most international hit, may confirm that tendency. Indeed, no one paid attention to the fact that the texts of the songs were in dialectal Arabic, probably because the singer's voice was considered part of the sound. Nevertheless, Khaled's record company used the Arabic words of his song as an artistic and exotic element of his CD jacket, which shows a Westernized portrait of the smiling Khaled's face in the foreground. In Algeria, on the other hand, the name of the artist and the song title are in Latin characters, because pop-raï singers sang in the Algerian dialect (Langlois 1996) and not in classical Arabic.

Therefore, the internationalization of raï not only required adapting music and sound to the Western audience's needs, but also required adapting the image and representation of raï to the Western consumer's ideology. Consequently, Barclay, Khaled's record company, organized a massive advertisement for the album *Khaled* (which includes "Didi") that brought the album to the surprising tenth position in the international Top 50.

With the success of the song "Didi," many French started to ask about the meaning of the mysterious songs Khaled was singing in dialectal Arabic. Khaled's later albums, *Sahara* and *Kenza*, resolved this problem in an unexpected way. Khaled has not always been the author of his texts, he has often taken the words from traditional Algerian songs and poems; consequently, his texts have always dealt with an Algerian cultural heritage.

Khaled's chance meeting with Jean-Jacques Goldman produced the first two of Khaled's French songs. However, Goldman wrote not only music but also the words of the French songs in the album *Sahara* (1996). The first, "Aïcha," was an incredibly successful hit speaking about an impossible love. The second, "Le jour viendra," dealt with political and Islamic Algerian issues.

The Khaled-Goldman French version of pop-raï is something very different from the Algerian raï.[6] This is certainly the case for *Kenza* (2000), which is the most international of Khaled's albums and the final one. Most people and journalists, in Algeria and in France, find this album "a Western product for a Western audience." The use of Egyptian string orchestra in "Raba-Raba" or "Aâlach Tloumouni," the duet with British-Pakistani singer Amar, the cover remake of John Lennon's "Imagine" (using Hebrew, Arabic, and English words) with Israeli diva Noa, as well as Goldman's texts, seem to radically change the meaning and the identity of Algerian raï.

This is the result of the Khaled's collaboration with two producers. On the one hand, Steve Hillage, who has been a relevant artist of British progressive rock in the '70s as leader of Gong and System 7; on the other, Lati Kronlund, who has been the founder of the New York collective project Brooklyn Funk Essential. Therefore most of the songs in *Kenza*, for instance "El Aâdyene" or "El Bab," strictly respect the orthodoxy of funk. The album has powerful horn sections, and rock-solid grooves, but at the same time, among funk guitars, there are 'uds, darbukkas, and bendirs.

Hence, Khaled became the ideal pop-raï singer in order to develop a Western commodification of raï music. In his French CDs, his voice represented the local heritage of raï, while Steve Hillage brought to the music "the global 'time-space' compression which *produce a sense of immediacy and simultaneity* about the world" (Brah, Hickman, Mairtin 1999: 3).

Cheb Mami and the New Exoticism

Khaled is not, however, the only raï singer who became an international success thanks to the Bobigny concert. Cheb Mami, alias Mohamed Khalifati, was born in 1966 in Saïda, a city to the south of Oran. After surprising success in Algeria thanks to his incredible voice, his Bobigny performance acted as a launching pad in much the same way it did for Khaled. Totem Records, nowadays affiliated with Virgin Records, offered him a contract to produce the album *Let me raï* (1990). This album, which was recorded in the United States, showed, two year earlier, the same characteristics of Khaled's successful album *Khaled*. The harmonies of its songs recall American pop and rock in the early 1960s. International musicians, such as saxophone player Ben Clatworthy, added jazz, reggae, and funk influences. However, *Let me raï* was not successful, probably because the Gulf War made it difficult to sell Arabic music to Western audiences.

On the contrary, *Saïda* and in particular *Meli Meli* are the albums that have allowed Cheb Mami to reach an international audience. In contrast to Khaled's album *Khenza*, Mami wrote the majority of the two album texts, recorded in 1994 and 1998, respectively. However, from the musical point of view, one notices the same alteration in the traditional rhythmic structure in favor of most Western dance styles that we have already observed in the case of Khaled's songs. Moreover, songs such as "H' Babi," in the album Saïda or even more "Trab," from the album *Meli Meli,* were composed to emphasize Mami's particular singing style, which is very distant from Western styles and deals with very wide melismatic ornamentation and a high pitch of the voice.

Many anecdotes surround the famous duet made by Sting and Mami for "Desert Rose." This has been attributed to the apparently casual meeting of the two artists, and Sting's attraction to Mami's voice. During an interview, Sting stressed that, "All last summer I lived with Cheb Mami's album. Eating, walking, all the time. His voice is an incredible instrument. He does whatever he wants with it; it really impressed me, as did his talent as a musician. I didn't have any idea of what he could sing, I didn't know raï music. Then I saw him in Bercy with Khaled, Rachid Taha, and this great orchestra . . . and Steve Hillage. Very impressed, I began to write a song on this experience, and we met. I asked him if he'd like to sing for me, in a way to 'authenticate' my experience."[7] I believe that the record company, which had signed both singers, may have been the principal promoter of this successful collaboration. Yet, it is interesting to note the post-colonialist use of the term "authentic" (Hobsbawm and Ranger 1983; Stratton 1983; Stokes 1997: 97–144; Chapman 1997: 29–34; Cohen 1997: 117–134) in Sting's words. Mami's voice is seen as an exotic and naturalistic element that is capable of transforming the "simple" rose into the "desert" rose.

His voice, as we have seen in the case of Khaled, is reduced to a decorative element of the song.

Therefore, it is no surprise that, even though Sting-Mami's "Desert Rose" won a Grammy in 2000, only Sting's name is registered in the list of the award winners. Additionally, only Sting's English textual part of the song appears on the jacket of the CD. The record company has transformed the dialectal Cheb Mami's Arabic text, which we listen to at the beginning and the end of the song, to an orientalized musical introduction and refrain. The artistic directors of Sting's album *Brand New Day* may have thought that the raï singer's voice would be sufficient to represent the "magical" and "mysterious" aspect of Sting's encounter with the Orient—an Orient that raï music increasingly symbolizes in the Western imagination.

On the contrary, Cheb Mami's text part is like a song within the song: "My night, Oh my night / This has been an eternity since I've been looking for my (*ghouzelleti*) gazelle. / Although I long to see her and finally meet her to hold her in my arms forever. / I would prefer to keep her in my mind like a secret poem to model and make her look more beautiful inside and out."[8] Mami's text comes from the *cheikhs'* and *ma'luf*'s poetic traditions in which words line "*ghouzelleti*" are often present. Additionally, the theme of distance is a typical subject of raï texts, as in the case of Cheb Hasni's songs. On the one hand, Sting's "Desert Rose" may be seen as the extreme example of the "globalization" of pop-raï. On the other, Cheb Mami's text and voice may be seen as the local heritage of a globalized raï.

In June 2001, Mami recorded his CD *Dellali* (My dearest one). The CD, like the last of Khaled's albums, focuses on the international crossover market and tries to attract, after Mami's American concerts, an American audience. Produced by Nile Rodgers and Nitin Sawhney and with the collaboration of Sting as a backup vocalist, this CD—including its first track, "Le raï c'est chic"—is a perfect example of the process in which raï music is involved today.

It is the voice of the raï singer that allows defining this music as raï. Rodgers reinvents Mami's raï music through a mix of different styles in which—as in Khaled's *Kenza* or, as we shall see, Taha's *Medina*—flamenco, *Africaines* (African rhythms), house, reggae, and techno rhythms and sounds support Mami's voice and melismas. As in *Kenza, Sahara,*

Front cover of Cheb Mami's *Dellali*

and *1 2 3 Soleils,* an orchestra, in this case the prestigious English Chamber Orchestra, has an important role in the reinterpretation of raï music. For instance, in the song "Yahamami" (a song in classic Arabic style) in which Mami's voice shows its range in a virtuosic style, the orchestra introduces the song with a classic harmonic cadenza. Although this album is very recent, many Algerian immigrants have not appreciated the deep Americanization of Mami's raï, in particular in this difficult political moment for the Middle East and the Palestinians. An Algerian friend of mine told me recently, "Singing in Arabic language is not enough. Raï music has lost its meaning and this Mami CD marks a point of no return."

The global and the local are, however, more entangled in the cultural production of the second-generation Algerian, for whom Western culture and Western music are neither the "exotic technoscape" nor the powerful otherness, but part of their daily life and identity. Indeed, with their music turned toward their Algerian heritage, the Beurs want to affirm a peculiar culture distant from both those of France and Algeria (Marranci 2000a).

Rachid Taha and the "1 2 3 Soleils" Concert

Rachid Taha, born in Oran in 1958, was one of the first Beurs to use raï in his music. His family immigrated to France during 1968 and he grew up in Alsace and Lyon. In 1981, he met two other young Beurs with a passion for music, Mohammed and Moktar, and they started playing together. Their group, Carte de Séjour, reached the height of their success in 1983 with the album *Rhoromaine*. After three years, a controversial remake in the Oriental music style of the song "Douce France," written by Charles Trenet, transformed Carte de Séjour into one of the most famous groups in France. During 1989, the group unexpectedly broke up and Rachid Taha started to work with Don Was. Yet Don Was preferred the Algerian Khaled to the Beur Taha in order to produce an international raï hit (the result was the famous "Didi").

In 1993, Taha wrote his first successful album as soloist and the song "Voilá Voilá," from which the album takes its name, crossed the sea and arrived in a number of discos and local clubs in London. Before this, pop-raï was almost unknown in these areas. The encounter with the lively London music life and its musical multiculturalism greatly influenced Taha's third album *Olé Olé*, yet again written with the help of Steve Hillage. Rachid Taha mixed together techno music, Algerian chaabi, and Mexican rhythms with Indian melodies, and used electronic effects and acoustic instrumentation in a variegated "ethno-melange" that characterized his particular raï style.

Nevertheless, the musical remaking of old Algerian hits has always been one of the most notable characteristics of raï music which "is rooted in the Bedouin tradition. In this tradition . . . the most important thing is the quality of the performance" (Daoudi and Miliani 1996: 206). In *Diwan* (1998) Rachid Taha recalled this raï tradition and remade some of Dahmane El Harrachi's and Mohamed El Anka's[9] *chaabi* songs into a powerful rock style.

Because of the positive responses Taha received from listeners about his last album, he tried experimenting with innovative musical styles, and the result was *Made in Medina* (2000). It has received positive praise from French critics, who have described this album as innovative, dealing with the complex identities of multicultural France. In addition, Steve Hillage and Rachid Taha claimed that the primary aim of the album has been to pay more attention both to the African soul and to the "other countries of black desire"[10] than to white America pop music. Therefore, rhythmical African traditions, such as voodoo rhythms, are used on *Made in Medina*, to try to capture the ecstatic and "mystic experience of the trance."

On September 26, 1999, Taha took part in the raï concert "1 2 3 Soleils," organized by Barclay Records in Bercy, with the participation of Khaled and Faudel. (Barclay Records is the recording company of all three raï singers.) It was the most international and commercial raï concert that a record company had ever organized. Furthermore, Barclay Records had planned the concert with the specific purpose of producing a double CD, a video, and a DVD for international distribution. Indeed, the record company has produced two different versions of the same CD for different audiences. The "European" version (with the exception of France, where we may find both CDs) includes a selection of the singers' most famous hits. The "Middle East" version is the complete recording of the concert. Hence, deep differences divide the Bobigny concert from the Bercy "1 2 3 Soleils."

On the one hand, the Bobigny concert was planned as a raï concert for the Maghrebian community in France. It was a "traditional" pop-raï concert with, darbukkas, bendirs, trumpets, electric keyboards, and guitars, in which the singer's improvisations and the singers' voices were at the center of the performance. On the other hand, in "1 2 3 Soleils" the "Orientalized" version of raï was not only promoted and sold as the Western acceptable version of raï but also indicated and represented as the "authentic" version of pop-raï. The principal symbol of such an exotic vision of raï was the prominent display, during this concert, of a fifty-string Egyptian Umm Kulthum-style orchestra. Hillage gave more prominence to the string orchestra in this concert than he did in Khaled's album *Sahara*. However, this powerful orchestration is something completely new in raï and has not affected the local Algerian production of this repertoire, where raï seems to preserve, more or less, its 1980s style (Virolle 1995, Daoudi and Miliani 1996, Shade-Poulsen 1999). In this style, electronic keyboards perform the accompaniment, the rhythm is cyclic, and the singing style plain. At the beginning of the songs, there are dedications, and sometimes some *yu-yu* or *twalwil*[11] are added like cadenzas.

In a certain sense, in the later development of raï, the concept of global and local are so entangled in a multidimensional representation that raï music becomes a "fluidity of meanings involved in the act of constructing and rearticulating identities" (Guilbault 1997: 32). Indeed, until the concert at Bobigny, rap and reggae music were the only musical domains where Beurs could express themselves. In Taha's style, for instance, one may observe the search for a middle ground between the Algerian cultural heritage of his parents and the multicultural aspects of France. Consequently, many young people, born of Algerian parents, started to set up groups to play raï music in Maghrebi locals at the periphery of the French cities.

Faudel and the New Commodification of Raï

One of these young singers was Faudel Bellou, who, at the age of 12, organized, with some of his Magrebi friends, the group Les etoiles du Raï (Stars of Raï). His group performed covers of Khaled and Cheb Mami's songs to enliven weddings and neighborhood parties in the suburban quarter of Mantes-la-Jolie in Val Fourré. A meeting with the guitarist Mohammed Mestar (Momo), who became his manager, inspired Faudel to pursue performance opportunities beyond his local neighborhood. In 1993 he began collaborating with different artists, and played in a few Cheb Mami and MC Solaar concerts as well. In France, moreover, there was a particular attention to the so-called Question Beur (the Beurs' issue). Hence, the producers from the private television broadcaster, Canal+, decided to invite him to their program *C'est pas le 20 heures*, on which Faudel performed a duet with Khaled. As a result of this media attention, in 1997, Faudel published his first album for Virgin, *Baïda*.

Baïda is an eclectic album where tradition and innovation are mixed. As in Khaled and Mami's last albums, the sound of *Baïda* is more hip-hop, rock, and flamenco then traditional Algerian raï. Nevertheless, unlike Khaled's or Mami's CDs, Faudel's texts and the rhythmical cyclic structure of darbukkas recall the musical heritage of Algerian raï as well as pop-raï in Algeria today. For example, in "Baïda" Faudel sings, "Baïda you have spoiled my life / I told you that I have had enough of you / I did not know what was happening. / I discovered your game, but it was too late/she is in my mind and my life. / To whom could I tell my happiness and my sorrow (*el mahana*)? / I cannot understand this pain / Tell me why I do love her, still." In another song, however, Faudel sings in French and this time it is not the pain of love and the *femme fatale* he sings about but the harshness and suffering of his generation. In "Dis-Moi" (Tell me), he put questions to an invisible interlocutor (the French society?), asking, "Tell me how to understand all these things / Hey you! Do you think I have the right / To believe in something that does not exist any more? / Tell me how I could understand all these things / There are some moments in which I do not know what I might think / Do not lose yourself within the oblivion / Do not waste your time / But I can see that all is decaying around me / Without any respect / I tell myself that life is a long battle / How could I understand all these things?"

Faudel's music represents the Beurs' difficult hyphenated reality, that Faudel, in an interview, described in this way, "When I go to Algeria, I am not at home. At the same time, here [in France] I am not completely at home as well. The integration bothers me. Where do we [the Beurs] live? Where are we? We, the young people coming from suburban quarters are deranged."[12] Nevertheless, Parisian suburban life has some contacts with *le blad* (the country: Algeria). In fact Faudel points out that, "in France suburbs are like the *blad*. People know each other. The *banlieues* (suburbs) are like villages. Everyone knows what you are doing."[13] Local and global, France and Algeria, are part of the everyday life of this generation that shares the same difficulties and disorientation of today's youth.

Hence, Faudel's *Baïda*, which sold 300,000 copies, had success in attracting not only a Maghrebian audience but also some French listeners, who were attracted by both his pop-raï style and his image. French critics, however, were less receptive to Faudel's next album, *Samra*. For example, in an article entitled "'*Samra*'s Colorless Mix: New Faudel with International Ambition," Ludovic Perrin, writes that "the album dissolves the Arab blood in an incongruous marriage" of styles "as lukewarm as it is colorless, which should open the way to export."[14]

Thus, according to the viewpoint of some French critics, the relentless search for a wide international success has reduced Faudel's raï music to an "inauthentic" patchwork of different styles.

Between *Glocalization* and Postcolonial Orientalism

Far from the international music business, however, new singers and groups of raï, such as Khaled Habib, Yahia Mokeddem's raï Kum group, Cheb Aïssa, and Cheb Tarik (to name just a few), are increasingly using electronic and synthesized sounds, such as funk, techno, and reggae, to explore new musical languages, in much the same way as Faudel and Taha.

For example, Khaled Habib, who lives in Sweden, is an Algerian musician and composer. He performs both traditional and modern raï developing personal musical approaches to the style. In his compositions, often only instrumental, he homogenizes raï, style with complex classical arrangements and jazz influences. His artistic activities, however, are very eclectic: from concerts to music for films and theater. In fact, raï music is no longer the only cultural place in which Beurs express themselves.

Moreover, a number of young singers, such as Cheb Tarik, who work in both Algeria and France, are increasingly beginning to criticize the texts of Khaled and Mami. For example, in a recent interview, Cheb Tarik argues that, "I do not think that raï has improved. On the contrary, I think that it has regressed. I do not like what they [raï singers] are doing at all and as for raï texts, the 'catastrophe' is more serious; it is disgraceful. I do not know whether this is a result of the commercial influences or not. Yet we need to work hard with the song texts. They should have a certain meaning."[15]

Beginning in the late '90s, this new generation asserted that raï musicians should rethink the "local" heritage of raï, from their "daily life" experience of music. Some films about the Maghrebi community living in France have misrepresented the lives of second-generation Maghrebi. They describe them as being linked with the "local" Algerian conflict between Islam and society, which does not exist within the Maghrebi quarters of Paris. Thus, pop-raï, as we have seen above, becomes the improbable barrier, the "antibody" against an Islamization of the Maghrebi quarters of the French cities.

Mahmoud Zemmouri's film, *100% Arabica* (1998), is a perfect example of the misconception of what raï means in the context of Parisian life. In the film, Khaled and Mami play two raï singers living in a low-income housing project located on the outskirts of Paris, renamed "100% Arabica" by its inhabitants (African and Maghrebi immigrants who live together). The two singers, with their powerful raï songs, triumph over the extremism and violence of an orthodox Islamic religious group that controls their neighborhood. Once again, raï music is represented not only as the "good" side of the Arabic world over the "evil" side of Islam, but also as local and immigrant repertoires dealing with Algerian local issues.

Although the music industry has played an important role, it was not uniquely responsible for the transformation of raï from a local tradition to a globalized music. Indeed, these transformations include a number of different factors, such as artistic collaboration, disjunctive places, identity complexity, as well as market strategy. In other words, this "French raï" or "international raï" has its own "authenticity" that is not the same as the "authenticity" of Algerian raï.

In order to produce raï styles acceptable to Western audiences, the major record companies have developed two different strategies. First of all, during the period from the end of the 1980s to the mid-1990s, they encouraged, through a series of artistic collaborations, the predisposition of pop-raï toward "musical transculturation" processes (Marranci 2000a). Since that time, the record companies have promoted pop-raï to take advantage of what Breen defines as "cultural mobility." Breen explains that "Music is moving rapidly into fresh areas. Likewise, the corporations that own and control music business are strategically using music to develop new markets for consumer products, while developing new products" (Breen 1995: 422). But this process would be impossible without the agreement of the raï singers. Major record companies could "strategically [use] music to develop new markets" only if there existed the conditions necessary for such developments. In pop-raï, local and global are often entangled (e.g., within the text, sometimes within music, or within both). In other words, the last developments of pop-raï may be inscribed in the process of *glocalization* in which the Mediterranean area is involved today.

Roland Robertson, writing about glocalization (1995: 35), argues,

"The global is not in and of itself counterposed to the local. Rather, what is often referred to as the local is essentially included within the global. In this respect globalization ... involves the linking of localities. But it also involves the 'invention,' of locality, in the same general sense as the idea of the invention of tradition, as well as its 'imagination.'" Hence, nowadays, funk, techno, reggae, but also Steve Hillage, Don Was, and Goldman, belong to a certain style of pop-raï.

Of course, record companies are involved in this process, and probably they are one of the most important "motor forces" in the development of raï. Nevertheless, it would be absolutely naïve to consider major record companies and the music market the only things responsible for the transformation of raï from a local tradition to a globalized repertoire. Yet both mass media and record companies were, and are, responsible for the orientalized and anti-Islamic image of raï. That is another aspect of the globalization process in which raï is involved, and it shows how raï "musicians are moderns who face constant pressure from westerns to remain musically and otherwise premodern—that is culturally 'natural'—because of racism and western demands for authenticity" (Taylor 1997: 126).

Indeed, the "French pop-raï" and "Raï-Beur," as one may name them, are linked with the immigration flow from Algeria to France. This has resulted in the development of new complex identities that deal with the experience of the reconstruction and deconstruction of musical and cultural memories. In this sense, the globalized "French pop-raï" and "Raï-Beur" are not less authentic than local Algerian raï played in Algeria today; they are only different.

Notes

1. As some of my Algerian informants living in Oran have told me.

2. I suggest reading Khaled's autobiography (Khaled 1998). About Mami, Taha, and Faudel more biographical notes may be found in Daoudi 2000, and Daoudi and Miliani 1996.

3. WOMAD (World of Music, Arts and Dance) was created by Peter Gabriel in 1980 as a World Music festival to introduce talented unknown artists to an international audience both through concerts and recordings realized under the label WOMAD.

4. This is an influence of the Spanish *corrida*.

5. The first one was the concert at Bobigny.

6. An Algerian friend of mine argued that "there is only Khaled's voice to remind us that this song deals with raï."

7. Sting, in *Music Up* 9/1999.

8. I have tried to translate the text of the song as carefully as possible, but due to the style of Mami's singing, some words may be not exact. However, the meaning of the text is respected.

9. Mohamed El Anka was born in Algiers in 1907. During 1918 he started to sing, and in 1928 recorded his first recording. After performing in Algeria and France, he was asked to be in charge of the first program of popular music on the Algerian radio. His style defined chaabi (popular). He died in 1978. Dahmane El Harrachi was born in 1925 at El Biar, a residential neighborhood of Algiers. After his studies, he began playing and singing chaabi. Immigrating to Paris in 1949, he performed in the Maghrebi bars of the French capital, writing numerous successful songs. He died in a fatal car accident in 1980.

10. *Le Monde*, October 7, 2000.

11. The typical ululation of the North Africa women during wedding and especially pre-wedding parties, mourning, circumcision processions, and at women's gatherings.

12. *Inrockuptibles* 138, February 17, 1988.

13. Ibid.

14. *Le Monde*, February 8, 2001.

15. *Elwatan*, August 24, 2000.

Bibliography

Appadurai, Arjun (ed). 1999. "Disjuncture and Difference in the Global Economy," *Theory, Culture & Socety* 2–3: 295–310.

——. 2000a. "Grassroots Globalization and the Research Imagination," *Pubic Culture* 12: 1–9.

Boucher, Manuel. 1998. *Rap: Expression des Lascars*. Paris and Montréal: L'Harrmatan.

Brah, Avtar, Mary Hickman, and Mairtin Mac an Ghaille. 1999. *Global Futures: Migration Enviroment and Globalization*. London: Macmillan Press.

Breen, Marcus. 1995. "The End of the World as We Know It," *Cultural Studies* 9: 437–503.

Chapman, Malcolm. 1997. "Thoughts on Celtic Music," in *Ethnicity, Identity and Music*, edited by Martin Stokes. Oxford and New York: Berg. 29–44.

Cohen, Sara. 1997. "Identity, Place and the 'Liverpool Sound'," in *Ethnicity, Identity and Music*, edited by Martin Stokes. Oxford and New York: Berg. 117–134.

Danielson, Virginia. 1997. *The Voice of Egypt Umm Kulthum, Arabic Song, and Egyptian Society in the Twentieth Century*. Chicago & London: The University of Chicago Press.

Daoudi, Buziane and Hadji Miliani. 1996. *L'aventure du raï*. Paris: Edition du Seuil.

Daoudi, Bouziane. 2000. *Le Raï*. Paris: Libro musique.

Derderian, Richard. L. 1996. "Popular Music from the North African Immigrant Community: Multiculturalism in Contemporary France 1945-1944," *Contemporary French Civilization* 20: 203–16.

Gross, Joan, David McMurray, and Ted Swedenburg. 1992. "Arab Noise and Ramadan Nights," *Middle East Report* 22: 120–155.

Guilbault, Jocelyne. 1997. "Interpreting world music: a challenge in theory and pratice," *Popular Music* 16: 31–44.

Hall, Stuart. 1991. "The Local and the Global: Globalization and Ethnicity," in *Culture, Globalization and the World System*, edited by A.D. King. New York: Macmillan.

Hannerz, Ulf. 1989. "Notes on Global Ecumene," *Public Culture* 2: 66–75.

——. 1999. *Cultural Complexity*. New York: Columbia University Press.

Hobsbawm, Eric and Terence Ranger (eds). 1983. *The Invention of Tradition*. Cambridge, U.K.: Cambridge University Press.

Khaled, Hibraim. 1998. *Khaled, Derrière le sourire*. Paris: Michel Lafon.

Langlois, Tony. 1996. "The Local and Global in North African Popular Music," *Popular Music* 15: 259–73.

Lorai, Marcello and Senouci Chawky. 1999. *La battaglia del raï*. Milano: Zelig.

Marranci, Gabriele. 2000a. "A complex Identity and its Musical Representation: Beur and *raï* music in Paris," *Music & Anthropology* 5. <http://www.muspe. unibo.it/period/MA/index/number5/marranci/marr_0.htm>

——. 2000b. "Le *raï* aujourd'hui: entre metisage musical et world music moderne," *Cahiers de Musiques Traditionnelles* 14: 139–149.

Miliani, Hadji. 1995. "Banlieues entre rap et raï," *Homes & Migration* 1191: 24–30.

Mitchell, Tony. 1996. *Popular Music and Local Identity*. London and New York: Leicester University Press.

Robertson, Roland. 1995 "Glocalization: Time-Spaced and Homogeneity-Heterogeneity," in *Global Modernities*, edited by Mike Featherstone, Scott lash and Roland Robertson. London, Thousand Oaks and New Delhi: Sage. 25–44.

Shade-Poulsen, Marc. 1997. "Which World: On the diffusion of Algerian *raï* to the West," in *Siting Culture*, edited by Karen Fog Olwig and Kirsten Hastrup. London: Routledge. 143–156.

——. 1999. *Men and Popular Music in Algeria*. Austin: University of Texas Press.

Sorce Keller, Marcello. 1992. "La 'popular music' come riflesso dei contatti culturali nell'area mediterranea," in *Antropologia della Musica e culture mediterranee*, edited by Tullia Magrini. Bologna: Il Mulino. 133–145.

Stokes, Martin (ed). 1997. *Ethnicity, Identity and Music*. Oxford, New York: Berg.

Stratton, Jon. 1983. "Capitalism and Romantic Ideology in the Record Business," *Popular Music* 3: 143–56.

Taylor, Timothy D. 1997. *Global Pop. World Music, World Market*. New York and London: Routledge.

Virolle, Marie. 1995. *La chanson raï*. Paris: Karthala.

Discography

Cheb Faudel. *Baïda*. Mercury MC 5583314. 1997.

——. *Samra*. Mercury CD 3460373. 2001.

Cheb Khaled. *Kutché*. Pathé. 1988.

——. *Le meilleur de Cheb Khaled*. vols. 1–2. Blue Silver. 1991.

——. *Khaled*. Barclay CD 511815.2. 1992.

——. *N'ssi n'ssi*. Barclay CD 527480–2. 1993.

——. *Sarha*. Barclay CD 8238741. 1996.

——. *Kenza*. Barclay CD 3654741. 1999.

Cheb Malik. *After raï*. Aladin le Musicien CD 2342609. 1992.

Cheb Mami. *Fatma*. MCPE. 1989.

——. *Let me raï*. Totem CD 8554282. 1990.

——. *Saïda*. Totem CD 840680.2. 1994.

——. *Meli meli*. Totem CD 724384. 1998.

——. *Dellali*. ARK21 CD 3735921. 2001.

Khaled Habibi. *Nostalgia*. D.A.M. 2001.

Taha, Rachid. *Barbes*. Polygram CD 2014671. 1990.

——. *Rachid Taha*. Polygram CD 1986725. 1993.

——. *Olé Olé*. Uni/Mango CD 9364991. 1995.

——. *Carte Blanche*. Polygram CD 8283195. 1997.

——. *Diwan*. Universal/Island Cd 8404558. 1998.

——. *Made in Medina*. Universal CD 3237881. 2000.

CHAPTER FIVE

"NEW SOUNDS, OLD TUNES":
TUNISIAN MEDIA STARS REINTERPRET THE
MA'LUF

RUTH DAVIS

Between 1992 and 1994, the Tunisian Ministere de la Culture copro-
duced with the Maison des Cultures du Monde in Paris a series of five
compact discs entitled *Tunisie Anthologie du Malouf.* The series is devoted
to the Arab urban tradition of Tunisia known as *ma'luf* (literally, "familiar," "customary"), believed to have originated in the Islamic courts of
medieval Spain. Each volume presents a performance of a *nuba* (plural
nubat), one of the thirteen cycles of vocal and instrumental pieces that
constitute the ma'luf's core repertory.

Volumes 1–4, subtitled "enregistrements historiques," reproduce
four nubat (*al-dhil, al-ramal, al-asbahan,* and *'al-'iraq*) from the canonic
studio recordings made by the Radio Ma'luf ensemble around 1960;[1]
since then, the studio recordings have served as the standard sources
for the Radio's routine broadcasts of the ma'luf. Conducted by
Abdelhamid Belelgia with chorus master Khemais Tarnane, the Radio
Ma'luf ensemble comprised 10 violins, 2 cellos, a double bass, *nay* (side-
blown bamboo flute without mouthpiece), *qanun* (trapezoidal plucked
zither), *'ud sharqi* (Middle Eastern lute with five or six strings), *naqqarat*
(pair of small kettle-drums), *tar* (frame drum with jingles), darbukka
(vase-shaped drum), and a chorus of 10 men and 10 women.

Volume 5, in contrast, is a contemporary performance of nubat *al-*

sikah by the Ensemble de Musique Traditionelle de Tunis, formed especially for the occasion. Led by Fethi Zghonda, head of music in the Ministry of Culture, the ensemble comprises 5 violins, cello, nay, 'ud *tunisi*, qanun, tar, naqqarat, and a chorus of 5 men and 5 women. Despite the ensemble's reduced size, its basic performance principles mirror those of the historic recordings; in both cases, the instrumentalists perform a fixed version of the melody from notation, the vocalists sing the same by ear, and the dominant sound is that of bowed strings and chorus in unison and at the octave. Introduced into Tunisian music in the mid-1930s by the Rashidiyya, a specialist ensemble for the ma'luf, this distinctive performance style was subsequently adopted by the Radio Ma'luf ensemble and it was promoted throughout Tunisia by the Ministry of Culture after independence in 1956.[2]

In 1993, the Maison des Cultures du Monde produced a recording representing an entirely different approach. Entitled *Lotfi Boushnak: Malouf Tunisien*, it presents three *waslat*, or abbreviated nubat (al-asbahan, rast al-dhil, and sikah) sung by the Tunisian media star Lotfi Boushnak, famous throughout the Arab world and beyond for his interpretations of an eclectic range of Tunisian and Egyptian styles.

Here, Boushnak sings solo throughout, replacing the impersonal, perfectly coordinated choral renderings of the Radio ensemble with an expressive, virtuoso style and subtle nuances of articulation, backed by an ensemble of nine instrumental soloists on violin, nay, qanun, 'ud sharqi, cello, double-bass, naqqarat, darbukka, and tar. Boushnak had been including the ma'luf in his programs for gala concerts and festivals in Tunisia and abroad since the early 1990s; the Maison des Cultures du Monde made this recording following a successful tour given by Boushnak. The CD was followed by cassette recordings for the Tunisian market. By the mid-1990s, Boushnak's renderings of the traditional love songs vied with the latest hits of other popular singers, blasting from the cassette stalls along the Avenue Bourguiba in downtown Tunis.

Around the same time, in April 1995, the young media star Sonia M'Barek was featured as a solo singer in the concert "Ya Zahratan" ("O Fleur") celebrating the centenary of the birth of Shaykh Khemais Tarnane (d. 1966), the legendary ma'luf authority and the original chorus master of the Rashidiyya ensemble.[3] The program was devoted to

Lofti Boushnak

Tarnane's compositions, models of modern Tunisian song, considered as *turath*, or tradition, patrimony.[4] The concert was conceived and hosted by the Centre des Musiques Arabe et Mediterranéennes (CMAM) at "Ennejma Ezzahra" (Resplendent Star), the palace built by the pioneering scholar and patron of the ma'luf, Baron Rodophe d'Erlanger (1862–1932).[5] M'Barek sang solo, alone, or with a chorus of two male singers, accompanied by an ensemble of three violins, viola, nay, qanun, 'ud, tar, and darbukka.

In 1997, M'Barek made a cassette recording entitled *Tawchih* (literally, "ornament"), produced by the CMAM, in which she presents a 20-minute extract from nubat *al-asbain*, a sequence of *muwashshahat* from the ma'luf in *maqam sikah*, songs by the veteran composers of the Rashidiyya, Shaykh Khmais Tarnane, and Muhammad Triki, and a new song by the young Tunisian composer Abdelhakim Belgaied. M'Barek's supple, full-bodied, carressing voice is offset by a light instrumental backing of violin, nay, 'ud, qanun, cello, *riqq*, and darbukka. *Tawchih* was released on compact disc in 1999 by Club du Disque Arabe ("Artistes Arabes Associes").

In the same year, World Network produced *Takht* (literally, "platform," the term used to designate the traditional solo instrumental ensemble of urban Arab music) featuring M'Barek with the same lineup as *Tawchih* in a live concert recording at the WDR-Funkhaus in Cologne, Germany, in June 1998. Similarly biased toward the ma'luf, *Takht* comprises solo renderings of four waslat (sikah, *kurdi, hsin,* and asbain), a *samai* (an Ottoman derived instrumental genre), and two new songs by the Tunisian composers Muhammad Mejri and Abdelhakim Belgaied.

With their English titles and extensive notes in French and English (*Tawchih*) and in German, French, and English (*Takht*), M'Barek's compact discs are clearly aimed at foreign, non-Arab audiences. However, her name is known to every taxi driver I rode with in Tunis (my personal benchmark of a singer's popularity) and her voice is heard more or less daily on Tunisian radio singing an eclectic repertory of Tunisian and Egyptian songs, including the ma'luf.

In certain respects, Boushnak and M'Barek seem to represent throwbacks to the performance style that prevailed before the Rashidiyya, characterized by a solo vocalist alternating with choral responses, accompanied by an ensemble of up to five solo instrumentalists; typically, the instrumentalists doubled as chorus, sometimes with additional vocalists (El-Mahdi and Marzuqi 1981: 49). This traditional type of performance is still being perpetuated by the veteran singer and 'ud *'arbi* player Tahar Gharsa and his son Zied. As he approaches his seventieth year, Tahar is considered the leading authority of the ma'luf in Tunis; celebrated for his live performances and broadcasts, he has never made a commercial recording.

Zied, in contrast, is featured on a compact disc produced in 1997 by the Tunisian company Soca Music in a program of songs by veteran composers of the Rashidiyya, including his father, in the traditional solo and choral response style.

Unlike Tahar and Zied Gharsa, Boushnak and M'Barek maintain a strict separation between the instrumental and vocal roles, and they sing solo throughout, dispensing with the chorus altogether. Moreover, whereas Gharsa and Zied specialize in the ma'luf and related Tunisian repertories, Boushnak and M'Barek sing a broad spectrum of Tunisian and Middle Eastern styles.[6] Indeed, the novelty of both Boushnak and M'Barek's recordings lies not only in their uncompromisingly soloistic interpretations but more fundamentally, in the very fact that such high-profile media stars are performing the ma'luf at all. Since the creation of an Egyptian-style national radio ensemble in 1958 and the production of an recorded canon to substitute live broadcasts of the ma'luf, the traditional repertory had become divorced from the commercial mass media; when I began my research in Tunis in the early 1980s, public performances of the ma'luf were more or less confined to the ensembles of the state music clubs and the national conservatory, the Rashidiyya, and occasional broadcast offerings from the archives of the RTT (Radio diffusion et Television Tunisienne). In this context, the reappearance of the ma'luf in the 1990s among the eclectic repertories of the top media stars, Lotfi Boushnak and Sonia M'Barek, seemed to herald a new popular revival.

This impression is reinforced when Boushnak's and M'Barek's recordings are considered in the context of representations of the ma'luf in the mass media earlier in the twentieth century. Performances of the ma'luf by top singers and instrumentalists appear among the earliest recordings made in Tunis from around 1910. When the national radio station was founded in 1938, it presented weekly live concerts of the ma'luf by the Rashidiyya ensemble, and during the decades leading up to independence, musicians, singers, and composers of the Rashidiyya were independent media stars in their own right.

In a previous article (Davis 1996b), I challenge the appropriateness of the dualistic art/popular paradigm in relation to Tunisian music, noting that in terms of its historical credentials and its representation in local discourse, the ma'luf would seem to qualify equally in both categories. My argument focuses on relationships between "traditional" and "popular"—categories that are generally considered mutually exclusive in Western music—and I question whether a musical culture that places so high a premium on the aesthetic and symbolic values of turath (literally, "heritage") could support a genuinely popular musical culture comparable to that of the West (Davis 1996b: 313).

Other scholars, notably Harold Powers (1980), Jihad Racy (1981; 1982), and Virginia Danielson (1988; 1996) have made comparable observations with respect to music of the core Middle East, particularly Egypt. Racy in particular points to the leveling role played by the Egyptian mass media in promoting many different types of music equally, without discrimination, noting that "the classical-popular division, with all its familiar implications, can be particularly misleading" (Racy 1981: 6). Danielson also argues for an eclectic approach toward identifying "popular" music in Cairo, observing that, "Some widely popular mediated music is located in the turath, or heritage of Arabo-Egyptian music. . . . 'Popular' then does not exclude classical nor 'folk' nor religious music which also draws from sources within the turath" (Danielson 1996: 301). She concludes that "no single word accounts for this [widely popular mediated] music; and it is not analogous to the large corpus commonly called 'popular' in the West."

In the present chapter, I question the existence of a distinctive category of "popular music" representing the vast body of mediated repertories in Tunisia. In particular, I consider the ma'luf interpretations of Boushnak and M'Barek in the context of earlier representations of the ma'luf and its related secular repertories, collectively known as turath,[7] in broadcasting and the record industry. In so doing, I argue that while appearing innovative and exceptional in their time, singers such as Lotfi Bushnak and Sonia M'Barek represent well established phenomena in Tunisian music and by extension, in Middle Eastern music as a whole.

The Ma'luf as a Popular Tradition

The ma'luf is the Tunisian musical repertory that allegedly originated in the Arabic speaking communities of medieval Spain. With the expulsion of the Muslims and Jews during the Christian reconquest, their musical traditions were transplanted into towns across North Africa where they acquired distinctive local traits.[8] The ma'luf thus shares a common history as well as musical and poetic similarities with the urban Arab repertories known as ala (literally, "instrument") or ala al-andalusiyya in Morocco; gharnati (from Granada) in Tlemcen and the west of Algeria; san'a ("work of art") in Algiers and central Algeria; and ma'luf in Constantine and the eastern part of Algeria, and in Libya.

The ma'luf is essentially a vocal repertory based on a system of melodic modes called *tub'* (singular, *tab*) and rhythmic metric genres called *iqa'at*. The song texts, in the literary Arabic genres of *muwashshah* and *zajal*, were recorded in special collections called *safa'in* (literally vessels; singular, *safina*). With their archaic mix of literary Arabic and dialect, their focus, resonant of Sufi mysticism, on love unfulfilled or otherwise unattainable and their rarefied imagery depicting human and natural beauty, precious jewels, and the intoxicating effects of wine, the song texts reinforce the mythical associations of the ma'luf with an idealized and irretrievable past.

In the sixteenth century, Tunisia was absorbed into the Ottoman Empire and the ma'luf was adopted by the new Turkish rulers, or beys; in the eighteenth century, Muhammad al-Rashid Bey (1711-59) was allegedly responsible for arranging the main body of the repertory into thirteen vocal cycles, or *nubat*, and introducing instrumental pieces into the canon (Guettat 1980: 214-15). But the ma'luf was not confined to the aristocracy: its principal patrons were certain Sufi brotherhoods, popular religious organizations open to all social classes.[9] The Sufi musicians cultivated the ma'luf alongside their religious repertories as a deliberate act of preservation; they gave public concerts in their meeting places, or *zwaya* (singular, *zawiya*), and they also performed the ma'luf in cafes and communal festivities. In the same communities, Jewish musicians adapted the melodies to Hebrew texts, both traditional and new; the songs, called *piyyutim*, were sung in the synagogue and at home, in worship, and in family celebrations.[10]

The Sufi musicians sang in chorus accompanied by percussion or handclapping in a style called ma'luf *kham* (literally raw, unrefined ma'luf). In the beylical palaces and in towns such as Tunis and Bizerte, there developed a type of performance with melody instruments: typically, a solo singer was accompanied by three to five solo instruments such as *rabab* or *kamanjah*, 'ud 'arbi, naqqarat, tar, and, from the beginning of the twentieth century, a piano or harmonium (El-Mahdi 1981: 49).[11] The solo singer might also be an instrumentalist and the instrumentalists doubled as chorus, sometimes with additional singers. Professional musicians—generally Jews, barbers, and artisans of the lower social strata—performed the ma'luf at weddings, circumcisions, and in cafés, while amateur musicians formed ma'luf ensembles in the privacy of their homes.

Jihad Racy has observed that

> in each major Near Eastern or Asiatic "high culture," one should expect
> to find a self-contained, indigenous musical repertoire, which is authen-
> tic, ancient, musically sophisticated, and socially exclusive. Such a reper-
> toire is usually described as "classical music," "art music," "court music,"
> and "serious music." (Racy 1981: 4)

To the extent that it was cultivated by trained professional musicians in the courts of the Ottoman aristocracy, conceived as a distinct
repertory with a continuous history dating back more than a thousand
years, and connected both historically and theoretically to the broader
traditions of urban Arab, Persian, and Turkish music, the ma'luf would
appear to qualify, according to Racy's criteria, as "art music." It
acquired an academic status comparable to that of Western art music
with the founding of the Rashidiyya Institute in Tunis in 1934. The
Rashidiyya compiled and edited the texts of the ma'luf, transcribed the
entire melodic repertory into Western staff notation for use by the
ensemble, and established a school to provide systematic teaching in
modern Tunisian and Middle Eastern Arab music theory. In academic
and governmental circles, the ma'luf is described accordingly in terms
such as *musiqa fann* (literally, "art music"), *musique classique,* or *musique
savante.* However, in the historic ma'luf centers of Testour and
Zaghuan, where ma'luf kham still plays an essential role in traditional
wedding celebrations, the townspeople describe their local tradition as
musiqa sha'biyya (literally, "music of the people") or *musique populaire.*

In popular mythology, the ma'luf is perceived as a homogeneous,
uninterrupted tradition, connecting contemporary Tunisian communities directly to their ancestors in medieval Spain. The official transcriptions of the repertory in *Al-Turath al-Musiqi al-Tunisi/Patrimoine
Musical Tunisien,* published in nine volumes by the Ministry of Cultural
Affairs, appear to support this myth by presenting the ma'luf as a
closed canon of anonymous compositions. However, even Salah El-
Mahdi, who compiled the volumes, maintains that once transplanted
in Tunisia, the ma'luf absorbed so many indigenous elements as to
become "almost purely Tunisian" (El-Mahdi 1981: 10). Moreover, it is
commonly recognized that the ma'luf includes formal and stylistic ele-

ments reflecting Ottoman and Middle Eastern influences. In addition to the instrumental pieces of the 13 nubat, popularly attributed to Muhammad al-Rashid Bey, volume 1 is devoted to the *bashrafs*, an Ottoman-derived instrumental genre, while volumes 2 and 9 are devoted to miscellaneous songs of the genres muwashshahat, *azjal* and *funduwat*, many of which clearly reflect Ottoman and Middle Eastern influences from the eighteenth and nineteenth centuries.

Despite its courtly patronage, the ma'luf was never primarily an elitist or otherwise socially exclusive repertory; historically it was "popular" in the most general sense of belonging to the people as a whole (Manuel 1988: 2). When performed by solo vocalists and instrumentalists, the Rashidiyya or the Radio Ma'luf ensemble, the ma'luf does indeed require specialist expertise; ma'luf kham, however, demands no special training or skills, and membership of a Sufi ensemble was traditionally determined by commitment to the lodge and its practices rather than by any particular musical criteria.[12]

Thus alongside its "art" music credentials, an equally valid historical profile emerges for the ma'luf as a "popular" music genre in the sense that it was enjoyed by all social groups, its repertory was continually self-renewing and open to new musical forms and styles, and its performance could be unsophisticated enough for anyone to join in, regardless of talent, training, or expertise.

The Ma'luf and the Origins of the Record Industry in Tunis

Gramophone was the first company to record in Tunisia, at the beginning of 1908, under the label of its French company, Zonophone. In his pioneering study on "*Les premiers engegistrements de musique tunisienne par les compagnies discographiques,*" dealing with the period up to the 1930s, Bernard Moussali describes how the new medium was at first regarded with great suspicion by the majority of artists and shunned by the best. In particular, "scholarly musicians, Muslim religious singers and Jewish cantors refused to co-operate . . . and feared the diabolical operations of the strange machines which might well 'steal' their voices or pervert the divine message. Their decision clearly explains the virtual absence of the ma'luf from the earliest recordings" (Moussali 1992: 5).[13]

Moussali's study demonstrates above all the eclecticism of the recorded repertory during this period, apparently reflecting the eclecticism of the live musical scene in Tunis. Certainly, no single category emerges above any other to qualify as a genre of "popular" music, associated specifically with the record industry. The first catalogue edited by Gramophone devoted specifically to Tunisian recordings appeared in 1910.[14] The list of double-sided discs includes a series of records by the Jewess Layla Sfaz devoted to the ma'luf and to Middle Eastern songs; Shaykh al-Sadiq ibn 'Arfa singing qasa'id (singular qasida; a solo improvisatory genre in classical Arabic) on traditional Tunisian and Near Eastern modes;[15] Shaykh Hasan ibn 'Amran singing mystic hymns of the Sulamiyya brotherhood and verses of the Qur'an; monologues and comic sketches by the Jewish actor Kiki Quwayta' (Guetta); an assortment of Tunisian, Egyptian, and Ottoman marches by the beylical fanfare; and unspecified performances by the Egyptian qanun player Mursi Barakat and the Jewish singer Tayra Hakim from Damascus, both resident in Tunis (Moussali 1992: 6–8).

The eclecticism of this list was partly the result of Egyptian and other foreign Arab musical influences, introduced by visiting artists and stimulated by the record industry. According to Moussali, "The growth of the record industry, its invasion by Syrio-Egyptian productions, the fashion for songs from Tripoli (tarabulsiyyat) and Algiers (dziriyyat), the increase in musicians' play and their emulation, if not the competition between them, resulted in a greater variety of choice in the realm of Tunisian music which became positively protean" (Moussali 1992: 6). Moussali's observations echo those of Salah El-Mahdi, who describes the pervasive influence of Egyptian and other Middle Eastern music as one of the principal factors underlying the founding in 1934 of the Rashidiyya Institute, devoted to the conservation and promotion of Tunisian traditions, particularly the ma'luf (El-Mahdi 1981: 23–25).

The 1926 catalogue of Tunisian recordings by the French company Pathé[16] demonstrates, in addition to *une egyptianisation progressive du repertoire*" following World War I, a striking preponderence of Jewish artists and composers. The celebrated Jewess Habiba Msika (niece of Layla Sfaz) performs a series of Tunisian, Tripolitanian, and Egyptian songs, including taqatiq and monologues by the famous Egyptian composer Sayyid Darwish al-Bahr (1892–1923) and duos with Maurice

'Attun or Hasan Bannan from operettas and theatrical pieces; Fritna Darmon performs songs by the famous Jewish composer from Cairo, Dawud Husni; the Jewish singer Israel Rosio (born of a Moroccan father and a Tripolitanian mother) known as Shaykh al-Ivrit ("the Hebrew master") or Shaykh al-'Afrit ("the master devil") makes his debut; the Jewish violinist Gaston Bsiri (Bishi Salama) presents new works with al-Bashir Fahma, recently arrived from Tripoli; Shaykh Khemais Tarnane presents both the ma'luf and Middle Eastern songs; the beylical fanfare performs *"une serie de pieces d'inspiration traditionelle,"* which may well have included arrangements of the ma'luf;[17] an ensemble of five players on piano / harmonium, 'ud / qanun, violin, second violin / mezwed, and percussion, presents Middle Eastern style pieces and improvisations. Other repertory listed includes Bedouin songs, Sufi religious songs, Sephardic Jewish songs, and a rendering of the Zionist song "Hatikvah" by one Babi Bismut (Moussali 1992: 9–10).

It was the Lebanese company Baidaphone that appears to have had the greatest long-term impact on Tunisian musical production. In 1928, the company mounted a massive publicity campaign in Tunis, inviting the greatest artists, including Habiba Msika, the pianist and qanun player Muhammad Qadri, and Khemais Tarnane, to record in Berlin alongside musicians from other Arab countries, using state-of-the-art German equipment. Baidophone's Tunisian catalogue appeared in June 1928. Habiba Msika recorded a series of Tunisian, Lebanese, Egyptian, and Syrian patriotic songs and Middle Eastern qasa'id, including "Ma li futintu" and "Li ladhdhatun" by Umm Kulthum, as well as traditional Tripolitanian songs and Tunisian love songs, wedding songs, and circumcision songs, with both ensemble and piano accompaniment.[18] Shaykh Khemais Tarnane recorded songs from the ma'luf, as well as Middle Eastern, Tripolitanian, and Algerian songs, and improvisations in Tunisian modes on the 'ud 'arbi, while Muhammad Qadri recorded *"sur un 'piano oriental' de facture inconnue . . . une veritable anthologie"* of Tunisian, Egyptian, and Ottoman instrumental pieces (Moussali 1992: 14).

According to Salah El-Mahdi, it was their experience with Baidaphone in Berlin that brought to the attention of the Tunisian delegates and their colleagues their lack of a specifically Tunisian repertory suitable for recording. Their experience was followed by an upsurge of mediocre compositions by second-rate composers, often with corrupt and even obscene texts. It was in response to these events that the Rashidiyya launched its second main project (after the conservation and promotion of the ma'luf), to encourage the production of new Tunisian compositions of the highest quality[19] (El-Mahdi 1981: 90–91).

The Rashidiyya, the Ma'luf, and the Media during the French Protectorate

In order to achieve this goal, the Rashidiyya held competitions and commissioned songs from its most respected composers (El-Mahdi 1981: 90–91). Included among these are Khemais Tarnane, Muhammad Ghanem, Muhammad Triki, Kaddur Srarfi, and among the younger generation, Tahar Gharsa, Salah El-Mahdi, and Muhammad Sa'ada. For the shaykhs of the Rashidiyya, as for subsequent generations of Tunisian musicians, the ma'luf was the foundation of all Tunisian composition. Thus far from being in opposition with or representing a new direction from the traditional repertory, the new songs promoted by the Rashidiyya were perceived as being in harmony with it: the old and new were seen as a continuum, the older repertory providing the inspiration for the new.

When the Tunisian Radio station was established in 1938, less than four years after the Rashidiyya, it adopted a policy to promote Tunisian music exclusively. Its Artistic Director, Mustafa Bushashah, was brother-in-law of Mustafa Sfar, President of the Rashidiyya Institute, and the Radio had positive relations with the ensemble from the outset. At first, the Rashidiyya more or less monopolized music programming; later, two evenings a week, eventually decreasing to one, were devoted to live broadcasts of the ensemble, while several of its members also broadcast independently on other evenings. From the 1930s through the 1950s, the Rashidiyya ensemble provided the springboard for some of the most popular media artists of the time, in particular, the legendary female singers Chafia Rochdi, Salihah, Fathiya Khayri, Oulaya, Na'ama, and Shabilah (daughter of Salihah). Today, songs of these and other media stars of this period associated with the Rashidiyya are considered as turath and they are sometimes loosely designated ma'luf.

The Ma'luf and the Media after
Tunisian Independence

After Tunisian independence in 1956, the Ministry of Culture published the Rashidiyya's transcriptions of the ma'luf in a series of nine volumes entitled *Al-Turath al-musiqi al-tunisi (Patrimoine Musicale Tunisien),* and distributed these to newly created amateur ensembles, modeled on the Rashidiyya, in state music clubs and conservatories throughout the county. At the same time, a gulf emerged between the ma'luf and the new commercial repertories promoted by the mass media.

A principal factor behind this division was the creation, in 1958, of a full-time, professional, state-funded radio ensemble. The ensemble was modeled on its contemporary Egyptian counterparts, with European instruments such as accordions, pianos, flutes, and clarinets added to the nucleus of violins, cellos, double basses, and traditional Arab instruments (e.g., qanuns, 'uds, nays, and percussion) characterizing the Rashidiyya. The Egyptian kamanjah player, Prof. Atiyah Shararah, was brought in as leader and the Egyptian qanun player, Prof. Fahmi 'Awad, was hired to train the chorus in Middle Eastern muwashshahat. The new ensemble concentrated on Egyptian and other Middle Eastern repertories and modern Tunisian songs in similar styles (El-Mahdi 1981: 57–58). Rather than present live broadcasts, the Radio systematically recorded performances of the ma'luf by the Rashidiyya and a special, reduced section of the Radio ensemble. Since that time, the RTT ("Radiodiffusion et television tunisienne") has relied upon these same archival recordings, mostly made around 1960, for its routine broadcasts of the ma'luf. When the television section was added in 1965, studio video recordings of the Radio ma'luf ensemble were made to provide sources for occasional television programs.

The RTT's bias toward Egyptian music and its relative disinterest in the ma'luf were mirrored in the catalogues of the Tunisian record and cassette companies. By the mid-1980s, both the two privately owned companies Mallouliphone (Tunis) and La Société de la Cassette (Carthage) and the state-owned Ennaghem were still relying mostly on contacts with other Middle Eastern record companies; music produced by Tunisians constituted only a very small proportion of their output (in the case of La Société de la Cassette, about six percent). Neither of the two privately owned companies had issued any recordings of the ma'luf, and Ennaghem had released only a handful of vinyl records, all of which were based on the original recordings made by the RTT.

However, the RTT's musical policies appeared only partly to reflect public taste. In the mid-1980s, the overwhelming impression I gained from musicians, journalists, and the music public generally was that Egyptian music was far more "popular" and highly regarded than Tunisian music; conversely, of all genres, the constant flow of new Tunisian media songs (al-haditha) churned out by the RTT (i.e., the repertory that would seem most obviously to correspond to Western notions of the "popular") was appreciated and valued the least. A survey made in 1980 of the musical tastes of "a representative sample" of students from various regions, aged between 20–25, ranked the following musical categories in order of preference: 1. orientale / al-sharqiya (Middle Eastern); 2. occidentale / al-gharbiya (Western); 3. tunisienne traditionelle / al-tunisiya al-'atiqa (traditional Tunisian, i.e., media songs dating from the 1930s to the 1950s or thereabouts); 4. al-ma'luf; 5. tunisienne recente / al-tunisiya al-haditha (modern Tunisian, i.e., contemporary media songs) (Noktar and Sallami 1980: 7).

As musicians, journalists, and government officials alike lamented the "crisis" of Tunisian music, many blamed the Rashidiyya and the state music clubs and conservatories for turning the ma'luf, supposedly the life source of Tunisian song, into a museum piece, far removed from contemporary musical taste and experience.

Nineties Sounds in Context

In a previous article (Davis, 2001) I consider the interpretations of Lotfi Boushnak and Sonia M'Barek in the context of wider trends in the ma'luf in the 1990s and more specifically, since the "Change" of 7 November 1987 when, in a bloodless coup, Zine El Abidine Ben Ali succeeded Habib Bourguiba as President of the Republic of Tunisia.[20] I argue that subsequent policies of decentralization have contributed to a cultural climate favoring individualism and self-expression in which the concept of the ma'luf as an emblem of national identity, forged by the Rashidiyya and promoted by the previous government, has given way to a variety of more fluid, personal approaches to the tradition.

In the first decades of sound recording, the ma'luf was just one of the many Tunisian and foreign genres represented in the companies' catalogues. Its diverse exponents included the famous singers Layla Sfaz, Habiba Msika, the respected Shaykh Khemais Tarnane, Shaykh al-Sadiq ibn 'Arfa (whose qasa'id on traditional Tunisian modes belong broadly to the ma'luf), and the beylical fanfare, whose traditional reper-tory included arrangements of the ma'luf. These and other artists recorded the ma'luf among a range of different repertories, including Middle Eastern.

The ma'luf acquired a privileged status with the founding of the Rashidiyya in 1934. For the Rashidiyya, Tunisian musical identity was embodied in the ma'luf: conceptually, if not aways identifiably, the ma'luf was the basis of all Tunisian composition, and the new songs commissioned by the Rashidiyya, popularized in the media by its lead-ing artists, were perceived as stemming from the same musical heritage, or turath. While the performance practice and institutional framework of the Rashidiyya were novel, its basic projects, to conserve and canon-ize the ma'luf and to promote new compositions, were historically grounded. Conservation was a deliberate aim of the Sufi brotherhoods; in the eighteenth century, Muhammad al-Rashid Bey supervised the canonization of the repertory and introduced instrumental genres. Songs embracing Middle Eastern and Ottoman genres and styles appeared during the eighteenth and nineteenth centuries, but the high value and prestige associated with the Andalusian heritage inhibited composers from acknowledging their works: instead, their songs were passed off as newly discovered items of the traditional repertory, con-veniently rescued at the last moment from the lips of a dying shaykh (El-Mahdi 1981: 89). The new compositions were thus absorbed anony-mously into an open-ended canon in which the nubat, with their well-defined forms and procedures, formed the "original" core and an "extra-nuba" corpus, receptive to new formal and stylistic elements, formed the "newer" periphery. Starting with Shaykh Ahmad al-Wafi (c. 1850–1921), d'Erlanger's original mentor, composers began to acknowledge their creations in the twentieth century, and the trend toward self-identification continued with the rise of commercial recording and the promotional activities of the Rashidiyya.[21] In time, the more durable of the named compositions formed a new level of turath, outside the official ma'luf canon.

Until independence, the Rashidiyya attracted leading composers and singers to its aims and it engaged fully with the mass media, particularly broadcasting; in addition, many of its individual artists pursued independent recording careers with songs commissioned by the Rashidiyya. After independence, the Ministry of Culture extended the Rashidiyya's mission to conserve, canonize, and promote the ma'luf, but unlike the Rashidiyya, it pursued its aims exclusively within academic and amateur musical frameworks. Meanwhile, the national radio station, controlled by the Ministry of Information, pursued an independent agenda that looked to the Middle East, particularly Egypt, for its sources and models. As the commercial record and cassette companies followed suit, a gulf was created between the ma'luf and the broad concept of turath on the one hand and the Egyptian-inspired *musiqa haditha* promoted by the media, on the other.

By the 1990s, the wheel had turned full circle. Like the media stars of the early record catalogues, neither Boushnak nor M'Barek has any special commitment to the ma'luf, and both singers include Middle Eastern repertories in their programs. Indeed, when I met Boushnak in his studio in Tunis in April 2001, he told me that he had lost interest in the ma'luf: *"Je ne suis pas un guardien du patrimoine."* He believed that an artist must mirror the problems of his time and that the archaic love songs had no relevance for today's world. However, he was in the process of composing a new nuba al-sikah with new, contemporary lyrics in collaboration with the Tunisian poet Adam Fethi. Sonia M'Barek, in contrast, claims that her choice of repertory reflects her personal identification with Tunisian culture and history. The ma'luf is one important aspect of that identity, but so too are the Middle Eastern and other Mediterranean styles she performs.

Both Boushnak and M'Barek claim to sing the ma'luf in their own way. Each cultivates a "personal" as opposed to a "Tunisian" vocal style, and neither acknowledges any particular influences on their interpretations. As media artists, they perform all their repertories as soloists, including the ma'luf, and their light instrumental accompaniments are designed in the first place to offset their own renderings. Moreover, they calculate the numbers of their players according to economic as well as aesthetic criteria. However, both singers adopt a special lineup for the ma'luf: influenced by the Rashidiyya, they include Western stringed instruments but exclude the fixed-pitch and electronic instruments used in some of their other recordings.

Boushnak and M'Barek contrast their own "personal" interpretations, as do their audiences, with those of Tahar and Zied Gharsa, universally recognized as bastions of the authentic Tunisian style.[22] In their pronunciation, vocal articulation, and melodic embellishments, as well as in their choice of instruments (Tahar plays 'ud 'arbi and Ziad plays rabab) and performance procedures, Tahar and Zied continue the legacy of the shaykhs. Their lineage is one of discipleship: Tahar's authority derives from that of his mentor, Shaykh Khemais Tarnane: not so much the media artist of the 1920s who specialized equally in Middle Eastern styles, but rather, the unrivaled ma'luf authority of the Rashidiyya, who designated Tahar his "heir." Tahar has passed his authority on to Zied, his son and student; now in his mid-twenties, Zied is Tahar's "heir."

Notes

1. Nubat al-dhil (r. 1959) and nubat al-ramal (r. 1960) were released in 1992, and nubat al-asbahan (r. 1962) and nubat al-'iraq (r. 1960), in 1993. See Davis 1996a: 425–30 and Guettat 1980: 214–226 for details on the structure and performance conventions of the Tunisian nuba.

2. In Davis 1996b, I give a general account of the musical characteristics of the ma'luf and its twentieth-century history, including the founding of the Rashidiyya and its novel performance conventions and cultural policies relating to the ma'luf after independence.

3. The title "Shaykh" was used to denote an authority or leader of an ensemble in the oral tradition. It is still used among practitioners of Sufi repertories and ma'luf *kham* (see p. 127).

4. I discuss the overlapping relationship between ma'luf and turath, pp. 135–137.

5. The baron Rodolphe d'Erlanger built his Moorish palace "Ennejma Ezzahra" in Sidi Bou Said on the bay of Tunis, between 1911 and 1921. A masterpiece of traditional North African architecture and decoration, it served as a center of Arab musical scholarship and performance until d'Erlanger's death in 1932. The fruits of this industry are published in his six-volume work *La Musique Arabe* (1930–59). In 1987, the Tunisian government acquired Ennejma Ezzahra from the d'Erlanger family and in November 1992, the Centre des Musiques Arabes et Mediterranéennes was inaugurated there, housing the Tunisian National Sound Archive. For a full acount of d'Erlanger's life and work including superb photographs of Ennejma Ezzahra, see Louati 1995.

6. I use the term "Middle Eastern music" to correspond to the Tunisian terms *musiqa sharqiyya* or "musique orientale," denoting music of Egypt and the Levant.

7. "Turath" also embraces the religious repertories of the Sufi brotherhoods, which may be closely related to ma'luf kham. I do not discuss the religious repertories in this article.

8. See Guettat 1980: 164–173 for an alternative perspective proposing North African origins for the ma'luf.

9. Numerous sources, including Abdul-Wahhab 1918: 116; Guettat 1980: 179–180, and el-Mahdi 1981: 26, testify to the prominent role played by certain brotherhoods, most notatbly the 'Isawiya and the 'Azuziya, in cultivating the ma'luf.

10. I give examples of such borrowings in Davis 1999 and Davis 1996a.

11. In the twentieth century, the Tunisian instruments were often joined or replaced by instruments such as 'ud sharqi, qanun, or violin taken over from Egyptian ensembles, with the mandolin as an additional fixed-pitch instrument.

12. Since independence, the Sufi groups have become secularized and function purely as musical ensembles. However, the principle of membership being open to all, regardless of musical expertise, still applies.

13. I am grateful to Mounir Hentati and Hatem Touil of the Centre des Musiques Arabes et Mediterranéennes for providing me with a copy of Moussali's paper.

14. "*Compagnie française du Gramophone: Disques Gramophones, double face, chant arabe, enregistres a Alger et a Tunis 1910, Imprimerie de Montmartre J. Aragno, Paris, 1910.*" Cited in Moussali 1992: 6.

15. Qasa'id may be inserted as introductions or interludes between composed items in performances of the ma'luf. A qasida in the tab of the nuba traditionally served as the introductory vocal genre, *al-abyat* (literally, verses), until the melodies were fixed by the Rashidiyya ensemble (Guettat 1980: 218).

16. "*Le Repertoire tunisien des disques Pathé a saphir inusable.*" Cited in Moussali 1992: 9.

17. The beylical fanfare of the Ecole Militaire du Bardo played arrangements of the ma'luf as well as military marches. The fanfare played an important role in the transcription of a large part of the traditional repertory (Zghonda: 8).

18. Habiba Msika was accompanied in her Middle Eastern songs by the ensemble from Baghdad comprising the Jewish 'ud player 'Azzuri Harun al-'Awadd (Ezra Aharon), the Jewish qanun player Sion Cohen, and the Christian violinist Jamil Iskandar; these musicians had arrived in Berlin with the celebrated Baghdadi vocalist, Muhammad al-Qubbanji.

19. The question of what constitutes a "Tunisian" composition is not readily definable. Tunisians agree that song texts should use literary Arabic or the Tunisian dialect and some specify Tunisian rhythms and modes. However, the ma'luf has long been receptive to Ottoman and other Middle Eastern influences, and in the twentieth century the best Tunisian composers used Middle Eastern and European modes and rhythms. In such cases the foreign elements are said to be integrated in such a way as to take on a Tunisian character, so that the result is purely Tunisian.

20. Leader of the Neo-Destour party under the French Protectorate, Habib Bourguiba led Tunisia to independence in 1956.

21. As late as the 1930s, some shaykhs of the Rashidiyya could only be persuaded to compose under pen names (El-Mahdi 1981: 90), apparently for similar reasons to the recording artists who remained anonymous rather than admit "un intérêt et un don pour la musique dans une société traditionelle qui confondait souvent l'artiste avec le domestique ou le deprave." Increased awareness of issues surrounding copyright undoubtedly played a role in reversing this tendency (Moussali 1992: 11).

22. I discuss the opposed but also related ideals of "authenticity" and "personal expression" in Davis, 2001.

Bibliography

Abdul-Wahab, Hassan Husni. 1918. "Le Developpement de la Musique Arabe en Orient, Espagne et Tunisie," *Revue Tunisienne* 24: 106–117.

Danielson, Virginia 1988. "The Arab Middle East," in *Popular Musics of the Non-Western World*, Edited by Peter Manuel. New York: Oxford University Press. 141–160. 1996. "New nightingales of the Nile: popular music in Egypt since the 1970s," *Popular Music* 15/3: 299–312.

Davis Ruth. 1996a. " Arab-Andalusian Music of Tunisia," *Early Music* 24/3: 423–37.

———. 1996b. "The Art/Popular Music Paradigm and the Tunisian Ma'luf," *Popular Music* 15/3: 313–23 (Middle East Issue).

———. 1999. "Piyyut melodies as Mirrors of Social Change in Hara Kebira, Jerba," in *From Iberia to Diaspora*, edited by Yiedida K. Stillman and Norman A. Stillman. Brill: Leiden, Boston, Köln. 477–495.

———. In press. "Al-Andalus in Tunis: Sketches of the Ma'luf in the 1990s." Paper read at the meeting of the ICTM Study Group on *Trends and Processes in Today's Mediterranean Music* at the Fondazione Ugo e Olga Levi, Venezia, 14–16 June, 2001.

D'Erlanger, Rodolphe. 1930–59. *La Musique Arabe*. Paris: Librairie Orientaliste Paul Geuthner. 6 vols.

Guettat, Mahmoud. 1980. *La Musique Classique du Maghreb*. Paris: Sinbad.

Louati, Ali. 1995. *Le Baron d'Erlanger et son Palais. Ennajma Ezzahra a Sidi Bou Said.* Tunis: Editions Simpact.

El-Mahdi, Salah and Muhammad Marzuqi. 1981. *Al-ma'had al-rashidi.* Tunis: Ministry of Cultural Affairs.

Manuel, Peter. 1988. *Popular Musics of the Non-Western World: An Introductory Survey.* Oxford: Oxford University Press.

Moussali, Bernard. In press. "Les Premiers enregistrements de musique tunisienne par les compagnies discographiques." Paper read at the colloquium *Liens et interactions entre les musiques arabes et mediterranéennes*, Programme d'inauguration du Centre des Musiques Arabes et Mediterranéennes, Hotel Abou Nawas, Gamarth, Tunisia, 9–12 November 1992.

Noktar, Fathallah and Rachid Sallami. 1980. *Musique Arabe et son Publique. Sondage des gouts des etudiants de l'ENSEPS de Tunis en Matiere de Musique.* Hammamet, Tunisia: Centre Culturel International de Hammamet.

Powers, Harold S. 1980. "Classical Music, Cultural Roots and Colonial Rule: an Indic Musicologist looks at the Muslim World," *Asian Music* 12: 5–37.

Racy, Ali Jihad. 1981. "Music in Contemporary Cairo: a Comparative Overview," *Asian Music* 12/1: 4–21.

——. 1982. "Musical Aesthetics in Present-Day Cairo," *Ethnomusicology* 26/3: 391–406.

Al-Turath. n.d. *Al-Turath al-musiqi al-tunisi (Patrimoine Musical Tunisien)*. Tunis: Wizarat as-su'un at-taqafiya (Ministere des Affaires Culturelles). 9 vols.

Zghonda, Fethi. n.d. *Al-musiqa al-nahasiya fi tunis (La musique pour harmonies en Tunisie)*. Tunis: Wizarat as-su'un at-taqafiya (Ministere des Affaires Culturelles).

Discography

Anthologie du Malouf Tunisien. La Nuba H'cin. Orchestre et Chorale de la Rachidia. Direction, Abdelhamid Belelgia. Ministere Tunisien de la Culture/MTC-Centre de la Musique Arabe et Mediterranéenne/CMAM-Ennejma Ezzehra. Sowarex/Bruxelles EE 002. 1999.

Boushnak, Lotfi. *Malouf Tunisien*. Maison des Cultures du Monde W260053. 1993.

Gharsa, Zied. *Soca Music*. CD 004. 1997.

M'Barek, Sonia. *Tawchih*. Les Artistes Arabes Associes—Club du Disque Arabe AAA 186. 1999.

——. *Takht*. World Network LC 6759. 1999.

Tunisie Anthologie du Malouf. Musique Arabo-Andalouse. Nuba al-dhil. Orchestre et Chorale de la Radio Tunisienne. Direction, Abdelhamid Bel Eljia. (Enregistrement historique: Tunis enr. mono 1959) Maison des Cultures du Monde W 260044. 1992.

Tunisie Anthologie du Malouf. Musique Arabo-Andalouse. Nuba al-Ramal. Orchestre et Chorale de la Radio Tunisienne. Direction, Abdelhamid Bel Eljia. (Enregistrement historique: Tunis enr. mono 1960). Maison des Cultures du Monde W 260045. 1992.

Tunisie Anthologie du Malouf. Musique Arabo-Andalouse. Nuba al-asbahan. Orchestre et Chorale de la Radio Tunisienne. Direction, Abdelhamid Bel Eljia. (Enregistrement historique: Tunis enr. mono 1962). Maison des Cultures du Monde W 260046. 1993.

Tunisie Anthologie du Malouf. Musique Arabo-Andalouse. Nuba al-Iraq. Orchestre et Chorale de la Radio Tunisienne. Direction, Abdelhamid Bel Eljia. (Enregistrement historique: Tunis enr. mono 1960). Maison des Cultures du Monde W 260047. 1993.

Tunisie Anthologie du Malouf. Musique Arabo-Andalouse. Nuba al-Sika. Ensemble de Musique Traditionelle de Tunis. Direction, Fethi Zghonda. Maison des Cultures du Monde W 260059. 1994.

Selected early recordings

Cheikh Elafrit. *La Musique Populaire Tunisienne. Anthologie de la Musique Arabe*. Club du Disque Arabe—Artistes Arabes Associes AAA 035. CDA 401. 1991.

Cheikh Elafrit. *Vol. II—Les Succes des annees 30. Musique Populaire Tunisienne*. Club du Disque Arabe AAA 057 CDA 401. 1992.

Musique Judeo-Arabe. Vol II—Tunisie. Club du Disque Arabe-Artistes Arabes Associes. AAA 072 CDA 401. 1993. [Recordings of famous artists, Jewish and other, made between 1908 and 1955].

Saliyha. *Ajmal Aghani* [The most beautiful songs]. Soca Music SO-CD 074. n.d.

Saliyha. *La Musique Populair Tunisienne: Fondo et Ardawi*. Club du Disque Arabe—Artistes Arabes Associes CDA 401 AAA 068. 1993.

Tunisie Chants & Rythmes. Club du Disque Arabe—Artistes Arabes Associes AAA 001 CDA 401. 1988.

Tunisie Chants & Rythmes. Vol. II. Club du Disque Arabe—Artistes Arabes Associes AAA 101 CDA 401. 1995.

Recordings made at the 1932 Cairo Congress

Musique tunisienne, Enregistrements du Congres du Caïre. 20 discs 78 rpm/25 cm. Gramophone HC 40–55 and HC 83–86. 1932.

Congres du Caïre 1932, Vol 2: Musique Citadine de Tlemcen/Algerie, Musique Savante de Fès/Maroc, Musique Citadine de Tunis/Tunisie. Edition Bibliotheque Nationale—France/l'Institut du Monde Arabe. APN 88–10. 1988.

Malouf Tunisien, La Musique Classique Tunisienne Congres du Caïre 1932. Artistes Arabes Associes—Club du Disque Arabe AAA 094 CDA 401. 1994.

CHAPTER SIX

SOME MEANINGS OF THE SPANISH TINGE IN CONTEMPORARY EGYPTIAN MUSIC

MICHAEL FRISHKOPF

Arab popular music from the mid-1990s onward strikingly displays the influence of Spanish and Latin music styles: the Spanish tinge. While these musical fusions are relatively straightforward (if varied) in execution, their meanings are more complex. Mere consideration of the Arabic adjectives associated with Spanish influence—*Latini, Andalusi, fil-imanku* (flamenco), *gharbi* (western), *bahrawsati* (Mediterranean), *ʿalami* (global)—as well as the multiple categories into which Spanish-tinged songs are sorted—*shababi* (youth), *hadis* (modern), *bub* (pop)—suggest the dense tangle of meanings that Spanish-tinged Arabic music presents to Arab listeners.[1] This chapter aims to begin the process of unraveling these meanings, as understood by Egyptians. It is neither my intention to document the Spanish tinge exhaustively, nor to explain it in "objective" historical terms. Rather, my aim is hermeneutic "ethnohistory":[2] to interpret how Egyptians themselves interpret the Spanish tinge as a historical trend; how they relate it to their past, explain its salience in the present, and assess what it means for the future. It is the production of historical knowledge, rather than reconstruction of history itself, which is the point of the study: to understand how people organize their own experience of music history. This chapter thus stands in the ethnographic more than the historiographic tradition. It constitutes a "second order" interpretation, the usual epistemological condition for cultural anthropology (Geertz 1973: 15), not history.

This task is triply valuable, for: (1) illuminating ongoing cultural processes by which Egyptians construct coherent patterns of historical self-representation, processes which carry additional significance as co-generators of future history; (2) producing subjective evidence, via Egyptians' reflection upon their own lived experiences through history, interpretable as a means of accessing that history; (3) illuminating objective history directly, insofar as Egyptians are (being close to it) well-poised to comprehend it (without denying or forgetting that another kind of more "etic" history, while not performed here, is also crucial).

Despite the theoretical value of (2) and (3), I cautiously do not submit this research as a piece of historical work, but rather as ethnohistorical only. But the new Spanish tinge turned out to be such a rich symbol that in attempting to explain and interpret it, Egyptians automatically revealed more general attitudes about culture and cultural change in contemporary Egypt. Thus in the final analysis, investigation of "the Spanish tinge" is perhaps most useful as a kind of Rorschach test, a catalyst for the articulation of diverse cultural thinking active in Egypt today.

The Scope of the Spanish Tinge in Arab Music Today

Ferdinand "Jelly Roll" Morton coined the phrase "Spanish tinge" to refer to Latin influence in jazz (Williams 1970: 28). Yet Spanish influence (broadly conceived to include Latin musics) has been strong worldwide, from the early twentieth century onwards, and has lately surged into the mainstream due to new fusions, and the powerful engine of the American music industry. In 1975 a "Best Latin Recording" category was added to the Grammy awards; their "Best World Music album" award (established 1991) has gone to Latin artists in five of the previous 10 years (Grammy Awards 2002). Latin megastars with broad appeal, such as Ricky Martin, Carlos Santana, and Shakira, have recently been dominating mainstream pop-music charts, while successive albums by the Gipsy Kings (from southern France but drawing on flamenco and Latin traditions: see Gipsy Kings 2002) have ranked high on Billboard's world music chart since its inception in 1990 (Taylor 1997: 5, 209ff).[3] All this has been marketed worldwide as Spanish/Latin culture, but also stands as "American," "Western," or "modern" culture (due to centers of production and popularity, mainstream industry status, and fusions: Latin-rock, Latin-pop, Latin-jazz), "global" culture (due to scope, "non-Western" origins, and syncretisms), and as a symbol of globalization itself. Within Arab culture, the Spanish tinge also carries particular cultural and historical meanings, via medieval Andalusia, the Mediterranean, Europe, North America, and Latin America, each of which is susceptible to multiple interpretations and valences.

Two factors, then, motivate this study. One is the striking rise of Spanish and Latin styles in Arab popular music over the last ten years. The other is the dense layering of its potential meanings within Arab culture, as linked to the broader significances attached to geographical regions, historical periods, and cultural processes. The Spanish tinge in Arab pop presents a rich symbolic lode for anthropological investigation.

The Spanish tinge in Egyptian pop music occurs primarily in the domain of *al-musiqa al-shababiyya* (youth music, already a fusion of older Arab music with Western rock and pop). Spanish influence includes instrumental, timbral, melodic, harmonic, rhythmic, textural, and occasionally linguistic resources. Most often, influence is manifested in acoustic guitar styles, both rhythmic and melodic (often an ersatz "flamenco"); in Latin grooves and percussion; or in distinctive harmonic progressions. Within a song, Spanish influence may appear vertically, in short segments: introductions, instrumental interludes, or fills (*lawazim*) separating vocal phrases. At the level of an album, influence is likewise vertical, because typically only one or two (out of 8–12) songs contain Spanish influence (although these are often the most popular). Or influence may appear horizontally, as one sonic layer within a *shababiyya* texture including also Arabic, Western rock/pop, and perhaps other styles as well. Occasionally the Spanish style constitutes the primary matrix for an entire song.

Amr Diab

Amr Diab[4] is the most popular music star in Egypt today, and among the three or four most consistently popular singers in the Arab world, from the 1990s to the present. Diab has consistently innovated since his first album in 1986; his great fame and financial success ensure that his artistic decisions reach a vast audience, and spawn many imitators. Since the mid-1990s, Diab's output has increasingly displayed Spanish influence. His broad influence in defining contemporary Arab pop motivated me to place him at the center of my ethnographic inquiry. A brief examination of his life, representing a microcosm of most of the trends to be discussed, is thus apropos.[5]

Diab was born in 1961, to a middle class family in Port Said. For Egyptians, this city carries considerable symbolic importance for modernity, nationalism, and Westernization, and Diab's modern image owes something to his birthplace. Located where the Suez Canal meets the Mediterranean, Port Said was founded in 1859 as the canal's Mediterranean port. Young by Egyptian standards, cosmopolitan, industrialized, Port Said was devastated by three wars (1956, 1967, 1973), but always returned to supply a wide range of goods, local and imported; after 1973 Port Said was declared a free-trade zone to encourage investments (Hamed 1981: 3). Inclining toward music at an early age, Diab received encouragement from his family to pursue a career in music, studying at the music faculty of the Cairo Academy of Art in the mid-1980s. His first album *Ya Tariq* (1986) soon followed, and was an instant success. Since then he has released sixteen albums, and garnered many awards for best-selling Arab artist.

Beyond birthplace and talent, Diab's social and generational positions were instrumental in catapulting him to the vanguard of Egyptian pop. His career has coincided with the rapidly increasing media sophistication of Arab pop styles; Diab was the first Egyptian singer to make extensive use of the *fidiyuklib* (videoclip, or music video), starting around 1990, and video broadcasts (especially to Arab communities abroad) have contributed greatly to his fame. His adoption of new Western fashions in clothes and hairstyle contributes to his au courant image, setting standards for millions of Egyptian youth, as well as establishing him as a source (hence symbol) of Western cool. His budding film career has further disseminated his image and music.

Gradually Diab's career has become more international. Besides touring abroad, his use of foreign musical styles has garnered international acclaim, and his fan base has increasingly extended outside the

Cover of Amr Diab's *Nur il-'En*

Arab world; this in turn reflects and necessitates continued deployment of those styles. Indeed, the most striking feature of his 1990s output is the increasing diversification of music styles, especially Spanish and Latin. Some Arabs began to refer to his as the "Mediterranean sound." His internationally acclaimed *Nur il-'En* (1996), became popular in European discos, often remixed with dance grooves.

Subsequently, Diab received a World Music Award (Monaco, 1998) for best global sales (in the newly established Middle Eastern category), alongside Mariah Carey, Puff Daddy, and the Backstreet Boys; the program (hosted by Gloria Estefan among others) was broadcast to 130 countries worldwide (although non-Western musics were evidently omitted in the American version) (Dezzani 1998). Diab reportedly stated that he considers this award as a first step toward popularizing Egyptian music internationally (Egypt Guide 2002). At the ceremony, his performance of the title track, cast in a flamenco/Gipsy Kings mold, was broadcast to an international audience. All this enhanced his image at home, even among those who do not ordinarily listen to (or even approve of) his music, for Diab's international recognition—as for Egyptian Nobel laureates Naguib Mahfuz (1988) and Ahmed H. Zewail (1999), whose works most Egyptians do not read—constitutes an important source of cultural pride and confirmation.

Although Spanish influence is most salient, Diab has experimented with other musical hybrids as well, including Turkish, North African, Greek, electronica, and hip-hop sounds. On his 1999 album *Amaren* he collaborated with Khaled, the star of French-Algerian *raï*, and the Greek pop diva Angela Dimitriou (also famous in Turkey). "Wala 'ala balu" (from *Aktar Wahid*, 2001) features a mix of classical Arab melody with techno and rap. A complex of features—Spanish, Arab, Western, Mediterranean, global—is thus evident in his life history and work.

The Spanish Tinge: Amr Diab, Egypt, and Beyond

What is the evidence for the Spanish tinge in Egypt? As principal trend-setter, a review of Diab's 1990s ouput (also foregrounded in my ethnographic investigation) is instructive; a few other examples can be mentioned to show that Diab is by no means alone. "Leli" (from the album *Shawa'na*, 1990) imitates lambada. "Eh bass illi ramak" (*Habibi*, 1992) opens with Spanish-style acoustic guitar, which returns for fills. On *Ayamna* (1993), "Hawak hayyarni" begins with conga sounds, and "Taba' el Hayah" features a Latin groove, plus Spanish guitar and Brazilian pop harmonies. However it is on *Wi yilumuni* (1995) that flamenco sounds appear in force, in "Ahlif bi il-layali" and "Wi yilumuni." *Ragi'in* (1996) features a Latin groove on "Balash tikallimha." The title track on *Nur il-'En* (1996) presents the clearest example yet of a Spanish-flamenco groove, instrumentation, and harmonic progression, displacing the usual Arab pop matrix. *'Awwiduni* (1998) features a Latin/flamenco groove and progression on "Kull il-kalam" and "Wi ghalawtik," while "Milk Idek" highlights Spanish guitar filigree. On *Amaren* (1999) the Latin/flamenco sound appears in the title track. *Tamalli Ma'ak* (2000) contains the Latin-based "Albi ikhtarak" (often compared to Santana's 1999 *Smooth*), and four songs infused with flamenco styles: "il-'Alam", "Allah", "Sinin", "Wi hiyya 'amla eeh", and Tamalli ma'ak. Finally his 2001 album (*Aktar Wahid*) contains no fewer than seven (out of ten) songs displaying deep Latin or flamenco influences, including the title track; by now one feels that for Diab the Spanish tinge has moved beyond color or novelty, to become incorporated in his musical language and identity.

However the Spanish tinge runs broader than Diab alone. Indeed, in the late 1990s most of Egypt's most popular contemporary singers

Front cover of Angham's *Leh Sibtaha*
(including *Habbetak leh*)

deploy the Spanish Tinge at least occasionally: Angham in "Habbetak leh" (Latin); Hakim in the introduction to his "Isma'ya illi" (2000); Hisham 'Abbas in "Sami'albi" (2000) and "Inti il-wahida" (1999), among many; Ihab Tawfiq in "La khatar, Mushta'", and "Amar il-layali" (1999). Mustafa Qamar deploys a rich Spanish texture in *'Ayshin* (2000) (including a flamenco singer) and *'Aynek wahshani* (1999), and a Latin groove in *Tal il-lel* (1997).

In 1997, Qatar's MusicBox International marketed a very popular cassette entitled *Arabica Latina*, featuring Spanish Gypsy/flamenco and Latin music with Spanish and Arabic words, through a production company in Cairo. The Gipsy Kings themselves have concertized in Egypt since the mid-1980s; today they are well known, performing on television and for weddings.

Furthermore, the Spanish tinge in Arabic music affects more than

Egypt. Latin influences are hot in Lebanon, as evidenced by productions of such top stars as Nawal al-Zughbi (particularly in *Tul Umri,* 2001), Julia Boutros (*Bisaraha,* 2001), or Raghib Allama, and many others. From Iraq, Ilham al-Madfa'i (*Ilham Al Mafda'i,* 1999) deploys Latin-flamenco textures. Within the wider sphere of Arab-Spanish fusions, Egypt represents an important case study, in view of the continued centrality of the Egyptian music industry to the Arab world as a whole.

Historical Sources for Musical Ethnohistory

What is the source of this Spanish tinge in 1990s Egyptian pop? The trajectories of musical culture are never easy to locate, not only because of the mass of musical data to be examined, or the difficulty in reconstructing the musical past, but because of the difficulty in assessing which phenomena are to be connected as historically continuous. But in this section I do not aim to analyze the objective sources of the contemporary Spanish tinge in Egyptian pop, much less to trace a continuous history from those origins to the present. Rather, I want to illuminate three historical periods that figure heavily in Egyptian interpretations of their own musical history.

Andalusia as Historical Past, and Contemporary Symbol

From North Africa, Muslim armies loyal to the Umayyad dynasty of Damascus took the Iberian Peninsula in 711–13, defeating the weak Spanish Visigoth kingdom, and establishing the Muslim Iberian domain of al-Andalus. After the Umayyads fell to the Abbasids in 750, 'Abd al-Rahman ibn Mu'awiya (one of the former dynasty) escaped to al-Andalus, where he managed to unify a fractious polity and establish the Umayyad Marwanid dynasty of Cordoba (756–912). Various Muslim dynasties followed, most notably the Berber Almoravids (1056–1147) and Almohades (1130–1296). Following centuries of conflict with forces of the Spanish Reconquista, the last Muslim kingdom (Granada) fell in 1492. By this time most Muslims and Jews had emigrated to North Africa; those who remained converted to Christianity (Moriscos) but were expelled (mainly to North Africa) from 1609 to 1614 (Levi-Provencal 1999a, 1999b; Wiegers 1999; Goldziher and Desomogyi 1966: 130).

The brilliant flowering of Arabo-Islamic Andalusian culture was catalyzed by rulers who patronized the arts and learning, and funded such architectural marvels as the Alhambra. In the late tenth century, al-Hakam II founded a great library at Cordoba containing 400,000 volumes, facilitating high achievements in philosophy, astronomy, mathematics, medicine, art and architecture, literature, and music (Goldziher and Desomogyi 1966: 131–132). Abu al-Hasan 'Ali ibn Nafi' better known as Ziryab, was a student of Ishaq al-Mawsili, court musician to Abbasid Caliph Harun al-Rashid in Baghdad (786–809). Ziryab captured Harun's fancy, thereby arousing al-Mawsili's jealousy; the latter forced him to flee. Thus did Ziryab arrive at the Andalusian court of 'Abd al-Rahman II (822–852), where he soon eclipsed all other musicians of al-Andalus, developing new musical forms, and establishing an influential music school at Cordoba (Farmer 1973: 128–130; Touma 1996: 11, 68–69). Andalusian culture developed two popular new poetic forms, thus breaking the dominance the *qasida* had formerly enjoyed: (1) the classical *muwashshabat*; (2) the colloquial *zajal*. Their stanzaic forms rendered these more suitable for music than the qasida's distiches (Goldziher and Desomogyi 1966: 135), and they continue to be used throughout the contemporary Arab world (al-Faruqi 1975).

The cultural efflorescence of Andalusia, situated at the interface between Islamic and Christian worlds, directly influenced the latter. Works by Andalusian scholars (such as the philosopher Ibn Rushd, known in the West as Averroës, d. 1198) were translated into Latin, and distributed throughout Christian Europe (Lapidus 1988: 383–384). There is also much evidence for musical influence; thus the European lute stems morphologically and etymologically from the Arabic one (*al-'ud*); "guitar" comes from Arabic "*qitar*," and Arab song appears to have influenced songs of medieval Europen minstrelsy (Farmer 1970: 4; Goldziher and Desomogyi 1966: 135). Though its extent has been debated, the putative facticity of this influence is key to constructions of musical history among contemporary Arabs.

In North Africa, the classical forms of *al-musiqa al-andalusiyya* (*nawba* or *ala* in Morocco, *san'a* in Algiers, and *ma'luf* in Tunis) are valorized (by dominant ideology) as the very musical forms of Andalusian courts (transferred by emigrants), whose contemporary stylistic differences result only from synchronic differences among various

Andalusian court traditions (such as Seville, Cordoba, and Granada) (Touma 1996: 70). Though this myth is sustained by anonymous ascription of musical pieces, and the symbolic value of Andalusia, musical and historical analysis suggests that Andalusian repertoires in different parts of North Africa developed quasi-independently, due to vagaries of oral tradition and contrasting regional histories (Davis 1996a: 423–4; Davis 1996b: 316).

Likewise, Egyptians and Levantines associate the *muwashshah* (*qua* musical genre) with Andalusia (*al-muwashshah al-andalusiyya*), though evidence suggesting a continuous musical linkage to Andalusia is even weaker than for North African music, and there is plenty of evidence suggesting discontinuities, including differences in poetic meter, and innovations by well-known composers of Syria and Egypt in the late nineteenth and early twentieth centuries, such as the Syrian 'Umar Batsh (1885–1950) and the Egyptian Sayyid Darwish (1892–1923) (Touma 1996: 83–84).

Five widely cited attributes render Andalusia a potent and affective symbol in the modern Egyptian imagination: (1) Muslim military victories over Christian Europe; (2) enlightened rulers; state patronage of arts and sciences; tolerance of religious diversity; and intellectual freedom; (3) consequently: the flowering of scholarly and artistic achievements; (4) the influence of Andalusian culture in kindling the European renaissance; (5) the romantic (almost Edenic) tragedy of loss and exile, a metaphor for all lost "golden ages" and utopias. These features combine to project Andalusia as asserting the greatness of the Arabs, inverting the contemporary power relations between the Arabs and the West, constituting proof that Western modernity is indebted to the Arabs, and suggesting that greatness is again possible. At the same time, Andalusia invokes powerful feelings of nostalgia.

While Andalusia has served as a potent literary symbol for centuries (Aboul-Ela 1999), it loomed particularly large in the ideological period of Arab nationalisms, from the 1950s onward. Andalusia resonates at many levels in literature of this period. Poets alluded to Andalusia as a symbol of lost beauty and hope (for example, Nizar Qabbani, who saw " . . . in the fading glories of Alhambra the possibilities for a rebirth of the Islamic nation and Arab aesthetics" [Woffenden and Mitwalli 1998]), or exile (in poetry of Mahmoud Darwish): Yusuf

Chahine's 1998 film *al-Masir* uses the decline of Andalusia as a means to critique contemporary Egyptian anti-liberalism.

Egypt's Liberal Experiment (1922–1936) and the Spanish Tinge

In the nineteenth century, urban Egyptian musical life centered upon varied folk and religious genres, and the more musically elaborate entertainments of popular singers with *takht* (Arab chamber ensemble) and choral accompaniment, incorporating much Ottoman influence. The latter, epitomized by stars such as 'Abdu al-Hamuli, Muhammad 'Uthman, and Yusuf Manyalawi, and patronized by elites, was associated with the ineffable aesthetic quality called *tarab*, "musical ecstasy" (Racy 1985). In performance, the tarab style features impeccable intonation, proper treatment of the melodic modes (*maqamat*), improvisation and variation, unison or heterophonic textures, stately tempos, slow solo expressive singing, concentrated listening, and emotional feedback from audience to performer (Racy 1991).

Alongside such "traditional" music were musical styles introduced from Western Europe following the Napoleonic campaign of 1798, and supported by the determination of Muhammad 'Ali (1805–1848) and his descendents to modernize the country along European lines. The late nineteenth century saw the first stirrings of Egyptian nationalism (Vatikiotis 1969: 136ff; Holt 1966: 211ff). Paradoxically, though turned against British oppression, such stirrings were inspired by European enlightenment ideals. Culturally, politically, and technically Europe presented the highest model for many educated Egyptians, the very definition and source of modernity (Hourani 1983). Broad admiration for European culture produced many attempts to emulate it. In music, these included European-style military bands, Italian opera, French-inspired theater, and Western instruments: especially violin, piano, and accordion (Racy 1985).

The pace of change accelerated rapidly in the early twentieth century, with a larger, more educated populace; urbanization; development of technical infrastructure (Hourani 1991: 333ff); and the corresponding rise of commercial media mass-markets, especially phonograms (from 1904), radio (from the 1920s), and musical film (1930s) (Racy 1978; Castelo-Branco 1987: 32–35). Pressured by change, the elaborate nineteenth-century musical genres swiftly declined in the 1920s (Racy 1988: 139). Flexible musical forms, improvisation, and small chamber ensembles gave way to more fixed arrangements, and larger orchestras. But the core aesthetic of tarab continued to dominate urban Egyptian music until the 1970s as what Racy calls the "neutral canvas" upon which all innovations were painted as "colors" (alwan) in the central domain of music in Cairo (Racy 1982: 391–397).

Forces of nationalism sprang forth violently as the Revolution of 1919 (Sayyid-Marsot 1977: 4), and Britain bestowed a nominal independence in 1922; thereafter the khedive became king, and a multiparty constitutional parliamentary democracy was installed featuring some measure of liberal political values until 1952 (but especially before 1936, when the Anglo-Egyptian treaty was signed) (Sayyid-Marsot 1977). The privileged status of Europeans, the presence of a large Mediterranean expatriate community, and French-speaking Egyptian elites ensured a cosmopolitan diversity and openness to foreign influences, at least in Alexandria and Cairo. Political, social, and economic modernization proceeded rapidly to "push Egypt squarely into the modern age" (Sayyid-Marsot 1977: 6). Political liberalization, combined with continued de facto British control, European economic dominance, a broad Egyptian acknowledgement of European cultural superiority, and the commercial forces of new entertainment media and industries, all encouraged incorporation of European musical styles into Arab music. But foreign influence was more free-wheeling prior to the Egyptian Revolution of 1952, after which foreigners were forced out, and Egyptian nationalism turned from European enlightenment ideals to the more rigid hegemonic forms of a military regime, including a purposive "cultural policy" (el-Shawan 1979: 113–115).

Composer and singer Muhammad 'Abd al-Wahhab (1897?-1991), whose artistic personality crystallized in the atmosphere of early nationalism, modernization, the monarchy, and Europe (including travels under the tutelage of his poet-mentor Ahmad Shawqi [Danielson 1997: 171; Armbrust 1996: 72]), was a famous exponent of European modernism within an "Eastern" matrix (Armbrust 1996: 63–93). He once stated that "most of our traditions now follow western lines, which have taken control of our life and the form of our social and artistic activities. There is no harm in this. Foreign influence, adapting to the world renaissance, is necessary for evolution. We must bring western instruments into Eastern music . . . and new melodies . . . but also hold to our Eastern spirit." But music, he said, should be a true Eastern creation, even if it appears in Western garb (al-Hifni 1999: 54–55).

John Storm Roberts's *The Latin Tinge* recounts the spread of Latin musics to North America (where new fusions and hybrids emerged) and around the globe. The motive force was the unique relation between the United States market power, media, capital, and attraction for "exotic" musical forms just south of the border. Fads were triggered through commercial entertainment mass media. Thus a craze for Argentine tango (deriving from Spanish Gypsy music via Cuba) swept the United States following the success of a 1913 musical show, *The Sunshine Girl*, featuring dancers Vernon and Irene Castle (Roberts 1979: 15, 44). Interest in Latin music affected Tin Pan Alley songs in the 1920s, which were disseminated widely (Roberts 1979: 50). In 1931 Don Azpiazu's hit "The Peanut Vendor" ushered in a new craze for the (Americanized) Cuban rumba (Roberts 1979: 76). In the 1940s Latin musicians received more publicity; new forms such as mambo and Latin jazz emerged (Roberts 1979: 100). Primarily driven by the engine of the American music industry, the popularity of Latin music soon became international (Roberts 1979: 50, 776, 100, 212ff).

Despite stylistic differences between tarab and Latin musics (especially the latter's use of functional harmony), early twentieth century Egypt was remarkably susceptible to this trend. 'Abd al-Wahhab frequently deployed Spanish influences in the 1930s, when the Latin tinge was so potent in Europe and North America: Spanish castanets in "Fi il-lel lamma khala"; Argentine tango in "Marreet 'ala beet il-habayib" and "Sahrat minnu al-layali" (al-Hifni 1999: 53). In the 1950s he composed "Ahibbak wa inta fakirni" (harmonized tango); and a rumba groove in "Khi khi." Such songs were extremely popular. Yet, true to his words, 'Abd al-Wahhab's music is founded on an "Eastern" tarab base, the "neutral canvas" upon which various colors, from Latin to Beethoven to tango, are layered, often obscuring but never permanently negating the tarab aesthetic (Racy 1982).

But while introduction of tango and other musical material was certainly innovative, the Western identity (as they were often heard) of such "borrowings" could also be ideologically critiqued, even as their meanings are subject to debate among Egyptians today. Along with many Arabs, 'Abd al-Wahhab believed that the West is indebted to the East. No doubt reacting to criticism, he stated that his Western borrowings are " . . . nothing more than the Oriental art of our ancestors, which had originally made its way into the western consciousness . . . being returned to us" (Okasha 2000). Here is a prefiguring of the Andalusian argument, elaborated below, which continues to strongly color Arab borrowings of Spanish and Latin musics today.

Similarly, Farid al-Atrash (1910–74), a Syrian Druze who lived most of his life in Cairo, innovated on the tarab tradition, without abandoning it. Farid was especially famous for his brilliant solo 'ud improvisations (taqasim); a style featuring flamenco melodies, harmonies, and rhythmic techniques, widely esteemed and imitated (Zuhur 2001: 271). Like 'Abd al-Wahhab, Farid used Latin music in a number of precomposed songs, including orchestrated tangos such as "Ya zahra fi khayyal" (replete with Latin harmonizations and accordion, from his 1947 film, Habib al-'Umr), and "Ana wa illi bahibbu" (from his 1950 film, Akhir kidba).

The lag between the Western tango craze of the 1920s and its appearance in Egyptian songs from the 1930s–50s, foreshadows a pattern, and a contemporary criticism of Egyptian musical borrowings: that they constitute delayed reactions to world trends, inferior imitations, rather than innovations indicative of cultural dependency and lack of self-confidence.

Despite the various overlays, the tarab style continued to flourish into the 1970s. But by then new changes were underway.

The Roots of the Contemporary Pop Explosion: 1970s to early 1980s

Following the Egyptian revolution of 1952, the development of Arab socialist nationalism by a popular and charismatic president helped restore Egyptian self-esteem. For the first time since antiquity, Egypt was boldly independent, a self-directed leader among the new Arab nations. The state strictly controlled the national economy; large businesses were nationalized, and most foreigners left. 'Abd al-Nasir's ideology, while it certainly did not preclude foreign cultural influence, discouraged imports and encouraged artistic self-confidence, self-suffi-ciency, and export. Already geographically and demographically central to the Arab world, Egypt under his leadership, became the ideological, political, and cultural center as well. Governmental support and monopolization of the media (radio, TV, film, and phonograms), and special attention to particular singers, such as Umm Kulthum and 'Abd al-Halim Hafiz, established Egypt's musical influence throughout the Arab world (Hourani 1991: 340, 393). Umm Kulthum's musical domi-nance is nearly a metaphor of state control: the Voice of Egypt (Danielson 1997). But by the mid-1960s, the system was faltering. Nasserism, as it came to be called, became inefficient and corrupt, and dreams of modern development, justice, and power were continually deferred (Aulas 1982: 7). Some of the hypocrisies of the system were revealed by Egypt's defeat in the 1967 war with Israel, and with the death of 'Abd al-Nasir in 1970 his eponymous ideology was fatally shaken too.

After the 1973 war, Nasir's successor Anwar Sadat took a new tack with his "open door" policy (*infitah*), laissez-faire economics opening the economy to foreign investment and imports, and establishing free trade zones in Port Said and elsewhere, in the hopes of attracting for-eign capital so that Egypt could follow in the footsteps of model nations such as Brazil (the Latin American model) and South Korea (Aulas 1982: 7–8). Culturally the infitah was a move toward the West, and away from the Soviets with whom Nasir had been close.

But the result was economic chaos and social upheaval, as Egypt's statist economy was rapidly integrated into the world market (Aulas 1982: 8). New economic opportunities (legal and illegal) beckoned from every direction (including commercial music ventures), and a nouveau riche of entrepreneurs emerged with new musical tastes. Those tastes would become increasingly important as the private-sector music industry developed its sophistication to target lucrative markets. But inflation was rampant, while government wages were nearly fixed. Many rural areas were impoverished, and the cities swelled with rural immigrants, providing ever greater markets for the new entrepreneurs. A rift between rich and poor opened. At the same time, the developing Gulf states were becoming rich with oil, and needed labor (Aulas 1982: 14–15). During the 1970s and 80s, Egyptians worked abroad, sending home remittances and returning with new gadgets, now also available in Egypt's newly expanded import market. Most relevant to the current discussion was the widespread purchase of tape players and television sets, which hastened musical commodification, and broadened markets. Though the infitah failed to attract much foreign capital, it did expand the internal market for imports (Aulas 1982: 11, 15). That market demanded capital equipment and media to fuel the cassette-music revolution. Cassette blanks, recorders, and duplication equipment, cheaper than their phonodisc predecessors, became available. Musicians could more easily import musical equipment, such as amplifiers and foreign-made instruments.

Suddenly it was more feasible for small businesses to produce recordings in private studios. The government could not easily regulate production, and the new culture of infitah was well disposed to entrepreneurial ventures. Decentralized production meant development of many more market niches: rather than a dominant "central domain" (Racy 1982: 391–392), multiple competing domains emerged, reflecting the newly competitive private sector (Castelo-Branco 1987).

But the infitah was also a cultural reorientation toward the West. Under Nasir, Egyptian radio broadcast a daily program of Western music called *al-Shari' al-Gharbi* ("The Western Street"). The Sadat years greatly increased direct Western media exposure. Two popular television programs, *Ikhtarna lak* ("We chose for you") and *al-'Alam yughanni* ("The world sings"), brought Western programming to all Egyptians with access to TV (and the percentage was rapidly increasing), including the West's culture of musical style, performance, and reception. Spanish flamenco and Julio Iglesias were popular on these programs. Cassettes of popular Western stars, in original or bootleg copies, became widely available.

The import of Western tastes and cultural products dovetailed with the import of Western modes of production and economic organization. Western popular music became more available, and more desirable. The largest market was the young generation, maturing under infitah, for whom the old tarab style was too heavy and old-fashioned. They longed for something new: shorter, faster songs, with more Western content.

Cultural influence was not only from the West, however. The rise of petro-dollars, combined with an increasing migrant worker population, increased influence from the East. Singers began to direct songs to rich Gulf (*khaligi*) Arabs summering in Cairo, or via media. Egyptian workers returned with a taste for khaligi musical styles. Islamism, inspired by Saudi and local preachers (and supported by Sadat for political ends), expanded rapidly in the 1980s, spearheading a new feeling of anti-Westernism.

Singers such as Warda, Nagat, and Hani Shakir continued the tarab tradition, as represented by Umm Kulthum, Farid al-Atrash, and 'Abd al-Halim Hafiz (though significantly all three passed away in the mid-1970s, and 'Abd al-Wahhab was no longer very active). Each of the younger tarab generation strove to be the *khalifa* (successor) of the predecessors, though none succeeded in revitalizing the tarab tradition. Correspondingly, the tarab style, until then the primary matrix for urban music, began to lose its status as the "neutral canvas" of a "central domain."[6] Instead two new (not entirely separable) types arose, rejecting that canvas: *musiqa sha'biyya*, and *musiqa shababiyya*. Both inhibited tarab via short fast songs, simple melodies, and a dance-like ethos (see also Danielson 1996: 301).

Musiqa sha'biyya ("popular" music) is based in rural song, combined with urban lower-class dance music, and some Western instrumentation (including synthesizers). This style is the musical response to rapid ruralization of the cities: low-brow, appealing to inhabitants of popular districts. Performers such as Ahmad 'Adawiyya, Hasan al-Asmar, and 'Abdu al-Iskandarani updated older traditions of *mawwal* and *zagal* (genres of folk song), and risqué-wedding songs, by modernizing the instrumentation and addressing urban life without losing a folk feel, full of improvisation and flexible interaction. Suggestive lyrics earned this material the moniker *aghani habta* ("low songs") (Armbrust 1996: 180–190; Danielson 1996: 307).

Musiqa shababiyya ("youth" music) fused Western popular music styles and instruments with Arab characteristics. This new *bub* (pop) music (sometimes mislabeled *jil* in the West [Werner 2000], a term Egyptians generally do not use) retains Arabic language, lyrical meanings, and elements of the tarab vocal style, thus addressing local aesthetic preferences. Arab percussion is typically retained as well. As one of my respondents put it, despite evident Westernization, there is an

"Eastern spirit" in this music. But this spirit blends with the grooves of Western popular musics (rock, jazz, funk, or disco), featuring trap set, keyboards, bass, and guitar, and often employs melodic and functional harmony as well. Composers and arrangers are central; performances are often multitracked; there is consequently less room for vocal interpretation or interaction. Unlike the tarab tradition, the music's social identity sometimes centers on the band rather than the singer. *Shababi* music is directed at educated middle and upper classes who appreciate Western styles, though it can be popular at many levels.

Out of these swirls of mixing cultures, several key musicians, bands, and styles emerged in shababi music. Hani Shanuda popularized the *org* (Arabic synthesizer)[7]; the first generation of Arab-Western bands included the Blackcoats, and the Petit Chats (with Hani Shanuda on keyboard) in the early 1970s. In 1977, Hani Shanuda's band, al-Masriyyin, became famous, paving the way for many of today's shababi stars (Ghazaleh 2001; Armbrust 1996: 186). Another popular 1970s group was the Jets, who blended western rock with Arabic lyrics and sensibilities.

Samir al-Iskandarani combined harmonic disco grooves with Arabic percussion and classical muwashshahat in his 1978 album *Layali Disco*. Around the same time, Muhammad Nuh combined disco with popular Sufi music. Muhammad Munir's upbeat blends of Nubian, Egyptian, and Western popular music were very popular, though media recognition was slow. Working with Hani Shanuda, he startled Egypt in the late 1970s with *Binitwilid*, featuring rock guitar, keyboards, trap set, and harmony on an Arab groove, with a non-traditional philosophical text by 'Abd al-Rahim Mansur. Jazzy and inimitable, Munir was one of the first Egyptian singers blending Arab and European styles to achieve popular acclaim in Europe—he recorded with German rock bands Embryo and Logic Animal (Swedenburg 1997: 95; Gehr 1997: 33).

Their postcolonial relationships made popular music cultural connections to Europe much stronger in North Africa than in Egypt. Two Libyans were central to the development of modern Egyptian pop. One is Nasir al-Mizdawi, whose songs feature Arabic lyrics and vocal style on a sophisticated pop-jazz base. Al-Mizdawi's first tape became extremely popular in Egypt in the mid-1970s, influencing Egyptian musicians. The other is Hamid al-Sha'iri, who came to Egypt in the 1970s.

Building upon al-Mizdawi's name and Libyan-European aesthetics, al-Sha'iri popularized the fast upbeat song in the mid-1980s.

Many of the innovators of shababi music continue to be active, though the field is much more densely populated today. Al-Mizdawi has continued to influence Egyptian musicians, having composed many songs for Egyptian pop stars, including Amr Diab's most best-known song, *Nur il-'en* (1996). Muhammad Munir and Hamid al-Sha'iri remain among Egypt's top singers. Besides producing his own material, al-Sha'iri composes and arranges for many other singers, including arrangements for many of Amr Diab's recent albums. Hani Shanuda composed four songs on Amr Diab's first cassette (*Ya Tariq*, 1985), and arranged all of them; he continues to compose and arrange for others.

In both new styles, the vocalist is a pop culture star (*nigm*), though not a *mutrib* (producer of tarab) in the strict sense. Since the broadcast media were still controlled by the state, these new types were at first largely excluded from TV and radio, and developed via the new cassette industry, especially *sha'bi* (Armbrust 1996: 184).

The 1970s witnessed a renewal in North American Latin music. In New York a developing hot, creative style, primarily combining jazz and Cuban influences, diffused under a new label: salsa. Latin rock emerged in the early 1970s (Roberts 1979: 186–191). These trends were to color Egyptian shababi music, or even transform it entirely.

Ethnohistory: Egyptians' Interpretations of the Spanish Tinge

I asked a variety of thoughtful Egyptians, living in Egypt, in Europe, and in Canada, to interpret and explain the recent profusion of Spanish and Latin sounds in Arab pop (shababi) music. Why Spanish, and why now? Discussions took place in person, by telephone, by e-mail, on list-servs, and Internet bulletin boards. I used the career of Amr Diab as my central example, though discussions ranged widely.

I have categorized their responses according to the kind of arguments used. Sorting responses was not an easy task, and required considerable interpretive activity on my part. For one thing, respondents didn't always fill in the logical chain and implications of their arguments. In what follows I have attempted to elaborate each argument while remaining true to what I perceive as its spirit. Second, responses frequently touched on a number of logically distinct positions, which I attempted to disentangle. Third, the various enumerated arguments are often interdependent, exhibiting a network structure that I attempted (with difficulty) to linearize. My occasional comments are relegated to footnotes.

Music, History, and Culture

Andalusia

Most respondents pointed to Andalusia as a key factor in the selection of Spanish (and Latin) music, indicating the enduring power of al-Andalus in the contemporary Egyptian imagination. Andalusian arguments for the contemporary Spanish tinge took two forms: (1) symbolic value, and (2) genealogical compatibility. Both are predicated on the notion that, at root, the Spanish tinge is connected to Arab culture.

Spanish (and by extension Latin) music is a symbol that invokes Andalusia, not merely due to its origins on Andalusian territory, but due to perceptions of a distant Andalusian source as well. Spanish and Latin musics are at least indebted to (or even represent the diffusion of) Arab culture. Egyptians hear flamenco, Spanish music generally, and Latin music by extension, as all pointing to the nostalgic glory of al-Andalus. They hear the 'ud in the guitar; flamenco's "*olé*" as a corruption of "Allah." The sounding of Andalusian symbols makes them all the more affective; as one respondent commented, "When you hear Spanish music you *feel* that you contributed to its construction." The Spanish tinge carries the positive value of Andalusia, reasserts the fact of Europe's debt to the Arabs, retrieves what was originally Arab (as 'Abd al-Wahhab emphasized), hence does not incur cultural indebtedness. All three factors are particularly important today, when many Arabs are feeling a sense of cultural despair.

Second, there is the argument of compatibility based on a shared genealogy. If Spanish and Arab musics flow from a common source, then it is only natural that they should produce a consonant mix. Arab constructions of music history (signaled by terms such as *muwashshahat andalusiyya* and *musiqa andalusiyya*) provide evidence of continuity, suggesting that other branches of the Andalusian genealogy should likewise be compatible. Emotionally, Arabs naturally respond to Spanish music. More generally, many Egyptians view Spanish and Arab culture as highly congruent, as if there were a distant shared bloodline extending back to Andalusia.[8]

Continuity of Western Influence

The Spanish tinge of the 1990s should be identified as a continuous extension to the use of Spanish musics earlier this century, but now within the context of shababi songs. This in turn is an instance of a more general propensity for Western styles in Egyptian music, e.g., the 1960s Franco-Arab fad (including such hits as "Mustafa ya Mustafa," sung in Arabic and French). Such eclecticism is longstanding, a product of Egypt's openness, reflecting a particular colonial history. Though strongly shaped by France and Britain, Egypt was never a formal colony of either (even among colonies, British indirect rule reduced cultural dominance). Large non-Egyptian populations (Greek, Armenian, Jewish, Italian) in Cairo and Alexandria ensured cultural diversity in centers of cultural production. Consequently, and most unlike North Africa, Egypt was open to a wide range of Western cultures, producing foreign musical influence. Even if the sound of the contemporary Spanish tinge is new, its acceptability is linked to the earlier popularity of the same styles. The adoption of Spanish music also followed naturally from the adoption of the guitar as a Western instrument in the 1970s. At first used to introduce jazz and rock styles, the acoustic guitar was associated by Egyptians with flamenco and Latin musics, facilitating entry of those musics. At the same time, from the 1970s onwards, Spanish music (with the growth of salsa, Latin rock, and Latin pop) was increasingly important in mainstream Western popular music. Egyptian musicians following Western trends thus introduced Spanish styles.

Modern Latin America

Since 1952, Latin America has carried a special significance in Egypt, more so than any other region of the developing world. At first there was a sense that Latin America was structurally and culturally parallel to the Arab world, comprising poor Third World countries (though not the poorest of the poor), manipulated by foreign imperialists. The struggles with poverty, against dictators, to achieve freedom, justice, democracy, and economic growth, were shared. Latin American liberation figures, such as Simon Bólivar, Fidel Castro, and Che Guevara (who met with Nasir) were cultural heroes to a segment of Egypt's revolutionary elites. Later, when Latin American countries achieved some measure of democracy and economic prosperity, Arabs wondered why, given their parallel conditions, they couldn't achieve the same thing.

Since the 1970s, Latin American writers such as Márquez and Borges have been extremely influential in Egypt, and admired for their worldwide influence. In music (as in politics) the history of Latin America sets a standard for Egyptians to match: a "Third World" music with European connections, which has become popular and influential world-wide, but especially in the West. By incorporating Latin music, Egyptians are identifying with Latin America and aspiring to what it has achieved.

Musical Compatibility

Without necessarily invoking Andalusian genealogy, respondents frequently pointed to the compatibility of Arab and Spanish musics, as ensuring the Spanish tinge's aesthetic success. The compatibility is timbral (both musics center on similar stringed instruments), rhythmic (Arab cycles such as *bamb* and *malfuf* mesh easily with *clave*), and formal. Unlike traditional Arab music, Spanish music is harmonic and does not use quartertones; however since the 1970s Arab music has developed harmony, and gradually reduced the use of quartertones. Furthermore, two Arabic scales lacking quartertones are central to Spanish musics: *nahawand* (analogous to the Western minor mode) and *kurd* (analogous to flamenco's Phrygian scale); furthermore, these two modes stir musical emotion quickly, an important quality for short shababi songs (in which there is no time for the longer modal developments and modulations of older tarab music).

Mediterranean

For some respondents, the presence of Spanish (and by extension Latin) music reflects more general cultural mixing and borrowing around the Mediterranean, including also North African, French, Greek, Italian, and Turkish influence. (For instance, Amr Diab has worked with Algerian, Greek, and Turkish musicians; Greek music of *Zorba* or Demis Roussos has been popular in Egypt.) Throughout history, Mediterranean peoples mixed and shared, due to proximity and similar environments. Mediterranean cultures are "hot," as opposed to the "colder" cultures of northern and eastern Europe. In Egypt, the Mediterranean cities, Alexandria and Port Said (birthplace of Diab), were important sites for cultural interaction, and the locus of much musical innovation. Mediterranean neighbor Libya also played a key role, because Libya maintained close ties to the West (especially Italy) until the 1969 coup, while Egypt was more closed. After 1969, when Qadhafi made conditions difficult, several Western-influenced musicians (including Nasir al-Mizdawi and Hamid al-Sha'iri) emigrated, and became influential in Egypt.

Passing of the Stars

Umm Kulthum, 'Abd al-Halim Hafiz, and Farid al-Atrash, three of the four greatest vocal stars of Egypt's mid-century tarab tradition, passed away in the mid-1970s. Due to a shifted zeitgeist, and (according to some) a paucity of equivalent vocal talent, younger singers found it impossible to take their places, though many tried. This fact created an aesthetic vacuum, which had to be filled with something new. The introduction of the Spanish tinge was a delayed reaction whose development required another fifteen years, after experiments with rock, disco, jazz, and other styles had run their course.

Rupture of History and Ahistoricality of the Musical Sign

Egypt is an ancient civilization, which has always borrowed from other cultures, while maintaining continuity through a cultural grasp of its own history. In the late nineteenth and early twentieth centuries, with advances in education, that grasp strengthened; the golden age occurred in the 1930s and '40s. The military-backed revolution of 1952 crushed this budding enlightenment; the educational system declined because revolutionary leaders were not themselves well educated; history was sacrificed to ideology. Blinded by the present, Egyptians lost their cultural memory, and an unprecedented rupture in historical continuity loomed.

The use of Spanish styles in post-revolutionary Egypt has nothing to do with Andalusia, or with Spanish-inflected music of the interwar period; it is rather an ahistorical musical sign designed to produce aesthetic pleasure for profit. Popularized in the 1990s, videoclip images (extending the power of musical products to dominate the visual as well as auditory field) play an important role in determining an ahistorical musical meaning, by gratifying and capturing more senses, riveting attention on the present. Watching videoclips of Spanish-tinged Arabic music, one sees white palaces, blue sky, clear water, beautiful girls dancing and singing, gorgeous sunsets. These are not signs of Andalusia, but rather ahistorical kitsch, designed to sell. Objectively the Spanish tinge may extend throughout history, but experientially one cannot connect present manifestations to that past.

Zeitgeist of Westernization, Globalization, Instability
Several respondents postulated that music necessarily reflects cultural ethos, or zeitgeist. As the Egyptian zeitgeist became more Western, Western musical styles became more appropriate for Egyptian cultural expression, and hence are appropriated in the new shababi songs. As Latin music mixed into the Western mainstream (over the past two decades), it naturally appeared (albeit delayed) in Egyptian music as well.

A related argument holds that in the 1990s the Egyptian zeitgeist was becoming not more Western, but more global; or that the concept (if not the content) of the global and globalization is itself central to the Egyptian ethos. Latin/Spanish music's popularity in Egypt results not from its Western, but from its global popularity and meaning. Latin/Spanish music *is* global; furthermore (due to global spread and internal hybridity) it represents the *concept* of the global.

A third version holds that Egyptians feel insecure; everything is unstable in Egypt today. Egyptians don't know who they are or even what they want; rapid stylistic change reflects this uncertainty.

Music, Politics, Ideology

Music, Politics, and Post-ideology
Several respondents stated or implied that Egyptian culture has been more open to foreign influence (interpreted as modernization) when its politics are more progressive. Two contrasting applications of this principle emerged.

In one interpretation, Egyptian progressiveness is associated with the pre-revolutionary period, particularly 1922–52, when foreign musical influence was strongest in the music of 'Abd al-Wahhab and others. In this period, models of modernity were drawn from European culture, through which came Latin music. During the Nasir years, socialist nationalism and statism caused Egypt to be more isolated. In the 1970s, with the infitah, and the decline of nationalism and Nasserism, Egyptian culture was again open to foreign economic, political, and cultural influence. But now diversity and globalism replaced Europe as a criterion for modernity. Throughout this experimental period a variety of musical influences appeared, to be sifted and sorted over the following decades; certain styles (including Spanish) ultimately emerged as most suitable (for any of the reasons presented earlier).

In a second interpretation, the pre-revolutionary period, as well as the mid-1960s, are viewed as progressive, in contrast to the reactionary 1970s. In the mid-'60s, Egyptians were optimistic and confident about their progress toward modernity and global greatness. Though politics were not free, they were forward-looking; reactionary Islamism was weak. Despite Nasir's anti-Western rhetoric, Western fashions were wildly popular. The 1960s thus represented a kind of cultural infitah, an acceptance of Western cultural modernity. Optimism and progressivism were extinguished by the 1967 defeat in the war with Israel, and the subsequent death of Nasir. The 1970s economic infitah was simultaneously a cultural closing (*inghilaq*), due to the rise in Gulf (khaliji) cultural influence, and the concomitant rise of reactionary Islamism, which did not decline until the early 1990s, by which time other ideologies were spent as well. The rise of more sophisticated musical fusions between Egyptian and compatible Western styles (including the Spanish) became more possible in the post-ideological 1990s.

Ideological uniqueness

Ideologically, Latin America is uniquely empowered as being both "Third World" and Western, among all musics of the world. Even today, Egyptians view Western culture as superior, yet they also seek symbols of resistance to Western dominance. Egyptian music producers want to fuse Arab music with a music fulfilling ideological criteria of

"Western," but also "global" and "Third World," opposing the hegemony of Anglo-American pop. Latin music, associated with Spain (hence Europe), popular in the West, global in diffusion and internal syncretism, nicely fits the bill. Egyptians regard African music, for instance, as *too* "Third World." (An additional advantage is the fact that Spain was not, for Egypt, a colonial oppressor.)

Ideological failures

Arab ideologies of unity and progress have failed. Leadership is poor; hypocrisy is everywhere. There is no democracy or political freedom; Palestine is still oppressed; there is economic distress and imbalance everywhere. The brutal 1991 United States-led Gulf War against Iraq, and an increasingly hard-line Israeli regime unconditionally supported by the United States, induced a turn away from American culture. Instead, the musical themes of Andalusia (ancient golden age) and Latin America (contemporary model) have come to the fore.

The Maturation of the Music Industry

The Rise of the Commercial Music Industry

With the decline in historical memory after 1952, Egyptian music began to be freed from its own past. The infitah of the 1970s, in both its technological and free-market economic dimensions, provided the critical push toward a totally commercialized market-driven music industry. The motive force is profit, and the shape of the market. Market forces, in the absence of historical memory, necessarily produced radical change. Egyptian music is no longer truly Egyptian. Music is created to please the foreign tastes of non-Egyptians (especially Gulf Arabs), or Egyptians alienated from their history. Poorer Egyptians maintained historical continuity, but with little financial clout they weakly influenced the market-driven system of music production. The age of unconstrained commercial music started in the 1970s, but marketing matured in the 1990s; during this period the market became less encumbered by ideological constraints. With the significant advent of the videoclip (popularized in the 1990s), musical meaning expanded to the visual sphere, to be more cunningly manipulated for a market seeking pleasure, not historical continuity. Because videoclips are intensively watched on ordinary Egyptian TV, as well as by Arab audiences living abroad, this mode of musical meaning increasingly determines musical content.

Egypt today is increasingly globalized, full of economic and cultural linkages to the outside world, particularly the West. Because of these interconnections, any outside commercial cultural trends will quickly penetrate Egyptian markets as well, though a short delay is to be expected. Because Spanish music is globally popular, a Spanish tinge in Arab music appeared: to sell to an international market, to sell to a local Egyptian market that has adopted foreign tastes, and to appear more international in the local market.

Maturation in Musical Tastes

A more sanguine view holds that the contemporary popularity of the Spanish tinge represents a delayed cultural selection from the infinite variety and confusion of the infitah era, when everything suddenly became possible. In the initial flush of enthusiasm, Egyptians saturated themselves with foreign cultural influences. Over the following twenty years, they gradually sifted through these influences, and selected Spanish musics as most compatible with their own.

Local Marketing

Particularly in post-Nasserist Egypt, Egyptian audiences want to feel importantly connected to global history, as a means of reestablishing cultural self-confidence and a sense of their own relevance to the wider world. Therefore they value global musical trends outside Egypt; they value Western culture (which largely controls those trends); they value that which signifies the concept of the global; and they value Egyptians who attain international stature. By blending Arab and Latin/Spanish, Egyptian music producers not only tap into an existing Egyptian fascination with Latin/Spanish music itself, but also with the very concepts of "Western trend," "global trend," and "global fusion," which that music signifies; "global fusion" being further symbolized by the Arab/Spanish mix itself. But one respondent reports that in Egyptian villages listeners don't recognize Spanish sounds at all, identifying such music only as "Western." In this case, the value of the Spanish tinge may depend on the foreign marketing argument.

Foreign Marketing

By incorporating global trends into Egyptian music, producers aim to capture foreign markets, or at least to give the impression (to local markets) of making Egyptian singers relevant to foreign markets. The foreign market itself comprises two essential segments: those of Arab descent seeking connections to the "home country" (expats), and the non-Arab "World Music" market. Those of Arab descent, but born abroad, seek music reflecting their dual identity, combining local aesthetic standards with Arabic language and sound. Aside from its privileged economic position and expanding population, in the 1990s the importance of the Western-Arab market has sharply increased with better distribution of Arab music CDs (largely via Internet), and widespread Western consumption of Arab music via satellite broadcasts of videoclips and music programs, in which song rankings are determined by viewers. Thus to a great extent Arab music is being driven by its foreign market. The worldwide popularity of Latin music (and its perceived connections to Arab music) make it an excellent choice for increasing sales abroad.[9] The non-Arab Western market seeks world music: the exotic in a familiar base; Latin/Spanish music, being both mainstream and "other," helps bridge Arabic and Western popular musics, and consequently markets.[10]

Maturation of Star-Creation Process

The music industry, including singers and their producers, has learned how to manufacture stardom. This ability has naturally produced a plethora of new stylistic syncretisms, as performers actively seek out visual and sonic material by which to forge a star persona, balancing continuity, imitations, and distinctiveness. The conscious control of this process naturally led Egyptian singers to incorporate the style of world famous Latin pop stars into a shababi pop base. Amr Diab is a good example. Though inspired by 'Abd al-Halim Hafiz's persona, he didn't insist on imitating 'Abd al-Halim too closely. Rather he followed the principle that had made 'Abd al-Halim successful, fusing continuity, modernity, and innovation in a musical style and image. Breaking free of Egyptian traditions, he sported Western dress and haircuts, benefiting as the cutting edge of fashion. More specifically, he imitated international Latin singers, such as Ricky Martin, in order to endear himself to Egyptian fans.

Arbitrary Difference

In the foregoing arguments, Latin and Spanish music do not carry any essential significance beyond representing trends happening in the West, or globally, or at least perceived as such. But this argument was also taken to a further extreme, by arguing that Spanish influence does not carry any particular significance at all, beyond the mere presentation of difference.

In the music mix, differentiation is necessary in three dimensions: differentiation from older tarab music to imply modernity; from the local to imply the global; and from previous mixes to imply innovation. If the first two establish Egyptian pop music as contemporary and international (like "World Music" in the West), the third establishes a particular product or artist as unique. As Egyptian music is increasingly driven by a sophisticated profit-seeking music industry, new albums are created and consumed more quickly. The commercial maturation of the music industry means that the music field is increasingly crowded and competitive. Each singer therefore attempts either to be unique, or to imitate others who are already successful; the latter must relentlessly seek out new musical styles. Not only cassettes, but entire styles are rapidly consumed. Whereas the tarab era favored musical craftsmanship and innovation within a stable style, today radical stylistic change has great commercial value. Marketers favor globally popular non-Egyptian styles, never previously fused with shababi music, to enable a new cassette to "burst" (*yitfar'a'*) on the scene, because, otherwise, the active bootleg cassette industry will reduce sales. Spanish influence is being used only to provide a new source of marketable difference.

Technological Change

Technological advancements enabled greater play of difference in Egypt since the 1970s. Previously, musical performances were recorded whole, with all musicians present and interacting, on one or two tracks. The unit of production was the song, for which creativity was credited to singer, composer, and lyricist. In the 1970s, the introduction of multitrack studio technology, with concomitant techniques of overdubbing and mixing, enabled inclusion of disparate musical factors, which could be recorded separately, then combined. The "song" unit, previously central to Arab music, was replaced by an aggregate of diverse tracks, contrived by the arranger, and combined by the sound engineer. Significantly, the names of arrangers and sound engineers were now prominently displayed on cassette boxes.

In the 1990s, availability of digital studio equipment, enabling "drag and drop" editing and digital effects, has pushed musical production further toward the art of manipulating and recombining tracks as the underlying musical units.[11] These technical operations enable any musics to be juxtaposed, opening Arabic music to wider ranges of foreign influences, indeed demanding such juxtapositions in order to ensure a constant supply of difference. The use of Spanish/Latin is only an instance.

Three other significant technological changes spread widely in the 1990s: videoclips, satellite television, and the Internet (web, e-mail, listservs, newsgroups, chat rooms, and filesharing). All contribute to the globalization of Egypt, further connecting young upper and middle class Egyptians (the prime market for shababi music) to global trends (such as Latin/Spanish music), while emphasizing the concept and importance of "the global" as a value in itself, and expanding foreign markets for Arab music, which responds by reflecting foreign tastes.

Postscript

If one grants them some historical validity, these arguments go a long way toward explaining the emergence and significance of the Spanish tinge in 1990s Egyptian pop music. In light of his biography, they also help to explain why Amr Diab became a leader in this trend, and why others followed him in it.

By asking Egyptians to reflect upon their own culture and history in order to explain a contemporary transnational musical phenomenon, this ethnohistorical study quickly uncovered a rich lode of meanings. Unpacking the answers to my questions reveals a startling diversity of theories, all deserving of a more in-depth "objective" historical treatment elsewhere, but also valuable in themselves for indicating how contemporary Egyptians conceptualize their music, its historical and cultural predicament, and its relation to the wider world.

But one of the most remarkable outcomes of this research does not concern Egyptian musical history or even ethnohistory, but rather the extent to which a seemingly innocuous question about popular culture catalyzes the generation of wide-ranging and heartfelt discourse of broader and more profound significances. Beyond their importance for understanding transnational flows of music and meaning, the arguments enumerated above provide evidence for the varied ways in which Egyptians construct and interpret their own history and culture.

Through such research, ethnomusicology demonstrates its scholarly value, not only as a method for documenting musical culture per se, but as a mode of accessing cultural self-understanding in the broadest sense.

Acknowledgments

Many voices are woven into this chapter, and I am most grateful to all who contributed. I'd especially like to thank the following individuals, who shared insights and viewpoints unstintingly: Ahmed Farouk, Ahmed Hammad, Ashraf Elassaly, Elsayed Mersal, Enas Hammad, Fikri Rizkalla, Hakam Suleiman, Heissam al-Wirdani, Iman Mersal, Laura Salguero, Mahmoud Elbenhawy, May Telmissany, Walid Khachab, Yasser Abdellatif. Without their generous donations of time and ideas, this research could not have been carried out.

Notes

1. In this chapter, transliteration of classical Arabic is based on spelling, while transliteration of spoken colloquial Arabic is based on pronunciation of isolated words (disregarding elisions). Arabic words or names common in English are presented in their usual English forms.

2. Throughout this chapter, I use "ethnohistory" in the sense of ethnomethodology, to mean "the study of the local construction of history" (analogous to "ethnobotany").

3. Another example is the 2001 World Music Awards, in which Ricky Martin is simultaneously awarded Best Selling Pop Male Artist, Best Selling Dance Male Artist, and Best Selling Latin Male Artist (World Music Awards 2002). And the examples could be multiplied: Christina Aguilera, Jennifer Lopez, Gloria Estefan, and the stunning success of *Buena Vista Social Club* (1997).

4. This spelling has become standard in English; a more standard transliteration would be 'Amr Diyab.

5. The following information has been culled from information duplicated among fan web sites (see Amr Diab 2002).

6. Composer Hani Shanuda criticized 'Abd al-Wahhab for never really rejecting Ottoman tarab, despite his innovations (Armbrust 1996: 187).

7. For a discussion of the *org* see Rasmussen 1996.

8. The Iraqi 'ud virtuoso Munir Bashir (1930–97) was convinced that flamenco was influenced by Arab music, illustrating his ideas in a recording entitled *Flamenco Roots* (Asmar and Hood 2001: 314). Likewise, Egyptian *sha'bi* star Hakim has justified his use of Latin influences since historically there is "a love between Arab and Latin rhythms" through a shared Andalusian heritage (Nickson 2001: 21).

9. Relatively large Arab populations living in Latin America, especially Colombia and Brazil, may also be significant. The great Lebanese singer, Wadi' al-Safi, lived in Brazil (Asmar and Hood 2001: 316). The Colombian vocal star Shakira is half Lebanese, and states that she is "devoted to Arabic tastes and sounds" (Shakira 2002).

10. Amr Diab's *Nur il-'En* is the outstanding example. Zirbel's claim that world music fans reject Egyptian pop (Zirbel 2000: 133) has yet to be verified; reviews by non-Arabs on music web sites (such as aramusic.com or amazon.com) and the incorporation of Egyptian pop on compilation CDs (Earthwork's *Tea in Marrakech* and Putumayo's *Arabic Groove*, both 2001) suggests otherwise.

11. International Arab artists such as Amr Diab have begun releasing multiple mixes of the same song for various markets and contexts.

Internet Sites

Amr Diab Web Page [accessed January 2002]. Available at www.amrdiab.net, www.mazika.com, www.amrdiab.info, www.amrodiab.com

Egypt Guide Web Page [accessed January 2002]. Available at www.egyptguide.net/entertainment/music/index_music.html

Gipsy Kings Web Page [accessed January 2002]. Available at www.gipsykings.com

Grammy Awards Web Page [accessed January 2002]. Available at www.grammy.com

Shakira Web Page [accessed January 2002]. Available at www.sonymusic.co.uk/shakira

World Music Awards Web Page [accessed January 2002]. Available at www.worldmusicawards.com

Bibliography

Aboul-Ela, Hossam. 1999. "Past rhetorics," *Al-Ahram Weekly*: 425.

al-Faruqi, Lois Ibsen. 1975. "Muwashshah: a vocal form in Islamic culture," *Ethnomusicology* 19/1: 1–29.

al-Hifni, Ratiba. 1999. *Muhammad 'Abd al-Wahhab: Hayatuhu wa fannuh*. Cairo: Dar al-Shuruq.

Armbrust, Walter. 1996. *Mass Culture and Modernism in Egypt*. Cambridge, UK: Cambridge University.

Asmar, Sami, and Kathleen Hood. 2001. "Modern Arab music: portraits of enchantment from the middle generation," in *Colors of Enchantment: Theater, dance, music and the visual arts of the Middle East*, edited by Sherifa Zuhur. Cairo: The American University in Cairo Press, 297–320.

Aulas, Marie-Christine. 1982. "Sadat's Egypt: a balance sheet," *MERIP Reports* 107: 6–18.

Castelo-Branco, Salwa el-Shawan. 1987. "Some aspects of the cassette industry in Egypt," *The World of Music* 24/2: 32–45.

Danielson, Virginia. 1996. "New nightingales of the Nile: popular music in Egypt since the 1970s," *Popular Music* 15/3: 299–312.

_____. 1997. *The Voice of Egypt: Umm Kulthum, Arabic Song, and Egyptian Society in the Twentieth Century.* Chicago: University of Chicago Press.

Davis, Ruth. 1996a. "Arab-Andalusian Music in Tunisia," *Early Music* 24/3: 423–37.

_____. 1996b. "The art/popular music paradigm and the Tunisian Ma'luf," *Popular Music* 15/3: 313–23.

Dezzani, Mark. 1998. "World Music Awards Win Praise," *Billboard* 110/21: 59–60.

Farmer, Henry George. 1970. *Historical facts for the Arabian musical influence.* Hildesheim, Germany: G. Olms.

_____. 1973. *A History of Arabian Music to the XIIIth Century.* London: Luzac.

Geertz, Clifford. 1973. *The Interpretation of Cultures: Selected Essays.* New York: Basic Books.

Gehr, Richard. 1997. "Pyramid Selling: Richard Gehr Finds Racism and Censorship as He Searches Cairo for the Roots of Egyptian Pop," *Folk Roots* 18/7–8: 32–34.

Ghazaleh, Pascale. 2001. "Hani Shenouda: in concert," *Al-Ahram Weekly* 539.

Goldziher, Ignác, and Joseph Desomogyi. 1966. *A Short History of Classical Arabic Literature.* Hildesheim, Germany: G. Olms.

Hamed, Osama. 1981. "Egypt's open door economic policy: an attempt at economic integration in the Middle East," *International Journal of Middle East Studies* 13/1: 1–9.

Holt, Peter Malcolm. 1966. *Egypt and the Fertile Crescent, 1516–1922: a Political History.* Ithaca, NY: Cornell University Press.

Hourani, Albert Habib. 1983. *Arabic Thought in the Liberal Age, 1798–1939.* Cambridge, U.K.; New York : Cambridge University Press.

_____. 1991. *A History of the Arab Peoples.* Cambridge, MA: Harvard University Press.

Lapidus, Ira M. 1988. *A History of Islamic Societies.* Cambridge, U.K.; New York: Cambridge University Press.

Levi-Provencal, E. 1999a. "'Abd al-Rahman [I:81b]," CD-ROM v. 1.0 ed. Koninklijke Brill NV.

_____. 1999b. "al-Andalus [I:486a]: (vi) General survey of the history of al-Andalus," CD-ROM v. 1.0 ed.Koninklijke Brill NV.

Nickson, Chris. 2001. "The year of desert rose," *Saudi Aramco World* 52/6: 16–23.

Okasha, Saeed. 2000. "The man who would have lived forever," *Cairo Times* 4/10.

Racy, Ali Jihad. 1978. "Arabian music and the effects of commercial recording," *The World of Music* 20/1: 47–55.

_____. 1982. "Musical Aesthetics in Present-Day Cairo," *Ethnomusicology* 26/3. 391–406.

_____. 1985. "Music in nineteenth-century Egypt: an historical sketch," *Selected Reports in Ethnomusicology* 4: 157–79.

_____. 1988. "Sound and society: the takht music of early twentieth-century Cairo," *Selected Reports in Ethnomusicology* 7: 139–70.

_____. 1991. "Creativity and ambience: an ecstatic feedback model from Arab music," *The World of Music* 33/2: 7–26.

Rasmussen, Anne K. 1996. "Theory and practice at the 'Arabic org:' digital technology in contemporary Arab music performance," *Popular Music* 15/3: 345–65.

Roberts, John Storm. 1979. *The Latin Tinge: The Impact of Latin American Music on the United States.* New York: Oxford University Press.

Sayyid-Marsot, Afaf Lutfi. 1977. *Egypt's Liberal Experiment, 1922–1936.* Berkeley: University of California Press.

el-Shawan, Salwa. 1979. "The socio-political context of al-musika al-'arabiyya in Cairo, Egypt," *Asian Music* 12/1: 86–128.

Swedenburg, Ted. 1997. "Saida Sultan/Danna International: Transgender pop and the polysemiotics of sex, nation, and ethnicity on the Israeli-Egyptian border," *The Musical Quarterly* 81/1: 81–108.

Taylor, Timothy Dean. 1997. *Global Pop: World Music, World Markets.* New York: Routledge.

Touma, Habib. 1996. *The Music of the Arabs.* Portland, OR: Amadeus Press.

Vatikiotis, P. J. 1969. *The Modern History of Egypt.* New York: Praeger.

Werner, Louis. 2000. "Arab Pop on the World Stage," *Saudi Aramco World* 51/2: 2–9.

Wiegers, G. A. 1999. "Moriscos [VII:241b]," CD-ROM v. 1.0 ed. Koninklijke Brill NV.

Williams, Martin T. 1970. *The Jazz Tradition.* New York: Oxford University Press.

Woffenden, Richard, and Mohammed Mitwalli. 1998. "They have announced the death of Nizar Qabbani," *Cairo Times* 2/7.

Zirbel, Katherine E. 2000. "Playing it both ways: Local Egyptian performers between regional identity and international markets," in *Mass Mediations: New Approaches to Popular Culture in the Middle East and Beyond*, edited by Walter Armbrust. Berkeley: University of California Press, 120–145.

Zuhur, Sherifa. 2001. "Musical stardom and male romance: Farid al-Atrash," in *Colors of enchantment: theater, dance, music and the visual arts of the Middle East*, edited by Sherifa Zuhur. Cairo: The American University in Cairo Press, 270–296.

Discography

Notes: Common informal transliterations are given in square brackets. The status of an item as CD or cassette does not imply lack of availability in other formats.

'Amr Diyab [Amr Diab]. *Aktar waahid [Aktar Wahid].* Cairo: Alam El Phan. 2001. CD.

——. *Tamalli ma'ak.* Amr Diab. Cairo: Niyusawnd. 2000. Cassette.

——. *Amaren.* Dubai: EMI. 1999. CD.

——. *'Awwiduni [Awedony].* Dubai: EMI. 1998. CD.

——. *Nur il-'En [Nour El Ain].* Cairo: Alam el Phan. 1996. Cassette.

——. *Ragi'in.* Cairo: Sawt al-Dilta. 1996. Cassette.

——. *Shawa'na.* Sawt il-Dilta. 1990. Cassette.

——. *Wi yilumuni.* Cairo: Sawt al-Dilta. 1995. Cassette.

——. *Ayamna.* Cairo: Sawt al-Dilta. 1993. Cassette.

——. *Habibi.* Cairo: Sawt al-Dilta. 1992. Cassette.

Angham. *Leih sebtaha [Leeh sibtaha]*. Cairo: Alam El Phan. 2001. Cassette.

Hakim. *Yaho*. Cairo. 2001. Cassette.

Hasan il-Asmar. *Mish hasibik*. Cairo: Two Stars. No date. Cassette.

Hisham 'Abbas. *Hisham*. Sharikat Niyusawnd. No date. Cassette.

——. *Kalam il-lel*. Cairo. 1999. Cassette.

——. *Habibi dah*. Cairo. 2000. Cassette.

Ihab Tawfiq [Ehab Tawfik]. *'Adda il-lel*. Sharikat Niyusawnd. 1994. Cassette.

Ilham al-Madfa'i [Ilham Al Madfai]. *Ilham al Madfa'i*. Dubai: EMI. 1999. CD.

Juliya Butrus [Julia Boutros]. *Bisaraha*. Dubai: EMI. 2001. CD.

Mustafa Qamar [Moustafa Amar]. *'Aynek wahshani*. 1999. CD.

——. *'Ayshin [Aisheen]*. Dubai: EMI. No date. CD.

Nawal al-Zughby [Nawal El-Zoughby]. *Tul 'Umri*. Dubai: EMI. 2001. CD.

Tal il-lel. Sharikat Niyusawnd. 1997. Cassette.

Various artists. *Arabica Latina*. Cairo: Al Rissa Artistic Production and Distribution. 1997. Cassette.

Filmography

'Amr Diyab [Amr Diab]. *New York '92: Amr Diab in concert*. New York: United Middle East Productions. 1992. Video.

C H A P T E R   S E V E N

YAM TIKHONIYUT: TRANSFORMATIONS OF MEDITERRANEANISM IN ISRAELI MUSIC

EDWIN SEROUSSI

Mediterraneanism (*yam tikhoniyut* in Hebrew) as a concept of cultural history appears in Jewish studies toward the end of the nineteenth-century in connection with the culture of the Jewish Diaspora around the Mediterranean as perceived from an Orientalist perspective by European Jewish scholars (see Bahloul 1994; Schroeter 1994; and for music research Bohlman 1993 and 2000). In this sense, the application of this concept is similar to the one used in general cultural history. The concept was perpetuated, in this inter-Jewish sense, in the Israeli cultural discourse in relation to the culture of the non-European Jewish component of the new Jewish nation-state (Elbaz 1994). Since the late 1950s, however, Mediterraneanism appears in the Israeli public discourse in a new sense, in connection with the identity of the emergent culture of the Israeli state.

The presence of the Mediterranean topos in Israel was notably intensified in the 1990s when geopolitical and economic developments related to the Middle East peace process, such as the Barcelona Process, put Israel into a closer relation with the European Union and the North African Arab states via a Euro-Mediterranean Association Agreement (Modena Terracini 1999). In its new sense, the Mediterranean became an optional location and a cultural utopia where the Israeli society and its new culture attempt to position themselves within a larger geopolitical and cultural frame.

The proliferation of Mediterraneanism in Israeli academic and public discourse since the 1980s is staggering (Shavit 1994: 314). Shavit even asks whether in the case of Israel academic research has actually influenced and inspired public discourse (1994: 317). For example, just in the handful of years that have elapsed since Shavit published in 1994 a checklist of academic initiatives in the field of Mediterranean cultural studies in Israel, one witnessed the establishment of the Forum for Mediterranean Cultures as a consortium of major governmental agencies and cultural institutions in Jerusalem and, more recently the creation of the Center for Mediterranean Studies at Tel Aviv University. Israeli scholars then relentlessly continue "to fish deeper into Mediterranean waters," to use an appropriate maritime figure of speech.

Interestingly, many authors participating in the Mediterraneanist debate in Israel frequently bring up music as the field where this concept can be grasped in its most concrete form. For example, several of the articles included in the special issue of the *Journal of Mediterranean Studies* dedicated to Israel refer somehow to music. Bahloul (1994: 197) recalls the transformations in the songs by the famous Algerian Jewish singer Enrico Macias immediately after his immigration from Algeria to France. Elbaz talks about music as the field of creativity where "osmosis and synthesis operate in the most natural and authentic manner." For this reason music became a barometer for measuring the relations between the dominant European culture of Israel and the challenging "Oriental and Mediterranean melodies and rhythms" (Elbaz 1994: 177). Shavit himself states that "music is the only type of artistic creation [in Israel] to which distinctively 'Mediterranean' characteristics were attributed" (1994: 316). He rightly suggests that the term "Mediterranean" in Israel was applied to diverse types of music in different historical and social contexts (Shavit 1994: 316–17). It is the goal of the present chapter to clarify within a broad theoretical perspective the various uses of the concept of the Mediterranean in Israeli music.

Models of Musical Mediterraneanism in Israel

The Mediterranean has been one of the most persistent metaphors in the Israeli discourse about music almost since Zionism became a tangible cultural enterprise in the early 1900s. It appeared in different contexts in relation to various types of music, usually as part of the ongoing debate over Israeliness, that is, the nature (roots, materials, meanings) of the culture of a new Israeli nation-state. Falling short of proposing an encompassing and rigid typology that covers all forms of Mediterraneanism in modern Israeli discourse about music, I would suggest here three models that may help to contextualize the diverse musical expressions that will be discussed.

First, there is the "synthesis model." In this model, the Mediterranean topos serves as an escape route from the East-West paradox in which the inventors of modern Israeli music were caught. This paradox has hunted Zionist cultural policies ever since the 1920s; the Mediterranean option appeared then as a viable solution, even if it represented a detour from the mainstream historical narrative of Zionism. The modern State of Israel, whose national myth traces its origins back to Biblical Judea (Zerubavel 1994), is actually an antithesis of its ancestor. Ancient Israel was a people of the inner Hills of Judea and of the desert, not a people of the sea. Contemporary Israeliness, on the other hand, developed along the Mediterranean shore, in the narrow seaside strip where the majority of Israelis dwell nowadays. In spite of the rhetoric about the return to Zion (i.e., Jerusalem), Zionism eventually chose the new seashore city of Tel Aviv as its cultural (and, for our purposes, musical) center.

The Mediterranean as a getaway from the East-West paradox was used both inwards, as an inter-Jewish process, as well as outwards, as a compromise between Israeli and Eastern Mediterranean cultures. It reflected the aspiration of the Zionist establishment (for which the Western nation-state and culture was the ideal) for some kind of synthesis between the Jewish cultures from East and West that was encapsulated in the Zionist slogan "ingathering of the exiles." Outwards, it described a synthesis between the Western-oriented Israeli culture and the civilizations of its Middle Eastern surroundings. Stretching this second argument to its limits, one may even argue that Mediterraneanism in the Israeli context can be also interpreted as a form of resistance to global "McDonaldization."

The perception of the Sephardi and Oriental Jew as the "aboriginal" or "noble" in the eyes of European Jews is the basis for the second model of Mediterraneanism, the "Orientalist mode." In this case, Mediterraneanism is related to the use of the authentic music of the "other" Jew, the Sephardi and Oriental Jew perceived from the standpoint of the Eurocentric establishment of the Zionist movement. The influence of scholarship on the shaping of this view can hardly be denied. For example, the work of the musicologist Abraham Zvi Idelsohn (who lived and worked in Palestine between 1908 and 1921) contributed to the perception of the musical lore of the Mediterranean Jewish communities as the most authentic expression of Jewishness in music.[1]

"Subversion" is the hallmark of the third and last model of musical Mediterraneanism in Israel. In this model, Mediterraneanism is perceived as a diluted form of Arabness, Turkishness, or Greekness that stands in opposition to the Western-oriented mainstream of Israeli culture. This model contrasts with the intellectual attempt for a synthesis between East and West or with the search for the authentic Mediterranean roots of Jewish musical traditions found in the first two models.

Texts that attempt to define musical Mediterraneanism in Israel present three different approaches. The first approach focuses on musical Mediterraneanism as a cluster of traits, such as particular scales, modes, rhythms, textures, musical instruments, and so forth. Following this approach, one may say that Mediterraneanism has a particular "sound." A second approach considers the particular contexts in which music of Mediterranean characteristics or origins is performed, such as the Greek *taverna*. Indeed the most popular Israeli TV show dedicated to Mediterranean music is called *At the Taverna*. Finally, Mediterranean music is sometimes defined as all music consumed by Mediterranean taste-publics. Although different combinations of elements from these three approaches appear in texts about musical Mediterraneanism in Israel, the traits list appears to be the most frequently used.

The Mediterranean topos entered Israeli musical discourse earlier than generally assumed and in a rather unexpected context. One of its earliest manifestations is found in the writings of Haim Arlozoroff (1899–1933), a prominent leader of the Zionist Labor movement, and a scholar who was murdered on the shores of Tel Aviv. In 1926 he wrote,

> [t]he cultural uniformity of the Mediterranean basin stands out very strongly. . . . In contrast to central, northern and western Europe . . . every-

body sings while they work—from all sides. The songs are the same throughout the Mediterranean, with the same melody and harmony, sung by Arabs, Jews, Italians . . . and the great popularity of Italian opera— Verdi, for instance—among the Jews, and the enthusiasm it arouses, is, in my opinion, by no means accidental. If we remain on the Mediterranean shore, we will set up a monument to honor Verdi rather than Bach, in Tel Aviv and in the Valley of Jezreel.[2]

Because Arlozoroff expressed himself in this curious manner, three distinctive expressions of substantial musical Mediterraneanism can be located in Israeli music discourse. Each of these expressions shows aspects of the three models of musical Mediterraneanism already suggested. The first one appears in the late 1940s in the field of "art" or "serious" music (see Bressler 1985; Hirshberg 1995, chapter 15) under the title of the "Mediterranean" or "eastern Mediterranean" school. This phenomenon can be understood in terms of the synthesis model, although it shows aspects of the Orientalist model as well. Soon after, Mediterraneanism appears in connection with the Israeli folk song as being inspired by a most "authentic" form of Mediterranean Jewish music, the Sephardi (Judeo-Spanish) folk song.[3] Finally, in the 1980s Mediterraneanism reappears in its most contemporary and prominent manner in relation to a genre of Israeli popular music called *musiqa mizrahit* (literally, "Oriental music"; see Halper, Seroussi and Squires-Kidron 1989, 1992; Horowitz 1994, 1997). This last case represents the "subversive" model of musical Mediterraneanism in Israel.

This rest of this chapter explores in more detail the transformations of Mediterraneanism in the Israeli discourse about music. It stresses in particular the evolving sociopolitical connotations of this topos, first by the *Ashkenazi* (Eastern European) elite, then by *Sephardi* (Judeo-Spanish) intellectuals, and, finally, by the subversive *Mizrahi* ("Oriental") Jews.

Eastern European Visions of the Mediterranean: A Synthesis Model

The concept of Mediterraneanism in the art music of Israel is generally associated with the Hungarian-born Jewish composer Alexander U. Boskovitch (1907–64), who immigrated to Palestine in 1938. In an essay elaborated in several stages and published in its final version in Hebrew in 1953, titled "The problems of Jewish music," Boskovitch maintained that music is a function of time and place, not a universal language. He then argued that "music appropriate for the misty seclusion and melancholy of northern Europe would be out of place in the Mediterranean countries 'where everything is sharply delineated'" (Hirshberg 1995: 262ff). Hirshberg, in opposition to Brod (see below), maintains that Boskovitch was influenced by Nietzsche's concept of the "ancient man's public speech" (*Jenseits von Gut und Böse*) in his vision of the "dynamic landscape" of "the sorching Mediterranean sun, the sand dunes of Tel Aviv, . . . and the excited vocal gestures of spoken Arabic and Hebrew" (Hirshberg 1995: 263).[4] Following this rationale, Boskovitch argued that only the Jewish composers living in Palestine, nourished by the spirit of their time and place (the eastern Mediterranean), would be able to create a true Jewish national style of music.

Despite Boskovitch's application of these ideas in some of his works in the 1940s, especially in the *Semitic Suite* of 1946, it was actually the composer and critic Max Brod (Prague, 1884–Tel Aviv, 1968) who was the first one to use, in his book *Israel's Music*, the concept of a "Mediterranean style," attributing it to Boskovitch. According to Brod, Boskovitch employed the term to refer to musical works that were influenced by the "Oriental" Jewish folk songs collected and made public by the Yemenite Jewish singer Bracha Zefira (Brod 1951: 57–58).[5] The label "Mediterranean" also appears in the name of musical compositions about the same time (early 1950s), such as Menahem Avidom's *Mediterranean Sinfonietta* of 1951.

As Bressler (1985) pointed out, Brod's approach to the Mediterranean topos was mainly based on a list of musical traits. Works of Mediterranean music, according to Brod, had

> [t]heir rhythm in the harsh irregular meters, the obstinate repetition but also the manifold ceaseless variation which enchants by its apparent freedom from rule and impulsiveness. The structure of the movement is sometimes linear, unisonal, or at least not polyphonically overburdened. The influence exerted by the melodies of the Yemenite Jews, the neutralization of the boundaries between major and minor keys, the return to

ancient modes the neglect of the augmented second, so characteristic of the Diaspora[6]—in all these respects, lines of connection can be drawn with Arabic music. . . . Climate and landscape, shepherd's song, oboe and clarinet, play their part. Accompaniment by tympani or tambourine, real, only hinted at, or imaginary, add to some of these songs . . . a strangely monotonous, even hypnotic character; but whoever immerses himself in this apparent monotony is enabled to hear delicate and subtle nuances which have been denied to European ears. (Brod 1951: 57)

The model of Brod's "Mediterranean music" then is "Arabic music." This music is described as "southern," "infused with the bright light of the Mediterranean air," "utmost attractive," "tense," and "anti-bourgeois" (see Bressler 1985: 138, after Brod 1951: 57). His Mediterraneanism is a true, if anachronistic, echo of late nineteenth-century European musical Orientalism. "Arabic" music as an abstract concept does not exist in reality, for many contrasting types and styles of music co-exist in the different Arabic cultures. One may also wonder how much Arabic music Brod actually had the opportunity to listen to.

Criticizing Brod's generalizations, Hirshberg vehemently argued against the very existence of a "Mediterranean school" of Israeli music, referring to this label as a "fallacy." According to Hirshberg (1993), Boskovitch never spelled out Brod's concept of Mediterraneanism. Moreover, one could not talk about "schools" of music among the small circle of European Jewish composers of art music active in Tel Aviv in the late 1940s. Hirshberg concluded that "the so-called Mediterraneanism did not constitute a coherent musical style but a set of semiotically loaded musical patterns which were frequently juxtaposed with other similar sets, such as that of Diaspora-related patterns. Nor did Mediterraneanism effect any significant change on the level of selection of musical genre" (Hirshberg 1995: 271–72).

Despite these weaknesses, the Mediterranean concept coined by Brod, after Boskovitch, reverberated in the historiography of Israeli art music. It reappears in a survey of art music in Israel by the musicologist Peter Gradenwitz as the "Eastern Mediterranean school" (Gradenwitz 1978: 63–101). Later on Bohlman (1989: 189) speaks about "eastern Mediterraneanism" as a bridge between the founder fathers of Israeli music and a younger generation born in Israel who had "internalized the sounds presumably unique to that region." More recently, Fleisher discusses the "Mediterranean school" in some detail, as an expression of the East-West encounter in the music of the 1950s (Fleisher 1997: 49–52, 318, n. 87).

The Mediterranean topos did not lose its appeal and persists in contemporary Israeli musical discourse. A most recent manifestation of this presence is found in the title of a concert by Musica Nova, one of Israel's most prestigious ensembles of contemporary Western art music: "Mediterranean Fantasy: On the Search for an Israeli Musical Identity" (which took place in Tel Aviv in June of 2000). The concert included works by Israeli composers from different periods and styles, such as Paul Ben Haim (a representative of the founding school of Israeli art music, born and educated in Germany), Ami Maayani, Mordecai Seter, and Zvi Avni (three representatives of the second generation of composers, born or educated in Israel), and Joseph Bardanashvili (a new immigrant from Georgia in the former Soviet Union). By relating the Mediterranean to the realm of "fantasy," the designers of this concert apparently implied that there is a certain link between Mediterraneanism and a fantastic reality in which the musical identity of Israeliness can be located. We can detect here the persistent relation between the "synthesis" and the "Orientalist" models of musical Mediterraneanism in Israeli art music. This relation was stressed in the program of this concert by the inclusion of the renowned Yemenite folk singer and dancer Leah Abraham as a soloist.

Music of a Noble Jew: A Judeo-Spanish Model for the Israeli Folk Song

Another type of Mediterraneanism in Israeli music that had fewer repercussions in the literature than the former one is an instance of the model we called "Orientalist." According to this model, the new Israeli folk song has to lean on an authentic form of Jewish music, that is, on the music of the Jews who dwelt on the rim of the Mediterranean for many generations. For the past five centuries, these Jews were Sephardim, Jews expelled from Spain and Portugal at the end of the fifteenth century.

The chief exponent of this second form of musical Mediterraneanism was the Sephardi singer and folk song collector

Isaac Levy. Born in Turkey in 1919, Levy immigrated as a child to Palestine. He attended the Academy of Music in Jerusalem. In the early 1950s, Levy became interested in his cultural roots and became a systematic collector of Judeo-Spanish folk songs. In the mid-1950s he started to broadcast the Judeo-Spanish program at the state Israeli radio station. In these programs, he broadcast Judeo-Spanish folk songs from his original field recordings and also arrangements of the same songs that he commissioned and sometimes performed himself.

In 1959, Levy published the first of his four-volume collection of Judeo-Spanish folk songs (see Seroussi 1995). In the introduction to this volume, Levy proclaimed his vision of Mediterraneanism in Israeli culture. He predicted that Israeli culture would transform itself from a European culture into a Mediterranean one. He vaguely explained this adjective as the juncture of the "ancient Eastern civilization of Israel and early Christianity" with contemporary Western culture. The Sephardi Jews were, according to Levy, the natural carriers of this legacy because they

> always dwelt around the rims of the Mediterranean and were never separated from the air and the atmosphere of this marvelous sea, cradle of the so-called "Western" culture and civilization.

Therefore the future of Israel should be linked to this synthesis:

> The melos in the new Israel has changed . . . and I am convinced that in due time our national music will be entirely Mediterranean. As the Sephardi pronunciation of Hebrew was adopted [in Israel], so will the Judeo-Spanish melodies serve as the basis for its music. (Levy 1959: VI)

The concept of an Israeli "national music" should be understood in the historical context of the 1950s. This was a period when the European Jews dominated, through the Labor movement, the cultural institutions of the new country in accordance with secular Zionist ideology. During the same decade, masses of Jews from Islamic countries arrived in Israel. The governmental policy of absorption set the basis for an ongoing process of political, social, and cultural confrontation between the leadership of the state and the new immigrants. At this juncture, Levy was ambivalent. As a musician trained in the Western tradition and a state radio employee, he was part of the establishment. At the same time, he became, from within the system, an advocate of Mediterranean culture.

It is interesting to note that Levy's vision of Sephardi music as the authentic model for the music of the Jewish people in its old/new land was predicted many years before by no less than Haim Nahman Bialik, Israel's national poet. In his introductory remarks to an anthology of religious Hebrew poetry published in Istanbul in 1921 titled *Shirei yisrael be-eretz ha-qedem* (*Songs of Israel in the Near East*), Bialik (after attending a musical performance of these poems) stated that

> [t]he [Turkish] Hebrew folk songs and their Oriental melodies, that undoubtedly are more valuable than the [Ashkenazi] folk songs, even if they are borrowed, are closer to the spirit of the Hebrews than the songs of the mixed languages coming from the Northern West. And if the Hebrew music is going to be renewed sometime, there is no doubt that it will turn to this well, to the well of the Oriental melody, and it will absorb from it the energy for its renewal.

This is then a most concrete expression of the Orientalist model of musical Mediterraneanism.

Mediterraneanism as Subversion and Compromise: The *Musiqa mizraḥit* Model

The third and most recent appearance of the Mediterranean topos in Israeli musical discourse occurs in the 1980s when *musiqa yam tikhonit* (Mediterranean music) or more specifically *musiqa yisraelit yam tikhonit* (Israeli Mediterranean music) becomes the alternative name for the genre of popular music that was until then called *musiqa mizraḥit* ("Oriental music") exclusively (see Horowitz 1997). The evolution of labels used to designate this genre reveals a change of attitudes by its creators and consumers. The shift of the 1980s to musiqa yam tikhonit was intended to differentiate musiqa mizraḥit from other non-European musics, particularly Arabic music. By adopting this strategy, both the creators and consumers of musiqa mizraḥit prevented European Israelis from confusing them with the Arabs whom they resembled in musical tastes and other aspects of culture. Such a distinction also lent legitimacy to musiqa mizraḥit's claims to being truly Israeli music.

Musiqa mizraḥit is a complex and unique genre within the field of popular music in Israel whose definition is quite elusive.[7] In its initial stages, musiqa mizraḥit was not specifically Israeli, but mainly imported Greek, Arabic, or Turkish popular music adapted from records, cassettes, or radio performances and "made" Israeli merely by substituting Hebrew lyrics for the original ones. Prominent among these imported musical styles were the songs performed by Greek singers, like Aris San, who appeared or established themselves in Israel or mellow Mediterranean ballads in the style of the Sanremo festival in Italy.

In the 1970s and 1980s, musiqa mizraḥit could be also defined by its public, mostly working-class Jews of North African and Middle Eastern origin (called 'edot ha-mizraḥ, "the Oriental communities"). Rejecting the label 'edot ha-mizraḥ, these Jews consolidated a pan-ethnic sense of identity called mizraḥiyut. The rise of the right-wing Likud party to power in 1977, largely on the votes of working-class Easterners, which empowered the Mizraḥi Jews politically for the first time since the massive immigration of the 1950s, is sometimes perceived as a major factor in the rise of public attention to musiqa mizraḥit. A feeling that their "own" were governing the country gave the Mizraḥi Jews a sense of added legitimacy and allowed them to express their ethnicity without endangering their status as Israelis. It was in this social and political context of the late 1970s that the original, authentic musiqa mizraḥit fully emerged into the general public scene.

In the 1980s original songs in the more specifically Israeli Mizraḥi style started to outnumber the covers of foreign songs. Mediterranean music basically became Western popular music with distinctive features: quality of voice emission (specifically Yemenite Jewish singers), use of particular instruments (especially the bouzouki), the disproportionate use of the Phrygian mode, and loci in free rhythm (defined by the Arabic concept of muwwal). The resulting sound of musiqa mizraḥit fluctuates, recalling intermittently the Turkish arabesk, Greek laïkó, "rocked out" versions of traditional Yemenite Jewish tunes, and ballads in the Sanremo festival style.

In the 1990s the fusion of musiqa mizraḥit with diverse forms of rock and mainstream popular music brought it to the center of national attention. Musiqa mizraḥit, whether adopted whole cloth or originally composed by Israeli composers, became Israeli and not ethnic music. From this viewpoint, musiqa mizraḥit departs from the traditional music of the Jews from Islamic countries that was either "museumized," "ethnicized," or plainly rejected in Israel (see Cohen and Shiloah 1985).

Two major social themes of musiqa mizraḥit are discrimination against it by the Israeli establishment and its aspirations to become a representation of authentic Israeliness, not just of Mizraḥi Israeliness. Musiqa mizraḥit artists and producers felt rejected by the establishment, particularly by the state-funded media. This rejection was perceived as a delegitimization of musiqa mizraḥit as an authentic form of Israeli popular music. Radio programs dedicated to musiqa mizraḥit, perceived by the producers of this music as "ghettos" (in itself a loaded term within Israeli discourse, with the clear connotation of harsh discrimination), bear names such as *Me'orav yam tikhoni* ("Mediterranean Mix").

The new Mediterranean identity of musiqa mizraḥit seems to emerge from this feeling of discrimination. One can best understand this transformation from "Oriental" to "Mediterranean" by analyzing the public airing of the "narrative of discrimination" that developed among Mizraḥi composers, performers, and producers. For example, discrimination became the theme of a relentless campaign by Avihu Medina, one of the most influential composers of this style (who wrote over 400 songs) and one of its performers too. To argue that Mediterranean music is "the" Israeli music, Medina stressed four basic related ideas: 1) there is a conspiratory discrimination against musiqa mizraḥit by music editors of radio and television stations; 2) this conspiracy dates back to a period when Israeliness equaled Westernness and this period is over; 3) until the start of his own public campaign there was no protest by musiqa mizraḥit artists against discrimination because Eastern Jews are submissive to structures of power due to their education in totalitarian regimes and their lack of experience in open democracies; 4) there is no power now to halt the cultural integration of Israel in the Middle East, and this integration means adopting an Orientalized culture: "Everybody here will be a Middle Easterner. We go in that direction and those who do not see it are blind." As a result of this analysis, he concludes that musiqa mizraḥit is the only authentic Israeli music because it reflects "a synthesis of East and West." It should therefore be allowed slots of airtime in the electronic media that are akin to this status:

> The [music] editors fight against the *zemer mizraḥi* [Oriental song], they are afraid of it. They know that the moment they will give the right of speech to this song, there will not be space for their thing. . . . Because our music is the Eretz Israeli [music]. . . . The media still does not broadcast consensus. It is the media of the establishment, people that work on behalf [of the establishment]. They do not reflect the existing reality. . . . They created ghettos to play our music. . . . In my opinion the [music] editors and disk jockeys in these stations should be thrown out. . . . They betrayed the public's trust.[8]

The campaign against the alleged media discrimination led to the establishment of "Azyt," a non-profit organization dedicated to promoting the interests of musiqa mizraḥit. From its inception, this organization adopted the Mediterranean label as its presentation card: "Azyt" is a Hebrew acronym that stands for *Amutat ha-zemer ha-yam tikhoni*, "The Mediterranean Song Association." In support of its claims, Azyt recruited statistical research prepared by academics. Academic research "proved" the conspiracy against musiqa mizraḥit with facts. Moreover, scholar Ayelet Ben-Zvi warned that

> when [musiqa mizraḥit] is removed from the consensus [e.g., by not broadcasting musiqa mizraḥit songs in the prime time programs], Israelis are stripped of their mizraḥiyut ["Easternness"] and the *mizraḥim* from their Israeliness.[9]

Azyt succeeded in creating public debates on the issue of discrimination of musiqa mizraḥit/musiqa yam tikhonit and even a parliamentary intervention on this issue. The committee for education of the Knesset debated Azyt's grievances in 1997, in a meeting in which the director general of the Israel Broadcasting Authority and the head of the state radio stations participated. Politicians expressed their sympathy for the arguments of Azyt. However, they politely avoided the issue by not taking any specific measures except for vague recommendations to the Israel Broadcasting Authority.

The "Mediterraneanization" of musiqa mizrahit is thoroughly linked to its growing "Israelization" and "rockization," as exemplified by the songs of the most popular Mizrahi singers of the late 1990s and early 2000s, Eyal Golan, Sarit Hadad, and Amir Benayun. These songs are successful crossovers of Mizrahi and mainstream Western pop styles (e.g., disco). The cultural "cost" of this success however has been, besides the watering down of the Mizrahi sound, a dilution of the sense of identity that had long been associated with it. Musicians who refused to melt down classic musiqa mizrahit in favor of a softer "Mediterranean" sound and continued to produce in the late 1990s musiqa mizrahit in the style of the 1980s, paid with the persistence of marginality, inferiority, and labeling as non-mainstream Israeli.

This split between the *yam tikhoni* (Mediterranean) and hardcore mizrahi (Oriental) labels in relation to the same genre reflects the ambivalence of Israeli Mizrahiyut in general. The "story" of musiqa mizrahit can be read in terms of "resistance" and "subversion." Using neo-Gramscian subcultural theory, it could be argued that musiqa mizrahit is in fact the authentic and rebellious expression of mizrahiyut against its marginalization and inferiority within Israeli culture. In accordance, the success and "crossover" of musicians such as Golan and Hadad under the label of Mediterranean can be interpreted as the appropriation of musiqa mizrahit by dominant Israeliness and its accommodation to the patterns and interests of mainstream Israeli popular music, that is, Israeli rock. In other words, this would be a reading of Golan's and Hadad's success as a "failure" of the original subversive aim of musiqa mizrahit.

Given the essential commitment of musiqa mizrahit artists and producers to national Israeli culture, however, the general "Mediterranization" of popular music in Israel, could be interpreted as a goal achieved. That is, musiqa mizrahit speakers have persistently argued that their music is Israeli, and that their interest is to be recognized as legitimate and authentic. With musiqa mizrahit turned into Mizrahi/yam tikhoni placed at center stage of Israeli popular music, with rock and pop musicians influenced by the Mediterranean sounds of musiqa mizraḥit, and with Mizraḥi/yam tikhoni musicians such as Avihu Medina and Zohar Argov canonized as "all-Israeli," one could hardly interpret the situation as a cultural failure. The nationalist impetus underlining musiqa mizraḥit has achieved its own self-declared goal of bringing musiqa mizraḥit, under the disguise of Mediterranean music, into the mainstream of Israeli popular music and of Mediterraneanizing the sound of popular music in Israel.

Militant "new journalists" perceive this wide public recognition of musiqa mizraḥit and its embrace by the media as a threat to its primordial authenticity. Because the cultural hegemony in Israel is Western oriented, musiqa mizraḥit has to retain, according to these critics, its oppositional status. Rock journalists became concerned with the success of musiqa mizraḥit to appeal to wide audiences under the Mediterranean label. A review of *Ha-ossef ha-yam tikhoni* ("The Mediterranean Collection"), a four-CD pack edited by Shimon Parnas, the chief exponent of musiqa mizraḥit/yam tikhonit on Israeli radio and TV, asks rhetorically, "Is the culture war [between mainstream rock and musiqa mizraḥit/yam tikhonit] of Israeli pop behind us?" The reviewer responds:

Whoever did not pass through the old Central Bus Station of Tel Aviv in the '60s, '70s or '80s, will find in this collection a fine introduction to the different trends and faces of this music, that was called with names such as musiqa mizraḥit and *musiqat qassetot* [cassette music] before it earned its present name, musiqa yam-tikhonit [Mediterranean music]. . . .

Musically, the songs represent well the yearning of most of the creators of musiqa yam-tikhonit to find for themselves a good place in the middle. The history of the musiqa yam-tikhonit in Israel is a short history of anger and offense, of longing for legitimacy and of the will to create a bond with the centers of power of the popular culture and of the Israeli society at large. The continuous coupling of "starts sing in couples" has a proper symbolic meaning: the songs reflect the will to connect, to contribute, to merge.

All this is very nice and harmonic, of course, but for the sake of the coming generations it is worthwhile to remember that in less commercial circumstances, it could be possible to make another anthology. The spirit of fraternity that invades this record cannot conceal neither the critical relations between some of the participants in the anthology, nor that which is not included in it.

The connection between rock and musiqa mizraḥit—one of the fascinating connections of the local pop—is almost not documented. . . . Also within the yam tikhoni [Mediterranean] genre itself there is perhaps room for wonder. In an era of natural longing for unity, there is something natural in the will to locate "Yeladim zeh simḥah" by Ha-brera ha-tiv'it between "Ani Gedaliah" by Natan Alterman and Moshe Vilenski and "Ha-peraḥ be-ganni" performed by Zohar Argov.

However, it seems that the tension between these songs is more interesting than their relations. They are collected here one after the other, but the split seconds that separate them conceal emotional dramas, social tensions and musical experiments that well reflect such dramas and tensions.[10]

These recent approaches to musiqa mizraḥit reveal yet another paradox. While celebrating what appears to be the final acceptance of musiqa mizraḥit as a legitimate expression of Mediterranean Israeliness, there is also a sense of a loss of authenticity. Mediterraneanism signifies in this context the concessions made by Mizraḥi artists to accommodate the technological and aesthetic demands of the Western-oriented popular music industry of Israel.

Conclusion

The Mediterranean topos is a constant feature in the Israeli discourse about music since the 1940s. Appearing first as an option between East and West or as a set of particular musical traits identified as characteristic "Oriental" music, all forms of musical Mediterraneanism in Israel can eventually be read as an escape route from the Middle Eastern predicament of the Israeli condition. Caught in the center of the Arab world and with a sizable part of its Jewish population originating in Arab countries or being itself Palestinian Arab, the Western-orientated Israeli culture is constantly faced with the challenges posed by its Arab surroundings. From this perspective, musical Mediterraneanism in its different forms was always a strategy to avoid full-fledged Arabness while at the same time developing a sense of belonging to the large Eastern Mediterranean cultural area.

The most modern form of Israeli musical Mediterraneanism, that is, the one represented by the recent transformations of musiqa mizraḥit, appears to be the most meaningful one. Born of the inherent desire of musiqa mizraḥit artists to become the mainstream of Israeliness, this Mediterraneanism, unlike all previous forms in art and folk music, appeals to the largest constituency within Israeli society. This "success" can be sensed in the growing gray-out between "mainstream" and "Mediterranean" Israeli pop found in the daily usage of these two terms. For example, the Israeli pop songs included in the in-flight radio program of El Al, Israel's national airline, are divided into two categories: *zemer yam tikhoni* and *pop yisraeli*, "Mediterranean song" and "Israeli pop."[11] The first category includes of course the hits of the Mizraḥi singers Eyal Golan and Sarit Hadad, both of whom are considered nowadays mainstream Israeli standards. Yet, included under the same category are the songs "'Aïcha" by the Algerian *raï* star Khaled and "Tip tipa" by the Israeli rock star Ehud Banai. On the other hand, the song "Oriana" by the renowned mizraḥi/yam tikhoni singer Avi Peretz is included in the "Israeli pop" category. The residual perception of Mediterraneanism as being "the other" in the Israeli discourse about music is concealed in the translation of zemer yam tikhoni in the English section of the same El Al in-flight program: "Ethnic Israeli Music."

Notes

1. See the discussion of this issue in Bohlman 1993.

2. Haim Arlozoroff, *Writings*. Vol. 6, Tel Aviv 1934, 177–178. Translated and quoted in Shavit 1988: 111.

3. The introduction to Levy 1959 is a key text on this regard.

4. See similar remarks by Mishori quoted in Fleisher 1997: 51.

5. For Zefira, see Flam 1986; Hirshberg 1984.

6. For this interval as an icon of traditional Eastern European Jewish music, see Slobin 1980.

7. The basic ideas presented in this section of the article are developed in detail in Regev and Seroussi, forthcoming, chapters 9 and 10.

8. Shimon Ifargan, "50 shanah le-Medina," *Kol ha-darom*, August 28, 1998.

9. Ayelet Ben-Zvi, quoted by Rami Hazut and Tamar Trabelsi-Hadad, "Nevadeh sheha-musiqa ha-mizraḥit tushma' yoter ba-radio," *Yedioth Ahronoth*, November 25, 1997 ("We shall verify that musiqa mizraḥit will be heard more in the radio").

10. Gidi Avivi, "Mitga'age'im la-beyaḥad," *Ha'aretz*, April 23, 1997 ("Yearning for integration").

11. See the music program in El Al's journal *Atmosphere* of October 1999.

Bibliography

Bahloul, Joëlle. 1994. "The Sephardic Jew as Mediterranean: A View from Kinship and Gender," *Journal of Mediterranean Studies* 4/2: 197–207.

Bohlman, Philip. 1989. "The Land Where Two Streams Flow." *Music in the German-Jewish Community of Israel.* Urbana and Chicago: University of Illinois Press.

——. 1993. "La riscoperta del Mediterraneo nella musica ebraica: Il discorso dell'altro' nell'etnomusicologia dell'Europa," in *Antropologia della musica e culture mediterranee,* edited by Tullia Magrini. Bologna, Italy: Il Mulino. 107–124.

——. 2000. "East-West: The Ancient Modernity of Jewish Music," *East European Meetings in Ethnomusicology* 7: 67–90.

Boskovitch, Alexander U.. 1953. "The Problem of Jewish Music," *Orlogin* 9: 28–93 (in Hebrew).

Bressler, Liora. 1985. "The Mediterranean Style in Israeli Music," *Cathedra* 38: 136–161 (in Hebrew).

Brod, Max. 1951. *Israeli Music.* Tel Aviv: Sefer Press Ltd. (published separately in English and German).

Cohen, Eric and Amnon Shiloah. 1985. "Major Trends of Change in Jewish Oriental Ethnic Music," *Popular Music* 5: 199–223.

Elbaz, Shlomo. 1994. "Israel, les Juifs et la Méditerranée ou: Une identité culturelle à Califourchon," *Journal of Mediterranean Studies* 4/2: 170–182.

Flam, Gila. 1986. "Beracha Zefira—a case study of acculturation in Israeli song," *Asian Music* 17: 108–125.

Fleisher, Robert. 1997. *Twenty Israeli Composers: Voices of a Culture.* Detroit: Wayne State University Press.

Gradenwitz, Peter. 1978 [1951, 1959]. *Music and Musicians in Israel.* Tel Aviv: Israeli Music Publications Ltd. (third edition, revised, rewritten, and enlarged).

Halper, Jeff, Edwin Seroussi and Pamela Squires-Kidron. 1989. "*Musiqa mizraḥit:* Ethnicity and Class Culture in Israel," *Popular Music* 8/2: 131–141.

——. 1992. "*Musiqa mizraḥit* and the Realignment of Israeli Society: The Case of Hayyim Moshe," in *1789–1989 Musique, Historie, Democratie.* Antoine Hennion, ed. Paris: Editións de la Maison des Sciences de l'Homme. 3 vols. III, 669–672.

Hirshberg, Jehoash. 1984. "Bracha Zefira and the Process of Change in Israeli Music," *Pe'amim* 19: 29–46 (in Hebrew).

——. 1993. "Alexander U. Boskovitch and the Quest for an Israeli National Style," in *Modern Jews and their Musical Agendas,* edited by Ezra Mendelsohn. New York: Oxford University Press. 92–109.

——. 1995. *Music in the Jewish Community of Palestine.* Oxford: Oxford University Press.

Horowitz, Amy. 1994. *Musika Yam Tikhonit Yisraelit [Israeli Mediterranean Music]: Cultural Boundaries and Disputed Territories.* Ph. Diss. University of Pennsylvania.

——. 1997. "Performance in Disputed Territory: Israeli Mediterranean Music," *Musical Performance* 1/3: 43–53.

Levy, Isaac. 1959. *Chants Judéo-Espagnols.* London: The World Sephardi Federation, vol. 1.

Modena Terracini, Sara. 1999. "The 1995 Euro-Mediterranean Association

Agreement between Israel and the EU," in *Towards a New European Ius Commune*, edited by A. Gambaro and A.M. Rabello. Jerusalem: The Harry and Michael Sacher Institute for Legislative Research and Law. 699-704.

Regev, Motti and Edwin Seroussi. [Forthcoming.] *Popular Music and National Culture in Israel*. University of California Press.

Schroeter, Daniel J. 1994. "Orientalism and the Jews of the Mediterranean," *Journal of Mediterranean Studies* 4/2: 183-196.

Seroussi, Edwin. 1995. "Reconstructing Sephardi Music in the 20th Century: Isaac Levy and his *Chants judéo-espagnols*," *The World of Music (Jewish Musical Culture—Past and Present)* 37/1: 39-58.

Shavit, Yaacov. 1988. "The Mediterranean World and 'Mediterraneanism': The Origins, Meaning, and Application of a Geo-Cultural Notion in Israel," *Mediterranean Historical Review* 3/2: 96-117.

——. 1994. "Mediterranean History and the History of the Mediterranean: Further Reflections," *Journal of Mediterranean Studies* 4/2: 313-329.

Slobin, Mark. 1980. "The Evolution of a Musical Symbol in Yiddish Culture," in *Studies in Jewish Folklore*, edited by F. Talmage. Cambridge, MA: The Association of Jewish Studies. 313-330.

Zerubavel, Yael. 1994. *Recovered Roots: Collective Memory and the Making of Israeli National Tradition*. Chicago: Chicago University Press.

Discography

Israeli Mediterranean art music
Pnina Salzman plays Mediterranean Piano Music. Helicon M11-CD19. 1996.

Musiqa mizraḥit: Artists
Zohar Argov Greatest Hits. 3 vols. Reuveni Brothers CDR 009, 0010, 0011. 1988.
Chaim Moshe Greatest Hits. 3 vols. Reuveni Brothers CDR 001, 002, 037. 1988.

Musiqa mizraḥit: Collections
Ḥalom yam tikhoni (Mediterranean Dream). 3 vols. B.M. Records CD B.M. 1190, 1191, 1192. 1992.
Chafla—Oriental Hits. Hataklit CD 136. 1991.

New Mediterranean music and rock crossovers
Ethnix—Golan, Eyal. *Ethnix ve-Eyal Golan, ha-mofa' ha-meshutaf* (The Joint Concert). Ben Zur Productions CD 00401. 2000.
Golan, Eyal. *Ḥayyal shel ahavah* (Eyal Golan: Soldier of Love). Ben Zur Productions BPS 0782. 1998.
Ḥadad, Sarit. *Kmo Cindarella* (Like Cinderella). Avi Guetta Productions, no matrix number. N.d.

C H A P T E R E I G H T

CROSSING THE BOUNDARIES: THE AKDENIZ SCENE AND MEDITERRANEANNESS

YETKIN ÖZER

Globalization hand in hand with Westernization is a catch-all term to which a number of issues in the study of local cultures and their dissemination are addressed. The latter is related to one-directional borrowings, from the West, by the non-West, while the former refers to a complex of exchanges that increasingly occur among various cultures around the world, though most exchanges concerned are still discussed on the axis of Western and non-Western dichotomy, or, "ours" and "theirs." Both terms have become self-defeating in the short run, due to the ambiguity of whether they reflect the imagination of the observer or the orientation of the people studied. Many observers once thought that Westernization would erase local cultures, but this has not come true. Now the worry is back with the advent of the globalization debate, though neither will it seemingly result in the stereotyped "one world, one culture," or "cultural cloning" (Zwingle 1999: 12). Such unpredicted consequences raise the need for these concepts to be elaborated for case studies where they have a clear import. Both denote a general framework, but are not sufficient to fully explain particular cases. Even the concept of Europe itself, as the origin of West, and its ramifications is far from being neatly concluded, as pointed out by Macdonald in her definition of "Western Europe" (1993: 2–3).

This chapter is about the *Akdeniz*, the "Mediterranean music," as a "scene" within Turkish popular music. But the topic permits, at the outset, a broader consideration on how a Mediterranean perspective may contribute to examine the coupling of globalization and Westernization, so that Mediterranean music can be studied properly out of that paradigm. The cultures in the Mediterranean rim have been attached to either side of Western and non-Western dichotomy, despite the fact that those cultures of the West and the non-West have been interacting in this region since well before the concept of Westernization came into play in social studies. The case suggests then that not all the cultural borrowings in the area, from the West by the non-West, can be easily explained through Westernization, and that these borrowings should not remark only on the exclusiveness of the cultures involved, but also the interdependence among them. The lack of such a perspective would lead us to disregard the potential of Western influence within the non-Western, or vice versa, in the Mediterranean, which may not necessarily be related to Westernization as an ideology.

Turkey epitomizes the interaction and exclusiveness of this dichotomy when addressing the cultural roots of its society. While Central Asia is emphasized as the origin of the Turks on one hand, ancient civilizations of the land still provide a source for many components of modern Turkish culture on the other, and these civilizations are presumably related to the roots of Western cultures. Anatolia, the Asian part of the land, is regarded as "the cradle of civilizations and cultures" among the elite who appreciate the multicultural heritage of the country. The duality that people experience provokes a controversy about the sense of belonging, but, it also implies the capacity of the people to interact with different cultures, closer or farther, Western or non-Western, as a source of formulating, or regulating, their own lives.

In general, the difference today is that, thanks to the improvements in communication, cultural exchanges increasingly become ever further reaching, and allow people to cross the confinement of acculturation within their vicinities. The inexact term "global" then may contribute to understanding musical changes world-wide, when it denotes the increase in contact among cultures, even distant ones, rather than a new category of cultural objects in comparison to those on the local level. The increase gives rise to both creating and disseminating multi-locality, but does not result in a "global style" in music; nonetheless I acknowledge the fact that there is a large corpus of pop music distributed globally. The nature of the relationship between the local and the global suggests a focus on processes, instead of objects, in the study of the movement of influences, in which not only globalization of the local, but also localization of the global is considered. The term process here refers to "the way in which moving objects and people are identified, assimilated, marginalized or rejected" (Friedman 1994: 1), and therefore, local and global do not generate two opposing arguments, but two fundamental and interdependent components of what goes on around the world.

With reference to music, the global, whether accepted or rejected by the local (and/or vice versa), generates some kind of global awareness in which musicians position themselves and formulate their own musics. I would argue then that both local and global processes, and the dialogue between them, find expression in music through stylistic and discursive features, the components of the concept of musicianly strategy. Process, in this respect, becomes an analytical concept that allows one to inquire "how": How do musicians relate their own music to their awareness of each other? How are extramusical processes (both global and local) translated into musical behaviors and articulated in one's own music? The following historical excerpt profiles Turkish popular music in relation to such processes, both local and global, to extend our understanding of it beyond the scope that Westernization could draw.

The Government's Project for Westernization and Rock 'n' Roll in Turkey

Although the putative relationship between musicianly strategies and governmental policies in many cases is not harmonious, the Turkish elite asserts otherwise. It is commonly presumed that the governmental project for westernization has also provided a ground for the advent of Western pop (including rock 'n' roll) in Turkey, and that the growth of popular music in Turkey is a concomitant result of this project.[1] However, the government's actions have not been completely irrelevant; Westernization was initiated by the government in the 1920s for reformation, but the approach has not produced results among musicians, because music-related parts of the project did not include any explicit, or even implicit, concern for popular music. Nor were those musicians who took part in the project involved in popular music. The project was strictly modeled on the "serious" music of Europe, or more precisely, of the Continent with a special interest in French impressionism and national schools in Eastern European countries. While it posed a channel through which Westernization has developed under control of the government, a historical overview illustrates that there were other processes to which popular music has been related in one way or another.

For instance, rock 'n' roll came into play in Istanbul during the late 1950s. At this time, Italian and French popular tunes, alongside tango and jazz, were enjoying popularity in the entertainment life of the upper class, but were not favored by the growing youth culture that cannot be thought of in isolation from the youth movement around the world, carrying no remarkable class or ethnic boundaries. "At the time," says Erol Büyükburç, the most prominent rock 'n' roll musician in the '50s, who even wrote songs in English, "the criteria through which youngsters viewed the world were quite different. There was a mosaic in Istanbul, with Armenians, Jews, Greeks, Turks and so on, building up Istanbul identity. It [his songs in English] was an adventure very much suited to that identity" (İdemen and Erol 2000: 58). Though not indicated specifically, English seems to have been used for its power to bring those communities together, as not belonging to any of them. Indeed, rock 'n' roll remained mainly within the "Istanbul identity" and did not find much response in other cities, so that, for his concert tours to cities in inner Anatolia, and later for his albums, Büyükburç included some folk tunes in his repertoire as well. Erol Büyükburç, named the "Turkish Elvis," led the rock 'n' roll movement through the late '60s, when the youth culture in Turkey turned its interest to local processes. Curiously enough, no other music idols of the time other than Elvis Presley were locally reproduced in Turkey.

Anatolian Pop and Rock

The rock 'n' roll movement of the '50s has resulted in syncretic forms of the Anatolian rock and pop, with the use of local music elements within rock and pop idioms in the late '60's in relation to two overlapping local processes. While the political climate among the youth against "Western imperialism" identified itself with the lower classes through the use of folk music in Western idioms, massive internal migration from rural to urban areas has permeated folk music into urban life more intensely than ever. The movement was also contemporary with the growing popularity of folk music around the world.

During the latter half of twentieth century, urban centers in the western part of Turkey—like Istanbul, Ankara, and Izmir—have witnessed great influxes from rural areas in Eastern Anatolia, mainly due to economic difficulties. The role of such difficulties in internal migration found its expression in a saying popular in Istanbul in the '60s and the '70s: "Stones and soil in Istanbul are golden" (*Istanbul'un taşı toprağı altın*). Even though rural to urban migration was considered successful from an economic point of view, for providing industry with cheap labor, and was suggested as a model for urbanization of rural people, it was certainly not only manpower but also culture that migrated to urban centers; and this unpredicted consequence created a striking conflict between migrants and city-dwellers. This conflict inspired film producers immediately to include among the themes for musical films desperate loves of dolorous migrants with high-class urbanites. While migrant musicians were involved in a search for adapting their music to the new environment on one hand, which resulted in popularized forms of folk music, many urban musicians have drawn on folk sources, which led to Anatolian rock and pop. Political pop and protest music have also developed in the same manner.

The growing interest in creating a national pop and rock found support in the *Hürriyet*, one of the most popular newspapers, that annually organized the song contest *Altın Mikrofon* (Golden Microphone), from 1965 to 1968. Dedicated to promoting music combining traditional tunes with pop and rock sounds, the contest has motivated not only those in search of new styles, but also band music and professional musicianship. Finalists having passed the first election by the committee were given the opportunity to perform on a tour of towns in inner Anatolia, and the audience voted for the winners. The organization has also sponsored the production of records by the winners, leaving the benefits to musicians. Many young musicians were inspired by the contest to start making music professionally. Note that it was folk music that musicians mainly focused on in this movement, although the organization was also intended to promote the use of Turkish classical music elements as well, by indicating "traditional tunes" under requirements.

The movement went into oblivion in the '80s when the political intensity dispersed after the military coup (1980). However the use of folk music in both idioms still occupies a large part of local music production but no longer under the rubric of "Anatolia." Rock songs using folk music elements are called "Turkish rock" today, giving a more nationalistic image of it. The '80s have also witnessed a shift in pop music toward the *arabesk*, which for many turned out to be an "entertainment form" lacking the values in Anatolian pop. Percussion was heavily emphasized in a way that stimulated the audience to participate actively with bodily movements, or dance, accompanying a vocal line that tended to be more "Oriental." The "pop-*arabesk*" was associated with "depoliticization."

Turkish Music and the Mediterranean

Music in Turkey, at least the western part of it, has been interwined with other Mediterranean musical cultures in many ways. Historical accounts show that Istanbul has been a center where musicians of different origins, including Greek, have come together to produce what is called "Turkish classical music" or "art music" in the twentieth century. The *rembetika*, the most popular genre of Greek music, is assumed today to have originated in the city of Izmir, Western Turkey, in the 1920s. Dario Moreno, a famous singer in Europe of the '50s was a native of Izmir, born a member of the Sephardic Jewish community. He started his career in Izmir with a repertoire of Italian and Spanish popular songs and left for Paris in the '50s. This is not surprising when considering that a large population of Greek, Italian, French, and Jewish communities existed mainly in the western part of Turkey until the '60s. Neither was it coincidence that the *aranjman*, French pronunciation for "arrangement," has mostly been nourished from French and Italian pop; the term was coined to describe the performance of borrowed Western pop songs with lyrics in Turkish, that may therefore be the most evident imitation of Western pop. Songs performed by singers like Mina, Enrico Macias, and Georges Moustaki became popular in

Turkey through records of the local aranjman singers, although many other pop singers like Adriano Celentano, Dalida, Gilbert Becaud, Jacques Brel, Charles Aznavour, and Demis Roussos have become known to the Turkish audience through their records as well. Note that Anglo-American pop did not occupy a considerable part in the aranjman practice, with some exceptions, like a Turkish version of "Strangers in the Night", presumably the first aranjman production.

Aranjman has provoked some nationalistic attempts to create an "indigenous Turkish pop" and dispel foreign material. Many pop music albums still include these songs, but an entire album of aranjman is no longer found in the music market since the late '80s, nor are such items perceived by the audience as aranjman. Accordingly, French and Italian pop tunes have almost disappeared under the overwhelming impact of globally distributed Anglo-American pop.

The influence of Egyptian popular music on Turkish classical music provides an example of the interaction of Turkish music with another Mediterranean culture. When film importation from Europe came to an end due to World War II, the Turkish film industry turned to the Egyptian market for European films, which inevitably brought in Egyptian films as well. The success of the first Egyptian film in Istanbul, *Tears of Love* (1938), featuring famous singer 'Abd-al Wahhab, was enormous. Concerned with the diffusion of this "Westernized" film, the government prohibited performance of the film's songs in Arabic, so the song "Tears of Love" was made available on record by a Turkish singer. The restriction was extended to the import of Egyptian films in 1948, when the Turkish film industry had begun to produce musical films bearing the heavy influence of Egyptian examples. Following their Egyptian colleagues in the film-music business, Turkish musicians recognized the demand for a popularized art music, abandoning traditional forms and performance styles (using only a few instruments), and attempted to establish larger ensembles, consisting of both vocal and instrumental groups. Numerous songs and background music were produced to be performed by such groups. Based on the idea that traditional ensembles were not sufficient to convey sentimentalism in musical films, new instruments like cello and piano were added, and violins were increased up to even twenty. The vocal form şarkı[2] has become the most popular form among contemporary composers, and, with an excessive sentimentalism, unique for the popularization of art music. Soon after, came the stardom of singers like Münir Nurettin Selçuk and Zeki Müren, again following in the footsteps of Arab stars like Umm Kulthum and Mohammad 'Abd-al Wahhab.

Musical films enjoyed a central place during and after what is called the "transition period" in the history of Turkish cinema (1939–45). A Turkish composer, Saadettin Kaynak, also wrote a number of scores for Egyptian musical films. Kaynak and his successors have been criticized by the elite, because their work resulted in the arabesk, the favorite form in popular music. The value of this music has been hotly debated because of the "inferiority" of its aesthetic and expressive quality as well as its social meanings, since its emergence in the 1970s. (For an extensive study of the arabesk, see Stokes 1992). Although it would be simplistic to define the arabesk only in relation to the influence of Egyptian music, an orchestra with a large group of strings has been used most prominently in the arabesk, along with the use of a multi-part score and orchestration. Large ensembles with multiple traditional instruments such as qanun, nay, 'ud, and the like, in addition to choir and strings, were later adopted as a model for government-operated performance organizations. Considering such aspects as number of performers taking part, dressing, conducting, performance regularity, and so forth, these ensembles resemble symphonic orchestras, and their wide-ranging repertoire includes historical items as well as the popular songs of the day.

This overview implies a discrepancy between the existence of historical links between Turkish music and other Mediterranean musics, and the absence of an awareness of it in musical discourse. The perspective drawn from the ideology of nation-building process in the republican era has overemphasized the "Turkishness" of the classical music in such a way that musicians of the Greek community as well as others were regarded later solely as "contributors." In the literature, there has been a considerable effort to demonstrate that Turkish music has not flourished upon the "remnants" of Byzantine music, and, on the contrary, made a great impact on Greek music throughout history. Due to the nationalism embedded in this perspective, music scholars have failed to study Turkish music in the context of other

Mediterranean cultures, nor was the existence of Western music treated by Turkish musicologists, beyond the axis of Western/non-Western.

The Akdeniz as a Scene

The Mediterraneanness has been initiated through the Akdeniz scene in Turkish popular music. The term "scene" as defined by Keith Harris "connotes a more flexible, loose kind of space within which music is produced; a kind of 'context' for musical practice" (Harris 2000: 14). He also points out that "no musical practice can take place entirely separately from social process" (ibid: 25). Flexibility of the concept allows us to avoid a distinct but unworkable definition, as has been with the case with "subculture." I refer to the "scene" in my analysis, because the Akdeniz practice suits the concept by being both interrelated with social processes and so flexible that it does not serve as a symbolic representation of a particular social group. Nor can it be regarded merely as a sonic structure.

The word Akdeniz, the Turkish term for the Mediterranean Sea, literally meaning "white sea," has gained a musical sense through the second album of the band Yeni Türkü (*Akdeniz Akdeniz*, 1983), whose first album, *Buğdayın Türküsü* (The Song of Wheat), was released in 1979. A comparison between the two reflects the impact of the military coup (1980) on their music. The first album was based on two sources, each associated with a particular instrument: Turkish folk music with the *bağlama*, the most popular folk instrument, and, Latin American political pop using recorder. The album also embodies the typical dilemma of musicians regarding what to emphasize in music, political commitment or musical taste. Derya Köroğlu, the leader of Yeni Türkü, experienced the dilemma when their first album was released:

I was involved in the political movement of the time as a member of the Students' Association at the University, but I have never put politics in the first place during my musical career. However, our first album included songs with a strong political content. The protest music of the time in Turkey had a pessimistic mode with slow rhythms and simplistic, mostly syllabic melodies, and, was "against'" something. In my music, however, I have never tried to be against anything, but instead, to unify people in music. Therefore, rather than Turkish protest music, I was very much

The band Yeni Türkü in 1990.

attracted by Latin American political pop, and notably music of the band Inti Illimani, which seemed to me more vivid and captivating. (Personal communication, January 2001)

Both local and global processes in the following decade encouraged the Yeni Türkü to further their search for "musical taste." After the military coup, the youth culture underwent drastic changes. As the revolutionary movement disappeared and solidarity among the "privates" of the movement was replaced by individualism, the Yeni Türkü turned in their album *Akdeniz Akdeniz* toward songs with more "musical taste" and less political content, questioning the self and comparing the before to the after. Such a substantial change was not only due to the military coup, but also related to ideological transformation around the world, in the words of Derya Köroğlu:

The '80s signaled that the world would no longer be the same as before, so we as musicians ought to correspond with the process. You could no longer just pick up a folk tune and sing politically loaded lyrics to the audience who were aware that things were changing in the socialist world. That is, you might have been defeated militarily. But, if the ideology just disappears, there must be something wrong with the ideology.

Note that all the albums but *Buğdayın Türküsü* were reproduced on CD with the advent of that technology in Turkey.

The Akdeniz scene emerged out of a reaction to "entertainment music" or "commercial music," which was associated with depoliticization after the military coup. It has shared with some other Turkish pop styles a meticulous concern with poetic values and/or political content in lyrics as opposed to the textual volatility and superficiality in mainstream pop. Many of these musicians employed works by well-known poets, including e.e. cummings, Nazım Hikmet, and so on, or even commissioned lyrics from contemporary poets, as Yeni Türkü did notably with Murathan Mungan[3].

Compared to many other productions of the time, the album *Akdeniz Akdeniz* was unique in including Greek musical elements. This was related to the dilemma of political commitment and musical taste, because they referred particularly to the music of Greek composer Manos Laizos, who seemed to have formulated a way out of the dilemma by being both a member of the Communist Party in Greece and a composer writing vivid and attractive music. *Akdeniz Akdeniz* included two of his songs, with lyrics by Murathan Mungan, and featured instruments like the bouzouki, the qanun, the *kemençe* (known as *lyra* in Greek music), and the accordion which were common in Greece and Turkey. The overall sound was not typically Greek or Turkish, but, according to Derya Köroğlu, "an abstraction of both on a ground provided by western idioms," and was also a musical representation of his definition of Mediterranean character: "Mediterranean people are those who express even their sorrow fervently" (personal communication, January 2001). The sound and the political background together have helped the band enlarge their audience throughout the decade, maintaining the Akdeniz music in many of their successive eight albums.

Yeni Türkü was joined by Gündoğarken (literally, The Day Dawning) in 1985 with the release of their first album *Bir Yaz Daha Bitiyor* (A Summer Ends), sharing its attitude concerning lyrics and the use of Greek musical elements in their own production, but differing as well in the rhetoric of Mediterraneanness in sound. Unlike Yeni Türkü, Gündoğarken does not espouse political engagement in their musical career. İlhan Şeşen, the leader and uncle of the two other members, had been a professional musician since the early '70s and established Gündoğarken by performing at pubs and clubs in Istanbul as well as in the Mediterranean provinces of Anatolia. The idea of producing an album occurred later, through the encouragement of the community in Bodrum (Halicarnassus), where they performed almost every summer.

Mediterraneanness serves as a means for Gündoğarken both to differentiate their own music from mainstream pop and to avoid the prevailing character of Turkish society, which they believe are overlapping. The group's leader explained his idea of Mediterraneanness in a published interview:

> Since Turks are mostly men of the soil, we have nothing to do with the sea. It is a pity. This is so obvious that we poured everything into sea . . . For some reason we dumped waste and everything into it . . . I never see myself as part of a nation. That I live in this territory does not mean I accept the culture here. In fact, everything begins with rejection. Perhaps, we started everything with rejection. (Bengi 1999: 20)

I observed that Gündoğarken's comparison between their own music and mainstream Turkish pop has resulted in their music being identified with marine culture and the mainstream pop with land culture (personal communication, January 2001). Although such a comparison may give an impression of what the Akdeniz is within Turkish popular music, defining it in reference to Mediterranean music(s) seems to be challenging, because musicians use the term as a general framing device for, rather than the denomination of, what they musically do. They dwelt on the difficulties in calling their music "Mediterranean," referring to the fact that the rim comprehends a large variety of musical cultures. Even the bouzouki does not directly address Greek music, because they do not consider their use of the instrument similar to the authentic playing technique of the instrument. Employing Western popular music forms and instruments, members of both bands and some other musicians agree that the Akdeniz music is related to the European part of the Mediterranean, acknowledging however that the label "Western" is not sufficient to define the diversity there.

This example suggests that the term "Akdeniz" does not depict traits of a musical style, but instead forms a context for particular ways of music making. Cengiz Onural, a former member of Yeni Türkü, pointed out that Akdeniz was introduced at the time when the military coup caused a political void among the left wing, and when there was a renewed interest in ethnic identities, by which Turkish popular music was heavily affected (personal communication, January 2001). Akdeniz was almost the most significant alternative to popular music with ethnic reference. The Akdeniz scene still survives in Turkish popular music, represented primarily by these bands, while the term Akdeniz has a wider variety of uses in Turkish popular music.

Musical Analysis

Even though it would be misleading to relate Akdeniz as a sonic structure to Mediterranean cultures, sound is undoubtedly related to the rhetoric of the scene in various aspects. Coming from different backgrounds and experiencing different processes, these bands have developed diverse approaches to Akdeniz. Comparing them to broader Turkish popular music can be a key to understanding a number of musical differences between them. Derya Köroğlu's tendency to choose "musical taste" over political message, for instance, establishes his basic argument together with his description of Akdeniz people. "Fervent expression of sorrow" is embedded in Yeni Türkü's music through the use of wide-ranged scales (usually divided into high and low parts), leaping notes, sudden changes in dynamics, and pounding rhythm. The track "Sorma Bana" (Don't Ask Me) in *Akdeniz Akdeniz* embodies the relation of such traits to the rhetoric. The text conveys individualism and the self-questioning tendency widespread among the left-wing supporters of the time, and thus one would expect this piece to be tranquil, or better, in a grave mode, according to the norms of political pop in the '70s (see Appendix A, pp. 218–219, for a translation of the full text).

Sor - ma - ba - na ki - mim   ner-den gel·dim bu·ra - ya

The first line of the song "Sorma Bana"
(from Yeni Türkü's album *Akdeniz Akdeniz*)

The piece however is in 5/8 rhythm and a vivid tempo. Frequent use of wide steps within a melodic unit is also peculiar to the Yeni Türkü.

Gündoğarken, on the other hand, deliberately avoids the use of such features as asymmetrical rhythms, because they are assumed to belong to traditional and ethnic cultures of Turkey. Furthermore, those who deal with the sea are, they believe, mild-tempered, peaceful, and modest, unlike the men of the soil, with their rigid and contentious character. On this distinction, their music is constructed with plain, unaccented, regular rhythms, and with melodies of narrow steps and ranges. (However, their earlier albums included more wide-ranging melodies.) All three members of the band have pointed to the song "Wind" as an example of what they musically mean by the Akdeniz (see Appendix B, p. 219, for a translation of the full text).

Pen - ce-re- min   per - de- se- ni   ha - va-lan - di-ran   rüz - gar

The first line of "Wind"
(from the Gündoğarken's album *Mest of Gündoğarken*)

The way the band relates to Greek music is also unique in the sense that they use the bouzouki as one of the main instruments and have had Greek singers performing on some of the tracks in the last two albums, but they have never performed original Greek songs themselves. Their collaboration with Nikiforos Metaxas as arranger and producer resulted in the album *Istanbul Atina Istanbul* (2000), which was recorded in Athens and produced in Istanbul. But even this album included only songs by the members of the Gündoğarken. Although the lyrics deal mainly with affection and love, the album *Mest* [sic] *of*

Gündoğarken is remarkable for including words like sea, waves, sky, clouds, wind, summer, sail as main motives. For this reason, the group regard the album as "one of the best of their Akdeniz albums."

In the process of song production, these two representatives of the Akdeniz scene follow the pattern most common in the Turkish popular music industry, even though they reject its products. The songwriter sets the vocal line and either collaborates with the other band members or cooperates with an arranger to create the instrumental parts and the final production. What is unique to Akdeniz is that the vocal lines are so abstract as not to invoke any ethnic or cultural origin, while the instrumental parts and sections occasionally, but also deliberately, refract the effect through the use of specific instruments whose cultural references are more obvious. That creates a dynamic contrast between the vocal lines and instrumental sections giving the most obvious character to Akdeniz music of both bands. Among those instruments are the 'ud, the kemençe, the bağlama, and the bouzouki, though the way the latter are played does not thoroughly resemble their authentic use, except in the Greek songs on Yeni Türkü's albums, in which the bouzouki sound is typically Greek. Such an "alienation" does not usually apply to the other instruments, which have strong cultural references by sound, being used both in Turkish classical music and in Greek folk music. That is, whatever a given instrumental section sounds like, it may be played on these instruments by using authentic ornaments, as seen in the intro for the track "Wind," in the *Mest of Gündoğarken*.

The intro of "Wind"
(from the Gündoğarken's album *Mest of Gündoğarken*)

Instrumental arrangement, according to Gündoğarken, is the main prop for constructing the Akdeniz sound in a given song. When asked to grade their albums in respect to Akdeniz, they selected three of their six releases as the most representative: *Another Summer Ends* (1985), *Mest of Gündoğarken* (1998), and *Istanbul Atina Istanbul* (2000).

When I reminded them that the *Mest of* included songs from the previous albums, their response emphasized the role of instrumental arrangement:

> Yes! But the arrangements are quite different. We were not happy with the arrangements until we met Nikiforos in the *Mest of*. Though what he had done in the album in 1999 did not satisfy us either, because we let him do whatever he wanted. But in *Istanbul Atina Istanbul*, we told him exactly what we wanted, so he did a good job on that. (Personal communication, January 2001)

Even the explicit use of bossa nova-like Latin rhythms and jazz strands did not restrain them from grading the album first, partly because it conforms to Akdeniz on the basis of "music to listen" as opposed to "music to entertain" through instrumental arrangements. In the previous albums, the excessive use of strings, made by pop-music arrangers sometimes jeopardized the Akdeniz, making the sound too close to mainstream pop music.

Akdeniz music has also been diffused through live bands performing at pubs and clubs where people simply listen to music, rather than actively participating by singing along or dancing. On a local level, Halicarnassus, the favorite town of tourists in summertime, epitomizes the adventure of the Akdeniz as well as changes in Turkish popular music throughout the last two decades. On the Barlar Sokağı (Street of Pubs) in its downtown area, Akdeniz was everywhere in the late '80s. But as the preponderance of mainstream pop increased in the '90s, bringing in faster and louder music, Akdeniz moved out to places in the suburbs, as the "entertainment music" has overwhelmed "audible music" in Turkey in general.

Akdeniz in a Broader Sense

In cultural terms, the word Akdeniz connotes in the Turkish language the contrast between the characteristics of the Black Sea (*Karadeniz*) region, the north of the land, with those of inner Anatolian culture, so that the word Anatolia sometimes means the central and eastern parts of the country. While the Karadeniz is a region of people with rough character, the Akdeniz is associated with modesty, peacefulness, and the passionate temper of the people in the Mediterranean region, including the Aegean coast. It is interesting here to note the analogy between such a differentiation and the Gündoğarken's definition of their own music as "sea culture" vs. "land culture," "peaceful" vs. "brisk," and so forth.

In musical discourse, the term denotes awareness and appreciation of the musical diversity of the Mediterranean rim, while Karadeniz music remains within the limits of folk music of the Black Sea region. I would argue then that the word Akdeniz has in its basic sense a connotation of "extroversion" as opposed to the "introversion" of the others. Introversion can also be found in folklore studies in which Turkish scholars can hardly be said to be studying folk music in relation to neighboring cultures. Perhaps that is why they are more interested in the study of the folklore of central and eastern parts, including Karadeniz, than in the Mediterranean and Aegean coasts.

The following examples illustrate the range of Akdeniz in music, in a broader sense. Janet and Jak Esim, members of the Jewish community in Istanbul, performing traditional songs of the Sephardic Jews, refer to "Mediterraneanness" as a common denominator for the heterogeneity of their audience. The extreme metal band Leviathan also relates to a Mediterranean character, considering the melodiousness of the riffs in their music.

"We grew up here," explains Selçuk, the leader of the band, "so, it is quite normal to sense in our music the taste of what we have heard as music on this land." Note that another black-metal band related to Mediterranean is Rotting Christ from Greece, who inspired Leviathan in "melodic progressive metal."

The intro of "Bleeding Clouds" (from the Leviathan's album *Cold Caress*)

In mainstream pop, however, Akdeniz is referred to when Greek, Italian, and occasionally Andalusian musical elements are employed in a musical production. Performance of Greek popular songs with lyrics in Turkish is included, but surprisingly not regarded as part of the aranjman, due to the "commonness" of Greek and Turkish musical cultures. The fact that the Egyptian musical film influence on Turkish popular music from the '40s did not generate the concept of the Akdeniz implies a tendency among these musicians toward the European part of the rim. An arabesk singer, Yaşar, referred to Mediterraneanness when he appeared on a TV show in 2000, but said it was "not to be regarded in the category with notorious arabesk singers." Several mainstream pop musicians refer to an "appreciation of Mediterraneanness" in their use of Greek, Italian, and Spanish-Andalusian melodies. Musicians from those countries have come together with their Turkish colleagues at Mediterranean Music Festivals in the late '80s. The popular music of those countries has been featured on many radio programs.

The Contribution of the Scene to the Broader Turkish Popular Music

The scene has long represented "band music," alongside rock and metal, as an alternative to the supremacy of "individual music," that is, music produced by and for star singers in mainstream pop. This is probably another significant point that distinguishes the scene from the Akdeniz in its broader sense as used by single musicians in Turkish popular music. The Akdeniz scene is so associated with band music that other bands sharing similar concerns about lyrics and alternative sounds have also been considered among the Akdeniz bands, though they do not define themselves as such. Accordingly, all the members of the Yeni Türkü except Derya Köroğlu, both the leader and the singer, have changed over time, but this did not result in a break up, nor did Köroğlu attempt to continue his career as a solo musician.

While folk instruments, notably the bağlama, have enjoyed a central place in Anatolian rock and pop, it was unusual to deploy classical instruments in popular music of Western idioms until the Yeni Türkü introduced the 'ud and the kemençe in the album *Akdeniz Akdeniz*. Nor was the bouzouki welcomed until then by pop musicians, while it has been the main instrument in the bands performing Greek music in taverns in and around Istanbul.

In regard to the music industry, popular music today rolls on two top-10-like lists, foreign and local. The former depends on globally distributed pop albums, mainly from Anglo-American pop, but recently welcomed some local contributions with the albums of Angela Dimitirou and Anna Vissi, as a consequence of sympathetic relations that occurred after the earthquake disaster in both Greece and Turkey (1999). The incident has provided the Akdeniz scene with a new context for emphasizing the closeness among Greek and Turkish people that has long been part of their discourse. The 1994 album *Külhani şarkılar* (Rembetika Songs) of the Yeni Türkü includes a song with lyrics on "closeness" among them. The fourth track in the album *Mest of Gündoğarken* was recorded in both Turkish and Greek, with the participation of Vasili Papageorgiou. The album *Istanbul Atina Istanbul* also includes remarkable contributions from Greek musicians, and on the cover is the following statement:

> We would appreciate if our travel of a musical purpose, back and forth Istanbul–Athens–Istanbul, receives acceptance as a "contribution to improving Turkish-Greek friendship."

While the impact of globally distributed pop is large enough to form an independent list, export of local pop to other markets has hardly occurred, except in a few recent accounts. "Rasputine" by Boney M was hotly debated in the 1970s due to its similarity to the "Katibim," a traditional Istanbul tune, but this similarity was denied by the band. A 1999 album by Ellisa, a famous singer in Paris, of Lebanese origin, featured four songs by Turkish musicians. On the other hand, several pop singers have found audiences today in the Balkan countries, Greece, and Central Asia with their own productions.

Musicianly Strategies, Scene, Local and Global Processes: Dialectical Aspects of the Akdeniz

Returning to the concepts I argued at the beginning, the Akdeniz scene demonstrates no explicit connection to globalization, or globally distributed pop music, but provides an example of the interplay between global and local processes. The comparative approach, focusing on two representative bands of the scene, suggests that the interplay is complex and multifaceted as the scene is flexible. While the Akdeniz resists such dichotomies as global-local, not all the musical configurations can be explained through the presumed impact of particular processes. The fact that these bands have different perspectives on what Akdeniz is, both musically and conceptually, also refers to its inherent flexibility.

Processes then, global or local, social or musical, become dynamics that musicians employ freely in the construction of their own music and rhetoric. The flexible nature of the "scene" suggests the concept of musicianly strategy as a key for the study of the unique trajectories of musicians within the concept of the scene. This is not to deny the impact of social processes on musicianship, but to define musicians as active participants who produce both music and discourse in relation to social processes, rather than being simply under the impact of them. Once a strategy for music making is attempted, there may be a variety of ways to relate the intended sound to surrounding processes, local or global. I find useful the concept in the study of scenes in popular music where production and consumption of music prevail, to which musicians adapt themselves through individual strategies. This concept explains the stylistic differences between Yeni Türkü and Gündoğarken.

The Akdeniz also suggests that it is not necessary to define a scene by its cultural origins, either historically or geographically. Musicians of the scene do not pinpoint any geographic origin and do not refer to any historical background for the characteristics of their music. There are however several other musicians using the term Akdeniz for their deployment of musical elements from other Mediterranean cultures, or as the identity of a culture area, including the western part of Turkey.

The concept of a scene also provides a means to define Akdeniz music as a distinctive unit within Turkish popular music in which stylistic ramification is so entangled that no definite categories can be distinguished for scholarly purposes. The music of Yeni Türkü and Gündoğarken for instance can be classified under "pop music with Western sound in which some local instruments are also used." However, the discourse explaining their ways of relating musical configurations to underlying concepts distinguishes their music, emphasizing their uniqueness as an alternative to the nationalistic tendency in Turkish popular music.

Appendix

A

"Sorma Bana." Translation of the full text (from the Yeni Türkü's album *Akdeniz Akdeniz*).

Don't ask me who I am
From where I came
Don't ask from which days came
The red clouds in my eyes
> Things that cannot be explained
> May have happened
> To the grapes I stole,
> I may have eaten
> Leaning upon the chest of blue sky

B

"Wind." Translation of the full text (from the Gündoğarken's album *Mest of Gündoğarken*).

The wind floating
The curtain of my window
The wind waving the sea
Covering with foam
Come on in gently
Get me rid of my troubles
You are a stranger
Where are you coming from
Sit next to me and rest
You must be tired
> Tell me about breezing
> Tell me about loving
> Tell me about breezing
> Tell me going with the wind
> Tell me so that my tongue would work
> I must say "I'm wind"
> Tell me about being wind
> So, I can breeze like you

Notes

1. Even the word "pop," as introduced by the government-operated radio station in the 1960s, was confined to Western popular music, or Turkish popular tunes with a Western sound. Local forms of popular music such as the arabesk, the *özgün* music, *fantezi*, etc. have never been regarded as popular music.

2. The *şarki* was but one of the forms taking part in the *fasil*, a cycle consisting of varying numbers in traditional performance practice. Since the late nineteenth

century, it has gained much popularity as being considered the "lightest" form in the fasil.

3. Murathan Mungan (b. 1955, Istanbul) is a well known, award-winning playwright and poet who started his career in the early '80s, contemporary with Yeni Türkü.

List of Interviews

Cengiz Onural (January 15, 2001, Istanbul).

Derya Köroğlu (january 18, 2001, Izmir).

Gündoğarken (January 14, 2001, Istanbul).

Leviathan (December 16, 2000, Izmir).

Bibliography

Bengi, Derya. 1999. "Mr. Gardener'a Soralım," *Roll* 36: 19–21.

Friedman, Jonathan. 1994. *Cultural Identity and Global Process*. London: Sage Publications.

Harris, Keith. 2000. "'Roots'?: The Relationship Between the Global and the Local Within the Extreme Metal Scene," *Popular Music* 19/1: 13–30.

İdemen, Siren and Merve Erol. 2000. "Erol Büyükburç,"*Roll* 44: 57–61.

Macdonald, Sharon. 1993. "Identity Complexes in Western Europe: Social Anthropological Perspectives," in *Inside European Identities*, edited by Sharon Macdonald. Oxford: Berg Publishers. 1–26.

Stokes, Martin. 1992. *The Arabesk Debate: Music and Musicians in Modern Turkey*. Oxford: Clarendon Press.

Zwingle, Erla. 1999. "Goods Move. People Move. Ideas Move. And Cultures Change," *National Geographic* 196/2: 12–33.

Discography

Gündoğarken. *Bir Yaz Daha Bitiyor*. Göksoy Plak. 1986.

——. *Mest of Gündoğarken*. Universal. FRS 19642. 1998.

——. *Gündoğarken 1999*. Universal FRS 21814. 1999.

——. *Istanbul Atina Istanbul*. Universal FRS 9723567. 2000.

Leviathan. *Cold Caress*. Poem Productions 10000–1. 2000.

Yeni Türkü. *Buğdayın Türküsü*. Ze Plak. 1979.

——. *Akdeniz Akdeniz*. Göksoy Plak CD006. [1983] 1990.

——. *Külhanişarkılar*. Göksoy Plak CD076. 1994.

C H A P T E R   N I N E

BETWEEN EAST AND WEST: CONTEMPORARY GROOVES IN GREEK POPULAR MUSIC (c. 1990–2000)

KEVIN DAWE

In piecing together a mosaic of the Mediterranean in music, the bits that make up Greece do not fit neatly or fall easily into place. However, one can see patterns emerging that, if correctly placed in relation to the backdrop of their social and cultural setting, provide interesting perspectives on a number of important issues. Greece is a major geographical, cultural, and political crossroads situated between the "East" and the "West," that is, a part of a region where the continents of Europe and Asia meet and run into each other around the Greater and Eastern Mediterranean area. It is this "between worlds" setting that today, perhaps more than ever before in the history of Greece, shapes Greek musical sensibilities. Here, in a region of contested homelands and shared cultural traits, an East-West musical orientation and indeed consciousness is explored, negotiated, contested, worked out, developed, defined, expressed, and given high profile in the popular music industry. In this chapter, I explore the work of a range of recording artists active in Greece in the 1990s and into 2000, focusing on performers of *laïkó* (popular music originating in the 1950s and 1960s). I concentrate on new wave laïkó (emergent in the 1980s) and its interaction with regional Greek "folk" musics, *rembetika* (originally "Oriental" songs from the Piraeus underworld from around

1900 that developed in various forms up to the 1950s), and global pop, rock, jazz, and rap.

The music industry in Greece is based largely in Athens, a city that is home to most of the major record labels and some of the largest recording studios in the Eastern Mediterranean area. The Minos Matsas corporation in Athens is but one music industry giant based in and around the city. For decades this musical powerhouse has helped to shape the Greek musical landscape, apprehending sounds from inside and outside Greece, leading to new musical formations, updating and revisiting older repertoires and genres, while grooming a number of talented Greek musicians for international stardom (such as George Dalaras). Naturally, this industry has had a profound effect on the Greek view of the musical universe. But, as elsewhere in the world, a constant stream of Euro-American pop and rock continues to enter Greek airspace, having an equally profound effect on local music making.

In Greece there has been a general shift toward use of global media communications, satellite TV and radio, the Internet, link-ups between Greek and international music corporations, and an increase in touring by major Greek music stars. This activity has opened up the country and its musicians to a new sound world, to audiences around the world, and to the "world music" scene. Nearer to home, Egyptian radio can be clearly heard in Crete, while Turkish radio carries across the Green Line (and vice versa). A broad range of musical influences have had a huge effect on the Greek music scene, and Greek musical exports have in turn enjoyed enormous success in countries across the Eastern Mediterranean area. There have been a number of phenomenally successful collaborations between Greek musicians working in different musical genres, musicians from around the Greater and Eastern Mediterranean, and from further afield (for example, Egypt, Israel, Armenia, Turkmenistan, and India). A number of highly influential producer-composer-musicians have, in two to three decades, virtually revolutionized and updated the local music scene (whether they are based in Athens, New York, London, or Cyprus).

This work has built upon the international success of talented Greek singing superstars such as Nana Mouskouri and Demis Roussos (born in Egypt), where the seeds were successfully sown for the packaging of Greek music in an international setting. The appeal of these

The largest Greek music selection in the World:
Trehantiri Record Shop, London (2001)

artists abroad (and outside the Greek diaspora) is due in no small way to sensationalized notions of "Greek-ness" as exploited in the media, advertising, and tourism from at least the 1960s. The popular imagination traded on notions of an Oriental and primitive Otherness emerging from the bush of Southern Europe. From island idylls (Happy to be on an Island in the Sun) and sun-drenched Acropoli (The White Rose of Athens) to sexy, gyrating Zorba-types displaying their manhood on a deserted Cretan beach (long before Ayia Napa happened); "kebab culture" (to borrow Haji Mike's phrase) has had its fatal attractions. The popularity of this dubious reflection upon Greek culture was aided and abetted, first, by a bouzouki-driven sound that intersected with the sound of Greek Nights in tourist villages, and second by the accessibility of the song lyrics (Mouskouri, Roussos, and others sing in several languages). Interpretations of the ways Greeks "do" popular music have often been inaccurate and misleading (kaftans and plate smashing are, of course, not obligatory). And Greek music is certainly much more than "bouzouki music." Greek popular musicians continue to work out what is "traditional" and "exotic" about their music (as these things can mean quite different things to Greeks than to non-Greeks) as they explore the dynamic interplay between the local and the global in music in the "between worlds" setting of Greek musical culture. Greece then, is a place of musical cross currents.

Greek Music in the Global Soundscape

Little has been written of the ways in which traditional music genres, languages, instruments, and songs feature in contemporary pop, rock, jazz, and rap within Greece. In this chapter, I present a series of case studies to illustrate the ways in which Greek musicians and recording artists have engaged with new musical resources and creative opportunities offered by today's global—or globally accessible—soundscape. I focus on commercial recordings and chart-topping artists—mass-mediated music—rather than on the vibrant live music scene (from village feast days to music festivals), and I do not consider regional and island music industries (such as the one in Crete; see Dawe 1996, 1998, 1999, 2000, forthcoming). This chapter is but a glimpse of the popular music scene in Greece.

Greek popular musicians are fully conversant with the *global*[1] language of contemporary rock and pop, using synthesizers, drum machines, sequencers, samplers, and overdriven electric guitars, along with other Western stylistic and technical models from exotica to ambient, hip-hop to heavy metal, cool jazz to chill out, and so on. However, they continue to exploit the nuances of the Greek language in song, much as they turn to *local* regional sounds and musical styles for inspiration.[2] Thus synthesized backing tracks may provide the musical ground for rhythms, melodies, and instruments that have their origins in particular communities (even villages) in a particular mainland or island region of Greece, past or present.

On top of all this, Turkish, Arab, and a variety of other Eastern Mediterranean sounds and musical instruments have been brought into the mix to arguably freshen up and spice up once conservative and inward-looking Greek popular styles. In familiar rhetoric, some would say this is merely a return to earlier times and sounds (from the Ottoman and post-Ottoman periods). But the cultural flows of the past in the Eastern Mediterranean region now come up against the Green Line. There is, in fact, no reason (apart from the obvious political ones) why the shared repertoires and instrumentation of Greek and Turkish musical worlds should not work together as *music*. In fact, in Greek and Turkish popular musics today, there is a limited degree of interaction, just enough to show that these musical worlds are not quite as distinct as they are often made out to be.

However, Greek popular music reaches out of the confines of an Aegean sound and extends its musical palate by incorporating music from around the world. Therefore, Greek clarinet, sampled Pygmy hoots, didgeridoo, a whirling Turkish pops/Eurovision string orchestra, programmed house and dance-style percussion, Madonna-style vocal lines and Cher-style synth-vocal treatments can all be heard in the space of one CD if not one CD track. One only has to listen, for example, to the first two tracks or track 10 on CD 1 of the Ana Vissi album *Kravgi* (Shout, Cry) (2000). In this type of mix, the Greek lyrics and the clarinet act as crucial signifiers and authenticating references of "Greek-ness," two examples selected from among a small selection of vocal and instrumental resources that have become the standard and essential ingredients of the Greek-Mediterranean or Greek-world music sound.

It might be said that Greek musicians have tried to establish a territory in popular music that is all their own. Greek popular musical productions are not only about what it is to be young and Greek at the turn of the century (and therefore explore exciting and new soundworlds). These productions also confront sensitive, challenging, and deep-seated issues relating to a cultural identity formed out of a mixture of "Eastern" and "Western" cultural elements (see Herzfeld 1982, 1987). The mix *really is* a mix. As musician-composer-producer Nikos Papazoglou notes:

> Our musical culture, if this is indeed the right word, is a farrago [confused mixture], and this is stark evidence we should pay attention to the music we compose or to the choices we make whenever we are on the

horns of a dilemma; we are thus compelled to make a stand. Nevertheless, whatever our decision might be, we still betray a part of ourselves, since we are composed of heterogeneous elements and by choosing one, we automatically reject the others. Love is more powerful than heterogeneity; the whole question lies in whether we can intermingle our musical contradictions, that also constitute our own, private contradictions, into a "mixed" but widely accepted musical genre. (Nikos Papazoglou, liner notes to *Haratsi*)

In an attempt to establish the "right" mix in *sound*, Nikos Papazoglou, along with other folk-rock experimenters, such as Dionysius Savvopoulos, played a major role in the creation of the *neo kima* (new wave) music of the late 1970s and 1980s. This artistic movement helped many young musicians move beyond the almost suffocating musical orthodoxy previously imposed by the Junta, the military dictatorship that ruled until 1974. Particular forms of music had been suppressed by a regime that had a penchant for safe music. The bouzouki music of the late 1960s and 1970s dominated Greek music to the detriment of all else; indeed, bouzouki music was pushed forward as *the* national music. However, given its use in the traditions of mainland Greece, some have suggested that this role might be reserved for the clarinet. With the fall of the military dictatorship came a resurgence of interest in Greek music in all its forms that exploded in the 1980s. A new generation discovered a rich tapestry of regional styles and almost forgotten urban musics, including rembetika and other vernacular musics.

Since his earliest recordings in the late 1960s, Greek music superstar George Dalaras (b. 1950) has performed music from most of the musical traditions found within Greece, from rembetika to Byzantine hymns, as well as drawing on a number of rock and pop styles. Dalaras released his first LP in 1968 with the Minos Matsas record company and has remained there ever since. Among his many collaborations, guitarists Paco de Lucia and Al Di Meola have even featured on Dalaras's more Latin-flavored albums, while Dalaras sang on Al Di Meola's *Orange and Blue* album (Verve, 1994).

Two of his live albums offer examples of how Dalaras has melded traditions in his music: *Zondanes Echografeseis* (*Live Recordings*) from

1986 and *To Elliniko Prosopo Tou Giourgou Dalara* (*The Greek Face of George Dalaras*) from 1996. The 1986 album features the classic and ever-popular song "Me Teleoses" (You Have Finished Me). In the basic plan of the piece, note the instrumentation used.

Basic plan of *Me Teleoses*

Opening *outi* (Turko-Arab fretless, plucked lute) solo (played by Dalaras) with piano, bouzouki, and percussion interjections, and held synthesized bass.

Riff (repeated figure) played by outi, bouzouki, electric violin, synthesizer and electric bass guitar.

Verse One (melismatic vocal style).

Chorus.

Riff as before.

Verse Two.

Chorus.

Extended electric violin solo in "Orientalized" Cycladic island style over riff. (Riff carried by outi and electric bass guitar and keyboards with percussion accompaniment).

Extended bouzouki solo over riff.

All instruments play descending runs into the Chorus to end.

The ever-present eclecticism that informs Dalaras's work as shown in this piece became part of standard practice in the Greek popular music of the 1990s. Ten years later, Dalaras's 1996 album features an all-acoustic set with a stripped-down approach, quite a contrast to the pop, rock, and traditional instrumental mix of the 1986 album (although this orchestration can still be found on other recently released Dalaras albums). On the album *To Elliniko Prosopo Tou Giourgou Dalara* (*The Greek Face of George Dalaras*), Dalaras sings and plays guitar, outi, and bouzouki. The accompaniment is provided by a backing group consisting of nylon-string acoustic guitar, double bass, and, on one track, piano. The set opens with a Byzantine hymn, followed by a traditional song from Asia Minor that features an extended outi solo (a *taximi* or "unmetered improvisation") at the beginning. (I have heard this song performed many times in Crete.) Arguably, the outi provides the essential "Oriental" ingredient, pulling Greek music eastwards just as the guitar and other instruments continue to pull Greek music westwards. The songs of art music-based composers Mikis Theodorakis and Manos Hadjidakis are also featured on the album, along with the laïkó and rembetika-style songs of Apostolou and Konstantinou Kaldara. The Dalaras model, as shown in these two examples, is one that many artists have adopted or customized to achieve great success.

Between East and West

Eleftheria Arvanitaki (b. 1958) is currently Greece's first lady of song. In a recent interview in the *Rough Guide to World Music*, she remarked that

> [b]ecause we are between the West and East we know very well the music of Europe and America, but we know the music of Asia as well. We are well-positioned to take the best from both worlds, but we keep doing our music in our own way. (Broughton et al. 1999: 135)

In an attempt to demonstrate how Eleftheria and her producers and arrangers put these theories into practice, I will briefly discuss her musical background and a song from her *Very Best of* album (1998). Her music has been described variously as "ethereal, synthesized Greek folk," "World music," "traditional-sounding world pop," "folksy Greek pop," and "a true revival of Greece's most loved laïka songs." Yet, however one may try to pigeonhole her music, it must be seen as consistently and persistently drawing on a number of Greek traditional and popular musics, while not being afraid to engage with the latest developments in global pop. Her first group was Opisthodromiki Compania (Backwards Band) dedicated to singing old rembetika songs. In the early 1980s, these songs—which are largely about drugs, love, and lust—resurfaced and became popular with a whole new generation. This brought Eleftheria and her group to the attention of the general record-buying public. The retrospective *Very Best of* album draws largely on a trio of best-selling solo albums: *Meno Ektos* (I Still Remain an Outcast)

(1991), *To Kormia ke ta Maheiria* (The Bodies and the Knives) (1994), and *Tragoutihia yia tous Mines* (Songs for the Month) (1996), all of which went gold or platinum in Greece. The song "Meno Ektos" is dedicated to Armenians and others "who have lost their homes." Indeed, the music for six of the tracks on the *Very Best of* album was written and arranged by New York-based Armenian composer and musician Ara Dinkjian.

Basic plan of "Meno Ektos"

Low-pitched, short solo on the *nay* (Turko-Arab end-blown flute).

Verse 1: wistful solo female vocal with strident synthesizer arpeggios.

Chorus: solo female vocal, synthesiser arpeggios, strings, electric guitar-with-reverb interjections, and light cymbal crashes.

Solo: short phrases on sitar and bendir with strings and synthesizer arpeggios.

Verse 2 and Chorus as before.

Solo: electric guitar (restrained, Pink Floyd style) with synthesizer backing.

Chorus: as before.

Chorus with male choir added.

The Greek lyrics combined with a range of Eastern and Western musical elements help to create a "between worlds" sensation. Some tracks feature Greek traditional dances and instrumentation, such as "Lianotragoudo" (Songs of the Sun), which features a 9/8 *zeybekiko* rhythm, bouzouki, clarinet, and *sandouri* (hammered dulcimer or zither), and "Skies ke Chromata" (Shadows and Colors), which features outi and bendir.

Although Eleftheria Arvanitaki might be regarded as the supreme songstress of Greece at the present time, a number of female singing superstars' recordings demonstrate an engagement with both traditional Greek and world musics. Angela Dimitriou, for example, featured Egyptian singing superstar Amr Diab on the track "Eleos" (Sun) on her album *Kane Stin Akri* (Get a Move On) (1999). The song and the album were an instant hit in Egypt as well as in Greece. Dimitriou is so popular in Egypt that all the album track titles were written in both Greek and Arabic. Angela went on to sing on an album by Amr Diab.

The release of the album *Ethnic Beats* in 1995 by Glykeria features dance and video remixes of some of her best-known songs, including "Kane Kati" (Do Something), first released on the album *Ola Mou ta Mistiki* (All My Secrets; 1990). This immensely popular song originally mixed "Eastern"-sounding synthesizer (sitar and nay), outi, and Turkish pops orchestra with a late disco beat accentuated by funky electric rhythm guitar and a heavy drum beat. The *Ethnic Beats* version is dominated by a heavy dance beat, sequencers, synthesizers, and the "Oriental" pop strings of the previous hit. Glykeria has achieved as much success and critical acclaim in Israel as she has in Greece, and indeed she mixes songs sung in Hebrew with those sung in Greek on her recent albums (for example, "Shabechi Yerushalayim" on *Ethnic Beats*). She continues to feature songs by rembetika composers, such as Vasilis Tsitsanis, although these receive the now-familiar dance-beat and Orientalizing outi treatment.

Along with Eleftheria, Glykeria, Angela Dimitriou, and Ana Vissi, Melina Kana appears just as interested in singing traditional Greek music as she is in engaging with global pop and world music. On the album *Lafyra* (Loot) released in 1998, Melina Kana uses a mixture of musicians from Turkmenistan and Greece. The instrumentation on the album features violin, accordion, clarinet, *tar* (plucked, long-necked lute found in Persian music), and percussion played in Turkmeni style. This is fused with bouzouki, nay, *gaida* (bagpipes), *kanonaki* (plucked, trapezoid zither), and a range of percussion from bendir to *toumbeleki* (goblet drum). Acoustic and electric guitars, cello, double bass, and kit drums are also used. The rhythms range from *zeybekiko* to *tsifte-teli* (loosely, the "belly dance") and jazz swing. In the liner notes to the album it is said that

> *Loot* is the coming together of three distinct expressive forces. Melina Kana, the most arresting voice to come out of Greece lately, Thanasis Papaconstantinou, the composer who thinks that the city of Ashkhabad is as close as a nearby village, and Ashkhabad, the finest soloists of Turkmenistan, who can turn a mere gathering into a banquet.

Listening to the music of Ashkhabad I did saw the soul like an ivy thickened with the notes, rhythms, and voices. I felt that its vein would definitely mate with some of my songs [*sic*]. (Thanasis Papaconstantinou, liner notes to *Lafyra*)

The instrumental solos are mostly performed by the Turkmeni musicians whose incredible virtuosity is evident on the very first track. The blend of instruments and performance practices provides an impressive backdrop to Melina Kana's vocals that also display an impressive versatility across a range of genres and styles. Sometimes the tar performs the role normally reserved for the bouzouki in Greek song. The instrumental tracks give the musicians a chance to show off their skills, including the virtuosic bouzouki solos that play off the accordion, clarinet, and violin solos of the Turkmeni musicians, producing exciting and breathtaking music that explores new musical terrain between East and West. The clarinet sound and performance techniques appear not that different from those produced and used by Greece's own virtuoso clarinetists, such as Petro-Loukas Chalkias and the late Vasilis Soukas. Such crosscultural connections also fascinate Ross Daly, a musician, composer, and arranger with whom Chalkias and Soukas have worked.

The Music That Connects

The one non-Greek in this chapter (except for guest musicians on the Greek records mentioned and Demis Roussos) is Ross Daly, an eclectic musician whose influence upon the Greek music scene has been great. He has been a facilitator, reminding Greeks of the connections between their music and music throughout the Balkans, the Middle East, and beyond, as well as bringing together musicians from an apparently diverse range of musical traditions. Daly, who was born in England in 1952, spent some of his formative years in Ireland, and has lived in the United States, Canada, and Japan, is a musical polymath. Daly studied a variety of musical traditions and musical instruments in North India, the Middle East, and the Balkans. If there is anyone in Greece with experience of the music of a wide range of cultures it is Ross Daly. He has performed and collaborated with many of the great names in Greek music and has appeared on several landmark albums. He is a composer in his own right, recording several albums that have been critically acclaimed if not commercially successful.

In his arrangements, improvisations, and compositions, Daly explores the connections between Greek music and music of the Middle East and South and Central Asia:

> The musical reality of this vast region [from the Balkans, through the Middle East to India] is based on a modal-rhythmic principle. These great modal systems (*maqam, raga, tropos, dastgah*) are not confined by political or religious boundaries yet they seem to be linked by a common origin which might be based quite literally on one note. Apart from myself, quite a few others have sought these trans-ethnic, trans-regional and trans-personal origins. And in doing so, you come across spiritual traditions, and find yourself in search of a common origin of nature. (Liner notes to *Mitos*, 1992)

The track "Thalassa Mavri" (Black Sea) from the 1989 album *Oneirou topoi* (Dream Places) illustrates Daly's approach to his work. The piece was composed by Ross Daly and features the poetry of Dimitris Stavrakakis from Crete. It was released on the Cretan label Aerakis. Section A, played on the outi (short-necked, fretless, plucked lute—the Turko-Arab outi), explores characteristic phrases of the mode in which the piece is written (North Indian Rag Bhairavi). The North Indian *swarmandal* (zither) interjects a sustained chord before the outi sets the 2/4 tempo of section B. It is joined by the *laouto,* which embellishes the melody throughout, and then the Cretan *lyra.* The *daouli* (a cylindrical drum usually played with a beater) plays on the first beat of every bar throughout. The *mantinades* (sung, recited poetry) of the next section (C) are sung on the themes of section B and are connected by short instrumental passages. Finally, the mantinades give way to the longer instrumental passage (section D), providing contrasting passages with and without the lyra and swarmandal, and ending by fading and cadencing on note E with outi and swarmandal. Daly plays all the instruments himself.

In a version of this piece recorded in 1992 (from the album *Mitos*), Daly plays the opening improvisation on the Afghani lute, the *rababa* "in the style and technique of an Arab outi and an Indian *sarod* (fretless plucked lute), combined with Greek and Turkish phrasing" (*Mitos* liner notes). Turkish *fasil kemençe* (bowed lute, similar to the Cretan lyra and used in Turkish "art" music), Persian *zarb* drum, and Indian *tampura* drone are also featured.

Ross Daly has rarely used electronic instruments such as the synthesizer in his work; he is committed to using a range of acoustic instruments whether in the studio or in live performance. His attention to detail is legendary: not only in his insistence on accurate tuning and suitable acoustics in live venues but also in the time he takes to make a record. He told me that it took him eleven months to record the track "Elefthero Simio" (Free Point) as featured on the album of the same name (1996). This extraordinary composition plays for over twenty-one minutes, features a range of instruments (from *yayli tambur* [bowed, upright lute] to Cretan lyra), and takes the listener through a range of sections or movements and "scenes" using multitracked bowed and plucked acoustic instruments, featuring the nay and kanonaki. The clarinet playing of the late, great Vasilis Soukas from Epirus is also featured. On this track, Daly gives the instruments an echo treatment reminiscent of the way they would sound in a concert setting.

Daly adheres to the working out and movement to and from various modes in the way he was taught by a succession of master musicians (in Greece, the Middle East, and South and Central Asia). He acknowledges that these traditions are similar but distinct, in that they each have a particular ethos and set of performance practices attached to them. Daly has a vast and sensitive musical imagination matched by his ability to play a range of musical instruments well, and by his outstanding virtuosity on the Cretan lyra. His music, that is, the compositions of Ross Daly (along with his understated ability as a first-rate performer of Cretan music), merits serious musical and academic attention. This is a part of his work that is often eclipsed by his interpretation of a range of Greek and Middle Eastern compositions, and by his influence upon the Greek and Middle Eastern music scenes.

Repercussions and Developments

In his percussion-driven albums, Alexis Boulgourtzis shows a similar concern with bringing together instruments and musical styles from around the Greater Mediterranean area, although through his focus on percussion he also reaches into Latin America and India. It is not quite clear from the album title whether Boulgourtzis is really concerned about the recognition of "borders" in his album *Borders* (1998) (in the way that Ross Daly adheres to, though he mixes, the performance practices of various traditions in the space of one of his compositions). Perhaps it is the crossing of borders that he is concerned with, or their eradication through music. However, lines gouged into a wall by a rusty nail, as featured on the record sleeve, suggest that he has demarcation points in mind in this collection of contemporary "grooves." The tracks include "Percussions' Odyssey," "Armenian," "Samba," "Hitjaz," and "Borders."

Not surprisingly, the instrumentation featured comes from a wide range of cultures. It includes, along with a host of percussion, darbukka (goblet drum), *tabla* (North Indian drums), and timbales. Other instruments used include the Greek and Middle Eastern based outi, kanonaki, clarinet, violin, and *zournas* (a shawm played in parts of northern Greece), sequenced keyboard parts, tenor saxophone, heavy metal guitar, and electric bass guitar. Drawing on a range of ambient, techno, and house grooves, exciting percussion tracks are layered beneath a variety of instrumental riffs and solos, with the percussion coming to the fore at various points to display Bouigourtzis's obvious virtuosity as a percussionist extraordinaire. A number of contemporary grooves are, to my mind, very effectively employed to kick-start Greece-based music that soon becomes something else.

This basic plan shows the structure of the "Introduction" and "Karshilamas" [*sic*] tracks on the CD.

Basic plan of "Introduction" (track 1)

Opening processed (echo) kanonaki improvisation; melody also etched by synthesizer. Leads into:

Riff on Hammond-organ sounding keyboard and electric bass guitar accompany virtuosic percussion workouts on toumbeleki.

Basic plan of "Karshilamas" (track 5)

(A *karsilamas* is a traditional island dance in 9/8 meter, originally from coastal Asia Minor.)

Deep breathy bass note held on synthesizer provides the background for the kanonaki solo. Leads into:

Fast and furiously rhythmic beat provided by toumbeleki and drums behind the improvisations of the distorted electric guitar and nay.

Short percussion interlude and nay solo.

Zournadhes (two shawms) soloing with Joe Satriani-style "dives" on distorted electric guitar with percussion accompaniment.

Ends on *nay* solo.

Leads into next track: "Dream Theater"/sandouri-style piano with outi joining in.

One can also find jazz grooves on Alexis Bougourtzis's albums, although I have not heard him play "straight" jazz, by which I mean everything from Stan Getz to Pat Metheny. A musician who is jazz-based is the versatile guitarist and composer Takis Barberis. Barberis plays a range of electric, synth, and acoustic guitars with a style of playing that is distinctive (especially his sitar imitations on electric guitar), although owing a debt to both John McLaughlin and Pat Metheny (among others). It is clear that Barberis is an eclectic composer in the mode of Boulgourtzis and Daly. Indian percussionist Trilok Gurtu appeared on the *Episodes* album (1995), along with Petro-Loukas Chalkias on clarinet. On the album *Naiva* (1998), Barberis features four Indian musicians (along with Petro-Loukas Chalkias) on sitar, tablas, and tampura (a plucked lute that performs the drone in Indian music). Both these albums combine extended improvisations with carefully crafted tunes, all performed by some of youngest and brightest names in modern Greek jazz. But this is jazz with a "world music" feel, not a million miles away from the soundworld of Boulgourtzis's *Borders* album, but more restrained.

Mode Plagal is one of the better known Greek jazz groups, combining virtuosic and Greek traditional music-influenced alto saxophone playing with blues-grunge-electronica-influenced guitar, electric bass guitar, kit drums, and percussion. The album *Mode Plagal II* (1998) moves from bebop to jazz-funk to free jazz, making various musical stops on the way (including a heavy rock beat one minute and an African guitar riff the next). The album also features a traditional *kalamatianos* dance rhythm, a traditional Greek carol, and various traditional tunes from Epirus (featuring, in turn, a chorus of voices, alto sax solos, and overdriven and feedback electric guitar with traditional percussion and kit drum accompaniment), Roumeli, Thrace, and Bulgaria.

Drawing on a similarly wide range of musical influences, some of which intersect with Mode Plagal and Ross Daly, the liner notes to Kristi Stassinopoulou's album *Echotropia* (1999) state:

> As the heliotrope turns its face towards the sun, so does echotropia follow the orbit of a wide landscape of sounds deriving from Greek traditional music, psychedelic rock and electronica.

Working with multi-instrumentalist and composer Stathis Kalyviotis, Kristi has come up with an intriguing blend of traditional and contemporary sounds. The "traditional" acoustic instrumentation features zournas, clarinet, violin, accordion, and Turkish *saz* (bağlama). These instruments are used within a rock-electronica band setting. Thus shimmering guitar chords and slowly picked-out arpeggios provide an accompaniment to the vocals, with a heavy (drum and bass) beat underneath and zournas or synthesized bagpipes on top. All the time we have Kristi's "folkie" sounding voice, often processed, with its intriguing melismas and Trio-Bulkarika-style choral effects. An ethereal yet earthy sound is produced, somehow giving the feeling of being "rooted" in "folk tradition" (with traditional songs taken from Epirus and Persia), yet right up to date in the use made of synthesizers, electric guitar, and effects. The sense of space created in these recordings captures the feeling of a mountain landscape, as if the sound of celebrations from a number of villages are echoing through the valleys and merging into one.

Conclusion

I conclude by examining Greece's hip-hop scene, because it pulls together concerns that must be addressed in an article on Greek popular music. Little has been written about this scene at the time of writing, although the better known artists, such as Imiskoumbria and Haji

Mike (despite the language barrier in the case of the former) are starting to break through internationally. Haji Mike, the star of "Greek-reg-
gae," has a solid following in both British-Greek communities in
Cyprus, where he now lives. His music features a mix of Greek "traditional" references with careful use of the bouzouki and Greek dance
rhythms combined with reggae, house, and drum and bass beats. His
lyrics—a mix of Greek and English that he calls "Glinglish"—satirize
Greek-Cypriot life in London and contain strong condemnation of the
political situation in Cyprus. An excerpt from Haji Mike's web page
reads:

> Welcome to Haji Mike's web page home of reggae artist, outernational
> producer and lyricist based in Cyprus. Long before Ayia Napa became the
> second "Ibiza" he was making music. Played in over 30 countries world-
> wide and a genuine doctor of philosophy. A unique artist on a difficult
> mission.
>
> As one of many victims of this act of modern day colonialism I feel
> gutted by the continued occupation of my homeland.

Haji Mike's web page has a link to the Cyprus home page, just one
of his attempts to raise awareness of the problems there. The site also
features the poignant and bittersweet "Cyprus Is My Name," which can
be found in different versions on *Haji Mike on the Mike* (1994) and
Aphrodite's Dream (1997). Its lyrics include:

> Bury me somewhere in between
> In that no persons land
> On that line which they call green
> And there my spirit will rest and wait
> To greet the date
> To celebrate
> The time and day so great
> When Cyprus becomes One.

The "mix" and the "blend" might well have been perfected in Greek
popular music but the political problems do not go away. There is a
genuine push for peace in the "between worlds" grooves of contempo-

rary Greek popular music. However, "between" is just not good enough for many.

Acknowledgments

Special thanks to Laki and all the Pattalis family at Trehantiri record shop in London (www.trehantiri.com).

Notes

1. Here, I take "the local" to mean in general terms, a source of cultural continuity rooted in notions of "the local" held by Greeks. Their "local" has become clearer to me over a long period of fieldwork in Greece. On the other hand, "the global" can be seen as a source of change as problematized by a number of authors including, Featherstone (1990, 1995), Hall, Held and McGrew (1992), Appadurai (1996), and Hannerz (1996). These issues are also considered in, for example, Slobin 1993, Lipsitz 1994, Mitchell 1996, and Taylor 1997 with a focus on music. The observations made in this essay are guided by this reading, by ethnographic fieldwork, and by the belief that, "Globalization . . . is not brand new, it can move back and forth, it comes in many kinds, it is segmented, and it is notoriously uneven; different worlds, different globalizations" (Hannerz 1996: 18).

2. Jane Cowan (1998) provides a useful and up-to-date overview of the history and regional variability of Greek music. See also Cowan's seminal study of Greek dance (Cowan, 1990). Broughton et al (1999) is also a useful starting point.

Bibliography

Appadurai, Arjun. 1996. *Modernity at Large. Cultural Dimensions of Globalization*. Minneapolis and London: University of Minnesota Press.

Broughton, Simon Mark Ellingham, and Richard Trillo (eds). 1999. *The Rough Guide to World Music. Volume 1: Africa, Europe and the Middle East*. London: Rough Guides Ltd.

Cowan, Jane K. 1990. *Dance and the Body Politic in Northern Greece*. New Jersey and Oxford: Princeton University Press.

——. 1998. "Greece," in *Europe* (*The Garland Encyclopedia of World Music,* vol. 8), edited by Timothy Rice, Christopher Goertzen, and James Porter. New York and London: Garland Publishing, Inc. 1007–1028.

Dawe, Kevin. (1996) "The Engendered Lyra: Music, Poetry and Manhood in Crete," *British Journal of Ethnomusicology* 5: 23–44.

——. 1998. "Bandleaders in Crete: Musicians and Entrepreneurs in a Greek Island Economy," *British Journal of Ethnomusicology* 7: 23–44.

——. 1999. "Minotaurs or Musonauts? Cretan Music and World Music," *Popular Music* 18/2: 209–225.

——. 2000. "Roots Music in the Global Village: Cretan Ways of Dealing with the World at Large," *The World of Music* 43/3: 47–66.

——. Forthcoming. "Lyres and the Body Politic: Studying Musical Instruments in the Cretan Musical Landscape," in *Popular Music and Society*, special issue on *Reading the Instrument: Techniques and Technologies in Popular Music*. Bowling Green, OH: Bowling Green State University Press.

Featherstone, Mike. 1990. *Global Culture: Nationalism, Globalization and Modernity*. London, Newbury Park, and New Delhi: SAGE Publications.

———. 1995. *Undoing Culture: Globalization, Postmodernism and Identity*. London, Thousand Oaks, and New Delhi: SAGE Publications.

Hall, Stuart, David Held, and Anthony McGrew. 1992. *Modernity and Its Futures*. Cambridge, U.K.: Polity Press.

Hannerz, Ulf. 1996. *Transnational Connections: Culture, People, Places*. London and New York: Routledge.

Herzfeld, Michael. 1982. *Ours Once More: Folklore, Ideology, and the Making of Modern Greece*. Austin: University of Texas Press.

———. 1987. *Anthropology Through the Looking-Glass: Critical Ethnography in the Margins of Europe*. Cambridge, U.K.: Cambridge University Press.

Lipsitz, Gorge. 1994. *Dangerous Crossroads: Popular Music, Postmodernism and the Poetics of Place*. London and New York: Verso.

Mitchell, Tony. 1996. *Popular Music and Local Identity: Rock, Pop and Rap in Europe and Oceania*. London and New York: Leicester University Press.

Slobin, Mark. 1993. *Subcultural Sounds: Micromusics of the West*. Hanover, NH, and London: Wesleyan University Press.

Taylor, Timothy D. 1997. *Global Pop: World Music, World Markets*. London and New York: Routledge.

Discography and Further Listening

Arvanitaki, Eleftheria. *The Very Best of 1989–1998*. Mercury/Universal Music S.A. 558 636-2. 1998.

Barberis, Takis. *Episodes*. Musurgia Graeca/LYRA ML 0177. 1995.

———. *Naiva*. Musurgia Graeca/LYRA ML 0661. 1998.

Boulgourtzis, Alexis. *Borders*. FM Records FM 962. 1998.

Dalaras, George. *Zondanes Echografeseis* [Live Recordings]. Minos Matsas & Son Co. Ltd. MCD 651. 1986.

———. *Ta Tragoutiia Mou* [My Songs]. Minos Matsas & Son Co. Ltd. MCD 461/2. 1988.

———. *To Elliniko Prosopo Tou Giourgou Dalara* [The Greek Face of George Dalaras]. Minos Matsas & Son Co. Ltd.. 007. 1998.

Daly, Ross. *Oneirou Topoi* [Dream Places]. Aerakis Records SA 521. 1989.

———. *Selected Works*. Oriente Musik Rein CD01. 1994.

———. *Elefthero Simio* [Free Point]. Oriente Musik Rein CD 11. 1996.

Daly, Ross and Bustan Abraham. *Abadai*. Nada Productions NADA 9. 1996.

Daly, Ross and Labyrinth. *Mitos* [Thread]. WDR World Network 54.035. 1992.

Daly, Ross, Petro-Loukas Khalkias, Daya Shankar, Rakesh Chaurasia, et al. *Ellines kai Indoi* [Indians and Greeks]. Saraswati SARA001 and SARA002. 2000. (2 separate CDs. Number one also features Gregoris Kapsales on clarinet and voice.)

Dimitriou, Angela. *Kane Stin Akri*. Minos/EMI 7243 52091720. 1999.

Glykeria. *Ola Mou Ta Mistika* [All My Secrets]. WEA 903171354-4. 1990.

Glykeria. *Ethnic Beats*. Music Circle 5001 002 4. 1995.

Glykeria. *Rembetika, Folk and Traditional Greek Songs Vol 2*. Eros Music S.A. 01722. 1999.

Hadjineophytou, George. *E Hora Tou Perithoriou* [Marginal Land]. Bonjour Records CAVA 007. 1996.

Imiskoumbria. *2030*. Def Jam/Universal Music S.A. 542286 2. 1999.

Kaná, Melina, Ashkhabad, and Thanasis Papakonstantinou. *Lafya* [Loot]. LYRA CD4919. 1998.

Mike, Haji. *Haji Mike on the Mike*. Kebab Culture Music KKM CDLP001. 1994.

——. *Aphrodite's Dream*. Orpheus Musical Imports Ltd. HMP CDLP002. 1997.

——. *Haji Mike Meets Dirty Harri*. Minos-EMI/Axion Production HMP CDLP003. 1999.

Mode Plagal, *Mode Plagal II*. LYRA ML 0668. 1998.

Musurgia GRAECA/LYRA Anthology 2000. ML 0676. 1999.

Nikoloudis, Michalis. *Aeolia*. Libra Music Ltd. LM 001-2. 1995.

Papathanasiou, Vangelis and Papas, Irene. *Odes*. Polydor Records 833 864-2. 1980.

Papazoglou, Nikos. *Haratsi* [Tax]. LYRA CD3369. 2000.

Stassinopoulou, Kristi. *Echotropia*. LYRA ML 4942. 1999.

Vissi, Ana. *Kravgi* [Shout, Cry]. Columbia/Sony Music Greece COL 501513-2. 2000. 2 CDs.

C H A P T E R   T E N

KLAPA SINGING AND *ČA-VAL*: THE MEDITERRANEAN DIMENSION OF POPULAR MUSIC IN CROATIA

JOŠKO ĆALETA

In the time when globalization[1] is slowly, yet unstopably, conquering the world in all fields of human life, there are still local and regional music genres that surpass the frames of local and regional community and become characteristic of a wider community. *Klapa* singing and *ča-val* are examples of a Mediterranean dimension of music that has passed the boundaries of the local and regional in Croatia.[2] Both have originated from the local framework, one as a traditional music that has become popular (klapa singing), and the other as popular music linked to local Istrian cultural tradition and dialect (ča-val). I will be dealing with klapa singing as an insider, based on my rich personal experience (singer, leader, and consultant in klapas). With ča-val I will be dealing as an outsider, concentrating on the media coverage of the musical phenomenon (newspaper clips, radio and TV production, audio recordings), attending concerts of ča-val performers, and field research in Istria. I consider an ethnographic approach that "focuses upon social relationships, emphasizing music as a social practice and process" (Cohen 1993: 123) to be the most suitable for such research. This approach is comparative and holistic; historical and dialogical; reflexive and politically oriented, emphasizing the dynamic complexes of situations that contain abstract concepts and models. At the same time, "it will have to be sensitive to both macro processes of state formation, . . . media networks, and to the micro level of individual experience within these structural coordinates" (Erlmann 1993: 7).

From an average Croat's point of view, the term "Mediterranean" would probably be associated with a number of stereotypes: "sea and sunshine, fish, wine and song, physically appealing and jolly people, noisy street-life, and macho men" (Povrzanović 1989: 166). Music—that is song, its simplicity, and the flourishing melodic line that irresistibly remind one of the musical idea that a person from the continent (the North) has when thinking about the sea, and a southerner (a Mediterranean) instinctively feels as a continuation and a part of his or her musical preoccupations—is a part of the Mediterranean cultural identity of the Croats. The term "Mediterranean" is mainly associated with the expression of both popular and traditional music, but does not coincide with state borders, indicating the importance of continuity in contacts at all levels of communication (Ćaleta 1999: 183). It should be mentioned that neither the traditional nor the popular dimension of Mediterranean music are the most popular genres of musical culture in Croatia. The most represented musical genres in the media are global musical genres, primarily from English-speaking countries. "Although the process of globalization has been going on for decades in this area, a global culture, as a result of it, does not exist" (Kalapoš 2000: 68).[3]

Traditionally, in Croatia, Mediterranean music refers to the music-making of the coastal area and the islands in the regions of Dalmatia, Istria, and Kvarner.[4] This area is rich in diverse, traditional and new vocal and instrumental styles in both secular and spiritual traditions, which is one of the basic conditions for a rich musical practice and production. Popular Mediterranean music in the Croatian context refers to the local musical genres that combine "global" music styles with local elements according to the formula: "A cultural element which is considered to be local, original and one's own (such as a dialect) plus one of the contents of culture which is considered to be global (pop or rock music)" (Kalapoš 2000: 70). It can be concluded from this statement that all popular music performed by the "Mediterranean", that is by people from the coastal area, need not to be characterized as Mediterranean music.[5]

The spread of both traditional and popular music in Croatia cannot be understood without taking into consideration the social and political changes in the last decade of the twentieth century. The "Homeland War" (1991–95), economic, and political changes have put Croatia into an entirely new position.[6] With the rise of the new state of Croatia—at the beginning of the 1990s—there was a need for a (re)definition of national identity. Mediterranean identity grew from a regionally based identity to an important factor in the formation of the national identity of today's Croats.[7] The music-making of the Croatian coast is increasingly recognized as a model for Croatian musicians. The term scholars use for the phenomenon of the wide dissemination of Mediterranean influence into areas with different and even converse musical characteristics is "Mediterraneanization."[8]

What common features of popular and traditional music are considered Mediterranean? First of all, they have the same local framework, the place of origin. Popular music has a better chance to spread these styles, through recordings, media appearances, and concert activities.[9] Their origin gives a local overtone to the term "Mediterranean" because it refers exclusively to the traditional and popular music developed in the local framework. Although both have elements of other Mediterranean cultures, communication does not exist at this level.[10] The audience that supports them is partly local. There is an increase of interest of not only older but the younger generation for some genres of traditional music (particularly klapa singing) as well as an increase of interest of both the younger and older generations in the popular Mediterranean music (pop entertainment music, ča-val). Third, and possibly the most important, the specific quality they share is the dialect as a form of musical expression. Their music in the dialect sings about universal themes (love), understandable and present in the lives of the people of all local communities.

Popular music sung in dialects did not emerge in the 1990s with the political and economic changes. The dialect in popular Croatian music, and throughout Europe, has been a characteristic of locality and region, present only in the local media, in the local cultural manifestations, often presented "as an expression of the *authentic, autochthonous, traditional* and *undiscovered,* whatever that may mean in the given context" (Kalapoš 2000: 70). Some of popular songs—*šlager*[11]—crossed the local borders and modified in another environment. Šlagers, some of which date as far back as the beginning of the twentieth century, have persisted until today, mostly in the repertoire of folklore groups that treat them as traditional tunes.[12] The other segment of popular music—rock music—primarily associated with the young population, has mostly used the standard Croatian for its lyrics. There were also some very successful groups "whose sound might be called local, Yugoslav (Bijelo dugme) for their concrete musical and textual folklore motifs, and Azra and Riblja čorba for the folkloric atmosphere created by successfully expressing the domestic mentality" (Bobinsky 1985: 70).

The dialectal/regional trend that appears in the 1990s does not refer exclusively to pop music anymore, but also greatly to rock and alternative music, whose audience is mainly the young population. One of the reasons for the sudden popularity of the dialectal trend is a possible answer to the growing media campaign promoting the repertoire of *tamburica* music as Croatian national music.[13] The dialectal trend is a phenomenon in different parts of Croatia, especially in the regions where the *kajkavian* dialect (bands like Dreletronic, Zadruga, Vještice) or the *čakavian* dialect (bands like Kvartet Gorgonzola, šo!Mazgoon, Kuzma & Shaka Zulu) is used (Knezović et al. 1994). The most recognizable among dialectal trends is the wave of the Istrian and Kvarner bands that have become known as the ča-val.

Dalmatia and Klapa Singing

If one were obliged to select a single aspect of music-making as most representative of the Mediterranean as far as Croats are concerned, it would definitely be the phenomenon of klapa singing, "a coming together of the traditional and the popular with a positive tendency of spreading outside the imagined borders of the Mediterranean" (Ćaleta 1999: 193). Klapa singing is a continuing and relatively old tradition, which was pointed to by researchers and musicologists at the end of the nineteenth century.[14] It is a style of traditional homophonous singing. Nowdays, this organized form of singing, because of the way it is presented, is perceived as a style of popular music rather than traditional. Klapa was never an isolated phenomenon. The character, musical content, and style of klapa "were dynamically modified, through the time, freely adopting new changes" (Ćaleta 1997a: 142). This is one of the reasons for the present-day popularity of klapa, especially among the younger generation, and it is a certain sign of a longlasting future of it.

The differences of the various forms of the klapa became in time so significant that we can speak of three models of the klapa: the traditional, the festival, and the modern klapa.

The traditional klapa represents an informal group of singers who sing occasionally, for the sake of singing. Oral tradition and simple music-making were the main characteristics of this style. Traditional klapa songs have been sung on different occasions, "in wine cellars, at home, in town squares, or in some acoustically favorable space, so common in traditional Mediteranean architecture, as serenades to a girl and at pauses during fishing or some other work" (Povrzanović 1989: 162). Despite the existence of new contexts and changes in musical content, the authenticity of the performance practice still exists today, especially in smaller (Dalmatian) Mediterranean towns, usually among older people.[15]

The term "festival klapa" is associated with the beginning of Omiš Festival of Dalmatian Klapas, established in 1967, the annual competition and great promoter of klapa singing, a bond between amateurs singing and scholars directing. Festival klapa is a formally organized group of singers with clear aims and intentions. Although the joy of singing binds them, "the performance and presentation of the singing are their main objective" (Ćaleta, 1997a: 130). All of this is realized with the help of a trained leader who selects the singers and the repertoire, and regularly practices with the klapa. The popularity of the Omiš Festival has encouraged the formation of many klapas, from around 15 organized klapas in the 1960s to more than 200 registered male klapas at the end of the 1980s.[16] Most klapa leaders and singers have evaluated their work through their success at the Omiš Festival. Formation of female klapas, which have inherited the structure, the repertoire, and the performance style practice from their male counterparts,[17] was also encouraged by the Omiš Festival. Klapa singing has in this period been increasingly defined as a symbol of the Dalmatian (Mediterranean) identity.[18] In this period, a trend began of forming klapas outside the borders of Dalmatia, and even Croatia.[19] A great number of klapas that differ by gender, age, reasons for singing, and locality has provoked interest in different genres of vocal music, both traditional and popular.[20] In the 1970s, they became the choral accompaniment to pop singers at festivals of popular music (especially the Split Festival).[21] The first commercial klapas emerged as a part of tourist entertainment, usually performing with the accompaniment of mandolins and guitars,[22] thus spreading the positive Mediterranean spirit among the tourists, both Croatian (northerners) and foreign.

In less than 30 years, klapas have outgrown the local traditional framework. It should be mentioned that such a rapid increase of popularity was helped by a positive relation between politics and klapa singing. The answer to the question in what manner is music used for certain political objectives and, particularly, what kind of music is used on politically important occasions (Ceribašić 1998: 111), will confirm the thesis that politics doesn't pass by music, traditional or popular. From the beginnings of its organized existence, the klapa has been a favorite of the politics of the system it has existed in.[23] The klapas have mainly been organized as parts of the local KUDs (Cultural Artistic Society), and actively participated in all local cultural programs.[24] For such an occasion, the klapas usually had an appropriate repertoire of songs attached to the partisan movement from World War II and songs that celebrate the brotherhood and unity of socialist society. The Omiš Festival was also recognized and sponsored by the Ministry of Culture as an event of regional importance (Marošević 1988: 86).

The social, cultural, and political changes in Croatia at the beginning of the 1990s provoked changes in the klapa singing movement. In order to distinguish this new style from the klapa of the previous period (festival klapa), I use the term "modern klapa," for a number of reasons. First of all, the term "modern" denotes something innovative, suiting the aspirations of the new klapa singers. For the singers, klapa is an advanced musical form that widens their musical horizons. "Modern" means experimental, and this is characteristic of the contemporary klapa that is capable of dealing with the vocal styles of traditional, classical, and especially popular music. "Modern" also means popular and this is what the klapa of the 1990s accomplished—from the popularization of the klapa movement to the widening of the circle of interest of audiences of all ages beyond their local and regional limits.

The center of klapa singing in the 1990s is no longer Dalmatia; Zagreb and Rijeka are these days the bearers of klapa singing. An increasing number of klapas have been formed among Croatian emigrants (Australia, New Zealand, Canada, Germany, Sweden), but also among people fond of part-singing.[25] The Mediterranean identity is still omnipresent; although now the singers are not always Dalmatian Mediterraneans; the audience perceives them as klapa groups based on the sung (čakavian) lyrics, the melodious tunes, the temperament that they display when performing, and their repertoire. The number of female klapas has increased.[26] While in the 1980s most klapa leaders and singers evaluated their work through their success at the Omiš Festival, being exposed to the media is becoming a success factor of increasing importance for the klapas in the 1990s.

Changes have also occurred in the formal organization of the klapas themselves. Although the leader of the klapa is still very charismatic and crucial for its results and accomplishments, an increasing number of klapas do not have a permanent leader. A number of successful klapa leaders share their knowledge and experience with several klapas through various short-term programs that result in festival performances, studio recordings, or individual concerts.

What is the cause of the change in relations between the leader and the klapa? Most singers of the festival-klapa type have had a direct contact with the tradition of klapa singing; they have had personal experience and visions about the manner of singing, acquired through listening to the elders and imitating their manner of singing (oral tradition). In a modern klapa, the singers are young, educated people who have acquired their experience through listening to the performances of certain klapas and to numerous recordings. The singers of a modern klapa are more aware that practice is a certain way to success, as well as the choice of repertoire and the specific way of singing. The role of the leader is slowly but certainly being taken on by the member of the klapa in charge of public relations, contracting the concerts, and arranging the media promotion of the klapa. The role of a professional manager will soon be an indispensable part of every successful klapa. One of the tasks of a professional manager will be successful audio and video production, which in the 1990s rapidly grew due to the decrease of cost and the simplifying of production technology.

I have on several occasions been able to listen to the conversations and comments during the rehearsals and spontaneous singing on informal occasions of modern klapa groups. Comments such as, "This performance is like the one of the klapa Trogir in the 1989 concert in Lisinski" or "Why don't we sing as openly as klapa Ošjak on their second album?" speak of modern klapa singers and their approaches toward klapa singing. They are able to imitate various styles of singing and through them find their own expression. Their models are the best klapas and singers of their choice, not the locality they come from. With the new way of thinking and presenting their music, modern klapas have won over a new audience. Their audience is drawn from the relatively young (the student population) and middle-aged (the educated) who enjoy listening to the music with complete attention during the performance.[27]

As in the previous periods, the klapa movement owes its popularity and media exposure to the cultural politics of society as a whole. Social and political changes at the beginning of the 1990s have made changes in the repertoire and the occasions for the performing of klapas. Klapa groups no longer have songs from World War II or the socialist period in their repertoire. On the other hand, a whole new repertoire has been created, consisting of patriotic songs ranging from nationalist songs from the time of the Illyrian Movement (mid-nineteenth century), performance of which originally resulted in imprisonment ("Vila Velebita"), to patriotic songs composed during the "Homeland War" ("Bože," čuvaj Hrvatsku," "Na Omiškoj stini," "Vjerujem u te"). The klapas keep performing for all local cultural and political manifestations, but also during election campaigns.[28] With the new social and political system, the attitude toward religion has changed, so that a modern klapa now has on its repertoire a number of compositions on sacred subjects (some of them composed for a klapa), which they perform during mass or in concerts in sacred premises.[29]

The repertoire of the klapa has gone through the most perceptible changes. While cooperation with pop singers was the main characteristic of festival klapa, cooperation with rock musicians and even "alternative" musicians, experimenting with new forms and new sounds, is characteristic of modern klapa. The challenge in incorporating elements of rock, soul, and even rap into klapa singing is that these modern styles feature a solid rhythm, a movement that encourages dance, as opposed to klapa song, which is by itself wide and slow, sung in free *parlando-rubato* rhythm not suitable for dance.

The greatest promotion of klapa singing in this area has been made by certainly the most popular klapa of the 1990s: the klapa Cambi.[30] Their success and media popularity was mostly helped by cooperation with the famous Croatian rock musician Zlatan Stipišić Gibonni.[31] Although he incorporates rock, blues, funk, and soul into his musical expression, his lyrics are written in the *čakavian* dialect. In his projects, Gibonni treats the klapa as an equal partner, and not as chorus accompaniment.[32] The concerts of the klapa Cambi are organized like rock bands' concerts: they perform in open-air arenas and sport halls, and they tour regularly. Their lives are not so exposed to the media as the lives of singers of popular music, their names (maybe with the exception of the first tenor) are not remembered, only their figures are identified with the name of the klapa, not individually.

Another example of a klapa that has been influential in the 1990s is the klapa Kumpanji from Blato on the island of Korčula. In cooperation with a local band, Kvartet Gorgonzola, in the summer of 1998. they recorded a rap song whose base were quotes of a klapa song "Vila moja projde." Besides klapa quotes, the lyrics of the rap were quite unusual. While typical rap topics are social problems of the urban culture of the young, the topic of their rap was a typical klapa and Mediterranean one: unrequited love (of a high school boy in a small island village).[33]

Media attention to klapa "excursions" into various styles has resulted in the founding of a festival that promotes the cooperation of the traditional and popular Mediterranean music in the area. The Kaštela Festival was conceived as two days of socializing of klapas and musicians of various styles who cooperate with klapas or look for inspiration in any form of traditional music-making of Mediterranean Croatia.[34]

It can be concluded that klapa in the 1990s is a part of a movement of popular music, with which it freely experiments and that it integrates into its repertoire. At the same time, musicians of popular music arrange klapa songs in the manner of their music-making style, thus widening the generally accepted positive spirit of the Mediterranean identity.

Istria and Ča-val

The Mediterranean coast of Croatia, apart from the southern region of Dalmatia, includes the area of the northern Adriatic, consisting of

Istria and Kvarner. With the exception of recent geographers who considered the Upper Adriatic a sub-Mediterranean zone (Ogrin, in Baskar 1999: 124), the peninsula of Istria is generally considered the northernmost part of the Mediterranean. For the rest of Croatia, this region is recognized as "Mediterranean" because of its geographic characteristics (the sea, the coast, and the islands) and the unavoidable symbols (sunshine, wine, song, happy and optimistic people, tourism, temperamental lifestyle).

The peninsula of Istria is also a very specific area in the historical and cultural sense. Istria had been governed by various authorities, and during the centuries several ethnic groups have lived and have a claim upon it. Constant interactions created a specific and a unique regional picture, a cultural mosaic of ethnic groups that call themselves Istrians (Banovac 1996, 1998). At the same time, Istria was the scene of mixing of different traditional music styles that came to the region, lingered there, blended, and were reborn or disappeared. The image of the area's musical heritage has usually been incorrectly created in the field by researchers who focus on particular cultural communities using different criteria.[35] Older layers of traditional music are characterized by untempered singing or two-part singing and playing: descant, *na tanko i debelo* (thin and thick), *bugarenje* (wailing), and sacral ritual singing in a so-called Istrian scale. The more recent musical tradition consists of tempered (tonal) music created under the influence of Middle European urban traditions. In all ethnic communities, the recent tradition has influenced the untempered, two-part music-making, mainly by introducing new tempered instruments (manufactured). This repertoire is limited exclusively to dances performed by various small ensembles, called *gunjci,* known in very narrow local circles, completely unexposed to the media.[36]

Popular music in Istria established its first connection with Istrian traditional music in the 1960s, at the height of the festival-founding trend throughout Croatia. In 1964, the "Melodies of Istria and Kvarner Festival"[37] was founded with the aim "to popularize domicile folk musical heritage" (Marušić 1995: 38). The festival has been able to inaugurate a type of song based on pleasant-to-the-ear refrains (Mediterranean melodies), with only a few quotes of the traditional music. Regional music has been reflected only "in stereotyped lyrics, patterns appropriate for tourist postcards with little boats, *kažun,*[38] small walls and wine"

(Marušić 1995: 39). Only a few singers (Mirko Cetinski, Lidija Percan, Radojka Šverko) have emerged from this festival and become popular to the wider audience by singing not only their local hits (in the Istrian or Italian dialect) but also in the Croatian standard language.

Istria, especially its biggest urban center, Pula, has an important role in the Croatian musical scene as far as the popular music of the young—rock music—is concerned.[39] Pula's rock and alternative scene is represented by Atomsko sklonište,[40] whose standards from the 1980s are still often played on radio stations. Franci Blašković, a cult performer of the Istrian region, whom many consider to be the originator of the ča-val, came from Pula, too. In the 1980s, Istrian rock musicians tried to combine elements of traditional music, the dialect, with "musical realities," such as rock, blues, and country, but these attempts didn't have a significant response on the old Yugoslav market.

The sudden popularity of Istrian musicians in the 1990s can be linked to the general situation in Croatia. The independence the state gained through a war was followed by the forming of national, regional, and local identities, parallel with the forming of new musical genres, caused a need for new musical expressions. The media-promoted performers from Istria, regardless of their stylistic differences, became known in the Croatian scene under the joint name of ča-val.[41] The term itself[42] was not constructed by the musicians or the local audience, but by the press, music critics, and media promoters who follow the movements in the musical scene, and who sensed the possibility of promoting this type of music nationally.

The first significant success in the Croatian popular scene was made by Alen Vitasović, a singer from Orbanići near Pula, in 1992, with his hit *Gušti su gušti*. It was the first in a series of hits, created in cooperation with Livio Morosin, which first won over the critics and then the audience (Vitaljić 2000).[43] The čakavian dialect in which Vitasović (and all ča-val performers) sang his hits was the local essence, which was joined to differently-oriented Western musical styles, that gives them the Istrian-Mediterranean overtone. Vitasović has on various occasions spoken about the reasons for singing in the čakavian dialect: "I sing in the čakavian, Istrian dialect, and what more can you do for your region if you are a musician? You get it? I don't need to wave little flags with goats[44] on them" (Brnobić, 1994). At the same time, Vitasović warns that the use of the dialect has no direct connection with the music he sings. "My aim is good music, sincere, my music, American rhythm and blues, and only the lyrics are Čakavian. Why shouldn't they be, if I use it?" (Balen 1994). The meteoric career of Alen Vitasović did not last very long, but it paved the way for other Istrian musicians.

One of the greatest and and longest lasting bands of ča-val is the band Gustafi. I will use their example to illustrate the making of popular music in Istria. The most eminent Croatian music critic described their music in this way:

> Gustafi are my favorite domestic live band. When listening to it for the first time it's Tex-Mex and blues that you hear, but if you go on listening you can learn a lot about the emotional realism and the sensibility of the people who live on a miserly ground, and who want to live their lives to the fullest. (Glavan, in Bakić 1999)

This description raises the basic question: "Where is the Mediterranean in this and what is Mediterranean about it?"

Edi Maružin, an Istrian from Svetvinčent, a small village in the interior of Istria, formed his band—Gustaph i njegovi dobri duhovi—in 1980 playing music in an alternative, avant-garde style.[45] Unburdened by "greatness," they played everywhere "from a ship to a tavern, from a wedding to a hotel" (Maružin, in Bakić 1999). Soon they surpassed the local framework, and from a local band they turned into a well-known band. They performed all over the former state of Yugoslavia, although without significant media success. However, a change occurred in the 1990s, when by merging traditional music, rock and roll, and the specific Istrian (local) pop entertainment sound with rhythm and blues, they managed to build an audience. The Homeland War made them focus their performances in the Istrian region in the beginning of the 1990s. They began giving a series of concerts—*štala* (stable)—playing in small villages, inns, taverns, civic community centers, in order to entertain the local population. They began with the Oštarijada in 1991, together with Franci Blašković, and then alone with a number of štala-type concerts, working continually.[46] The ensemble varies from 6 to 13 musicians, according to the size of the space, purpose of the concert, and the financial resources of the organizer.

Front cover of Gustafi's *Vraćamo se odmah*

Edi Maružin, the frontman and key member of the band, feels that he lacks musical experience because he has never played in another band.[47] He calls his music popular music[48] that "unites everything we have heard that affects us in a positive way," while Istrian music for him is "a specific music, very simple . . . and the person has to have some ethnical preconditions (genes) to understand it."

At the beginning of their project, Gustafi cooperated with Livio Morosin, the key person in building the media popularity of ča-val, who deserves the most credit for the promotion of Alen Vitasović. His last project CD, *Bura-tramuntana*, realized in cooperation with the musician and ethnomusicologist Dario Marušić, maintained the popularity of ča-val in this decade. Besides rock and pop music, Morosin has experimented in his project with other musical styles, from jazz to electronic music and hip-hop.[49] In this project, we can hear a number of Istrian traditional untempered instruments that fit into various musical styles:

> I claim that the *sopile*[50] and *roženice* can function in any kind of music, as well as any kind of a brass-section. People simply listen to music and if it has quality, it is completely irrelevant which instrument you are playing, and in what context. . . . I am a man who always has to review his own attitudes, who has to change, learn. So, in the meantime, I have realized that electronic music can be of a very high quality. (Marušić, in Vitaljić 2000)

What conclusions can we draw from these various ča-val musicians? All of them consider music part of their lives. Listening to all sorts of music and styles has widened their horizons and visions when building a personal musical outlook. Their music is progressive, changeable, open to diverse influences, and not limited to one musical style. It is customary that local musicians who succeed in the region move to the capital (Zagreb), for better media promotion, which is not the case locally. All of them live contentedly and perform musically in Istria. Although the majority of musicians deny any connection with the traditional music of their childhood, they cannot walk away from it and, in fact, it is the most important factor of their popularity beyond regional boundaries. I do not wish to state categorically that their popularity would not have occurred had they played rock music in standard Croation or in English, but the fact remains that they did not. There was something that encouraged them to turn to their roots, their own way of life, which they appreciate and care about. Therefore, music in their case is everything *they* think music is: the experience acquired by following the global musical trends they join with their musical reflections, thus gaining a new, specific expression, understandable to a wider audience, interesting exactly because of the specific local additions that they add into the melting pot of global reflections, as a dose of inheritance unconsciously integrated into their minds. All of this is a part of a great mosaic, which, in this specific case, promotes the music of the Mediterranean.

Although in their statements they never comment on or emphasize their political affinities, their music-making has skillfully been exploited for political purposes. Their sudden media popularity was the reason for the interest the state political scene has shown for their music making:[51] "By frequently presenting the ča-val in the media, the makers of cultural politics wanted to show that Istria, even on such a symbolic level as art, is an integral part of Croatia, and in that they succeeded" (Kalapoš 1998: 8). The most famous representatives of the ča-val have become an obligatory part of the scenery of political election campaigns. They played for the national governing *HDZ* party (Vitasović)[52] and more often for the popular Istrian regional governing party *IDS* (Šajeta and Gustafi).[53]

This brief description of ča-val music and musicians is based on what we, the outsiders, know or can find out about ča-val and what was exposed by the media. When researching the musical phenomena in central Istria, I had the chance of talking with the local population and asked them about their relation toward ča-val. Their answers did not always coincide with the image I had developed by researching the media sources. The majority of people knew of the most popular interpreters of ča-val, but only after I mentioned the name of a certain band or a singer. Through these conversations, I gathered information about bands I had not heard of until then, which could be a part of ča-val according to their music (Magnolija, Battifiaca), as well as some singers (Elio Pisak) unknown to the wider audience. As a source of listening to these interpreters, the majority of the informants named local radio stations. Listening to the program of local stations (Radio Pazin, Radio Buzet, Radio Pula) for several days, I noticed that their music can frequently be heard.[54]

These examples show that the relations of the foreign and close, in the world of the mass media, are difficult to define, "and it is increasingly difficult to locate and identify consistent, insoluble communities or bodies of texts and practices which can be taken as constitutive of the culture of the community" (Grossberg, in Cohen 1993: 125). In this case, the local population identifies with one part of the repertoire, which doesn't coincide with the media-formed repertoire that the wider population enjoy (Vitasović, Gustafi, Šajeta). Numerous questions arise: Does something popular have to be a widely spread phenomenon? And does narrow or local popularity mean that it is not truly "popular" music? Does popular music rise from the people who constitute its audience, or is it superimposed upon them from above (Manuel 1988: 8)? Considering these questions is an important act in forming conclusions about the musical activity of a certain environment. Musical tastes of the local audience do not coincide with the media image we have of ča-val. In this particular case, the music-making of local interpreters, such as Elio Pisak or Magnolija, are more important for the local audience then the music-making of Gustafi or Morosin, known to the wider audience as ča-val representatives.

Both klapa and ča-val are a part of the popular music identified with the Mediterranean in today's Croatia. The Mediterranean dimension as a part of cultural identity is accepted, and thus from the local and regional becomes a significant national identity. Popular music of Mediterranean dimension develops according to the formulas: a little (ča-val) or a lot (klapa) of the local and traditional; and a little (klapa) or a lot (ča-val) of the globally popular, surpassing the local framework. By approaching the two phenomena differently, I wanted to point out the diversity and stratification of the musical phenomena, in which, because of the extraordinary saturation, the borders between the popular and the traditional are not clearly drawn.

Notes

1. I understand globalization as "a dynamic process of restructuring and transformation of the political and economic world order" (Guilbault 1993: 33).

2. Being an ethnomusicologist whose research has been focused mainly on the research of local musical traditions, I am interested in the relation between global musical phenomena (popular music) and local musical tradition. In this way I join the majority of my colleagues within popular music studies, and even more cultural studies generally, which recently shifted "from the study of the global to the local, and from work on production to consideration of consumption, subjectivity and identity in the context of everyday life" (Cohen 1993: 127). There is an extensive literature on this topic written in the 1980s and later: among others, Morley 1986; Csikszentmihaly and Rochberg-Halton 1981; De Certeau 1980; Erlmann 1993; Guilbault 1993; Stokes 1994.

3. "It can be 'global,' its products can be sold in millions of copies, . . . it can be transmitted all over the world, by means of satellites, local radio and TV networks, but there still is no popular 'hit' which has been accepted or even known to every person of the 'global village'" (Muršić 1996: 59-60).

4. The term "traditional music," as an integral part of the traditional culture, I conceive in Hobsbawm's sense, as a "set of practices, normally governed by overtly or tacitly accepted rules and of a ritual or symbolic nature, which seek to inculcate

certain values and norms of behavior by repetition, which automatically implies continuity with the past. In fact, where possible, they normally attempt to establish continuity with a suitable historic past" (Hobsbawn 1983: 1). It is defined from an ideological point of view, which usually redefines locally as new political orientations arise.

5. This mainly refers to the musicians from the area, which follow popular global musical trends (rock, jazz, techno, hip-hop, rap) in English (as a global language) or in the Croatian standard language.

6. The "Homeland War" is a perspective that cannot be avoided in the considering of the local-global relations. The war was going on in the time when the world was attempting to define the term "local" for small and developing countries. For some, defining local has come as a "reaction linked with the fear of losing cultural identity in the face of worldwide homogenization" and for others has been "perceived as an opportunity to redefine and promote local identity" (Guilbault 1993: 34).

7. The majority of Croats see their identity rather as a part of Mediterranean identity (Adriatic) or Central European identity (sub-Alpine, Panonnian), than as Balkan identity (Dinaric). In order to strengthen this argument they are inclined to point to a number of issues that differentiate them from their neighbors to the East, the East to them having an absolutely negative connotation. For more information, see Čapo 1999; Rihtman-Auguštin 1999.

8. The term "Mediterraneanization" was introduced by Pettan: "While migrating from the Dinaric to either the Panonnian or the Adriatic zone (and not vice versa), people think they are moving from worse to better . . . more modern, and more Western in comparison to their own heritage. As a result, parallel with the growth of tourism along the coast, one can predict further *Mediterraneanization* of Croatia. This *Mediterraneanization* will certainly emphasize Western values, at the expense of Croatia's Eastern cultural traits, here synonymous with the Dinaric heritage" (Pettan 1997). For those who create a new social identity (moving into a city) popular music may serve as a powerful and meaningful symbol of identity. Popular music may serve "as a metaphor for the creation of a distinctive world of common meanings and shared cultural ideologies on the part of the new urban classes" (Manuel 1988: 16–17). There are two elements in the Mediterraneanization that Pettan mentioned: littoral/coastal migrations or village/city migrations and tourism. There are a few more elements that I consider integral parts of the phenomenon: music festivals, popular music, discographic production, radio and television broadcasting.

9. In the field of entertainment/popular music, singers from the Mediterranean part of Croatia hold a leading place on the Croatian popular music scene in both number and popularity. This started with the festivals of pop entertainment music (*zabavna glazba*) in the 1960s, modeled on the famous Sanremo festival of Italian *canzone*, and continued with the founding of many well-known or lesser-known festivals of popular music whose output formed a large part of the music broadcast by radio stations throughout the country, and their increasingly popular presentation in TV videoclips.

10. Popular music which comes from, for example, Italy, people in Croatia will identify as a "global" rather than Mediterranean. The same applies to the traditional or popular music, which comes through mass media from more distant Mediterranean countries. Many of my fellow citizens would, in that case, surely identify the term "Mediterranean music" as "world music."

11. *Šlager* is a term used for easily remembered popular melodies that have a stereotyped musical structure and codified textual messages, ranging in a very narrow circle of permitted topics (patriotism, Puritanism, tragic, sentimental, or platonic love, exotics, etc.). Any concretization or real problematization of current social, ethical, or sexual dilemmas is avoided, and the impression is given that the sung contents refer directly to the life experience of the listeners (Glavan 1978: 18).

12. Elaborating the "transition from the realm of composed (popular) music to the realm of folklore music life," Grozdana Marošević states that "most people who are singing or listening to these songs today have no idea that they were composed by individual authors; the songs are considered anonymous products of a folk (collective) creativity" (Marošević 1988: 77).

13. This promotion was executed by politically dictated state media as a typical case of a centralized political system against regional political aspirations. *Tamburica* orchestras, mostly made up of younger performers, for the lyric use Štokavian dialect which is, at the same time, the base for the Croatian standard language. For further information on *tamburica* music in the 1990s, consult Bonifačić 1998; Ceribašić 1995; Ćaleta 1999.

14. For more information on klapa singing, see Povrzanović 1991; Ćaleta 1997a.

15. By "traditional klapa" I do not consider spontaneous singing of informal groups in organized (weddings, baptisms, birthdays) or unorganized gatherings, nor spontaneous singing of several members of various klapas during common gatherings.

16. Primary sources for the history of the festival are the Bulletins of the Festival of Dalmatian Klapas in Omiš (1/1970–70/2000) and programs and catalogues which are regularly published by the Festival Committee, and especially three miscellanies of Dalmatian Klapa Songs, which with some 900 tunes performed at the Festivals, bring a series of information of the participants, melographs, composers, arrangers, and klapa leaders.

17. The first female klapa to compete at the Festival appeared in 1976. Before that year female klapas appeared sporadically in the non-competitive part or as individual members of male klapas. In the 1980s the number of female klapas slowly increased as well as their quality. It resulted in female klapa winning expert jury prizes, as well as audience prizes (especially klapa Zadranke, from Zadar). For more information about women klapa singing see Stremšek 1994: 197–217.

18. Zvuci Dalmacije from Perth, Dalmacija from Sydney, formed by Croatian, mainly Dalmatian emigrants, and the klapa Sokoli from Seattle, formed by singers of Croatian and American descent, performed at Omiš Festival in the 1980s. For further information on the klapa in diaspora, consult Ćaleta 1997b.

19. All the songs of the klapa repertoire are sung in the local čakavian dialect. The singers perform in stylized national costumes, characteristic parts of national

costumes (linen belts, hats), or in sailor T-shirts or peasant shirts which symbolize the region they come from.

20. With the help of the Omiš Festival and the media, the klapas have discovered the charms of singing on stage, which has become the almost exclusive place of performing. Microphones, stage lights, TV broadcasts have become a part of the klapa singing have ritual, and klapa singers have become better stage performers. Besides klapa songs, they also perform "Russian, Serbian, and Macedonian folk songs, urban romances, Renaissance compositions, Negro spirituals" (Povrzanović, 1989: 161).

21. The most popular singers usually choose the best klapas. The collaboration of the klapa Trogir with the most popular Dalmatian singer, Oliver Dragojević ("Oprosti mi pape", "S ponistre se vidi šolta", "A vitar puše"), is well-known. The klapa Šibenik has sung with Mate Mišo Kovač and Jasna Zlokić with the klapa Ošjak. In the 1980s, klapa Trogir and Oliver Dragojević gave a number of joint concerts, which were always all sold out. The result of one of those concerts is the first live recording made by one of the klapas. The practice until then was releasing only studio recordings.

22. The klapa Šibenik is certainly one of the best representatives of this style of klapa singing. It has proved itself by winning with their *a capella* performances at the Omiš Festival several times during the 1970s and 1980s, as well as with commercial repertoire that was more often played on radio stations due to the instrumental accompaniment (mandolin ensemble). Many other klapas have followed in their footsteps (e.g., the klapa Bonaca, Maslina). To accommodate media demands, they started experimenting by adding other electronic instruments (synthesizer, rhythm machine, sound samples), simplifying the already simple harmony and emphasizing one solo voice. It resulted in more media attention than regular *a capella* klapa singing.

23. The vocal ensemble Dalmacija (with instrumental accompaniment), the predecessor of a festival klapa, was one of the favorite ensembles of the Yugoslav president Tito. An ensemble entertained him during his diplomatic visits, during his stay in Zagreb and the Brioni Islands, and for the various celebrations (New Years' parties, parties for foreign statesmen).

24. Peter Manuel points out that "the constraints and pressures on musical style and content in socialist countries tend to derive less from market concerns than from bureaucratic or ideological factors. . . . The limits that have been and are still imposed upon artists in the socialist world may not be structurally inherent to socialism; in that sense, such a social economic system—regardless of its other assets or defects—may continue to offer one kind of alternative to the dialectic contradictions which popular music may never transcend under capitalism" (Manuel 1988: 15–16).

25. During my stay in Canada (1989–96), I attended klapa singing workshops on several occasions. One of them, East European Folk Music Society Campus, was held every summer in Mendocino, California. The workshops were attended by people of Croatian descent but also by an exceptionally large number of people who simply enjoyed learning and performing traditional music of various nations.

26. Because of the growing popularity of female klapas, the Omiš Festival in

1992 dedicated one festival night exclusively to them, and in 1994, a whole parallel festival where they competed according to the same rules as the male klapas (24 klapas in two semi-finals, 10 klapas in the final night performance). The groups were chosen by auditions organized in the centers of klapa singing (Zagreb, Rijeka, Split, Dubrovnik). This might be the greatest influence that the Omiš Festival had on the klapas in the 1990s.

27. Although the concerts in Zagreb (which are sold out in advance as a rule) are attended by a great number of young people, especially students, there is a chamber atmosphere during the performance, like that of classical music concerts. The seated audience is carefully listening to the performance; they know exactly when to salute the performer with applause, they call the klapas to perform an encore. The spaces where such concerts take place in Zagreb are smaller (Glazbeni zavod) or bigger halls (Lisinski), theaters (HNK, Komedija, Kerempuh), student clubs (SKUC, Pauk) and even places for the alternative culture of the young (Tvornica).

28. President Franjo Tudjman, like his predecessor, Tito, liked the klapa and klapa singing. He was the sponsor of Omiš Festival, and was present on the final night of the 30th jubilee Omiš Festival. Klapa Cambi sang an appropriate composed klapa song ("Sutra će te ponit") at his funeral.

29. The new relation of the church and klapa singing has resulted in an official visit of the representatives of the Omiš Festival and the chosen klapas to the Pope at the Vatican in 1996.

30. Like all famous klapas, Cambi began competing at the Omiš Festival, where they were, for several years in a row, absolute winners of traditional klapa singing. The leader of klapa Cambi, Rajmir Kraljević, has arranged most of Gibonni's hits for klapa performance, using an emphasized syncopation as a base, unknown in klapa performing before. Klapa Cambi won the prestigious Porin-Croatian media award (Croatian version of the American Grammy or the British Britt Awards).

31. Zlatan Stipišić Gibonni is a musician who began his musical career as a singer with the heavy rock group Osmi putnik, and continued it by making a very successful solo career as a composer, lyricist, and singer of entertainment music (*zabavna glazba*). Gibonni grew up with the klapa tradition of his father, Ljubo Stipišić, one of the most highly appreciated klapa leaders, melographs, and especially composers of newly-composed klapa expression. Gibonni's songs have won numerous festivals of popular music, performed by him or the most popular Croatian pop singers (Oliver, Tedi Spalato). Besides klapa Cambi he has worked on *Ljudi, zviri i beštimje* with the Macedonian guitar player Vlatko Stefanovski, whose band Leb i sol was in the 1980s the recognized Yugoslav jazz-rock group. At the moment, Gibonni is finishing his seventh CD, in cooperation with leading musicians—drummer Manu Katche and bass guitar player Pino Palladino. As journalists report, "A Welshman of Italian descent, Palladino, the Frenchman, Katche, and Gibonni have found a meeting place in the Mediterranean spirit of his songs" (Zagorac 2001).

32. The biggest Croatian daily newspaper *Večernji list* gives an annual musical award, *Ruža* (The Rose), in several categories, by the readers' choice. Because of the media popularity of *tamburica* music during the 1990s, the *tamburica* players had their own category until this year, when it was renamed the ethno music category.

33. The sudden popularity enabled this young klapa to perform in concerts outside their island, on TV, where their videoclip was played for a long time. The media popularity was reflected in their treatment at the Omiš Festival. For their performance at the Omiš Festival, 1999, which until then did not recognize the qualities of this klapa, they were awarded both the audience and the expert jury awards. In cooperation with Kvartet Gorgonzola, they have recorded a number of similar projects. "Splis'ke cajke" is a rap with an unusual theme—it warns of the growing popularity of "Eastern" music of Serbian origin, an act they consider to be treason.

34. Besides the two concerts, which are evaluated by a jury of music critics, journalists, ethnomusicologists, and musicians, round tables are organized, The ways of musical expression, the interaction of traditional and popular musical culture are themes of these discussions. The initiator and organizer of this festival is the above-mentioned klapa Cambi, which during the 1990s was the only klapa capable of making such a move. The step requires media, economic but also political support of the local and national environment.

35. The prevailing division in the Italian cultural circle is the one between Italian and Slavic music, a kind of in-group/out-group opposition, i.e., "us" and "them." But Slavic music can be either Croatian or Slovenian. In the Croatian cultural circle there is a division between Istrian music (understood as Croatian) and the music of the Italian ethnic community. This division is a rather general one because it can lead to the conclusion that Italian music is not Istrian. Slovenian experts deal only with Slovenian music and do not raise the question of divisions. (Marušić 1995: 11)

36. "*Gunjci*" is term used for an ensemble originally consisting of a violin and a double bass, performing exclusively dance music (polka, mazurka, waltz, march) at village fairs, weddings, and dances. In time, the ensemble was joined by other instruments: clarinet, *triestina* (diatonic accordion), and *trombeta* (trumpet) (Pernić 1997: 95). The revitalization of the gunjci, whose popularity decreased in the second half of the twentieth century, was realized by means of gunjci festivals, which take place annually in small villages in the interior of Istria (Roč, Grožnjan), and thus popularize the almost forgotten musical forms and customs.

37. Speaking of regional festivals in Croatia, Marošević wrote that "Melodies of Istria and Kvarner (since 1964) is a traveling festival which is held at a number of places in Istria and Kvarner over eight days. . . . Pop singers are the most frequent performers at these festivals, sometimes already known for their performance of other genres of popular music. Interpretation is more seldom entrusted to a group of singers. It is the solo singer who is emphasized and his or her performance is sometimes followed by a festival vocal group and the obligatory festival orchestra." She concludes that despite the evident quality of the songs performed at the festival and their media presentation (TV, radio, and recordings) their popularity does not last very long, and their acceptance usually does not go beyond regional boundaries (Marošević 1988: 89–90).

38. The *kažun* is a typically Mediterranean cabin made out of dressed stone or stone slabs, of circular or semi-circular form. They were built in fields, vineyards, and pastures, mainly with the intention of sheltering from the storm or storing the peasant's tools. Apart from the goat, the kažun is one of main Istrian symbols.

39. Because of its geographical position, Pula was a highly important military and naval center in the Austro-Hungarian empire. This function remained in the former Yugoslavia as well. The politics of equality, fraternity, and unity, which also applied to the army, made it common practice to send recruits and officers from the eastern regions to the western ones, and vice versa. Thus, the demographic image of Pula was in the last 50 years enriched with members of various nations and minorities, religions and persuasions that lived in the former Yugoslavia.

40. In the memory of the early deceased frontman of the band, Sergio Blažić Đoser, Đoser's Days take place each February. They are conceived as an encounter of Croatian pop and rock musicians through various concerts, socializing, and meeting with the media.

41. "Ča" is a grammatical pronoun meaning "what," and it is one of the main elements of distinction between the three Croatian dialects—kajkavian (*kaj*), Štokavian (*što*), and čakavian (*ča*).

42. Ča-val was the name of the top chart of *Čakavian* (Istrian and Kvarnerian) music on the radio of Rijeka. After the press and electronic media journalists began using it for the popular music of those regions in general, it came to be used in everyday speech.

43. The meteoric popularity culminated in 1994, when Vitasović won every festival in Croatia that he performed at. In the course of two years, as long as the interest for Vitasović's singing lasted, he visited almost every town in Croatia with his repertoire of some twenty songs. Vitasović was joined in popularity by rock bands Gustafi, Šajeta, the jazz singer Tamara Obrovac with her accompanying band TransHistria, and Livio Morosin and Dario Marušić, musicians who have for years collaborated with many ča-val interpreters (Gustafi, Vitasović, Istranova, Anelidi), but have also made excellent projects themselves.

44. The goat is the main symbol of Istria, representing Istria on the regional flag and on the Croatian coat of arms.

45. In 1983, Gustafi participated in the festival of new music in Zagreb, Musical Biennials, as one of the most avant-garde Yugoslav bands of the time.

46. Their formula for playing their *štala* concerts is interesting: three times for an hour—the first set *zagrijavanje* (warming up), the second one *razmrdavanje* (wiggling), and the third one *na punu forcu* (at full speed) (Maružin, in Bakić 1999). Their third album *Multo sentimento* was recorded in their favorite *štala*, the civic community center in Svetvinčent.

47. About his musical idols, Edi says, "Rock music was my main inspiration, bands like Slade, Sweet. . . . The first LP I bought was by Alice Cooper, T-Rex were very popular in that time, I remember the band In the Middle of the Road. After that I started listening to American rock music, some blues, a lot of country. In the course of time there has been an evolution so I started listening a lot to Alternative music and this is what influenced our music from the '80s, we played Alternative music. After that I got stuck on American pop music, like country, and then I switched over to the Irish, Celtic, Breton sound. In a way I was advancing towards us. Through Italian tarantellas I thought that our Istrian music could be just as good to play. I started listening to it more, learning how to play it and how to sing

it. This is how we started to play, in fact, it is how we live this music and how we work" (Maružin, in Bakić 1999).

48. "We play entertainment music (*zabavna muzika*) and we can't expect that someone will have fun listening to us if we don't have fun ourselves; the good vibrations must start from us. If we are endangered, stiff, frustrated it doesn't work for the audience. We don't even wear makeup or any special clothes for TV performances, unless someone goes crazy that day and puts on some kind of a hat or a shirt he particularly likes" (Maružin, in Bakić 1999).

49. Specifically, the conversation about hip-hop was crucial for their cooperation. "We have concluded that the Istrian folk dance *balun* is in fact an Istrian version of hip-hop. It may sound funny, but balun and hip-hop are both so-called street music. Both are danced in the street, it is like entertainment for the people. Besides, the rhythm of balun has the same speed as hip-hop, that is the 90–100 measure, the rhythm of the steps" (Morosin, in Vitaljić, 2000). Dario Marušić considers this project to be the "result of my sincere faith that what I'm doing is right."

50. *Sopile* or *roženice* are the conical oboe-type shawm with six finger-holes, found in Istria and Kvarner Bay. Usually, they are built in two sizes—the *vela* or large *sopila*, and the *mala* or small *sopila*—and played together or in two-part renditions. The playing of this instrument serves as an accompaniment to dance (balun, *tanac*) and as background music for festive processions (Ćaleta 2000: 434).

51. Although Croatian official government, at the beginning of the popularity of ča-val in the mid-1990s, partly judged the Istrian regional movement and their strong regional orientation as being separatist and anti-Croatian, it favored ča-val and promoted it through the state media.

52. In one of the interviews in 1998, Vitasović stated that the main reason of the decrease in his popularity was the fact that he supported the election campaign of *HDZ* by singing.

53. Ča-val musicians avoid talking about politics. However, they used to point out that for their work they don't get any media awards because they are not from Zagreb, considering the state system to be centralist, even where music is concerned (Jakovčev 1999).

54. On another occasion, I asked my colleague, a librarian, to bring me some relevant texts on ča-val, during her visit to Rovinj, Istria. Her colleague there was not familiar with the term ča-val. After naming Gustafi and Vitasović, she answered that it was *their* music and that they did not have the need of calling it by any special names.

Bibliography

Banovac, Boris. 1996. "Etničnost i regionalizam u Istri: povijesni rakurs i suvremeni kontekst," *Migracijske teme: časopis za istraživanja migracija i narodnosti* 12/4: 267–288.

——. 1998. "Etničnost i regionalizam kao izvori identifikacijskih procesa," in *Etničnost, nacija, identitet: Hrvatska i Europa*, edited by Ružica Čičak-Chand and Josip Kumpes. Zagreb: Institut za migracije i narodnosti. 249–262.

Baskar, Bojan. 1999. "Made in Trieste. Geopolitical Fears of an Istrianist Discourse on the Mediterranean," *Narodna umjetnost* 36/1: 121-135.

Bonifačić, Ruža. 1998. "Regional and National Aspects of Tamburica Tradition, The Case of the 'Zlatni Dukati' Neotraditional Ensemble," in *Music, Politics and War*, edited by Svanibor Pettan. Zagreb: Institute of Ethnology and Folklore Research. 131-151.

Ćaleta, Joško. 1997a. "Klapa Singing. A Traditional Folk Phenomenon of Dalmatia," *Narodna umjetnost* 34/1: 127-145.

———. 1997b. "Klapa u dijaspori: klapa 'Zvonimir' Vancouver, Canada," *Bašćinski glasi* 6: 71-93.

———. 1999. "The Ethnomusicological Approach to the Concept of the Mediterranean in Music in Croatia," *Narodna umjetnost* 36/1: 183-197.

———. 2000. "Traditional Musical Instruments," in *Croatian Folk Culture at the Crossroads of Worlds and Eras*, edited by Zorca Vitez and Aleksandra Muraj. Zagreb: Gallery Klovićevi dvori. 421-438.

Ceribašić, Naila. 1995. "Gender Roles During the War: Representations in Croatian and Serbian Popular Music 1991-92," *Collegium Antropologicum* 19/1: 91-101.

———. 1998. "Heritage of the Second World War in Croatia. Identity Imposed Upon by Music," in *Music, Politics and War*, edited by Svanibor Pettan. Zagreb: Institute of Ethnology and Folklore Research. 109-131.

Cohen, Sara. 1993. "Ethnography and Popular Music Studies," *Popular Music* 12/2: 123-139.

Čapo Žmegač, Jasna. 1999. "Ethnology, Mediterranean Studies and Political Reticence in Croatia. From Mediterranean Constructs to Nation-Building," *Narodna umjetnost* 36/1: 33-53.

Csikszentmihaly, Mihaly and Eugene Rochberg-Halton. 1981. *The Meaning of Things: Domestic Symbols and the Self*. New York: Cambrige Univeristy Press.

De Certeau, Michel. 1980. *The Practice of Everyday Life*. Berkeley: University of California Press.

Erlmann, Veit. 1993. "The Politics and Aesthetics of Transnational Musics," *The World of Music* 35/2: 3-16.

Glavan, Darko, et al. 1978. *Pop glazba i kultura mladih. Sondažno istraživanje publike rock-koncerata*, Zagreb: CDD SSOH.

Guilbault, Jocelyne. 1993. "On Redefining the 'Local' Through World Music," *The World of Music* 35/2: 33-48.

Hobsbawm, Eric. 1983. "Introduction: Inventing Traditions," in *Invention of Tradition*, edited by Eric Hobsbawm and Terence Ranger. Cambridge, U.K.: Cambridge University Press. 1-14.

Kalapoš, Sanja. 2000. "Cijeli svijet u mom selu. Globalna naspram lokalne kulture, lokaliziranje globalnog i globaliziranje lokalnog," *Etnološka tribina* 23/30: 65-79.

Manuel, Peter. 1988. *Popular Musics of the Non-Western World*. Oxford: Oxford University Press.

Marošević, Grozdana. 1988. "Folk Music in Croatia in the Period from 1981 to 1985," in *Contribution to the Study of Contemporary Folklore in Croatia*. Zagreb: Institute of Folklore Research. 75-96.

Marušić, Dario. 1995. *Piskaj—Sona—Sopi Svijet istaraskih glazbala*. Pula, Croatia: Castropola.

Morley, David. 1986. *Family Television: Cultural Power and Domestic Leisure*. London: Routledge.

Muršić, Rajko. 1996. "A 'Black-Box' of Music Use: On Folk and Popular Music," *Narodna umjetnost* 33/1: 59-74.

Pernić, Renato. 1997. *Meštri, svirci i kantaduri*. Buzet, Croatia: Reprezent.

Pettan, Svanibor. 1997. "The Croats and the Question of their Mediterranean Musical Identity," *Ethnomusicology on Line* 3 < http://research.umbc.edu/efhm/3/pettan/index.html>.

——(ed.). 1998. *Music, Politics and War*. Zagreb: Institute of Ethnology and Folklore Research.

Povrzanović, Maja. 1989. "Dalmatian Klapa Singing, Changes of Context," in *Folklore and Historical Process*, edited by Dunja Rihtman-Auguštin and Maja Povrzanović. Zagreb: Institute of Folklore Research. 159-170.

——. 1991. "Regionalni, lokalni i individualni identitet: primjer klapskog pjevanja," in *Simboli identiteta, (studije, eseji, grada)* edited by Dunja Rihtman-Auguštin. Zagreb: Hrvatsko etnološko društvo. 105-120.

Rihtman-Auguštin, Dunja. 1999. "A Croatian Controversy: Mediterranean—Danube—Balkans," *Narodna umjetnost* 36/1: 103-121.

Stermšek, Maja. 1994. "Ženske vokalne skupine na Festivalu dalmatinskih klapa u Omišu," *Bašćinski glasi* 3: 197-217.

Stokes, Martin (ed.). 1994. *Ethnicity, Identity and Music. The Musical Construction of a Place*. Oxford, U.K.: Berg Publishers.

Source Materials

Bakić, Goran. 1999. "Koraci; Edi Marožin & Gustafi—documentary film," *HTV 2nd Program*. 24. December. Zagreb.

Balen, Marko. 1994. "Čakavštinom do srca publike," *Slobodna Dalmacija* 24 November.

Bobinsky, Alenka. 1985. *"Novi val" u jugoslavenskom rocku: analiza jednog specifičnog fenomena*. Manuscript in the Institute of Ethnology and Folklore, IEF 1130.

Brnobić, Vesna. 1994. "Najbolje pjevam na istarskom!," *Večernji list* 9 September.

Glavan, Darko. 1999. "Roženice na 220 volti," *Večernji list* 31 December.

Hudelist, Darko. 1984. "Jugoslavenska diskografska laž," *Start* 2 June.

Jakovčev, Tanja. 1999. "Nagrade ne dobivamo zato što nismo iz Zagreba," *Jutarnji list* 12 November.

Kalapoš, Sanja. 1998. "Die Musik und die Sprache als Elemente einer Identitatskonstruktion: Ein Fallbeispiel aus Istrien," paper read at *16. Internationale Tagung der kommision für Lied-, Musik-, und Tanzforschung in der Deustchen Gesellschaft für Volkskünde*. Vienna, October.

Knezović, Pavica, et al. 1994 "Što?, ča, kaj!," *Vjesnik* 14 October.

Vitaljić, Sandra. 2000. "Sve pjesme na albumu 'Bura-tramuntana' napravljene su u ritmu polke iz žminja i baluna koji je istarska verzija hip-hopa," *Nacional* 19. January.

Zagorac, Vladimir. 2001. "Palladina Gibonni podsjeća na—Wondera!," *Večernji list* 7. March.

Discography

Gibonni. *Sa mnom ili bez mene*. Croatia Records. 1991.

——. *Noina arka*. Croatia Records. 1993.

——. *Kruna od perja*. Croatia Records. 1994.

——. *Koncert*. Croatia Records. 1995.

——. *Ruža vjetrova*. Croatia Records. 1996.

——. *Judi, zviri i beštimje*. Dallas Records.1999.

Gustafi. *Tutofato*. Adam Records. 1994.

——. *Zarad tebe*. Adam Records ACD 1023. 1995.

——. *Multo sentimento*. Adam Records. 1997.

——. *Vraćamo se odmah*. Dancing Bear DBCD 021. 1999.

Klapa Cambi. *Lipa slika*. Croatia Records CD 5224648. 1998.

——. *Kaštela—live*. Sound and vision-Makarska CD 002. 1999.

——. *Klapa CAMBI*. Sound and vision-Makarska CD 003. 1999.

——. *Vrime od nedije*. Dallas Records CD 227. 2001.

Klapa Kumpanji. *Klapa Kumpanji*. Orfej—HRT ORFCD 134v. 1998.

Kvartet Gorgonzola. *. . . iman osječaj da nas niko sluša . . .* Remix CD 01v. 1999.

Alen Vitasović. *Gušti su gušti*. Croatia Records CD 5036768v. 1994.

——. *Svi festivali*. Croatia Records. 1995.

——. *Come va*. Croatia Records. 1997.

——. *Ja ne gren*. Crno Bijeli Svijet. 2000.

JOŠKO ĆALETA

INVENTING ETHNIC MUSIC:
FABRIZIO DE ANDRÉ'S *CREUZA DE MÄ* AND THE
CREATION OF *MUSICA MEDITERRANEA* IN ITALY

GOFFREDO PLASTINO

In August 2001, *Rumori Mediterranei* ("Mediterranean Noises," the 21st International Jazz Festival, at Roccella Ionica, Calabria), one of the most important jazz festivals in Italy, was dedicated to songwriter Fabrizio De André and his album *Creuza de mä* (Path Along the Sea). Writing in festival program, Stefano Benni explained the reasons for this homage:

> *Creuza de mä* is a pathway for listening to the voices of the village, of the earth, and the sea—frequently a steep and narrow one. These days, we find "fusion" or "contamination" music born in the studio, mixing styles and discographers' precepts. We like to think of Roccella's music, on the other hand, as created while walking, listening, feeling. Not arising only from the idea of a homogenized uninspired global music, but a music sprung from variety and difference that achieves its own particular unity. Fabrizio De André was a composer, poet, instrumentalist, writer, and scholar of ethnic music. We have decided to dedicate this festival along the "creuza de mä"—the path upon which his life and ours have traveled, and upon which we can hear the dialogues, the dialect, and the songs of the people.

Many years after its publication, *Creuza de mä* still exerts an influence on musicians, writers, and music critics interested in *musica mediterranea*, "Mediterranean music"—so called. At the last Roccella Ionica Festival what linked the record to the concerts was their shared goal of expressing *mediterraneità* (Mediterraneanness) in music through jazz that De André in a different way was able to express in pop music: a mediterraneità reached through the collaboration between diverse musicians, to be found in the union of various and diverse musics; a mediterraneità opposed both to contemporary musical globalization and to the "contamination" between different musical genres. Looking back to *Creuza de mä* seems significant in this context, because it indicated that in Italian pop music one route to "Mediterranean music" had already been successfully achieved.

The best song album and the best rock album of the '80s in Italy, *Creuza de mä* came out in 1984. Sung in Genoese dialect, with an instrumentation in which the most important parts were assigned to such musical instruments as the 'ud, the *saz*, the bouzouki, mandolin, and mandola, the album was a turning point in Italian pop music, orienting future debate on musica mediterranea and subsequently also influencing the playing styles of numerous musicians, folk revival groups, and pop bands.[1] The importance of *Creuza de mä* as a symbol of mediterraneità in music was also recognized outside of Italy, notably through the praises of rock musician David Byrne (formerly of the Talking Heads): "*Creuza de mä* is a great album that succeeds in combining unusual and innovative elements in a highly emotional way. This in itself is extraordinary. . . . We should all be grateful to Fabrizio De André for the fact that a poet of his ability should have chosen pop music as his medium of expression" (Viva 2001: 193); "When a country has an artist capable of producing an album like *Creuza de mä* it can only be proud" (Videtti 1999). Even in Italy the record stimulated a discussion of Mediterranean identity as a synthesis of diverse cultural expressions.[2] In 1995, over ten years after it first appeared, *Creuza de mä* was remembered as the most successful attempt at synthesizing Mediterranean musical traditions—a synthesis to which Italian musicians "naturally" and "consciously" would be drawn, because Italy is "the ideal crossroads of Mediterranean sounds" (Brighenti 1995: 27–28).

Cover of Fabrizio De André's *Creuza de mä*

The influence that *Creuza de mä* exerted and continues to exert is also due to the charisma of De André himself, and to the role he assumed in Italian pop. Fabrizio De André (1940–99) was one of the most important and admired Italian singer-songwriters. After leaving law school to devote himself to music, De André studied guitar and violin, initially performing in jazz concerts (his favorite guitarist was Jim Hall), and then with an Italian country and western group. His long musical career began at the end of the 1960s, and was initiated, in fact, by Mina, a well-known Italian pop star, with a performance of his "Canzone di Marinella" (Marinella's Song). After 1968, De André's recording successes intensified; and he published virtually an album a year. His songs of the '60s and '70s exhibit discernible influences from

Jacques Brel, Georges Brassens, Bob Dylan, and Leonard Cohen (some of whose songs he translated and performed). He was esteemed for the poetry of his lyrics and was qualified, thanks to his background in music studies, to establish the musical characteristics of his compositions. De André over the years "'tuned,' 'Americanized,' and finally 'Mediterraneanized' his music, delegating to others the responsibility for his musical choices" (Fiori 1997: 150), although closely supervising the musical aspects of his songs. With *Creuza de mä*, De André effected an important change, abandoning in part Anglo-American pop styles in favor, first, of a Mediterranean, and then of the "ethnic" sound that characterizes his more recent works: *Le Nuvole* (Clouds), and above all, *Anime Salve* (Saved Souls).[3]

Many in Italy see *Creuza de mä* as the result of a recurring internal process in Italian pop music, which at various times in its history has been confronted with Mediterranean music of oral tradition. *Creuza de mä* is pivotal not only for De André's musical career, therefore, but also signified and concluded an epoch, representing a moment of passage, a clear "before" and "after." It has become an obligatory reference point for every Mediterranean music project in Italy. Like other albums that have attracted the careful attention of ethnomusicologists and pop-music scholars—Paul Simon's *Graceland* (Meintjes 1990; Feld 1994; Taylor 1997: 21–22; Erlmann 1999), comes to mind—*Creuza de mä* is a "complex polysemic sign vehicle" (Meintjes 1990: 37), whose multiple facets elucidate that musical practices can affirm the idea of a musica mediterranea.

"Where Is This Mediterranean Music?"

Usually attributed solely to Fabrizio De André, *Creuza de mä* was also the work of another author: violinist and poly-instrumentalist, composer, and musical producer Mauro Pagani's name is credited on every track of the record, and he is responsible for both the musical arrangements and the instrumentation. If many Italians consider *Creuza de mä* an album of musica mediterranea, it is above all due to Pagani's stylistic choices, choices whose story is interwoven with the development of a Mediterranean "style" in Italian music.[4]

Mauro Pagani's musical career began in the '70s, when he became a member of the Italian progressive rock band Premiata Forneria

Marconi. Initially, the band was inspired by such groups as Chicago, King Crimson, and Jethro Tull.[5] In 1972, in a quest for a new and more original sound, P.Г.M. issued *Storia di un minuto*, an album less influenced by English and American bands that has been called an example of "rock [music] with first-rate classical venation and Mediterranean influences" (Ruggeri 1990: 1389). It was a hit album in Italy. When he heard some tracks from P.F.M., Pete Sinfield (at the time the producer of Roxy Music), declared: "I like the warm Mediterranean quality of their progressive music." P.F.M. came out with eight LPs and singles in a few years (1972-76); and, thanks to live concerts with bands and musicians such as Deep Purple, Ten Years After, The Allman Brothers Band, Santana, ZZ Top, and Peter Frampton, it also became famous in Europe and the United States, where it also recorded a successful live album.

Pagani left P.F.M. in 1977. He was becoming more and more interested in the traditional oral music of the Mediterranean—Middle Eastern music in particular. He continued the work already begun by other Italian pop musicians and bands, such as Demetrio Stratos, Area, Canzoniere del Lazio, Carnascialia, and Teresa de Sio (Finzi 1999). In particular, the experience of Stratos and his group—Area, International POPular group—seemed at the time to point to an interesting way to conjoin Mediterranean melodies and rhythms to pop music and jazz. Led by the Greek singer Demetrio Stratos (Demetriou Efstratios, 1945-79), in the 1970s, Area was one of the most influential progressive-rock groups in Italy.[6] It began its activities in 1972, bringing out various albums that, taking off from a pop song structure, arrived at "radical" solutions, joining among other things, progressive rock, free jazz, and electronic music (through collaboration with such musicians as Steve Lacy and Paul Litton). The Mediterranean quality of Area's music resides in its use of certain Middle Eastern and Balkan melodies and rhythms, but above all in some of Stratos's vocal performances, rich in melisma, ornamentation, and leaps in register. In particular in the track "Luglio, agosto, settembre nero" (July, August, and Black September), Area used (at least partially) a melody that the band's drummer, Giulio Capiozzo, had heard in Egypt. Capiozzo had studied at the Cairo Conservatory of Music and had become interested in Egyptian music (Mirenzi 1997: II: 131). Another Area track that is considered Mediterranean is "Cometa rossa" (Red Comet), sung in Greek, and introduced and concluded by two symmetrically musical sections that reprise, almost note for note, the central part of "Gankino Krivo Horo", a dance tune performed by the Bitov Orchestra, a traditional group from Bulgaria.[7] These two cuts were enormously popular in Italy, rapidly becoming iconic for Area, and even though not really representative of the group's principal musical direction, they were responsible for its subsequent identity as performers of Mediterranean music (Mirenzi 1997: II: 120–21). Parallel to his activities as Area's lead singer, Stratos, incidentally, also had a very active career as a soloist, collaborating with John Cage and Merce Cunningham and taking a special interest in overtone singing techniques.[8]

Pagani took up and deepened an interest in the Mediterranean that was already present in Italian pop music. The quest for a *musica mediterranea*, essentially a synthesis of several musics of oral tradition, progressive rock, and jazz, became his most important musical goal, and crystallized in the album *Mauro Pagani* (1978). The album featured performances by Demetrio Stratos, some members of P.F.M., and other musicians involved in defining and exploring a Mediterranean musical language. It was favorably received in Italy. Pagani's quest had coalesced in a form that for Italian audiences constituted the best expression of a Mediterranean sound, with evident references to Italian and Middle Eastern musical traditions. The generous use of melodies in Balkan or Turkish style, the asymmetrical rhythms, the long improvised passages (some in a "jazz" style), use of acoustic instrumentation, and the space allotted to Stratos's vocals and to percussion assured the album's success. Many musicians began their careers taking *Mauro Pagani* as their model.[9] Six years before *Creuza de mä*, Mauro Pagani had established a canon, with an album that "can still today be considered one of the best and most authentic examples of 'Mediterranean music'" (Giugni 1990: 1254), and had positioned himself as the most influential and charismatic Italian musician in this field.

The collaboration between De André and Pagani was virtually foreordained. Pagani was inclined to accede to the singer/songwriter's wishes (Fabbri 1997: 167). *Creuza de mä* was born of a meeting between two musician/authors, who in the beginning of the 1980s, had different but converging motives. De André wanted to forge a new, less

American style for his songs,[10] while Pagani wished to present his Mediterranean musical synthesis in a new and different way. The idea was to realize an album that would be: "Italian, Mediterranean, alive not copied, ethnic not 'touristy,' poetic but not saccharine, that would be music and not little songs" (Pagani, in Fasoli 1999: 10–11). The album was intended to represent something authentically new, and above all to clarify what musica mediterranea might really be:

> Basically, I had had it up to here with all this talk of a so-called "Mediterranean idiom." The term "Mediterranean music" had been used for at least fifteen years, and I said, "But where is this Mediterranean music? I really want to hear it." And so I wanted to do it—this album. (De André, in Viva 2001: 188)

A Small World

De André and Pagani met by chance in a recording studio and discussed the possibility of working on a project together. At first, they wanted their record to tell the story of an Italian sailor who, after years of wandering about the Mediterranean, returns home speaking a language that had words from other, different languages: an invented language. The music was also to be the expression of a similar heterogeneity (Finzi 1999). As the work progressed, the division of labor became clear: Pagani took care of the musical part, De André of the lyrics and general direction of the work:

> [*Creuza de mä*] is dedicated neither to the Genoese nor to Genoa but to the Mediterranean basin. Now, where Mauro Pagani by means of his instrumental skill—as a musician—had succeeded in representing, even if *in vitro*, a little Mediterranean world, I had to find words that would somehow likewise reflect also *in vitro* (as well as in a "literary way," because these are song lyrics, after all) the Mediterranean world. (De André, in Fasoli 1999: 63)

When the work was already well underway, De André had the inspired idea of substituting the dialect of his native city of Genoa for the invented language. There were two reasons for this. In the first place, De André doesn't consider Genoese a dialect, but rather an independent language, his own maternal tongue in fact, in which he is as fluent as in standard Italian. Moreover, according to De André, the Genoese vocabulary "includes at least 2,500 words of Arabic origin—evidence of intense interaction with the Arab world" (Viva 2001: 189).[11] The choice of Genoese allowed De André to include the linguistic aspect of his musical project under a single criterion. Stressing the Arabic influence on Genoese suggests that the Arab world is an element linking the music and the texts. The Mediterranean imagined by the two musicians is therefore a region of different cultures that share a *langue* Arabic. *Creuza de mä* is an album that travels, explores, and, finally, declares the Mediterranean Arabic: in music, through the mediation of Pagani; in language, through the mediation of De André and his dialect, whose Arabic-derived lexicon affirms that a cultural synthesis was once, and still is, possible.

De André's imaginary voyage can therefore be accomplished, beginning and ending in the same city—Genoa—reached by way of language, as a place of coexistence, of syncretisms old and new. The seven songs of the album are discrete little worlds, complete in themselves but somehow connected, by Genoese and by the musica mediterranea developed by Pagani. The songs are about the environment and landscape of the maritime world, of the Ligurian hinterlands ("Creuza de mä," "Da a me riva"), and have such protagonists as the Genoese sailor, who in the second half of the fifteenth century, after having been taken prisoner by the Turks, went on to become Grand Vizier ("Sinan capudan pascià"), a tax collector ("A pittima"), and prostitutes and their clients ("A dumenega"); and themes such as sex ("Jamin-a") and death ("Sidun"). A joyous and sad humanity infuses the texts, creating finally a varied and quite unusual (in Italian pop music) portrait of the Mediterranean:

> *Creuza de mä* is nothing less than the depiction of a Mediterranean voyage—with the city of Genoa as both point of departure and arrival—whose characters move along the entire Mediterranean basin, including North Africa and the Middle East. All these characters—except in the two choral songs, "Creuza de mä" itself, and "A dumenega"—contribute in a singular fashion to give life to the entire canvas and to the entire little story. In fact, it is through its characters and the story of portions of their lives—if not the pré-

cis of their whole lives, as in the case of "Sinan capudán pascià"—that the entire album unfolds to become a unique story in the circumscribed environment of a unique cultural environment. (De André, in Fasoli 1999: 72)

A No-Man's Land

The choice of musical instruments and their well-planned sonorities also contribute to the mediterraneità of *Creuza de mä*. Pagani, who did the instrumentation, plays the 'ud, the saz, the bouzouki, mandolin, mandola, violin, and plucked viola (played with a plectrum rather than a bow), and various (unspecified in the liner notes) kinds of flutes. Other musicians play such traditional instruments as the *zarb* (the Iranian goblet drum) and the *shannaj* (the Indian shawm). The liner notes also mention other "medieval and ethnic instruments" and percussion. Aerophones are heard only in brief segments: the album's sound is composed mainly of chordophones, specifically those identifying different cultures or musical areas of the Mediterranean (the 'ud from the Arab world, the saz from Turkey, the bouzouki from Greece, the mandolin from Italy). Played together, they suggest the idea of a substantial unity of Mediterranean musics. The violin and viola also function as elements of this depiction of auditory unity; played with a plectrum, the two instruments resemble the higher registers of the 'ud, allowing Pagani to perform virtuoso passages that would have been harder to perform on that instrument (as in "Jamin-a").

Creuza de mä opens with a brief excerpt taken from another recording: "Aria per *Gaida* Sola," the *gaida* being the Thracian (Northern Greek) bagpipe.[12] These 49 seconds (surprising for a pop recording) of gaida music announce that in this album De André has changed musical direction, and create the expectation of something entirely different. They bear direct witness to the mediterraneità of the album and of the new musical project.[13] The bagpipe introduction was perceived by Italian audiences as "something oriental, Arabic,"[14] and functioned as an exordium to De André's imaginary voyage. Once accepted and shared, the Mediterranean sound of the album also ended up including instruments that are not actually Mediterranean, such as the shannaj, whose timbres, heard in the performance of the instrumental cut in *Jamin-a*, didn't seem incongruous.[15]

The instruments, above all the Mediterranean chordophones, are not played using their correct performance techniques, but instead are exploited for their sonorities.[16] *Creuza de mä* is a record in which the 'ud, saz, and above all the bouzouki function to provide a new auditory environment:

> I wanted to use Turkish musical phonemes and playing styles, which ought to have been the principal axis for a Mediterranean project. But original instruments like the *saz* have a scale that isn't transferable to our music. The bouzouki resembles it a lot, and so I thought of tuning it with Turkish instruments, thus obtaining a no-man's land on which to work to create something with a Western stamp, compatible with Western instruments and with tempered scale tunings. This also allowed the emergence of credible sounds, scales, and "ways of carrying music." (Pagani, in Viva 2001: 190)

Pagani was referring to the "credibility" that would allow the compositions to be recognized as songs. The project is "Western" in the sense that it respects the rules of composition and performance conventions of Anglo-American pop. In fact, it is not difficult to identify in every track features such as strophes, refrains, and solos. The novelty consists in the use by Westerners of musical instruments from diverse regions of the Mediterranean, instruments whose sound serves to characterize the songs, not to distort them.

To balance the exotic, distancing effect of the 'ud, saz, and bouzouki, the album makes generous use of more familiar pop music instruments: drums, bass, keyboard, and guitars. The keyboard mostly reprises the songs' harmonic progressions or performs long sections of drones; and "A dumenega" concludes with a guitar solo in progressive rock style.

Yet despite *Creuza de mä*'s careful balance between pop and Mediterranean, the foreground elements of the string instruments combined with the Genose dialect of the lyrics obscured (at least initially) the songs' reception. De André himself remembered the reaction of a music publisher's representative who, at first hearing, was disconcerted and predicted that the album would never be understood, even by the Genoese (Lanza 1999). *Creuza de mä* was "a work so unexpected for the period that its explosive novelty didn't immediately register"

(Liperi 1999: 390–391). Nevertheless, its intrinsic adherence to the formal and technical rules of Italian song, or *canzone d'autore* (Fabbri 1989: 123–127), assured its speedy success, propelling it into the Italian record market.

A Non-global World Music

The world music phenomenon at the beginning of the '90s (Taylor 1997: 1–37), prompted the reappraisal of *Creuza de mä* as belonging to this new musical genre, causing De André to declare that he had anticipated world music, because his album had preceded by two years Paul Simon's *Graceland*, which came out in 1986 (Fasoli 1999: 63). If *Creuza de mä* had at first looked like a rather extraordinary experiment on the part of the songwriter, the popularity of world music in Italy made it seem the most important—and for many years an unrivaled—example of the genre (Catalano 1999: 84).

Moreover, De André's *Creuza de mä* was arguably not only the first example of world music, but was also an overt reaction against "American" music, that is Anglo-American pop. Its affirmations more likely express a wish for a change of musical style, rather than an explicit declaration of a new aesthetic concept: "I shook American music off my back," De André asserted (Viva 2001: 188). "We didn't want to follow in the tracks of the Americans, of the Anglophone world and their music" (Lanza 1999). Pagani shared this sentiment (Viva 2001:189), and both reiterated it more than once. In the end the record became a representative Italian (Mediterranean) way of writing songs.

For many critics and commentators, who also considered the disc in the light of De André's declarations, *Creuza de mä* is the best answer of the '80s to the "resurgence of capitalism, to globalization and homogenization of thought," above all, because of the singers' use of dialect. From this perspective, Genoese is a metaphor for cultural survival against what some call "the annihilation of identity" (Pestalozza 1997: 175–76). These recent and most radical readings of the meaning of the disc lay stress on relationships between (musical) cultures, on the liberal use that can be made of rhythms not belonging to one's own (Western) culture, and on the use of dialect as an expression of identity. These aspects appeared in a positive light, because they allow the music to escape the uniformity of globalization, through a "disposition to confront those who are excluded by the process of standardization" (Lattarulo 2000). De André and Pagani's "world music" is valued positively in Italy (as shown by the tribute paid to the record even in a jazz festival), for its exemplary openness toward others, and as an essential rediscovery of Italian identity.

Roving Songs

De André and Pagani continued their collaboration for several years. A later disc, *Le nuvole* (1990), featured songs in the same Mediterranean style as *Creuza de mä*, also sung in Genoese, although without the same unity as its predecessor. De André frequently performed the songs from his Mediterranean disc live, along with Pagani; and he added to them, as though to emphasize a link, newer songs such as "Megu megun" and "A cimma". Even De André's 1996 disc, Anime salve, includes two pieces that follow in the direction laid out by *Creuza de mä*: "Le acciughe fanno il pallone," and above all "A cumba". Pagani did not collaborate on this disc either as instrumentalist or arranger, and De André appeared more intent on uniting world music with songs, using in his compositions a large number of musical instruments, from different countries and cultures.

Creuza de mä's success as "the keystone to the entire landscape of Italian music"[17] was such that it influenced Italian musicians of every extraction, folk-revival performers in particular. The record's sound was studied and reprised; the idea of an "Arab" Mediterranean spread and was finally accepted as a given; bands sprang up whose repertoires consisted of numbers that gave ample scope to Greek, Turkish, and Moroccan musical instruments, and Middle Eastern-sounding melodies. This trend shows no signs of abating and is today arguably one of the most vital in contemporary Italy. The publicity surrounding *Isettande* (2001), the latest release by the Sardinian group Tancaruja, stresses its "limpid acoustic sound, in which the *bandurria* [the guitar-like 12–string Spanish instrument] and the bouzouki meet drums and accordion, where intense Mediterranean rhythms alternate with pliant melodies."[18]

De André was well aware of his influence on many musicians and folk-revival groups, for whom *Creuza de mä* was something if not to imitate or copy, then certainly to take into account when trying to create new musical languages:

[Pagani and] I gave life to the desire to return to the ethnic manner. We chose a language that was not in use, with instruments no longer used. . . . We were not trying to confound ethnic music with "folkloristic" music, since folkloristic music is what people make to amuse those in social classes above them, while ethnic music is what people make for their own use. . . . After this record, many others began to play ethnic music in their local dialects, in the South above all. (De André, in Lanza 1999)

Italian folk revival musicians paid homage to De André, above all for giving their music credibility and visibility in Italy. They did this through *Canti randagi* (Roving songs), a 1995 album featuring De André's songs translated into various dialects (among them Neapolitan, Occitan, Tuscan, Friulan, Sardinian, Calabrian, and Genoese). The songs were performed to the accompaniment of diatonic accordion, mandolin, harp, *tabla*, *battente* guitar (a Southern Italian guitar), bouzouki, *darbukka*, hurdy-gurdy, violin, Galician *gaita*, and other Italian bagpipes. In a way, *Canti randagi* closed a circle for Italian folk-revival musicians: if a songwriter can make his pop songs sound more "ethnic," then it is also possible for folk musicians and groups to perform pop music.

Finally, perhaps contrary to De André's own intentions, *Creuza de mä* not only became a model for a new generation of Italian musicians, but also functioned as a new lens through which recent and modern Italian history could be interpreted:

It took Italy, a unified country only since 1860, some five generations, compulsory military service, two world wars, a Marshall Plan, and a national radio and television to forget its regional and local traditions, often to opt instead for a parody of (supposedly) Northern American cultural patterns. This is why *Creuza de mä*, recorded by Fabrizio De André and Mauro Pagani in the mid-Eighties stands as a turning point for the Italian roots scene, showing an extraordinary ability to combine old and new sounds from Italy and its neighboring nations. They produced a unique clothing of sounds for the old/new Genoese language finally on record after decades of nurturing the Italian lyrics of one of the most beloved Italian singers.

As Novalia [an Italian folk revival group] skillfully acknowledges, most of the labels and artists featured in this compilation[19] are spiritual daughters and sons of *Creuza de mä*, a "path along the sea." They rarely make use of the [official] Italian language and they rarely confine themselves within a single local tradition. They bear witness to a wide geographical and cultural spread. The traditional material is usually the first musical source, though the main focus is modern song formats. Windhunters on a boat in the crossroads between East and West, Italian roots-music groups have their Northern dock in continental Europe and their Southern anchor in the Mediterranean waters. (Surian 2001)

A Mediterranean Syncretism

Our intention was to invent an ethnic music.
(De André, in Lanza 1999)

Creuza de mä can be read, as through a filigree, as an idea of "Mediterranean music." The aesthetic of the disc is that of imitation and re-creation, and it is essentially oriented toward appropriation. The Greek, Turkish, and "Arab" instruments are used in such a way that it is not always easy or necessary for the listener to identify their provenance. Their cleaned-up sound renders them more enjoyable for Italian audiences. *Creuza de mä* is based on absence and evocation; the Mediterranean sound is obtained through the mediation of a Western pop musician (Pagani), so there is no need therefore for external collaboration. No Turkish, Greek, or Arab musicians were enlisted to participate in the recording. A Greek musician was present, but not identified as such: he plays the Thracian *gaida* for a few seconds at the beginning of the album. His name was not listed in the credits, which mention only the names of the Italian musicians. His short bagpipe performance, a traditional tune, was credited as being by De André and Pagani and was published in a simplified transcription.

Their compositions respect, as Pagani clarified, Western musical criteria and performance conventions. It is true that in *Creuza de mä* De André displays an infatuation with pretonality, and that the use of modes and the employment of "modal atmospheres derived from folk music" are accentuated to the point of a clear adoption of the mixolydian mode, as in "Jamin-a" (Fabbri 1997: 164–65). This did not prevent the recep-

The first 8 bars of *Creuza de mä*, showing a simplified transcription of an air for solo Thracian gaida. This traditional tune is credited as a composition by De André and Pagani. (By permission of BMG Ricordi S.p.A.)

tion of the disc as a sequence of pop songs, whose unconventional element resides in its musical arrangement.

Another interesting aspect of the disc is its lack of references to Italian traditional music. Apart from the mandolin and mandola (employed, like the other instruments, for their tone qualities), no other element harks back to Italian musical traditions. The link to Italy consists in the use of Genoese dialect. Once again, this anticipated a trend that would become more pronounced in the 1990s (Plastino 1996: 112–13). By using dialect, De André suggests a relationship with an element that, although seemingly local, in fact embraces the entire Mediterranean through its inclusion of an Arabic-derived vocabulary. Although none of the melodies sung in *Creuza de mä* have any relationship to the *trallalero*, the traditional vocal polyphony of Genoa, or to other Ligurian song traditions,[20] De André's use of sung dialect exerted a powerful stimulus on Genoese identity.

De André's claim that *Creuza de mä* anticipated world music was probably correct. Many of the questions that the new genre has raised, and which have been central to many ethnomusicological and pop-music studies, are already indicated in his work: questions of authenticity, of mediation rather than collaboration, of expropriation, invention, and revitalization; the question of musica mediterranea itself. De André and Pagani's musica mediterranea is the *in vitro* creation of an imaginary Mediterranean that has never existed. It is an artificial syncretism, an "ethnic" music that works only as re-created. The music of *Creuza de mä* is "Mediterranean" because it is distant from the musics of the real Mediterranean, which have been summarized, manufactured, and presented in an immediate and less problematic way. The Mediterranean that many Italians have imagined and continue to imagine, to which they turn their attention as listeners and render homage, is not the Mediterranean, but a representation.

Notes

1. Sometime after it appeared in 1984, *Creuza de mä* was the recipient of an award from a hundred Italian music critics, drawn from the magazine *Musica e dischi* (the most authoritative in the field), as the best record in the "light" (pop) and rock music categories. In 1989, the same magazine named *Creuza de mä* the best album of the 1980s (Viva 2001: 193).

2. In this sense, it is worth recalling certain remarks by the noted architect Renzo Piano: "For centuries the Mediterranean registered the sounds and images of different cultures, and it returns this patrimony to whoever has ears to hear and eyes to see. In Fabrizio [De André] you can hear concretely this extension in space and time, the Mediterranean echo that lives as a broth of civility. Of Italian, Spanish, Greek, and Arab. A heterogeneity that is our salvation, our only way out for us so-called wealthy nations" (quoted in Fasoli 1999: 28–29).

3. On Fabrizio De André, see Ceri 1999 (complete discography); Cotroneo 2000; Fasoli 1999; Franchini 2000; Giuffrida and Bruno 1997; Romana 2000; Videtti 1999 (another useful discography); Viva 2001; Zampa 1990. Texts and scores of De André's songs are in De André 1999, 2000.

4. On Mauro Pagani, see Giugni 1990.

5. On Premiata Forneria Marconi, see Ruggeri 1990. Useful information is available on the web site http://www.pfmpfm.it

6. On Area, see Assante 1990, Mirenzi 1997: II: 120–153. More useful information is available on the web site http://www.fariselliproject.com/bio-3.html

7. Thanks to Franco Fabbri for elucidating this piece.

8. On Demetrio Stratos, see Trân 1994: 124–125, El Haduli 1999.

9. "[The] solo project by Mauro Pagani, entitled simply *Mauro Pagani* (1978), arguably one of the most original by far of those years. It sounds as fresh and powerful today as when first released. When I interviewed Giampiero Mazzone and Enzo Rao of the Italian world beat band Shamàl, both acknowledged its great influence on their own music in those years. As a former member of Mazzone's group Ammaruvaja, I can personally testify that Pagani's recording caught me off guard. Pagani, a multi-instrumentalist, took inspiration from Turkish and Balkan music as well as from Southern Italian tradition. I was amazed by the power of his music. There was much musical prowess, but also a warm feeling to it, something that went beyond amazement at the sensational speed or other technical aspects of the music" (Catalano 1999: 82–83).

10. De André also made two live albums during this "American" period. These were recorded by P.F.M. (without Pagani) and released in 1979 and 1980.

11. According to Pagani, there are 1,000 or 1,200 words of Arabic origin in Genoese dialect (Finzi 1999).

12. The actual credits say: "*Introduzione a* Creuza de mä *da 'Aria per* gaida *sola' (Tracia) del gruppo strumentale diretto da Domna Samou, per gentile concessione Emial-Greece*" ("Introduction to *Creuza de mä* from 'Aria for solo *gaida*' (Thrace) by the intrumental group under the direction of Domna Samou, by kind permission of Emial-Greece").

13. The recording of the brief introduction for *gaida* was also reproduced in De André's live concerts to announce that selections from *Creuza de mä* were about to be performed (see De André, *1991 Concerti*, track 10).

14. This statement is based on numerous conversations that I heard after the publication of the record.

15. In live performances of the piece, the shannaj was replaced by the *ciaramella*, an Italian shawm (see De André, *1991 Concerti*, track 11).

16. In the video of *Creuza de mä*, Pagani plays the 'ud and De André the bouzouki, playing only chords, more or less as on a guitar (the video is included in De André 1999a).

17. See http://www.viadelcampo.com/html/creuza_de_ma.html

18. See http://cnimusic.it/newsitaa.htm. It's not possible to consider the varied Italian musical scene that referred to (and still does) "Mediterranean music" in the scope of this article. For "Mediterranean world music" in Sicily, see Catalano 1999.

19. *Travellin' Companion Vol. 2. A Musical Journey to Italy* (see Discography). See also http://www.humansongs.com/WWItaly.htm. Italian group Novalia composed a song inspired by De André's work: "Perzu pe 'na creuza de mä," published in 1999. Novalia wrote in the liner notes that it is an "homage to Fabrizio De André 'Creuza de mä', which has been an infinite source of learning."

20. For some examples of these vocal traditions, see the *Trallaleri of Genoa, Liguria: Baiardo and Imperia*, and *Liguria: Ceriana*, in Discography.

Bibliography

Assante, Ernesto. 1990. "Area," in *Il Dizionario della Canzone Italiana*, edited by Gino Castaldo. Milano: Curcio. 2 vols. 51–52.

Benni, Stefano. 2001. "Presentazione," in *Roccella Ionica 2001. 22–25 Agosto 2001. Rumori Mediterranei. Creuza de mä—Strade di suoni sul mare*. Roma: Associazione Culturale Ionica Onlus/XPress. 16.

Brighenti, Flavio. 1995. "Crocevia del sound mediterraneo," in *Mediterraneo/Il disco del mese*. Roma Edizioni La Repubblica. 26–31.

Catalano, Roberto. 1999. *Mediterranean World-Music: Experiencing Sicilian-Arab Sounds*. Unpublished Ph.D. Dissertation in Ethnomusicology. Los Angeles: University of California.

Ceri, Luciano (ed.). 1999. "Discografia completa," in Doriano Fasoli, *Fabrizio de*

André. Passaggi di tempo. Da Carlo Martello a Princesa. Roma: Edizioni Associate. 309-329.

Cotroneo, Roberto. 2000. "Una smisurata preghiera," in Fabrizio De André, *Come un'anomalia. Tutte le canzoni,* edited by Roberto Cotroneo. Torino: Einaudi. V–XIII.

De André, Fabrizio. 1999. *Fabrizio De André. I testi e gli spartiti di tutte le canzoni.* Milan: Mondadori.

———. 2000. *Come un'anomalia. Tutte le canzoni.* Edited by Roberto Cotroneo. Torino: Einaudi.

El Haduli, Janete. 1999. *Demetrio Stratos. Alla ricerca della voce-musica.* Milan: Auditorium.

Erlmann, Veit. 1999. "Hero on the Pop Chart. Paul Simon and the Aesthetics of World Music," in *Music, Modernity, and the Global Imagination. South Africa and the West.* New York and Oxford: Oxford University Press. 179-198.

Fabbri, Franco. 1989. "The system of *canzone* in Italy today (1981)," in *World Music, Politics, and Social Change,* edited by Simon Frith. Manchester and New York: Manchester University Press. 122-142.

———. 1997 "Il cantautore con due voci," in *Fabrizio De André. Accordi eretici,* edited by Romano Giuffrida and Bruno Bigoni. Milan: Euresis Edizioni. 155-167.

Fasoli, Doriano. 1999. *Fabrizio de André. Passaggi di tempo. Da Carlo Martello a Princesa.* Roma: Edizioni Associate.

Feld, Steven. 1994. "Notes on World Beat," in Charles Keil and Steven Feld. *Music Grooves. Essays and Dialogues.* Chicago and London: University of Chicago Press. 238-246.

Finzi, Paolo. 1999. "Da Carimate a Genova via Maghreb. Colloquio con Mauro Pagani," *Rivista Anarchica Online* 252 <http://www.anarca-bolo.ch/a-rivista/252/29.htm>

Fiori, Umberto. 1997. "'La canzone è un testo cantato.' Parole e musica in De André," in *Fabrizio De André. Accordi eretici,* edited by Romano Giuffrida and Bruno Bigoni. Milano: Euresis Edizioni. 145-154.

Franchini, Alberto. 2000. *Uomini e donne di Fabrizio de André. Conversazioni ai margini.* Genova: Fratelli Frilli Editori.

Giuffrida, Romano and Bruno Bigoni (eds.). 1997. *Fabrizio De André. Accordi eretici.* Milano: Euresis Edizioni.

Giugni, Riccardo. 1990. "Pagani, Mauro," in *Il Dizionario della Canzone Italiana.* 2 vols. Edited by Gino Castaldo. Milano: Curcio. 1254-1255.

Lanza, Luciano. 1999. "Gli anarchici, i poeti e gli altri. Intervista a Fabrizio De André," *Rivista Anarchica Online* 252 <http://www.anarca-bolo.ch/a-rivista/252/34.htm>

Lattarulo, Alessandro. 2000. "De André e il Mediterraneo," *Cupa cupa.* <http://www.cupacupa.com/italiana/de_andre.asp>

Liperi, Felice. 1999. *Storia della canzone italiana.* Roma: RAI-ERI.

Meintjes, Louise. 1990. "Paul Simon's *Graceland,* South Africa, and the Mediation of Musical Meaning." In *Ethnomusicology* 36: 37-73.

Mirenzi, Francesco. 1997. *Rock Progressivo Italiano. La storia, i protagonisti, i concerti.* 2 vols. Roma: Castelvecchi.

Pestalozza, Luigi. 1997. "La canzone dell'altro mondo," in *Fabrizio De André. Accordi eretici*, edited by Romano Giuffrida and Bruno Bigoni. Milano: Euresis Edizioni. 169–180.

Plastino. Goffredo. 1996. *Mappa delle voci. Rap, raggamuffin e tradizione in Italia*. Roma: Meltemi.

Romana, Cesare. 2000. *Amico fragile. Fabrizio de André*. Milano: Sperling & Kupfer.

Ruggeri, Roberto. 1990. "Premiata Forneria Marconi," in *Il Dizionario della Canzone Italiana*, edited by Gino Castaldo. 2 vols. Milano: Curcio. 1388–1390.

Surian, Alessio. 2001. *A Path Along the Sea*. Introduction to *Travellin' Companion Vol. 2 : A Musical Journey to Italy*. WeltWunder Records.

Taylor, Timothy D. 1997. *Global Pop. World Music, World Markets*. New York and London: Routledge.

Trân, Quang Hai. 1994. "Le chant diphonique: description, historique, styles, aspect acoustique et spectral, demarche originale, recherches fondamentales et appliquées." In *EM* II: 123–150.

Videtti, Giuseppe. 1999. "De André: la discografia," *Musica! Rock & altro* <http://www.repubblica.it/supplementi/musica/19990121/artic_dischi.html>

Viva, Luigi. 2001. *Vita di Fabrizio De André (non per un dio ma nemmeno per gioco)*. Milano: Feltrinelli.

Zampa, Fabrizio. 1990. "De André, Fabrizio," in *Il Dizionario della Canzone Italiana*. 2 vols., edited by Gino Castaldo. Milano: Curcio. 489–494.

Discography

A Harvest, a Shepherd, a Bride: Village Music of Bulgaria/In the Shadow of the Mountain. Bulgarian Folk Music. Collected in Bulgaria and produced by Ethel Raim and Martin Koenig. Elektra/Nonesuch 9 79195-2. 1988 (first released 1970/71). (Includes *Gankino Krivo Horo*.)

Area—International POPular Group. *Arbeit macht frei*. Cramps/EMI 7243 8 57424 2 2. 1998 (first released 1973). (Includes "Luglio, agosto, settembre nero.")

_____. *Caution Radiation Area*. Cramps/EMI 7243 8 57425 2 1. 1998 (first released 1974). (Includes "Cometa Rossa.")

_____. *Are(A)zione*. Cramps/EMI 7243 8 57427 2 9. 1998 (first released 1975). (Includes live recordings of "Luglio," "agosto," "settembre nero" and "Cometa rossa.")

_____. *Parigi-Lisbona*. Cramps CRSCD 018. 1996.

_____. *Concerto Teatro Uomo*. Cramps/EMI 7243 8 57539 2 3. 1998. 2 CDs.

Canti randagi. Canzoni di Fabrizio De André. Ricordi TCDMRL 6509. 1995.

Carnascialia. Mirto/Phonogram 6323/50. 1979.

De André, Fabrizio. *Creuza de mä*. Ricordi SMRL 6308. 1984.

_____. *Le nuvole*. Ricordi/Fonit Cetra CDL 260. 1990.

_____. *1991 Concerti*. Ricordi ACDMRL 26478. 1991. 2 CDs.

——. *Anime salve*. Ricordi TCDRML 392352-74321392352. 1996.

De André, Fabrizio/P.F.M. *In Concerto Vol 1*. Ricordi SMRL 6244. 1979

_____. *In Concerto Vol 2*. Ricordi OR 8431. 1980.

Liguria: Baiardo and Imperia. Recordings by Alan Lomax. Rounder Records 1816. 2001.

Liguria: Ceriana. Recordings by Alan Lomax. Rounder Records 1817. 2001.

Novalia. *Arkeo*. CNI Ludos LDL 11133. 1999. (Includes "Perzu pe 'na creuza de mä").

Pagani, Mauro. *Mauro Pagani*. Ascolto ASC 20093. 1978.

Premiata Forneria Marconi. *Storia di un minuto*. Numero Uno ZSLN 55055. 1972.

_____. *Live in USA*. Numero Uno DZSLN 55676. 1974.

Trallaleri of Genoa. Recordings by Alan Lomax. Rounder Records 1802. 1999.

Travellin' Companion Vol. 2 : A Musical Journey to Italy. WeltWunder Records CD WW 502-2. 2001.

Filmography

De André, Fabrizio. 1999. *Parole e canzoni*. Edited by Vincenzo Mollica. Torino: Einaudi.

_____. 1999. *De André in concerto*. Milano: Mondadori.

GOFFREDO PLASTINO

SACRED POPULAR MUSIC OF THE MEDITERRANEAN AND THE JOURNEY TO JERUSALEM

PHILIP V. BOHLMAN

Passage through the Jubilee Year

"Jubilee 2000 in the Holy Land: A Musical Journey to the Land of Jesus." The promise proclaimed by the title for the contents of a CD jewel box is not inconsiderable. In addition to the "musical journey," the "Limited Millenium [*sic*] Edition" provides a CD-ROM containing fifty sacred sites in the Holy Land, which the producers "hope . . . will be useful, on your pilgrim [*sic*] to the Holy-Land, or help bring the Holy-Land closer to you." There is no reason to doubt the claim, for in the spine of the CD jewel box are two minuscule flasks, one filled with olive oil, the other containing holy water.

CD technology and marketing design conspire to popularize the experience of a millennium in the Mediterranean. The jumble of images on the CD cover iconically offer something to every potential pilgrim, from the blond-haired, New Age Jesus to the Palestinian village serving as a simulacrum for the everyday presence of sacred sites, to the sanctuary of St. Catherine's Church in Bethlehem, the ethnographic site for the several field recordings that authenticate the music of the Holy Land. We might even be tempted to react to the cover as kitsch, but the more we unravel its images, the more their familiarity acquires mean-

Cover of *Jubilee 2000 in the Holy Land*

ingfulness and intensifies the intimacy of the CD and its recorded tracks.

In the Jubilee year of the Christian church, the Mediterranean itself underwent a transformation into an extensive landscape of sacred popular music. Songbooks appeared in countless editions and in seemingly limitless print-runs. Cassettes and CDs were available everywhere, and the music they offered represented the Jubilee in every possible way. The music of Jubilee 2000 was popular music writ large—and appropriated and mediated even larger.

The 21 tracks on *Jubilee 2000 in the Holy Land* provide a small sampling of the sacred musics popularized for the Jubilee year, and in so doing they also raise crucial questions about sacred popular music in the Mediterranean. Employing a format increasingly popular with pilgrimage cassettes and CDs (Bohlman 2000a), the CD opens and closes with tracks containing the bells of St. Catherine's Church in Bethlehem, thus evoking a sense of ambient sound that might surround the pilgrim entering the church. Several tracks at the beginning and end of the CD (2 and 3; 19 and 20) also contain performances from the church itself. The authenticity that these tracks attempt to mediate is striking, for the singers make no attempt to capture a professional sound, or for that matter, to sing in a consistent tuning system.

The repertory is highly Protestant, with its core anchored to the hymn-singing traditions of American evangelicals. Critical to the coherence of the hymnody on the CD is its inclusion of several of the most popular hymns among evangelical Protestants (for example, J. B. Dykes's "Holy, Holy, Holy" and C. H. H. Parry's "God Is Love"). Popular Christmas songs punctuate the tracks, one of them ("Adeste Fideles") among the ethnographic tracks. The CD tracks are liberally drawn, therefore, from the most popular sacred-song tradition of English-speaking Protestants, but for *Jubilee 2000 in the Holy Land* they have been repackaged to make them popular for use in entirely different ways. Produced by a recording studio in Israel that uses the Hebrew name, Derech Ha'ozen Music (literally "Way of the Ear"), the hymns not recorded in Bethlehem are sung by professional choirs in modern arrangements. Neither choir nor arrangers are acknowledged here.

The core repertory of evangelical hymnody on *Jubilee 2000 in the Holy Land* might not fulfill the usual conditions we attribute to music in the Mediterranean, much less to popular music in the Mediterranean. Contrary to our intuition about those conditions, however, it is the intersection of the sacred and the popular that transforms these hymns into a popular music of the Mediterranean. English and American evangelical hymns may not be products of the Mediterranean, but they are among the most common repertories used to represent the sacred sites of the Christian Levant. Whether or not one thinks of their nineteenth-century, four-voice texture as popular in a contemporary sense, that texture lends itself to virtually every textural permutation and rock vocabulary of the late twentieth century. If they are not produced in the Mediterranean, they nonetheless meet the criteria that popular repertories of the Mediterranean have fulfilled for centuries, perhaps millennia, if we are to accept the claims of those who package and market them for popular consumption. As sacred popular songs, they collapse local and global categories. They define sacred sites by placing them on the CD-ROM interactive track, yet they use recording technology to move the Jubilee pilgrim along a cyber-sacred journey.

In this chapter, I examine the multifarious repertories that constitute the sacred-popular musics of the Mediterranean. Metonymically drawing on the historical imagination of the Mediterranean as a place of in-betweenness, I concern myself with the ways in which sacred musics in the Mediterranean become popular through their articulation of senses of place and journey. Sacred-popular musics empower and mobilize religious practice and practitioners—worshipers or the faithful whose music-making maps the Mediterranean as sacred—to move into and out of spaces that are contested or that occupy boundary positions between sacred and secular worlds, or between modern political realities and memorialized religious ritual. Moving from section to section in the chapter, I rhetorically chart the mediated terrains that sacred-popular musics make visible and audible, and in so doing I attempt to rethink the ways in which the larger geographical and historical spaces of the Mediterranean emerge: as a landscape of pilgrimage, diaspora, and religious revival that is constantly in flux because of the shifting signification of sacred-popular musics.

Religious Music and the Instantiation of Sacred Space

The sacred enlivens the popular, and the popular intensifies the experience of the sacred. The sacred and the popular interact in particularly powerful forms of mutual dependence. The intensity with which the sacred and the popular interact may seem counterintuitive, especially in an era of late capitalism and postmodernism that has espoused many claims for a globalized secularism. That same era, however, has witnessed the globalization of religious revival and the proliferation of diverse forms of popular religion. Indeed, in an era of global connections, religious practice has benefited in countless ways from mass mediation and the growing presence of religion in the public sphere. But this is not new, and that is precisely the point of this essay.

In the religions of the Mediterranean specific sacred musical forms have undergirded the popularity of religious practice, even mass participation in religion. The broad range of participatory practices that coalesce as hymn-singing are one of the most obvious examples of the popularizing of religion through music. In the broadest generic terms, hymns form repertories that lend themselves to congregational participation in many religions. Hymn texts are frequently strophic and often metric in order to facilitate ease of learning and performance. Whereas hymn texts may begin as sacred texts, they often undergo extensive adaptation to local conditions, for example by employing translations into the vernacular. Hymn melodies often begin as well known contrafacts, borrowed or appropriated from popular repertories. At moments of extensive religious transition, such as revival or persecution, hymn repertories grow in size, and their popularity intensifies as a means of providing social solidarity. During moments of mass pilgrimage in the Mediterranean world, whether Muslim, Jewish, or Christian pilgrimage, it is the hymn that becomes the popular musical genre of choice.

The musical intersection of the sacred and the popular is one of extraordinarily intense cultural intimacy (Herzfeld 1997). Popular religion and popularized expressions of religion are redolent of the metaphors of sacred intimacy: intense expressions of love, physical and spiritual; witness to the sacred through pain and suffering; abandonment of the self in order to fulfill a religious commandment. Writing about cultural intimacy in the modern nation-state, Herzfeld points out the ways it provides "insiders with their assurance of common sociality, the familiarity with the bases of power that may at one moment assure the disenfranchised a degree of creative irreverence and at the next moment reinforce the effectiveness of intimidation" (ibid.: 3). In popular forms of religion cultural intimacy assumes somewhat different, albeit closely related, forms, for example by engendering what might be called "creative reverence" that reinforces the effectiveness of "fervor through shared worship." The symbolic surfeit of cultural intimacy that seems to crush the real religious efficacy of a CD such as *Jubilee 2000 in the Holy Land*—to turn it into just so much kitsch—instead undergirds its power to mobilize religious community at the millennium.

Music provides one of the catalysts that makes such forms of intimacy possible and, I wish to suggest, popular. It is music, again, that has the potential to expose and open the intimate experience with the sacred as public and popular. Private worship takes on public forms; intimate genres of private litany engender mass participation. Music provides a performative context for the public display of religious intimacy, enhancing the popularity of that intimacy. Sacred music, thus, creates a space in which the intimacy of the sacred experience itself is opened for intensive and extensive participation.

In this chapter, I focus on two types of sacred space that are exposed and opened through popular musical practices. The intimacy of sacred musical experience is particularly intense at these sacred spaces, further emphasizing processes of mediation that they unleash. Viewed together, the sacred spaces with which I concern myself in this essay suggest ways of metaphorically mapping the Mediterranean—historically and geographically—as a domain of complex religious interaction. The spatial character of the sacred spaces therefore function metonymically for the sacred landscape of the Mediterranean itself.

The first type of sacred space I examine seems at first glance to be a fixed space, as if sacred musical practice accrues to the geography of the Mediterranean, defining sacred space by bounding and ultimately fixing it. In contrast, there are sacred spaces that are fluid, or rather, that undergo repeated redefinition and rebounding. The second type of sacred space, it follows, facilitates passage. Historically, the two types of sacred space with which I concern myself in this essay coexist in a kind of religious and geographical tension. Passage connects sacred spaces that are otherwise fixed and bounded. The tension that accrues to the sacred geography of the Mediterranean is set in motion by worshipers, those who follow the passages of sacred journey and gather to sing at sacred sites. Rhetorically, my essay also follows a path from sacred site along a sacred passage toward yet another sacred site. The essay thus attempts to represent the ways in which sacred musical practices become popular through the creative use of music by worshipers moving along personal and collective sacred journeys, pausing at those stations along the way that make their songs especially meaningful by allowing them to share the intimacy of a music shared with fellow believers.

Sacred Site 1: Pilgrimage

Maria abit in montana.
Mary's icon is represented in thousands of faces in the history
and tradition of Christian devotion. . . . Hers is a pilgrimage in
faith which takes place in time.
(Pilgrim Prayers *2000: 76*)

Time and history converge at the sacred sites toward which the pilgrim multitudes of the Jubilee year move. The convergence itself swells from the narrative power of time and history, and from the performative capacity of song to empower the mass popular movement that pilgrimage sets in motion. That several specific pilgrimage sites dominated the sacred landscapes of the Mediterranean during the Jubilee was crucial to the popularity and popular culture that it engendered. Most popular of all, surely, was the mass movement of young pilgrims to Rome, where they celebrated the founding of the Catholic Church. For these pilgrims, however, the great age of Rome was secondary to the vitality of the popularity that charted their movements in and around the Jubilee sacred site of Rome itself. They moved with an official prayer book clasped in one hand, and a portable CD-player in the other, alternatively moving through ritualized space and the arenas dominated by the spectacles of popular culture. Their pilgrimage, like that of St. Mary, to whom they raised their songs, took place in time—time they had recalibrated as their own.

Historically, pilgrimage has provided one of the most persistent of all templates for the expression of sacred-popular music in the Mediterranean. Pilgrimage begins, ironically, with a vision of its goal, in other words the sacred site that lies at the end of the pilgrim's journey. That beginning, moreover, is a site of extraordinarily intense intimacy, an iconic juncture between the pilgrim's physical life and the life that lies beyond. It is also at the sacred site that the pilgrim joins most physically with others, thus sharing the intimacy that envelops the site. The sacred site at the end of the pilgrim's journey is therefore one of active performance, thus it is here that the meanings converging at the site are most fully performed into being.

Music is crucial to achieving the intensified intimacy that suffuses the sacred site, and the music that most effectively achieves intimacy is that which unifies through popularity. Accordingly, sacred music is produced and distributed in massive proportions at the sacred site. There is a flourishing local cassette industry, and small presses churn out prayer and song books, as well as song sheets and broadsides of all kinds. Local radio stations inundate the airwaves. Professional musicians, secular and sacred, offer their services as a colportage of popularity (Bohlman 2000a). Hymn production is redoubled, connecting familiar repertories with popular contrafacts. The Mediterranean sacred sites that the performative pilgrim texts of the Jubilee year document realize a virtual reality of many different forms popular culture (e.g., *Pilgrim Prayers* 2000). The Mediterranean itself became a map of history, charted by the movement of pilgrims, their songs amplified by the technologies available to the purveyors of the sacred-popular songs that ceaselessly memorialized the two millennia defining the present.

Passage 1: The Way of the Pilgrim

The way of the pilgrim maps and remaps the Mediterranean, transforming the region into a landscape of intersecting sacred journeys. The pilgrim's journey is musical at every station, and the journey itself assumes its context as the continuously unfolding texts of song. As a landscape of intersecting sacred journeys, the Mediterranean may well display its most historically musical character (Bohlman 1997). The in-betweenness of Mediterranean geography itself has historically emerged from the pilgrimages of the three world religions dominating the region. Indeed, the sacred in-betweenness of the Mediterranean results from passage across the borders that the three religions contest.

The music of the pilgrim's passage embodies the most intimate of all forms of sacred-popular music. The way of the pilgrim does not simply stretch across the geography of the Mediterranean, but rather it is a highly personal journey that reaches into the self, that is, penetrates in profoundly intimate ways the body of the pilgrim. The songs of the pilgrim succeed in negating the physical demands of the journey—the passage by foot of extended distances—while at the same time heightening the awareness of the physical nature of worship as a pilgrim. Song becomes, thus, a metaphor for life through its paving of the sacred route through life, but in so doing it draws the pilgrim closer to the journey's end, to the border between the mortal and the immortal (see Bohlman 2000c).

The signifiers of popularity in the music accompanying pilgrimage through the Mediterranean are many and complex. Throughout this essay I show that that designating such sacred musics as popular extends our understanding of what popular music is and how it functions. At the beginning of the twenty-first century we are confronted by the obvious, namely the resurgence of pilgrimage's popularity, both in the religious revivalism of the 1990s and then in concert with the Christian Jubilee year of 2000. The proliferation of pilgrimage repertories has been unchecked, with new technologies of song production—cassette culture and the internet—driving the mass distribution of pilgrimage songs. Songs such as the "Medjugorje Song," composed to respond specifically to Marian apparitions in Bosnia-Herzegovina in the early 1980s, appeared on countless cassettes and CDs by the early 1990s at the height of the war between Serbia and Bosnia-Herzegovina. It was as a popular song that the "Medjugorje Song" could and did intervene in the Bosnian crisis (ct. Rupčić 1989).

The sacred song of the pilgrim opens the way of the pilgrim. The song itself becomes the template for the sacred journey, with alternative routes opened for setting forth on the journey. As intimate as the individual sacred journey is, however, it is not taken alone, but rather in communion with those sharing the way. As the song swells in volume and gains in popularity, its sacredness spreads, indeed across entire historical regions like the Mediterranean.

Sacred Site 2: Saints' Shrines

The shrines of saints chart one of the most complex historical geographies of the Mediterranean, providing a map for some of the most intensive and intimate forms of devotion expressed through music. Saints' shrines are at once shrouded with local, individual functions and capable of generating a sense of community through worship that spreads across the faithful (cf. Avishur 1986; Dubisch 1995). Because it may contain the remains of a saint, a shrine attracts worshipers for very specific reasons, and it builds communities through centralizing the musical repertories that speak to the life of the saint her- or himself. The musical repertories that accrue to saints' shrines, such as those accompanying *hillulah* at the graves of Moroccan Jewish saints, survive because of the types of exchange they tolerate and encourage (Ben-Ami 1998: 105–24). Musically, they must embrace the popular, for example the melodic store of *piyyutim* and *qasidot* that Moroccan Jews muster when participating in *hillulot* at saints' shrines. Such genres already enable the mixing of sacred texts in Hebrew with vernacular texts, sometimes in verses with bilingual texts (see also Avishur 1986). Traditional sacred and popular vernacular texts, therefore, provide two different types of connective fiber, the former to historical narratives and the latter to contemporary expression that emphasizes exaltation and veneration.

Shrines form the nodes along complex sacred passages through the Mediterranean. The passages between shrines may serve as individual legs of longer sacred journeys, or they may provide localized networks for journeys that articulate the holidays or historical events defining regional communities. The musical repertories of the two different types of passages to and from saints' shrines take shape from distinctive processes of mixing the sacred and the popular. One of the most sustained studies of the impact of passage between Jewish saints' shrines in North Africa has been Robert Lachmann's analysis of song in the Jewish communities on the Tunisian island of Djerba (Lachmann 1978 [1940]). The passage through these communities of pilgrims *en route* to saints' shrines proved crucial to the defining of local musical traditions, defining the traditions, however, through constant processes of mixing and remixing. Those passing through the villages of Hara Kabira and Hara Saghira replenished sacred traditions in effect by introducing music from outside the local tradition (cf. Davis 1984/85).

It is not my point to argue that all the musics that accrue to saints' shrines are popular, but rather that saints' shrines serve as particularly intensive sites for mixing the sacred and the popular. "Mixing" itself has both sacred and popular meanings in the contexts of the shrine. Recordings of popular Sufi music may well be the most effective illustration of this type of mixing. Whereas many forms of mixing suggest that popular styles can overwhelm certain aspects of the sacred when appropriating them for recordings, recordings at Sufi shrines reveal that popular sounds themselves may undergo a mixing process that yields sacralization. The popular style is subsumed to the sacred sound (for example Azrié and Rabih Abou-Khalil 1998). The mixed sacred sound, however, intensifies the experience of exaltation at the shrine by renewing it and revealing the increasingly contemporary meanings of its pastness.

Passage 2: Border-Crossing

Oh madre, yo sé que un dia tú verás
Que también puedo cambiar
Oh madre . . . yo volveré . . .
(Tekameli, "¡Oh Madre!")

Popular musics of the Mediterranean do not shun the sacred. The rhetoric about anti-Islamist repertories from North Africa or anti-Orthodox styles from Israel too often turns a deaf ear to the deeper religious message that pervades popular song. The failure to perceive the sacred stems from an accompanying failure to perceive not only the border between the sacred and the secular, but also the ways in which popular music crosses and recrosses that border, blurring it while also intensifying the intimate forms of sacred music-making that contest it.

Themes of passage provide the connective tissue that link the sacred and the secular in the imagery of Mediterranean popular music. The themes of passage are perhaps most explicit in the repertories of diasporic peoples, for example, Roma bands in Spain or Sephardic Jewish bands in Bosnia. For its 1999 CD, *Ida y vuelta,* the Roma ensemble, Tekameli, draws upon a rich stock of metaphors that express the forms of passage that define its past. At one level, the passages with which Tekameli is concerned are historical, the historical diaspora from South Asia to the Mediterranean. At another level, passages that intersect in the texts and musical styles of *Ida y vuelta* serve as metaphors for human interactions, particularly between Europeans and their Mediterranean others. At still another level, the passages on the CD draw the sacred and the secular together, profoundly so, for *Ida y vuelta* devotes itself entirely to a sacred imagery that accrues at the border between Mediterranean Christianity and the other religions through which Mediterranean Roma pass.

That imagery is powerfully present, for example, in the song, "¡Oh Madre!," that provides the epigraph above (*Ida y vuelta*, cut 5). For this song, with its expression of overt Marian worship, Tekameli is joined by the *raï* singer, Cheb Khaled. The collaboration is by no means random, for it offers a testament to the very passage across religious and musical boundaries that map the entire album on the Mediterranean as a terrain of contested boundaries. Stylistically, "¡Oh Madre!" explicitly mixes flamenco in the accompanimental parts with the North African vocal genre, *layali,* which permits Khaled at once to sing a Marian text and to do so in Arabic. Sacred themes of several types are not foreign to raï (Schade-Poulsen 1999: 148–53). The theme of return that closes "¡Oh Madre!" serves as a refrain in many raï songs, among them Khaled's "Alech taadi" and "Abdel Kader" (*N'ssi n'ssi*: cuts 6 and 10).

During the 1990s the Bosnian Jewish trio, Vladah, similarly transformed the diasporic Jewish repertory that defined the Jewish past of Bosnia and invested it with a new popular sound to evoke the metaphors of the late twentieth-century passages of Balkan Jewish communities. The "new" sound chosen by Vladah, however, was deliberately sacred, and it was mustered by consciously crossing borders. Traditional genres, such as the *copla,* were recharted to fit religious holidays (e.g., "Coplas de purim," which celebrates the early-spring holiday, Purim, *Vladah Trio,* cut 4). Songs celebrating the Hassidic past of northeastern Europe ("Als der Rebbe," cut 5) migrate to southeastern Europe, signifying the movement of pogrom in the course of the twentieth century. Borders run wildly across the Jewish landscape evoked by Vladah's mixing of past and present, self and other, and passage—constant passage—across Balkan borders is rendered normative by a sacred-popular style invented for diasporas still unfolding.

Sacred Site 3: The Musical Archeology of the Sacred

Musical traditions accrue to sacred sites to enhance the multidimensional layering that characterizes their historical archeology. The seeming stasis of a sacred site notwithstanding, they contain many rather than few meanings, and they lend themselves to constant interpretation and reinterpretation. Sacred music, in which multiple layers of meaning are also embedded, provides one of the most powerful forms of reinterpreting the layers of sacred meaning that accumulate at a sacred site. This capacity of music empowers it to serve what we might call a musical archeology.

The archeological complexity of a sacred site in the Mediterranean is most commonly recognized in Jerusalem. Sacred layers separate not only different historical eras one from another, but also the major religions—Judaism, Christianity, and Islam—that compete for the spaces of Jerusalem. Within the major religions, different sects and denominations focus their worship and political activities on different levels. Christian sects, for example, work out distinctive ways of using ritual sites in their worship activities, mapping their own forms of Christianity on the city's many levels (see Bowman 1991). Other major pilgrimage sites of the Mediterranean also form multilayered complexes of sacred practices, with archeological depth often unearthed as a simulacrum for the *longue durée* of religious history.

Sacred song does not so much penetrate the many layers of contested sacred sites as rise above it, filling the spaces that worships create as they move through the spaces of the sacred site. The soundscape of Jerusalem, for example, shifts constantly through the mixing and remixing of the Muslim call to prayer, the voices of praying Jews, and the rhythmic movements of Christian processions. Sacred music liberates the spaces above the archeological layers, not so much laying bare the layers as aurally revealing the meanings embedded in them. Pilgrimage sites elsewhere in the Mediterranean, too, undergo continuous transformation to dense sonic spaces, where song draws the worshiper to sources of the sacred not otherwise palpable.

It is the ways in which sacred music lends itself to mixing and remixing that establish the link to its archeological potential—and by extension to the domains of the popular. Through formations of new popular sounds, sacred repertories reconfigure more vividly what would otherwise remain hidden, buried in a layer few could reach. Through mixing and remixing, moreover, sacred-popular musics breach the boundaries that could stultify religious practice. Again, the sacred and the popular intersect in order to reflect the multidimensional character of the sacred site, enhancing it as a space where many, rather than few, can worship.

Passage 3: Freighting of *Qur'anic* Recitation

The very universality of the *Qur'an* endows it with the power to transport its teachings to Muslims across the vast distances and historical spaces of the Islamic world. Recitation of the Qur'an, however, resists being torn from the meanings that the individual believer invests in it through localized performance. Recitation must be both personal, and at the same time it must convey varying degrees of communality, concentric rings of cultural intimacy radiating outward from the text itself. Knowledge of the practices of recitation (*tajwid*) lies at the core of its performance, but perception of the Qur'an's musicality—its use of melodic and modal principles from Arabic musical systems, especially in the eastern Mediterranean—relies not on vocal production, but rather on aural reception, that is, on *sama* (Nelson 1985).

The basic principles of qur'anic recitation notwithstanding, the mass production of LPs, cassettes, and CDs containing the Qur'an has become so extensive as to make it the core of recording in the Mediterranean. Recordings of the Qur'an circulate about the Mediterranean, conducting star reciters (*muqri*) in one part of the region to consumers in communities elsewhere, in Mediterranean communities and beyond. The distribution network that connects record companies in Cairo or Istanbul to markets (e.g., the *soqs* of Paris, Milan, or Berlin) form trade routes for the trafficking of the most sacred of all forms of Muslim expressive culture as postmodern popular music. The key sites for the transformation of Qur'an recitation to popular recordings lie at opposite ends of the distribution networks.

In Egypt, record producers tap into the genealogy of reciters that accrues to specific schools of recitation, recognizing that a star system existed for generations (Asad 1993). The recordings of recitation are marketed in such ways that they fit seamlessly into the soundscapes of open-air markets and shopping districts of Muslim communities about the Mediterranean, especially in those communities in Europe that comprise the Mediterranean Muslim diaspora. At the ends of such modern trade routes, production and consumption of sacred music differ not at all from those of other popular music. On CDs, the Qur'an is experienced almost as other popular musics of the Mediterranean are experienced. The mutual interdependency of the sacred and the popular collapses the difference between them.

Sheikh Abdel Basset Abdel Samad has for the past generation enjoyed the highest level of prestige in the Muslim communities of France. Though his career as a reciter was launched traditionally in Cairo, he secured an early recording contract with the French subsidiary in Egypt, Sono Cairo. The key to Sheikh Samad's success was that his recordings circulated widely in markets at both ends of the Mediterranean. Secondarily, Sheikh Samad was one of the first reciter-stars who took advantage of the technologies that would allow Sono Cairo to market entire Qur'an cycles, in other words, the successive performance of chapters stretching over the course of the Muslim year. From a marketing standpoint, his recordings were the equivalent of a *Gesamtausgabe,* or complete edition. It would not suffice to have a *sura* (chapter) or two, but rather it became almost a prerequisite to purchase as much of the entire *Qur'an* as possible.

Various processes of popularizing the Cairene sound of these recordings were quick to follow. By the 1980s, Sheikh Samad's recordings formed the canonic repertory of the Qur'an LPs and cassettes available in the largely North African and Algerian communities of France. During the 1990s, the recordings quickly underwent a transferral to CD technology, which effectively enhanced both compactness and marketability. As CDs, Sheikh Samad's recordings were quick to complement and parallel the exchange of popular music, especially *raï,* that passed between French diaspora communities and North Africa. Consequently, the cycle of production and consumption of the most sacred of repertories expanded and reached an ever-expanding audience in the Mediterranean, which was attracted to the availability of this most intimate forms of expressing belief.

Sacred Site 4: *Lieux de la Mémoire*

Zaljulja se mostarska munara,
Potrese se mostarska cuprija,
Mujezini ucit' prestadose,
Kad zapjeva Lakusica Zlata.

Mostar's minaret shuddered,
Mostar's bridge shook,

The muezzins stopped praying
When Lakusic's Zlata began to sing.
("Psenicice, sitno sjeme," traditional Bosnian song)

The sacred sites of the Mediterranean often survive because they are places of memory (*lieux de mémoire*) on a sacred landscape (see Nora 1989). Memory, however, renders the sacred no less real, no less palpable, for it is through memory that religion's intimacy can be made most real. Memory, too, relies critically on the narrative agency of music to make possible the return to the place that is no longer. As music maps the journey to the past, it acquires what Susan Slyomovics has called a "poetics of memory," wherein various pasts otherwise separate will converge and even coexist (Slyomovics 1998: 169-98). It is this poetics of memory that determines the sacred archeology of many of the Mediterranean's most contested regions, among them the multireligious, multicultural lands of southeastern Europe.

As *lieux de mémoire*, sacred sites in southeastern Europe mobilize various forms of resistance that ensure that voices from the multiple pasts of the region are not silenced by history. Many sacred sites, such as the minarets and bridge of Mostar in the epigraph opening this section, may survive most effectively through song and because of song's poetics of memory, having suffered repeated destruction in the long struggle between Christians and Muslims in Bosnia-Herzegovina. Bosnian songs themselves mix genres, but in so doing they articulate the several historical layers from which they come. The border between the Christian and the Muslim bounds one layer, while the border between the Serbian and the Turkish pasts bounds another. Crossing these borders is fraught with tension, for each border-crossing draws attention to the disjuncture between music and memory. Still, it is precisely such tension that unfetters a new signification of resistance in music.

The popular music of the Balkans resists being unfettered from the region's multireligious mix. Sacred imagery from memory returns again and again in popular song, whether in the Bosnian Muslim *shevdas* of exiled communities (see Hemetek 1996) or in the hardcore repertories of "turbo folk" in the former—and present—Yugoslavia (Longinović 2000). Sacred song proffers national imagery a new validity, modernizing in the process the sense of authenticity on which the poetics of memory depends. In Bosnia-Herzegovina, for example, sacred song may be wrenched from its place in traditional memory and resacralized for popular consumption (Lausević 1996). The poetics of memory reshapes the public spaces (e.g., athletic stadiums used for rock concerts) into sacred spaces, where popular music signifies myriad pasts but does so by resignifying them as sites where religious and national histories have converged as contested *lieux de mémoire*.

Passage beyond the Jubilee Year: Revival and Resacralization of the Mediterranean

Lauda Jerusalem Dominum
Lauda Deum tuum, Sion.
Hosanna, Hosanna,
Hosanna filio David.
(Pilgrim Prayers *2000*: 244)

Turn, turn, here we go again,
"Journey to Jerusalem" . . .
Life is a long, long journey
into Tomorrowland.
(Sürpriz, *"Kudüs'e seyahat"* [Journey to Jerusalem])

In 1999, on the eve of the Jubilee year, Jerusalem was the site for Europe's foremost popular-music pilgrimage, the Eurovision Song Contest. Jerusalem had won the privilege of serving as the site for the pilgrimage because in 1998 the Israeli entry, Dana International, had won the contest. For many of the European musicians who participated—each nation in Europe broadly defined (i.e., North African nations and, for that matter, Israel, have regularly contributed entries)—the metaphorical meaning of the journey to Jerusalem was not lost. Jerusalem had long served as a primary sacred site for all of Europe's major religions, and pilgrimages, crusades, and journeys into the sacred past recognized the ways in which Jerusalem's historical and geographic position in the Mediterranean in large measure defined Europe.

On the eve of the Jubilee year the potential of investing the world's major popular-song contest with added religious significance was also not lost on the competitors. For the first time, Germany chose a Turkish-German singer, Sürpriz, as its entry. Sürpriz, who had for several years before the Eurovision Song Contest sung with both German and Turkish bands in Germany, seized the opportunity to explore the various levels of meaning in a Jerusalem pilgrimage. For Germans at first hearing, the song explicitly referred to the children's game, "Reise nach Jerusalem," a form of musical chairs in which successive journeys about the inner circle led to the exclusion of more and more participants until "there were no longer any places left" ("kein Platz mehr frei").

In Sürpriz's version (music by Ralph Siegel and lyrics by Bernd Meinunger) the journey's meanings are turned inside-out, and Jerusalem is resignified as a sacred site open to the faithful of all religions. The various covers of "Kudüs'e seyahat" distributed in Europe together resignified Jerusalem as an ecumenical site. In addition to Turkish and German covers, there were English covers (for the Eurovision itself) and mixes with Hebrew and Arabic. Jerusalem, the sacred site of pilgrims approaching the millennium, emerged clearly in the midst of this intertexuality, the goal of an historical journey stretching beyond even the Jubilee year.

At the turn of the century, the passage to and then beyond the Jubilee year 2000 has witnessed two extensive phenomena of revival enveloping the public spaces of the Mediterranean. The revival of nationalism in its most extreme forms, and the revival of religion in its most intimate forms. These two forms of revival have formed a complex counterpoint, in which the voices of one respond to those in the other. More specifically, religious revival has served as one of the most trenchant responses to the resurgence of nationalism. The sacred music of religious revival, moreover, provides an alternative voice, audible and even extractable from the din of nationalism's insistence that only one nation can occupy the public sphere.

Sacred song enters the public sphere in a different way, sometimes quietly, sometimes with an arresting quality that is only possible in the fervor of revival. In so doing, sacred song at the beginning of the new millennium lays claim to the popular in ways more powerful than ever before. The religious revival that responds to the revival of nationalism also makes it possible for popular music itself to resignify the sacred. Together, then, the sacred and the popular, invigorated through the cultural intimacy accompanying their Jubilee and millennial passage, have set a resacralization of the Mediterranean in motion. Empowering the sacred journey unleashed by that resacralization is popular music, with its power to speak to and for the faithful as they journey to Jerusalem.

Bibliography

Asad, Talal. 1993. *Genealogies of Religion: Discipline and Reasons of Power in Christianity and Islam.* Baltimore: Johns Hopkins University Press.

Avishur, Yitzhak. 1986. *Shirat ha-nashim: Shire "am be-"aravit-yehudit shel yehude Irak* (Women's Songs: Folk Songs in Judeo-Arabic of the Iraqi Jews). Or Yehudah: Iraqi Jews' Cultural Institute.

Ben-Ami, Issachar. 1998. *Saint Veneration among the Jews in Morocco.* Detroit: Wayne State University Press.

Bohlman, Philip V. 1997. "Il passato, il presente e i popoli del Mediterraneo senza storia musicale," *Musica e storia* 5: 181–204.

———. 2000a. "Auf dem Weg zur Wallfahrt: Musikalische Kolportage an den Grenzen der Volksfrömmigkeit," in *Volksmusik—Wandel und Deutung: Festschrift Walter Deutsch zum 75. Geburtstag,* edited by Gerlinde Haid, Ursula Hemetek, and Rudolf Pietsch. Vienna: Böhlau Verlag. 504–521.

———. 2000b. "The Remembrance of Things Past: Music, Race, and the End of History in Modern Europe," in *Music and the Racial Imagination,* edited by Ronald Radano and Philip V. Bohlman. Chicago: University of Chicago Press. 644–676.

———. 2000c. "Pilgrimage," in *The New Grove Dictionary of Music and Musicians,* edited by Stanley Sadie. London: Macmillan. second ed., vol. 19, 743–745.

Bowman, Glenn. 1991. "Christian Ideology and the Image of a Holy Land: The Place of Jerusalem Pilgrimage in the Various Christianities," in *Contesting the Sacred: The Anthropology of Christian Pilgrimage,* edited by John Eade and Michael J. Sallnow. London and New York: Routledge. 98–121.

Davis, Ruth F. 1984/85. "Songs of the Jews on the Island of Djerba: A Comparison of Two Surveys: Hara Sghira (1929) and Hara Kebira (1976)," *Musica Judaica* 7: 23–33.

Dubisch, Jill. 1995. *In a Different Place: Pilgrimage, Gender, and Politics of a Greek Island Shrine.* Princeton: Princeton University Press.

Gross, Joan, David McMurray, and Ted Swedenburg. 1996. "Arab Noise and Ramadan Nights: Raï, Rap, and Franco-Maghrebi Identities," in *Displacement, Diaspora, and Geographies of Identity,* edited by Smadar Lavie and Ted Swedenburg. Durham, NC: Duke University Press. 119–156.

Herzfeld, Michael. 1997. *Cultural Intimacy: Social Poetics in the Nation-State.* New York and London: Routledge.

Idel, Moshe. 1997. "Conceptualizations of Music in Jewish Mysticism," in *Enchanting Powers: Music in the World's Religions,* edited by Lawrence E. Sullivan. Cambridge, MA: Harvard University Center for the Study of World Religions. 159–188.

Lachmann, Robert. [1940] 1978. *Gesänge der Juden auf der Insel Djerba.* Yuval Monograph Series 7. Jerusalem: The Magnes Press of the Hebrew University.

Lausević, Mirjana. 1996. "The *Ilahiya* as a Symbol of Bosnian Muslim National Identity," in *Retuning Culture: Musical Changes in Central and Eastern Europe,* edited by Mark Slobin. Durham, NC: Duke University Press. 117–135.

Longinović, Tomislav. 2000. "Music Wars: Blood and Song at the End of Yugoslavia," in *Music and the Racial Imagination,* edited by Ronald Radano and Philip V. Bohlman. Chicago: University of Chicago Press. 622–643.

Nelson, Kristina. 1985. *The Art of Reciting the Qur'an.* Austin: University of Texas Press.

Nora, Pierre. 1989. "Between Memory and History: *Les lieux de mémoire,*" *Representations* 26: 7–25.

Pilgrim Prayers: The Official Vatican Prayerbook for the Jubilee Year 2000. 2000. Rome: Continuum.

Rupcić, Ljudevit. 1989. *Erscheinungen unserer lieben Frau zu Medjugorje.* Jestetten: Miriam-Verlag.

Schade-Poulsen, Marc. 1999. *Men and Popular Music in Algeria: The Social Significance of Raï.* Austin: University of Texas Press.

Slyomovics, Susan. 1998. *The Object of Memory: Arab and Jew Narrate the Palestinian Village.* Philadelphia: University of Pennsylvania Press.

Sullivan, Lawrence E., ed. 1997. *Enchanting Powers: Music in the World's Religions.* Cambridge, MA: Harvard University Center for the Study of World Religions.

Discography

Abou-Khalil, Rabih. *Yara.* Enja ENJ-9360 2. 1998.

Azrié, Abed. *Les Soufis, d'après les textes mystiques du ixe au xiiie siècle.* Le Roseau 81021–81022. [1987.]

Bosnia: Echoes from an Endangered World. Smithsonian Folkways SF 40407. 1993.

Cheb Khaled. *N'ssi n'ssi.* Mango 697–124 012-2. 1993.

Hemetek, Ursula (ed). *Sevdah in Wien.* RST 91615-2. 1996. (Tondokumente zur Volksmusik in Österreich, vol. 5.)

Jubilee 2000 in the Holy Land: A Musical Journey to the Land of Jesus. Derech Ha'ozen Music Ltd. DHM 2000. 1999.

Sürpriz. *Reise nach Jerusalem/Kudüs'e seyahat/Journey to Jerusalem.* BMG 74321 65392 2. 1999.

Tekameli. *Ida y vuelta.* Epic EPC 493333 2. 1999.

Vladah. *Vladah Trio.* SW 028.

CONTRIBUTORS

Antonio Baldassarre since 1977 has been pursuing field work on musical anthropology in Morocco. Author of a number of writings appearing in edited volumes, he is record producer and concert manager for some of the most renowned Moroccan bands (Gnawa, B'net Houariyat, Rabita Andalousa, Sama Sufi of Fez). Among his publications: *Gnawa Leila: The Masters of Ganbri* (Nanterre, 1992/95, 5 CDs); *Morocco: Sound from an Ancient Land* (Firenze and Casablanca, 1998, CD-ROM).

Philip V. Bohlman teaches Ethnomusicology at the University of Chicago. His research ranges widely and includes Jewish music, music of the Mediterranean, folk and popular music, and music in the nexus of nationalism and racism. Among his most recent publications are *Music and the Racial Imagination* (coedited with Ronald Radano, Chicago, 2000) and *World Music: A Very Short Introduction* (Oxford, 2002). He is currently working on book projects on music drama in the Holocaust and the modern reception of Herder's writings on music and nationalism.

Joško Ćaleta is an associate of the Institute of Ethnology and Folklore in Zagreb, Croatia. After graduating music studies at University of Split, he received his MA from the University of British Columbia in

Vancouver. His main interests of research are the musical anthropology of the Mediterranean and the Dalmatian Hinterland. He is the author of many articles on traditional and popular music in Croatia, and coauthor of the CD *Croatian Traditional Music,* which presents a selection of fieldwork recordings of contemporary traditional music of Croatia. He is currently completing his PhD disertation on musical traditions of the Dalmatian Hinterland. Beside research work, he is also active as a singer, arranger, conductor, and composer (*klapa* singing).

Ruth Davis is Lecturer in Ethnomusicology at Cambridge University, and directs studies in Music at Corpus Christi College. She has broadcast and published extensively on Middle Eastern music, especially on her original field research in Tunisia. She is currently working in collaboration with the National Sound Archive and the Jewish Music Research Centre of the Hebrew University of Jerusalem on an edition of Robert Lachmann's writings and recordings from Palestine in the 1930s.

Kevin Dawe is Lecturer in Ethnomusicology at the University of Leeds. A music and science graduate, he has a MSc in anthropology (London) and a PhD in Ethnomusicology (The Queen's University of Belfast). Kevin has recently coedited the book *Guitar Cultures* (London, 2001) and made TV and video programs for the BBC on the music and cultures of Papua New Guinea and heavy-metal guitar music. He is currently editing a book called *Island Musics* and completing a single-authored book on the music of Crete.

Franco Fabbri has been a member of the Italian rock band Stormy Six since 1965. He was the chief organizer of the "Second International Conference on Popular Music Studies" in 1983, and chairman of the International Association for the Study of Popular Music (IASPM) in 1985–87. From 1992 to 2000, he chaired IASPM's Italian branch. His latest book is *Album bianco: Diari musicali 1965–2000* (Rome, 2001). He teaches Popular Music and the Media at the University of Turin.

Michael Frishkopf is Assistant Professor in the Department of Music, and Associate Director of the Centre for Ethnomusicology, at the University of Alberta. He lived in Egypt for nearly six years, where his research interests in musical-mystical experience, performance, and social structure were focused upon Islamic vocal forms, liturgies of the Sufi orders, and popular Sufi music of the *munshidin*. Among his publications are "Changing modalities in the globalization of Islamic saint veneration and mysticism: Sidi Ibrahim al-Dasuqi, Shaykh Muhammad 'Uthman al-Burhani, and their Sufi Orders" (2001-2), "Tarab in the Mystic Sufi Chant of Egypt" (2001), "Inshad Dini and Aghani Diniyya in 20th c Egypt: a review of styles, genres, and available recordings" (2001), and "al-Inshad al-Dini (Islamic religious singing) in Egypt" (in press).

Gabriele Marranci is a PhD candidate with the School of Anthropology at The Queen's University of Belfast. He obtained his MA at the University of Bologna with a thesis in Anthropology of Music, which was concerned with the relationship between pop-*raï* music and Algerian immigrants in France. Currently, his main area of interest relates to cultural aspects of the Muslim diaspora in Europe. His recent publications on *raï* music are "A Complex Identity and its Musical Representation; Beurs and Raï Music in Paris" and "La Musique Raï: Entre Métissage et World Music Moderne" (2000).

Sílvia Martínez was a researcher at the Department of Musicology of the CSIC (Spanish Council for Scientific Research) until 2001, and currently teaches Musicology in both the ESMUC (High School of Music of Catalonia) and the Universitat Autonoma de Barcelona. Among her publications: *Enganxats al heavy. Música, cultura i trangressió* (Lleida, 1999) and contributions to collective books: Ramon Pelinski (ed.) *Presencia del pasado en un cancionero castellonense* (Castelló, 1997), Carles Feixa i al. (eds.) *Música i Ideologies* (Barcelona, 2001).

Yetkin Özer is a PhD teaching Ethnomusicology at Dokuz Eylul University. He has conducted fieldwork in Turkey and produced two ethnographic films: *The Abdal: Professional Musicians of Anatolia* and *Urban Discourse on the Folk Instrument Called Baglama*. His recent studies include also popular music practice in Turkey. He is a founding member of the Turkish Society for Popular Music Studies and the chair of Turkish Branch of the International Association of Popular Music.

Goffredo Plastino is Lecturer in World Musics at the University of Newcastle. He taught also at the University of Calabria and at the University of Bari. He did fieldwork in Southern Italy and Spain, and has published on ethnomusicology, organology, rap, opera, jazz, and photography. Among his publications: *Tambores del Bajo Aragón* (Zaragoza, 2001); *Mappa delle voci: Rap, raggamuffin e tradizione in Italia* (Roma, 1996); *Lira: Uno strumento musicale tradizionale calabrese* (Vibo Valentia, 1994). He is currently editor of *Italian Treasury*, a 25-volume series of Compact Discs in the *Alan Lomax Collection*.

Edwin Seroussi is Professor of Musicology and Director of the Jewish Music Research Center of Hebrew University at Jerusalem. He was head of the Department of Music at Bar-Ilan University, and visiting professor at Binghamton University (New York) and at the University of California, Los Angeles. Among his publications: *Spanish-Portuguese Synagogue Music in Nineteenth-century Reform Sources from Hamburg: Ancient Tradition in the Dawn of Modernity* (Jerusalem, 1996); *Mizimrat Qedem: The Life and Music of R. Isaac Algazi from Turkey* (Jerusalem, 1989). His book *Popular Music and National Culture in Israel* (co-written with Motti Regev) will be published by the University of California Press.

INDEX